Embedding the Principles of Life Time Contracts

Embedding the Principles of Life Time Contracts

A Research Agenda for Contract Law

Luca Ratti (Ed.)

eleven international publishing

Published, sold and distributed by Eleven International Publishing
P.O. Box 85576
2508 CG The Hague
The Netherlands
Tel.: +31 70 33 070 33
Fax: +31 70 33 070 30
e-mail: sales@elevenpub.nl
www.elevenpub.com

Sold and distributed in USA and Canada
International Specialized Book Services
920 NE 58th Avenue, Suite 300
Portland, OR 97213-3786, USA
Tel.: 1-800-944-6190 (toll-free)
Fax: +1 503 280-8832
orders@isbs.com
www.isbs.com

Eleven International Publishing is an imprint of Boom uitgevers Den Haag.

ISBN 978-94-6236-773-9
ISBN 978-94-6274-738-8 (E-book)

Printed in The Netherlands

Table of Contents

Part II A Spectrum of Problems to Approach the Principles of Life Time Contracts

Preface

The Context of the Book

In 2015, when Luca Nogler and Udo Reifner first asked me to participate to a seminar on Life Time Contracts in Trento, their inspiring book on the topic had just been published[1] and the first reviews had just begun to circulate, particularly among private and labour lawyers.[2] After years of combined effort, the members of the European Social Contract group (EuSoCo) had created a wide network of peers, all of whom focused on the commonalities among those special private law contracts that are of crucial relevance in the life of every citizen.[3] EuSoCo identified common characteristics that revolve around the individual's medium- to long-term needs for housing, credit, and work, and determined that such contracts should be reflected in an encompassing set of rules, rights, and principles; EuSoCo's perspective was offered as an alternative to that taken by the EU Commission in its various reform initiatives over the last fifteen years – starting with its *Communication on European Contract Law* of 2001[4] – the fruits of which are now implemented and enforced all around the EU.[5]

The argument for tackling the inherent inequality between the contracting parties in such Life Time Contracts, by infusing them with some element of fairness, was not new in European contract law and had been elaborated upon by a number of scholars over the years, both individually[6] and in groups.[7] Nor was it the first attempt to subject such

---

1 L. Nogler & U Reifner (Eds.), *Life Time Contracts: Social Long-Term Contracts in Labour, Tenancy and Consumer Credit Law*, The Hague, Eleven Publishing, 2014.

2 D. Hiez, 'À propos de Life Time Contracts', 4 *Revue trimestrelle de droit civil* 2014, pp. 817-827; F.J. Arias Varona, 'Recensión', 21 *RPC* 2014, pp. 389-393; M. Tamm, 'Buchbesprechung', 1 *Verbrauecher und Recht* 2015, pp. 39-40; P.G. Ortega Lozano, 'Recension', *Revista española de derecho del trabajo* 2015, pp. 287-291; E. Hondius, 'Review', 37 *Nederlands Tijdschrift voor Burgerlijk Recht*, 2014, pp. 308-309; H. Collins, 'Review', 10 *Eur. Rev. Cont. L.* 2014, pp. 466-472; H.-W. Micklitz, 38 *J. Consumer Pol'y* 2015, p. 108; M. Graziadei, 'A proposito di Life Time Contracts', 69 *Rivista trimestrale di diritto e procedura civile* 2015, p. 1317 *et seq.*; C. Mak, 'Book Review: Life Time Contracts. Social Long-term Contracts in Labour, Tenancy and Consumer Credit Law, *edited by* L. Nogler and U. Reifner', 2 *Eur. J. Comp. L. & Governance*, 2015, p. 379 *et seq.*; M. Fabre-Magnan, 'Critique de la notion de contenu du contrat', *Revue des contrats*, 2015 n° 3, p. 639(II.C).

3 *See* the EuSoCo Declaration, Retrieved on 22 October 2017 from www.eusoco.eu/?page_id=685.

4 COM(2001) 398 final.

5 In particular, an ideal bridge may be established to connect the most important outcomes of this reformative process, namely the Unfair Commercial Practices Directive (2005/29) and the Consumer Rights Directive (2011/83), on which, *see*, among others, S. Weatherill, 'The Consumer Rights Directive: How and Why a Quest for "Coherence" has (largely) failed', 49 *Common Mkt L. Rev.* 2012, pp. 1279-1318, and J. Stuyck, 'The Court of Justice and the Unfair Commercial Practices Directive', 52 *Common Mkt L. Rev.* 2015, pp. 721-752.

6 O. Cherednychenko, *Fundamental Rights, Contract Law and the Protection of Weaker Party*, Sellier, European Law Publishers, München, 2007; C. Mak, *Fundamental Rights in European Contract Law*, Kluwer Law

contracts to rules that often appear to have little in common with the agreements from which they originate.[8]

Rather, EuSoCo's formulation was innovative due to its informal approach to the issue, thus distancing itself from the aforementioned institutional initiatives. Moreover, EuSoCo proposed a transversal analysis embracing housing, credit, and work contracts, all with the aim of extrapolating common principles therefrom. EuSoCo's 2014 book on Life Time Contracts represented the broadening of a theoretical discussion gathering together different perspectives, such as law *and* ethics, protection of the weaker party, *locatio conductio vs. emptio*, long-term *vs.* spot contracts, exchange of commodities *vs.* cooperative relations, and individual *vs.* collective.[9]

The 2015 Trento seminar was, therefore, intended to build on the intellectual project exposed in the 2014 book, by targeting certain common, fundamental principles, in their turn grouped in three main categories: general characteristics (including the definition of such common principles, the reference to the human dimension of the contract and certain basic human needs, and the collective and ethical dimension); contractual obligations (including access, information and transparency, price proportionality, and the aim of securing a livelihood); and relational obligations (including communication, confidentiality, adaptation, and termination). In addition, EuSoCo envisaged individual contributions on specific topics, such as adaptation and termination, access, fair price, and cooperation (namely good faith, mutual respect, and care) between the contracting parties.

For about a year after Trento seminar in September 2015, a number of scholars from the EuSoCo group worked to refine and further develop the Life Time Contracts project. They presented their results at the conference-symposium, entitled *"Life Time Contracts": Rethinking Contract Law*, held in Luxembourg on 30 September 2016.

In preparation for the Luxembourg conference-symposium, a call for papers was directed to scholars in their early careers, who were asked to present studies on three main

---

International, The Hague, 2008; M. Ylhäinen, 'From Obedience to Initiative? Precarious Work and Changing Subjectivities in Labour Law Discourse", *in* A. Griffiths, S. Mustasaari, & A. Mäki-Petajä-Leinonen (Eds.), *Subjectivity, Citizenship and Belonging in Law: Identities and Intersections*, New York – London, Routledge, 2016, p. 232 *et seq.*; L.K. L. Tjon Soei Len, *Minimum Contract Justice: A Capabilities Perspective on Sweatshops and Consumer Contracts*, Hart, Oxford & Portland, 2017.

7 *See* 'Social Justice in European Contract Law: A Manifesto', *in* M.W. Hesselink (Ed.), *The Politics of a European Civil Code*, The Hague, Kluwer Law International, 2006, pp. 171-195; G. Brüggemeier, A. Colombi Ciacchi, & G. Comandé (Eds.), *Fundamental Rights and Private Law in the European Union*, Cambridge, Cambridge University Press, 2011; H.-W. Micklitz (Ed.), *The Many Concepts of Social Justice in European Private Law*, Cheltenham – Northampton, Edward Elgar, 2011; C. Twigg-Flesner (Ed.), *Research Handbook on EU Consumer and Contract Law*, Cheltenham – Northampton, Edward Elgar, 2016; N.M. Pinto Oliveira & B. Mac Crorie (Eds.), *Pessoa, Direito e Direitos*, Braga, Universitade do Minho, 2016.

8 For this perspective, *see* C. Fried, *Contract as Promise: A Theory of Contractual Obligation*, 2d ed., Oxford University Press, Oxford, 2015, *passim*, but esp. pp. 103-105.

9 L. Nogler & U. Reifner, *Life Time Contracts: Evaluating Early Reactions*, EuSoCo working paper, 2016.

topics: (1) the collective dimension of Life Time Contracts; (2) Life Time Contracts, labour contracts, and the digital economy; and (3) Life Time Contracts, tenancy, and credit contracts. Five of the proffered papers were selected and became the backbone of the entire discussion in Luxembourg. They have been included herein.

In addition, Pascal Ancel graciously agree to open the Luxembourg conference, providing a stirring introduction to the Life Time Contracts project.

STRUCTURE AND COMMON THREADS

This volume collects and systematizes further-refined versions of the ideas initially presented at the Luxembourg conference-symposium in September 2016, as those ideas have been enriched by, among other things, the comments and contributions of a number of scholars outside the EuSoCo group. This book refocuses the reader's attention on the most important principles of Life Time Contracts, while expanding the reader's understanding of their interpretative potential in the broader context of general contract law.

As the reader will note, this volume republishes an updated version of the Principles of Life Time Contracts in their multilingual version (English, German, French, Italian, and Spanish), originally published in the 2014 book. The remainder of the book is divided into two parts.

The first part, on the "*The Idea of Life Time Contracts and General Contract Law*", seeks to influence the reader's reflections on the evolution of contract law in general, starting with the identification of principles and rules to be applied equally to contracts relating to the essential needs of every person. This first part reflects the authors' aspiration to define a proper *ius commune* applicable to contracts crucial to the existence and fair development of the individual within society at large (Nogler and Reifner, Fabre-Magnan, and Merlo), and scrutinizing both the material (Nicolussi) and the subjective (Albanese and Flos) scopes of influence of the *Principles of Life Time Contracts*. The rules on adaptation and change of circumstances, particularly important when applied to housing, credit, and work contracts (Pinto Oliveira and Schiavon), demonstrably play a pivotal role.

The second part of the book reflects the various authors' thoughts on "*A Spectrum of Problems to Approaching Private Contracts Using the Principles of Life Time Contracts*". It aims to explore as-yet undiscovered applications of the Life Time Contracts Principles to the distinctive fields of contract law at the core of the concept of Life Time Contracts. While some contributions share similar concerns regarding the need to fine-tune the legal approach and techniques used for such contracts in the wake of the digital revolution (Brahmeshuber and Defromont), with a particular attention to the collective dimension thereof (Szymanski, Razzolini), other authors attempted to embed specific Life Time Contracts principles in the already-established dynamics of the relationship between individuals and financial institutions, particularly those relationships that were stressed both during and after the global economic crisis (Beka and White).

Reflecting the bilingual approach to research and teaching at the University of Luxembourg, the contributions to this book are either in English or in French, at the discretion of the particular author.

I would like to acknowledge the institutional endowment by Luxembourg's *Fonds National de la Recherche* (FNR, Rescom scheme) and the Research Unit in Law (RUL) of the Faculty of Law, Economics and Finance at the University of Luxembourg. Substantial, active support for this project was provided by colleagues and friends, particularly Pascal Ancel, David Hiez, Elise Poillot, and Johan van der Walt, whose kindness and cooperation have helped to develop a fertile and constructive debate on this topic since I first joined the RUL in 2015. A specific mention needs to be addressed to our research assistant, Suzanne M. Larsen, for her support and competence from the early stages of this project and in the final editing of the various chapters.

This book is dedicated to the loving memory of my dear father.

Luca Ratti
Associate Professor of European and Comparative Labour Law
University of Luxembourg

Part I
The Idea of Life Time Contracts and General Contract Law

1 The Contractual Concept of Life Time Contracts under Scrutiny

Luca Nogler & Udo Reifner***

In its Principles on Life Time Contracts,[1] EuSoCo, an international research group focusing on European social contract law,[2] developed the following definition of its object:

> Life Time Contracts are long-term social relationships providing goods, services and opportunities for work and income creation. They are essential for the self-realisation of individuals and their participation in society at various stages in their life. Their subject matter is real-life circumstances. The role of the law governing them is to frame the power relationships of those contracts in terms of human development, so that on-going co-operation rather than the formation of the contract lies at the heart of the contractual relationship. Personal relations (such as the family) have to be taken into account. Mutual trust between the parties as to the durability of the long-term relationship must be protected, and early termination must have only future effect, having no bearing on the contract prior to that point.

After eight years of discussing the idea in a number of seminars, EuSoCo published a book on Life Time Contracts in 2014 (the '2014 Book').[3] We quote from its introduction:

> This book is concerned with *Life Time Contracts*, the group of contracts that generally have the most important role to play in people's daily lives and existence. These establish social long-term relations which, with regard to certain periods of the lifetime of individuals, provide essential goods, services, labour and income opportunities for self-realization and participation.
> Since all denominations such as social contracts, contracts with regard to social

---

* Professor of employment and labour law at the University of Trento.

** Professor emeritus of commercial law at the University of Trento and Hamburg.

1 'The Principles of Life Time Contracts', *in* L. Nogler & U. Reifner (Eds.), *Life Time Contracts: Social Long-Term Contracts in Labour, Tenancy and Consumer Credit Law*, The Hague, Eleven International Publishing, 2014, pp. 5-10.

2 For further details, *see* <www.eusoco.eu>. It might have been better to name the project the 'International Social Contract Group' or 'ISoCo', as people from Asia and the Americas have also participated in our discussions.

3 Nogler & Reifner (Eds.), *supra* note 1, pp. 29-30 (internal citations omitted).

existence or simply longterm [*sic*] contracts risked confusion we finally had to accept that our term could be confounded with a 'contract for lifetime'. Since such contracts are not legally accepted we occupy this notion in relation to the existing contract law as a counterpart to the sales contract model. We therefore use a spelling in which both words are separated from each other if it is feasible. If we refer to the period of time only, we will refer to it in a single word as lifetime. But similar to consumer contracts, commercial contracts and other economically defined categories of contract law, the term "Life Time Contract" serves as an umbrella for legal terms like social long-term contracts, relational contracts, *soziale Dauerschuldverhältnisse, contratti "di durata" per l'esistenza della persona, contrats de longue durée* or *de durée indéterminé, locatio conductio (ad longum tempus)*, which are equally used where the place of Life Time Contracts in the legal system is discussed.

Experience has taught us that in the modern world people share basic needs that are more than mere individual preferences and which do not tend to be conditioned by different cultural requirements. They also share the need for security and the necessity of a reasonable expectation of being able to satisfy their basic needs.

In any event, people are not generally in a position to conduct isolated and independent lives, and "no society can provide for people to be good friends/neighbours". Therefore, in order to satisfy their basic needs, people have to relate to the other elements of society. The fact remains [... that] the post-war constitutions oblige the State to ensure the minimum conditions for '*ein menschenwürdiges Dasein seiner Bürger* [a dignified existence for its citizens]'. Nowadays, entering into a Life Time Contract is the main and, for many, the most dignified way [...] of ensuring long-term satisfaction of the basic requirements to organise and plan their lives. Such contracts determine certain functions for the individual, but this does not hinder the other party from complying with ethical standards [...] and provisions aimed at safeguarding their personality nor, therefore, the competent authorities from setting out the required rules.

EuSoCo's 2014 Book set out sixteen Principles that started with the definition of Life Time Contracts in Principles 1 through 3, and were followed by thirteen additional Principles intended to guide future interpretation and the legal framework of certain contractual, long-term relationships in European contract law and beyond. While the initial multi-lingual publication, as well as a follow-up book published in Portuguese,[4] tried to develop this

4 N.M. Pinto-Oliveira and B. MacCrorie (Eds.), 'Em Torno de Life Time Contracts. Actas do colóquio internacional organizado pelo pelo grupo de investigação em Direito privado – phenómenos de constitucionalização, de materializaçãoe de socialização do Centro de Actas do colóquio internacional organizado pelo

idea in different areas of law (especially labour, tenancy and consumer credit law), this chapter will deal with the reactions to the debate initiated by the 2014 Book, which has been the subject of numerous presentation seminars,[5] as well as a range of reviews.[6]

1.1 The Form and Idea of Life Time Contracts

First, we have no regrets for having taken a multi-cultural approach in the 2014 Book, in the complete certainty that Europe's strength lies in its cultural pluralism. That strength was reflected in our choice to translate the Principles on Life Time Contracts into various languages that are used in the 2014 Book itself. It contains translations of the Principles in German, French, Italian and Spanish, but since its initial publication, translations have appeared in Portuguese, Japanese and Korean as well. Javier Arias Varona finds this a strengthening of the multi-cultural character of the work,[7] which is required by the impulses the authors want to promote. The 2014 Book's character was subsequently highlighted by Ewoud Hondius, who regretted that the Dutch contributions, which had been delivered in the English language, "did not dedicate enough efforts to a proper adaptation of the English to the Dutch environment."[8] He further regretted that the *centrale ondernemingsraad* had

grupo de investigação interdisciplinar em Direito privado – fenómenos de constitucionalização, de materialização', *Direitos humanos da Universidade do Minho*, no dia 15 de Maio de 2015, Braga 2016.

5 4 December 2013 (University of Luxembourg; speakers: H. Collins & D. Hiez); 17 March 2015 (University of Porto Alegre; speaker: C. Lima-Marques & J. Pulgar, Brasilcon; Seminar for doctoral candidates, professors and judges from the Academy of Judges, "Contratos de larga duracion y Credito"); 22 May 2014 (Internationale Konferenz zu Finanzdienstleistungen, Hamburg, Germany; speakers: D. Neuberger & U. Magnus); 17 October 2014 (Universito Santiago de Compostela; speakers: J.A. Varona, F. Gallardo; F. Hernández; J. Lete; & Á. Fernández Albor); 8 November 2014 (Chuo University of Tokyo; speakers: Katsutoshi Kezuka & Yasuo Suwa); 6 March 2015 (University of Pisa; speakers: V. Roppo; M. De Cristofaro; O. Mazzotta, & F. Padovini), 15 May 2015 (University of do Minho; speakers: N.M. Pinto-Oliveira; A. Cardoso Guedes; H. Sousa Antunes; C. Serra; J. Gomez; B. MacCrorie; J. Morais Carvalho; A.M. Taveira de Fonseca; S. Passinhas; & M. João Vasconcelos), 28 September 2012 (University of Trento; speakers: R. Fiori & G. Santucci); 26-27 September 2014 (Université McGill, Montréal, 'Le future du livre'); 28-31 May 2015 (Law & Society Ass'n Ann. Meeting, Seattle, WA); 29 June-1 July 2015 (Int'l Ass'n of Consumer Law, 15th Ann. Meeting, Amsterdam, "Early Termination in Life-Time Contracts").

6 D. Hiez, 'À Propos de Life Time Contracts', 4 *Revue trimestrelle de droit civil* 2014, pp. 817-827; F.J. Arias Varona, 'Recensión', 21 *RPC* 2014, pp. 389-393; M. Tamm, 'Buchbesprechung', 1 *Verbrauecher und Recht* 2015, pp. 39-40; P.G. Ortega Lozano, 'Recension', *Revista española de derecho del trabajo* 2015, pp. 287-291; E. Hondius, 'Review', 37 *Nederlands Tijdschrift voor Burgerlijk Recht* 2014, pp. 308-309; H. Collins, 'Review', 10 *Eur. Rev. Cont. L.* 2014, pp. 466-472; H.-W. Micklitz, 'Book Notes "Law"', 38 *J. Consumer Pol'y* 2015, p. 108; M. Graziadei, 'A proposito di Life Time Contracts', 69 *Rivista trimestrale di diritto e procedura civile* 2015, p. 1317 *et seq.*; C. Mak, 'Book Review: Life Time Contracts: Social Long-term Contracts in Labour, Tenancy and Consumer Credit Law', *in* L. Nogler & U. Reifner' (Eds.), 2 *Eur. J. Comp. L. Governance* 2015, p. 379 *et seq.*; M. Fabre-Magnan, 'Critique de la notion de contenu du contrat', *Revue des contrats* 2015 n° 3, p. 639(II.C).

7 Arias Varona, *supra* note 6, p. 391.

8 Hondius, *supra* note 6, p. 308.

been translated only as 'a participating body', which did not reflect its specific functions and originality. It supports our thesis that using the mother tongue of the authors may be better suited for understanding even if their language is less spoken in the world.

These translations are more than just a replacement of words with another language; rather, they are an attempt to insert the concept into the national legal culture. David Hiez, in particular, appreciated the choice we made:

> The *EuSoCo* group have decided to work in more than one language (English, German, French and Italian) rather than take refuge in the new Esperanto. Readers with limited language skills may go astray, but such a decision should be welcomed. This choice reflects a differing conception of how to build a body of European private law and responds in part to those who reject any such initiative on grounds of the untranslatability of law.[9]

Other commentators have also approved of the choice. Marine Tamm goes so far as to speak of "*gemeinsames europäisches Erbe*".[10]

Secondly, EuSoCo's phrase 'Life Time Contracts', which appears to be a typographical mistake to a native English speaker, is not used in its traditional English-language sense and, thus, is not even self-explanatory in English. It always requires further, careful explanation, and any such explanation is even more crucial when the concept is not being expressed in English. The phrase is simply a label (or a defined term, as it were) that has to be accompanied by definitions that express its two most important aspects (and challenges) in a more legal way: human relationships and long-term contracts. This has already been done in the different translations of our Principles in the 2014 Book. In his review, thereof, Hugh Collins suggested that:

> the issue posed in the definition of Life Time Contracts in Principle 1 is whether the contract is 'essential' for self-realisation and for participation in society. Depending on the circumstances, it must be possible to argue that virtually any kind of contract may satisfy that test. If a person needs to take a bus ride every day to reach her workplace, the bus service looks like it may be essential for self-realisation. The daily use of a bus service could also be described as a 'long-term social relationship' as mentioned in Principle 1. The problem I am raising with regard to the category of Life Time Contracts is that it has the potential to include most contracts that are regularly made by ordinary people when living their lives.[11]

9 Hiez, *supra* note 6, p. 819.

10 Author translation: "the common European heritage". Tamm, *supra* note 6, p. 39.

11 Collins, *supra* note 6, p. 468

David Hiez offered an answer to this, when he asserted that:

> so far as extending the category of *Life Time Contracts* to other types of contract is concerned, first of all it needs to be said that, essentially, the feature which characterises a *Life Time Contract* is on the one hand its duration, and on the other, its functional aim to achieve the personal and social self-realization of the [weaker] contracting party.[12]

In order to be classed as Life Time Contracts, the functional goal of personal and social realisation of the one contracting party is not enough: it must be a long-term contract. When contracts for immediate performance merely follow each other, from one to the next, and there is no provision linking them together from the outset, they are referred to as 'recurring contingent contracts';[13] they are not characterised by a single, on-going contractual relationship.

Life Time Contracts may better be read as Life *Time* Contracts. Indeed, they have nothing to do with contracts for one's lifetime, which were abolished – together with slavery and serfdom – in the bourgeois revolution, although perspectives have turned round since then. Today, many consumers, workers and tenants would appreciate it if their Life Time Contracts would continue for their lifetime. But, there is no systematic relationship because they themselves do not want to be bound for their lifetime; rather, they only want to have adequate protection against the early termination of contractual relationships they want to maintain. Contracts for life are nothing a free and socially minded society could truly wish for. Protection against early termination in the law of Life Time Contracts is not, therefore, categorical, but is an ongoing compromise between individual freedom and the social relationships that directly concern the life and time of workers, borrowers and tenants.

The concept of Life Time Contracts raises two levels of criticism with regard to the sales law model: a lack in the requisite time dimension and, even if the time dimension ('duration') is taken into account, the assumption that this time is only a quantitative dimension used to measure the interest, rent or salary, rather than a complex essential of certain contracts, in which time is connected with human life. But, both levels are only two sides of the same coin. The historic, capitalistic principle of *caveat emptor* continues to power a trade economy that permits contacts between people who do not know each other (and thus, are unlikely to like each other), such that, absent *caveat emptor*, they would be far less likely to willingly cooperate with each other. Capitalism's ability to reduce relations to spot contracts was an enormous achievement, one that enhances global cooperation and partition of labour. There is no question that this principle still

12 Hiez, *supra* note 6, p. 820.

13 Author translation of: *Wiederkehrschuldverhältnis.*

has a role in international trade and globalisation. The criticism is not that sales contracts should be replaced by Life Time Contracts; rather, it must be acknowledged that the sales contract model, described under different labels (such as the informational model in consumer law or the idea of free choice in labour and tenancy law), has conquered the general parts of international contract law, but it is not adequate for all legal relationships. Its greatest achievement – that is, supporting the establishment of the market through spot contracts – has become its basic flaw, by excluding labour, consumption and living from the nature of that type of contract. Since the predominance of the sales contract model became, over time, less and less convincing, thousands of exemptions endeavour to reintegrate relational thinking into contract law. 'Time', therefore, is not meant to be a span from now to then, or a future date, or a yardstick for establishing rent, interest or wages, but is, rather, the unquantifiable element of the time people spend simply living their respective lives. Sleeping, working, consuming, loving, suffering – all of these activities take their own time, which is not interchangeable. If the law accepts that time spent living, or Life Time, is an important dimension of certain contractual relationships, the path towards a general, second model of a contract is opened. Such contracts would make the use of things and services – ones that are linked to the life of one of the parties (typically the weaker party) – an essential element, as was the case in certain tenancy contracts of the early middle ages.[14]

The second and, perhaps, more challenging idea is, therefore, one of a uniform model of a long-term contract, similar to the sales contract model,[15] which should be developed, with its own legal structure in which the contract and the relationship are in harmony with each other.

Many observers see the focus of our work on the relation between human needs and contract law. As Marina Tamm rightly argued, an ethical choice lies at the basis of our approach, which approach is critical of the automatic tendency, in legal discourse, to take on the assumptions of neo-classical economics that pervades large swathes of the economic analysis of law.[16] As Michele Graziadei commented:

---

14 An interesting deviation from the modern use of the word 'time' can be found in the Bible (King James Version), Ecclesiastes 3, 1-22, which starts with "To everything there is a season, and a time to every purpose under the heaven." The verses go on to enumerate human activities and link them to *their* time. Each activity (verses 1-10) starts with the words "A time to [...]" while the second part of the passage makes clear that it is the duration and not the date. "That which hath been is now; and that which is to be hath already been; and God requireth that which is past" (verse 15). We are reminded of a social 'relativity of time', which, with regard to energy and material, has been acknowledged by physicists.

15 *See* G. Oppo's classic study, 'I contratti di durata', *Rivista di Diritto Commerciale* 1943, I , p. 143 *et seq.*, p. 227 *et seq.*, & 1944, I, p. 17 *et seq.*

16 Tamm, *supra* note 6, p. 40.

> in [the] neo-classical economy, all goods really are the same, and they are exchanged in markets where no one any longer takes account of their specific nature and the moral implications involved, as Debra Satz has asserted in a recent work.[17]

It is not by chance that one of the essays in the 2014 Book is fiercely critical of the work of Ronald Coase, presented rather in caricature, as the wicked prophet promoting similar behaviour among jurists. In reality, formalism at that time permeated the legal theory of law, too, which turned entirely on the concept of freedom of contract, against which writers, such as Gierke, reacted (who is often cited in the 2014 Book), as well as the standard-bearers of legal socialism and the jurists active in socially oriented movements. Muriel Fabre-Magnon argued that, for the authors, Life Time Contracts "are not necessarily contracts *for* life but contracts which play an important role *in* life".[18] She concludes:

> It seems for us that the underlying idea of this type of contract is the fact that one of the parties gets from it a means of subsistence. (this is the case of the three contract types cited [...]).[19]

She refers to her own proposition in which that function was invoked as an obligation of an employer seeking special justification for early terminations. She refers to Principle 14, in which such a function has been turned into one of the Principles of Life Time Contracts. But, she correctly determined "that the idea of the protection of the weak has its limits and looks a bit artificial. Even more the vulnerability of the weaker party".[20] "Protection", she went on to argue:

> is not justified by the type of contract but by the importance a contract has for one party and his existence. This is what justifies specific rules in contract law which especially have to stabilise the relation.[21]

Indeed, if the justification of labour, consumer, and tenancy protection law lies in the 'weakness' of one party, we do not need a special form of contract, since weakness can occur in all legal relationships. But, if legal 'weakness' is a function of an inadequate legal form and ideology in which the principle of equitable freedom is turned into the legit-

17 Graziadei, *supra* note 6, p. 1318, citing D. Satz, *Why Certain Things Should Not Be for Sale*, University Press, Oxford, 2010.
18 Fabre-Magnan, *supra* note 6, p. 639 *et seq.*
19 Id.
20 Id.
21 Id.

imation of subordination, dependency, and debt, it may be worthwhile to think about whether the sales law model needs a sibling that is better adapted to the modern credit and service economy. It is, then, the 'equality of law' that Anatole France evoked, that could change the perspective. Sales law models could then be seen, perhaps, as seller-, employer-, landlord- and lender-protection laws, which, itself, would need special justification instead of declaring the inequality of their counterparts as the effect of their personal weakness.

Here, we must clarify that we do not use a functionalistic approach;[22] rather, we use a technical approach on contracts. In contrast, the Social Justice Manifesto[23] used a functionalistic approach when arguing that contracts should fulfil the requirements of social justice, without making sufficiently clear how this could be achieved. The core of EuSoCo's project is to demonstrate that a social dimension is inherent in the time dimension of the Life Time Contracts. Time can only be considered if there is a period of time involved. The longer the period of time, the more relational aspects connecting the contract to one party's life will become apparent, until finally a particular type of contracts can even turn into an existential necessity. But, that would be the exception, rather than the rule.

We go back, here, to the criticism of spot contracts made at the beginning of the 20th century. It is 'social' insofar as it is for a long term, since 'long-term' logically implies social (legal) relationships. We, therefore, join the interrupted discussion between 'relational' and 'spot' contracts.

Secondly, the function of Life Time Contracts[24] is not defined outside the law, as when you approach the subject from the standpoint of social justice. While we start with the most dominant forms of socialised law (labour-, debtor- and tenancy-protection laws), we generalise the elements that these long-term contracts have already developed in order to provide a second general part to the law of obligations, which is currently restricted to the sales law approach. Coming from a bottom-up methodology, the new general top of the pyramid may fit with other areas that are currently not included in labour, credit and tenancy law, as was especially demonstrated in the labour law contributions.

1.2 The Definition of Life Time Contracts

At this juncture, it may be fruitful to return – briefly – to an analysis of the main elements of our definition of Life Time Contracts.

22 *See* Roelke, 'Funktionalismus', *in* J. Kriz, D. Nohlen & R.-O. Schultze (Eds.), *Lexikon der Politik: Politikwissenschaftliche Methoden*, vol. II, Munich, Springer, p. 141.

23 G. Brueggemeier, *et al.*, 'Social Justice in European Contract Law: A Manifesto', 10 *Eur. L.J.* 2004, p. 653 *et seq.*

24 On the difference between a functionalistic and a functional method, *see* L. Nogler, 'Die typologisch-funktionale Methode am Beispiel des Arbeitnehmerbegriffs', 11-12 ZESAR 2009, p. 465.

1.2.1 Duration

In civil law systems, long-term contracts mean those contracts implying the performance of one or more continuous activities (that is, those that are carried out, on an uninterrupted basis, for either the period of time specified in the contract or the period of time necessary to fulfil the obligor's contractual obligations to the obligee) or on a periodic basis (that is, an activity that is not continuous by nature, but is, rather, repeated at certain intervals). The differentiation between obligatory relationships, which can be either short-term or long-term relationships, reflects the different interests that are being satisfied by the particular obligation. In fact, whereas with contracts involving continuous or periodic performance, the creditor's requirements are such that, by their nature, they cannot be satisfied by a single act, but need a continuous or periodic performance by the obligor. In spot contracts, the obligee's interests can be served on one occasion. To conclude, a feature of Life Time Contracts is that "the performance in its entirety depends on the duration (*Länge*)".[25]

There are basically four interests that have, historically, justified the development of the category, in civil law, of 'long-term contracts': the first concerns the ability of the parties to terminate the contractual relationship at will; the second concerns the parties' ability to respond to an alteration of what, at least in German legal language, is known as the 'economic balance underlying the contract';[26] the third concerns the satisfaction of the parties' interests in the performance of the contractual obligations; and finally, the fourth concerns the fact that withdrawal, termination and the termination clause do not have retroactive effect.

1.2.2 'Life Time'

The civil law's historic 'long-term contracts' category discussed above has not been focussed – or, rather, has not been *sufficiently* focussed – on the human aspect of at least one of the contracting parties or on the fact that such contracts are related to that aspect. It is for that reason that we preferred to give a different name to them: 'Life Time Contracts'. As Principle 2 of Life Time Contracts, denominated 'Human Dimension', affirms:

> The subject matter of Life Time Contracts is real-life circumstances. The role of the law governing them is to frame the power relationships of those contracts in terms of human development, so that on-going co-operation[,] rather than the formation of the contract[,] lies at the heart of the contractual relationship. Personal relations ([such as,] for example, the family) have to be taken into account.

25 *See, e.g.*, K. Larenz, *Lehrbuch des Schuldrechts, I, Allgemeiner Teil*, Beck, München, 1987, p. 30.
26 Author translation of: *Geschäftsgrundlage, clausula rebus sics stantibus. Art. 313 BGB.*

More generally, we can say that new legislation in two special sectors of labour law and the law on residential leases have introduced rules into private law that relate to the principle of justice *with* regard to the person. As Hugo Sinzheimer stated, in relation to labour law, but with an assertion that is valid for all Life Time Contracts, the law must not just consider the freedom of the individual citizen as a formality, but project that concept into the real essence of freedom and recognise it in practical terms, when confronting the individual citizen's real relational needs.[27]

For this reason, EuSoCo decided that it was the human or existential aspect of social long-term contracts that interested us. Therefore, we developed the idea of emphasizing on Life Time Contracts. At the heart of this class of contracts, there is an individual human being, with his or her physiological and ethical requirements, in terms of security, belonging, success, and self-fulfilment, or in other words, the existential needs to be able to enjoy essential goods, services, labour opportunities, and income opportunities. The satisfaction of such needs is, normally, an essential precondition to the pursuit of a happy life, or for self-realisation and participation.

From this perspective, EuSoCo considers time to be in a dimension entirely different from the way it is conventionally treated by the law.

Let us take employment contracts as an example. The fact that needs to be recognised is that the work performed by the worker involves his or her time, not as a factor external to the individual (existing in time that, as such, does not belong to the business), but as a component that constitutes the very essence of the individual who *spends* his or her Life Time. Labour represents one of the main phenomena of social relationships; by participating in it, a worker may aspire, albeit with all the conditionality that the human state implies, to provide an answer to the basic existential question of why he or she is alive. In this sense, we can speak of the 'Life Time' of the worker.

Throughout the entire Taylor–Ford era, it was believed that work represented a period of existence in which the worker 'wasted' his lifetime, since the period itself was not part of time understood as *kairos*, but was ascribed to time understood as *chrónos*. Now, without doubt, it has become clear – absorbingly so – that the Taylor–Ford system brought about what can only be called the most negative aspect of involving the worker's very being in work performance. But, this does not detract from the fact that, from an axiological standpoint, a worker cannot surrender his very being – that is, his Life Time – to his employer. What's more, the optical illusion generated by Taylor–Fordism becomes obvious as soon as we reflect that, *mutatis mutandis*, such involvement may also affect self-employed workers, who survive on their own efforts and, for precisely that reason, must incur this 'expenditure' in preparing to carry out their work performance. It is not by chance that, so far as essential, personal performance is concerned, the view is gaining ground that, in reality, *utilitas* should be sufficient to justify the application of large por-

27 H. Sinzheimer, *Das Problem des Menschen im Recht*, Groningen, Batavia, 1933; and H. Sinzheimer, *Arbeitsrecht und Rechtssoziologie 2*, Europäische Verlagsanstalt, Frankfurt am Main, 1976, p. 53 *et seq.*

tions of labour law protecting the workers' existential sphere, as such *utilitas*, or benefit – which goes beyond work and service in the strict sense – accrues to the employer from the 'mere' link between the independent contractor and the producer organisation. The big question raised by the new legal dimension of time is whether the law, which necessarily operates through concepts, can give weight to time as a commodity, which belongs, ontologically, to the single individual and, if so, how it will achieve that weighing. Now, this definition of time, which may be referred to as 'in between' (that is, between one indicator of measurement and another) can only take on legal significance insofar as it is understandable and, at the same time, respects the relational needs that are the subject matter of the legal regulation.

The qualitative aspect of time, which is a direct expression of what makes each person a unique being, must, in short and of necessity, always be expressed through the law and, for this reason, by concepts that select typical or recurrent instances, such as sickness, poverty, unemployment, family needs, and so forth, and detach them from the individual cases that are involved in the relationship between individuals.

A feature of the jurist's life is to always run the risk of excessive abstraction from reality. Legal thinking, with categories such as the 'typical' case (*Typus*), has always striven to include a living substratum in its theoretical reflections (methodology), to which legal concepts must be anchored. But, in the pursuit of this very admirable objective – proposed by, among others, the fundamental movement to revitalise practical philosophy – jurists themselves must pay careful attention to avoid falling from the frying pan into the fire, by leaving to others – philosophers, economists, sociologists, and so on – the selection of the relevant interests present in the concrete case. Jurists, who do not want to lose their footing, must not avoid dealing with concepts, even for a moment. But, that does not imply that they should not, at the same time, aspire to keep – in as close contact as possible – with reality. In order to pursue such an understandable aim, however, private law jurists must, first and foremost, avoid bracketing off the very thing that inspires their actions: interpersonal relationships. If they keep the latter firmly in sight, there is no risk of removing – at the very outset – the necessary identification of presumptions about, and limitations of, the instinctive tendency of individuals to assert their subjective state and claim the importance of their will. Labour lawyers must indeed transcend this.

Labour and employment law developed because it promoted an axiological mission within the sphere of private law, in that it contrived legal rules governing who bears the costs of human action so as to take into account, within the limits of what is possible, the commutative principle, even the most significant cases of social pressure or, in extreme cases, coercion, that individuals may encounter over the course of their lifetime or existence. An example, highly relevant to the theme under discussion here, might be the use of information technology, to which individuals are increasingly exposed, to the point of making the evident tardiness in labour-law thinking on this subject seem beyond comprehension, given the basic framework of obligatory training that employers are meant to provide.

When one of the parties to the work relationship is exposed to an external reality around him in such a way that "things start to dominate humans",[28] the law should remind the other party in the relationship – again, always within the limits of the possible – that to be free "does not imply freedom from duty, but through rights and responsibilities".[29]

But, how can the subjective aspect of 'Life Time lived' or 'life' be strengthened?[30] Since the law must operate by reference to concepts, significance cannot be given to the Life Time of the worker directly. The contractual regime is always constrained by the need to collocate such Life Time within a chronological sequence and may, perhaps, expunge it, raising it to case types with typical characteristics. But, this is the work of the courts, which requires a reference to events that can be typified and that are, therefore, recurrent in the lives of a plurality of people (e.g., sickness, maternity leave, and paternity leave).

1.2.3 Basic Needs

All of the 2014 Book commentators emphasised that one of its strong points was its strict correlation between contracts of employment and consumer credit contracts. As Collins noted, these are:

> topics that are rarely treated together by lawyers. The basis of this connection is the insight that both types of contract provide immediate spending power for ordinary people, one through wages and the other through access to credit.[31]

In the same vein, David Hiez suggested that:

> it is unusual to consider these three contract types together, mainly because they are more or less independent of one another in private law. Nonetheless, this choice is particularly heuristic. In fact, it highlights points in common which are not immediately apparent to civil lawyers, who base their classification on technical rather than social considerations [...]. The authors convincingly demonstrate that in the consumer society, the arrival of a regular salary is no longer sufficient, but it is also necessary to be able to access more considerable sums at any given time, so that consumer credit ends up carrying out an analogous function to an employment contract.[32]

---

28 M. Weber, *Der Sozialismus*, Athenäum, Weinheim, 1995, p. 76 *et seq.*

29 K. Polanyi, *Una società umana, un'umanità sociale. Scritti 1918-1963*, Jaca Book, Milano, 1963, p. 136.

30 E. Borgna, *Il tempo e la vita*, Feltrinelli, Milano, 2015, p. 59.

31 Collins, *supra* note 6.

32 Hiez., *supra* note 6.

Focussing on the relationship between bankruptcy and credit law, Javier Arias Varona highlighted our innovative element with regard to the relationship between public bankruptcy and private credit law:

> The connection between the concept of life time contracts, credit contracts and the institutions of bankruptcy is not self-evident but according to the authors of the book, the examples provided make this relation apparent. Certain chapters concerning consumer credit and bankruptcy therefore offer innovative perspectives for the future. [... T]hey connect structural questions of bankruptcy law to general developments in law.
>
> With the contractual approach to bankruptcy 'a possible alternative to insolvency procedures (ex post) in the context of contractual credit relations (ex ante) becomes visible.' Anyhow the present credit law does not seem to be open to apply the *clausula rebus sic stantibus* to human conditions. [...] The book thus contributes in a methodologically unusual perspective to look at insolvency in a different way than one is accustomed to in bankruptcy law.[33]

In the current credit society, the work relationship has lost its exclusive status as guarantor of people's 'free and dignified life'. Unless we want this to remain a merely utopian wish, we need to find out – using the same approach as we have taken historically with productive activity – how to reinforce consumer acts that require an investment of people's Life Time, whether at present or in the future.

Big areas, such as financial services, old age pension schemes, insurance, and payment systems, seem to be arbitrarily excluded. The same seems to be true for contracts concerning basic services, as traced by Frey Nybergh.[34] It is obvious that the contracts we dealt with are basic examples and not an exhaustive enumeration of the types of contracts that can be subsumed within our definition of Life Time Contracts. In labour law, we already extended the idea to all kind of contracts through which labour is invested to earn one's living. The same could be said for financial services, where all contracts concerning the use of money for personal consumption or labour could be incorporated. In rental contracts, consumer leasing should also be incorporated, besides housing. Indeed, basic utilities (such as electricity, water, and communication services) are necessary, but have been totally omitted. Should we remedy this by creating a fourth area of 'service contracts' for such needs? There are many similarities connecting electricity to human needs and Life Time. But, there are also differences that, historically, placed electricity and similar services outside the marketplace and, thus, beyond the reach of the freedom of contract: there is often little choice and typically high governmental involvement. His-

33 Arias Varona, *supra* note 6.

34 F. Nybergh, 'Access to Longterm Banking Services in the Nordic States', *in* Nogler & Reifner (Eds.), *supra* note 1, pp. 331-348.

torically, such relationships were regulated by administrative, not private, law. The crucial alternative between 'having' and 'using' that divides dependent from independent labour, home ownership from tenancy, and the wealthy from the rest of the people, is absent. Utility companies, for example, do not rent out water or electricity for use, but 'sell' them. Instead, cultural activity (mass communication, theatre) seem to be closer to the 'capital-rent approach' typical of Life Time Contracts. This approach would also induce us to leave legal language and define our areas on the basis of the use of different forms of capital (e.g., means of production/labour; money/financial services; ownership/use of things (housing; leased consumables)). Legal dogmatics on the nature of Life Time Contracts would certainly have effects on sales law wherever the period for the exercise of the right of withdrawal or of warranties, for example, increasingly introduce Life Time elements into the relationship between the seller and buyer and are increasingly recognised in the duty of care imposed on the one party for the interest of the other party after the contract has come into force in international sales law. Basic services are often in-between both types of contracts and are, therefore, less prone to the development of an alternative contractual form for long-term use relationships.

Indeed, EuSoCo included, in the definition of Life Time Contracts, the concept of basic needs. But, it is not important for its categorisation. It is more an effect of a better adaptation of contractual forms to Life Time than the reason for it. Take, for example, David Hiez's comment that:

> the criterion based on the link between the contract and the self-realization of the contracting party is open to expansion, to an extent that would be difficult to circumscribe.[35]

In the 2014 Book's 'Introduction',[36] we mentioned that the case-law of the *Bundesgerichtshof*, for example, relates to that private-law dimension, which recognises a right to compensatory damages (including contractual claims) for the interruption of enjoyment (*Nutzungsentschädigung*) of goods or services that are of central importance to a self-maintaining lifestyle (*eigenwirtschaftliche Lebenshaltung*). However, other cases must be included, in which the interruption significantly impacts the material basis for leading one's life.[37] The reason for this has to do with both the principle of certainty in the law and the rule that non-economic loss can only be compensated to the extent provided for by law (§ 253 BGB).[38]

35 Hiez, *supra* note 6.

36 Nogler & Reifner (Eds.), *supra* note 1.

37 It is not the case if the enjoyment involves a private swimming-pool (*Bundesgerichtshof* 28 February 1980 – VII ZR 131/73), a camper (BGHZ 15 December 1982 – VIII ZR 315/80), a fur coat (BGHZ 12 February 1975 – VIII ZR 11/73), or a motor-boat (BGHZ 15 November 1983).

38 BGHZ 24 January 2013 – III ZR 98/12, in <http://juris.bundesgerichtshof.de/cgi-bin/rechtsprechung/document.py?Gericht=bgh&Art=en&nr=63259&pos=0&anz=1>, which recognizes a right to damages for interruption of internet services required for email services; further examples of compensable interruption

However, it is clear that the expression we used to circumscribe the interests to be regulated in the contract so that they fall within the category of Life Time Contracts – contracts that are "essential for the self-realisation of individuals and their participation in society at various stages in their life"[39] – refers to a legal specification that must be undertaken in strict adherence to fundamental rights recognised by legal tradition.

1.2.4 *Inequality and Justice*

Quite closely related to basic needs are responses to the 2014 Book that locate the idea of Life Time Contracts in the realm of market inequalities that have been cured by the concept of consumer law. Nuno Manuel Pinto-Oliveira[40] emphasised the element of the welfare state in contract law. European contract law, especially, has revealed the necessity of introducing protection of the weaker party into the general concept of consumer law. Mentioning the criticism that such developments have raised among German law professors, in particular, who denounce the destructive effects such materialisation of contract law would have on the formal equality of law, Pinto-Oliveira insisted that there is an ethical need to remedy the market asymmetries and inequalities that consumer law has brought to the forefront. Principle 8, in particular, recognises that effective access to Life Time Contracts is a fundamental element of such contracts, which justifies our translation of Life Time Contracts into Spanish and Italian as 'existential contracts'. Pinto-Oliveira referred not only to the evocation of ethics and contractual form in the contributions of Andrea Nicolussi and Helena Klinger to the 2014 Book, but also to the reference Geraint Howells made to consumer law. But, there is the danger of losing the specific difference in those developments in European contract law that built on the existing consumer law and the new trend of recognising the 'vulnerable consumer' as a legal person in his or her own right, who must be treated differently in order to become equal.

The concept of Life Time Contracts in its present state, however, argues that inequality in law is not the *effect* of the unequal circumstances of the contracting parties in Life Time Contracts, but more the *effect* of the ignorance the sales law shows with regard to the individual's Life Time. Thus, contract law is, thus, neither an unequal treatment of equal situations nor an equal reflection of unequal social situations, but rather it is a state of fundamental ignorance with respect to the decisive elements of the human relationship that it tries to regulate, tempered by myriads of case-by-case exceptions that render such law uncertain and often arbitrary.

include the use of a television set, a personal computer including lap-tops, a bicycle, kitchen furniture, and holiday home.

39 Principle 1 of Life Time Contracts, Nogler & Reifner (Eds.), *supra* note 1, p. 5.

40 N.M. Pinto-Oliveira, 'Uma introducao aos contratos existenciais', *in* N.M. Pinto-Oliveira & B. MacCrorie (Eds.), *Em Torno de Life Time Contracts*, Braga, 2016, p. 43.

It is true that, in several Principles, compensation for inequalities between capital and social interests, in all three of the areas of law, is defined as a goal and that the translation of Life Time Contracts into Romance languages uses the 'basic needs concept', in order to make readers understand the place our concept is intended to hold in a general political discussion on the prospects of the market economy. But, unlike social justice requirements, the concept of Life Time Contracts does not start from a social welfare principle in order to align contract law to the necessities of social justice from outside the law; rather, the concept presents the hypothesis that a more adequate treatment of both time and life in a historically well-known second contractual form of a rental contract (*locatio conductio*) would have those social *effects* that concepts on social-versus-formal law, materialisation, and protection of the weaker party require.

1.2.5 Use

To understand the difference of the Time dimension of Life Time Contracts – better understood as their term or durational dimension – from the typical Time dimension of sales law as a period or date in the concept of Life Time Contracts, an economic analysis of the nature of the relationship between capital and social interests can, perhaps, better illuminate why a separate form is needed. Psychoanalysts and philosophers have distinguished between 'having' and 'being'. The law does not know such distinctions. The existence of a person ('being') is the underlying fact for the application of norms that provide rights ('having'). A worker *has* the right to his salary, the tenant *has* a right to live in a flat and the borrower *has* a right to the capital owed, all of which are conditioned on the actor's own performance. Civil and common law turn all opportunities into rights that one can *have*, irrespective of whether that right is provided in the form of an absolute property right or in the form of a relative claim. They are all equal with respect to having. But, economics teaches us that, for at least practical reasons, it makes sense to distinguish between one's own and foreign capital, between exclusive and relative patrimony, and between having capital (savers, owners) and using capital (renters, borrowers). With the concept of the sharing economy, we recognise that from a macro-economic perspective, exclusive ownership may even hinder productivity (idle capital), ingenuity (unused patents), social welfare (e.g., governmental attempts to alleviate discrimination, unemployment, overindebtedness, and homelessness), and a sufficient supply of space for living (resulting in traffic jams, endless suburbs, empty homes, destroyed landscapes, etc.).

Since Life Time Contracts represent a 'use economy',[41] they seem to have enormous potential to overcome legal individualism, which increasingly jeopardises public good. If using, instead of having, becomes the prerogative of a future shared economy, legal devel-

41 That is, an economy in which goods and services are used directly, without requiring prior acquisition of its property. This historic difference between *emptio vendita* and *locatio conductio*, once even visible in the

opment – especially of the use element – in the Life-Time-Contract model would introduce a core element for the future. In the opinion of most reviewers, this connecting element has been properly identified between renting and borrowing. Both organise the use of capital in its fixed (things) or variable (money) form. There is no deeper justification for calling the person who rents a flat from another for his or her personal use a 'tenant', while the one who 'rents' money to acquire his or her home for personal use is called a 'debtor'. It is always the use of someone else's capital that defines the synallagmatic relationship.

Although labour law shares concerns for the Life Time of at least one of the parties, the 'use' element seems to be the reverse, if we assume that the employer 'rents' or 'uses' the labour force of the employee. Although this has to be investigated, we assume that labour contracts – in which the principles of care, cooperation, protection against early termination, collective interest, a special synallagma adapted to illness and human mishaps have a long legal tradition in civil law jurisdictions – provide, not just by chance, a model for understanding tenancy and consumer credit contracts. We also assume that, in labour contracts, it is primarily the human element that 'uses' capital. In the 19th century, dependent wage work developed in conjunction with machinery that required specific, ongoing labour that rendered individualised work, without access to capital, unproductive. Unemployment became more feasible than continuous individual work without such machinery. The use of machinery, the coordinating power of the employer, and the existence of a network of interactions in global markets became the core elements of the labour contract. Especially now, in a time in which, due to digitalisation, the use of foreign capital has partly turned into a rental relationship with seemingly independent workers, labour law will now have to pay more attention to this use relationship than to its opposite concept of using the labour force in a way that seems to justify the concept of subordination. Subordination may be much more the effect of using the organisation and machinery of a factory, rather than a consequence of the fact that the worker, in contradiction to his individual freedom, 'sells' his labour power to another party for a certain time.

A tenant who rents a home in order to live may, thus, not be very far away from a worker who rents the use of a complex labour organisation in order to offer productive work by which he or she is able to earn enough money for his or her family. Erich Fromm and Aristotle may, therefore, provide the key to a lost distinction in contract law: the fundamental difference in ideology and application between the right to use (*dominium utile, locatio conductio*) and the right to have (*dominium directum, emptio vendita*). Such research could be facilitated in this approach if contract lawyers in labour, consumer credit and tenancy law are bound to work together, when, formerly, they were of the opinion that they had nothing to do with each other.

distinction between *dominium directum* and *dominium utile*, gains momentum in the discussion on the shift from a trade to a service society or even the transformation into a shared economy.

1.3 Why (Social) Contract Law?

Neither national law nor European law nor, still less, Community law, has established a regimen for governing Life Time Contracts. Only individual types of Life Time Contracts have been regulated by national law, and no general discipline for the type of Life Time Contracts in fact exists, as has happened, on the other hand, for long-term contracts. Legal scholars in continental Europe, it is true to say, have recently endeavoured to emphasise on the need for a sort of "general part of the law of contracts and obligations of the weak party".[42] But, to base a new general contract-type on the weakness of one of the parties simply favours formal equality or, in other words, favours provisions that compensate for the information asymmetry between the contracting parties, mainly generalising the current legal setting of Community consumer protection law. Neither does the proposed criterion seem to be particularly selective, when one accepts the fact, affirmed by Andrea Nicolussi in his contribution to this book, that "in contracts, there is always, or almost always, one party which is weaker than the other".[43] For that matter, even under the 'economic contract theory', the category of relational contracts is only recognised as one aspect of the problem – namely the continuous, highly interactive contact between the contracting parties – without placing importance on the existential needs of the people involved.

This was the reason that stimulated EuSoCo to develop a range of Principles that should underpin any regimen governing Life Time Contracts. When we refer to these contracts, we cannot confine ourselves to only considering the formation of the contract and focussing on the will of the parties. Such contracts require non-derogable norms. We underline this point in answer to those who have commented that the response proposed by the 2014 Book's authors was unclear. According to David Hiez:

> the *Life Time Contract* is not a contract in the full sense, nor a category of contracts as generally understood. The authors indeed, assert this explicitly [...]. It concerns an abstract category, one might say an intellectual one, but not a legal one. Its purpose is not to produce immediate legal effects, but to provoke thought about the European law of contracts. Thus it is a work of a strictly academic kind.[44]

---

42 F. Gamillscheg, 'Zivilrechtliche Denkformen und die Entwicklung des Individualarbeitsrechts. Zum Verhältnis von Arbeitsrecht und BGB', *AcP* 1976, p. 197 *et seq.*; F. Gamillscheg, *Ausgewählte Schriften zu Arbeitsrecht und Rechtsvergleichung*, Nomos, Baden-Baden, 2006), p. 124 *et seq.*; P. Derleder, 'Unterlegenenschutz im Vertragsrecht. Ein Modell für das Arbeitsrecht?', 28 *Kristische Justiz* 1995, p. 320 *et seq.*; G. Höhn, *Kompensation gestörter Vertragsparität*, Beck, München, 1982; E. Roppo, 'Parte generale del contratto, contratti del consumatore e contratti asimmetrici', *Rivista di diritto privato* 2007, p. 669 *et seq.*; G. Gitti, La determinazione del contenuto, *in* G. Villa (Ed.), *Il terzo contratto*, Bologna, Il Mulino, 2008, p. 110 *et seq.*

43 A. Nicolussi, *infra* Ch. 3.

44 Hiez, *supra* note 6.

This observation remains true at this point in time. Obviously, we hope that, at some point in the future, our Principles will become accepted in the general law of contracts. Globalisation is bringing about an increasingly evident, indirect integration in market regulation. It is time to return to dealing with direct integration, produced, as far as possible, by the law.

The 2014 Book mainly dealt with contract law. This aspect differentiates our position from past treatments, which centred on the combination of contract law and rights *in rem*[45] or contractual and personal rights.[46] The experience of labour law shows that the contractualisation of the parties' positions in the legally binding relationship represents the debtor's primary guarantee that he is the "*porteur de valeurs liées à la liberté de l'homme*".[47] The contract is the means by which freedom and the formal equality existing between the parties can be associated. Clearly, it represents a negative guarantee, but, even so, it provides assurance that the contractual relationship, from the legal standpoint, is not unbalanced from the outset.

On the contrary, it is unrealistic to believe that a debtor holds a position similar to an owner (for example, the right to a job). This way of thinking leads to one-sided perspectives. In reality, or at least in that part of reality that is subject to the rules of contract, there are always at least two, if not more, fundamental rights at stake.[48] Contrary to the assumptions underlying the theories of the *Drittwikung*, which dominate the 'unilateral' academic frameworks, provisions relating to fundamental rights themselves must, in any event, be treated as 'principles' that, as such, are not only addressed to lawmakers, but also as conditions for the interpretation of statutes,[49] which remain the parties' only source of enforceable rights. Such integration must be conducted in a balanced way, using the noble arts of compromise and *proportio*, or whatever other way relational needs may be characterised. From such factors, we are well able to "draw elements of response and general indications"[50] since "questions of values [...] may be reduced to questions regarding the consequences of corresponding choices, transferring the discourse to a range of evaluations whose rationality can be more easily monitored".[51]

45 P. Grossi, *Locatio ad longum tempus: Locazione e rapporti reali di godimento nella problematica di diritto comune*, Morano, Napoli, 1963, p. 26.

46 O. von Gierke, 'Dauernde Schuldverhältnisse', *in Jherings Jahrbücher für die Dogmatik des bürgerlichen Rechts*, Vol. 64, 1914, p. 24 *et seq.*

47 G. Lyon-Caen, 'Défense et illustration du contrat de travail', *in* M. Villey (Ed.), *Archives de Philosophie du Droit, Archives de Philosophie du Droit*, 1968, p. 69.

48 Hence, the Aristotelian idea of justice is rediscovered. *See* Aristotle, *Etica Nicomachea*, M. Zanatta (Tr.), Milano, Biblioteca universale Rizzoli, 1993, p. 191.

49 Thus C.W. Canaris, 'Grundrechte und Privatrecht', *in Archiv für die civilistische praxis*, Vol. 184, 1984, p. 201 *et seq.*; and M. Ruffert, 'Die Rechtsprechung des Bundesverfassungsgerichts zum Privatrecht', 64 *Juristen Zeitung* 2009, pp. 389-390.

50 G. Vettori, 'Il tempo dei diritti', *Riv. trim. dir. proc. civ.*, 2014, p. 91.

51 L. Mengoni, *Diritto e valori*, Il Mulino, Bologna 1985, p. 46, n. 100.

Finally, we can only agree with Collins when he commented "if the authors are right that these Life Time Contracts are essential for well-being and self-realisation, so much so that they speak of a human right to these market opportunities, these provisions regarding access do not seem sufficiently powerful tools for ensuring access to these markets for everyone".[52] Private law needs to be supported by public policy.

BIBLIOGRAPHY

Arias Varona, F.J., 'Recensión', 21 *RPC* 2014, pp. 389-393.

Aristotle, *Etica Nicomachea* (M. Zanatta Trans.), Milano: Biblioteca Universale Rizzoli, 1993.

Borgna, E., *Il tempo e la vita*, Milano: Feltrinelli, 2015.

Brueggemeier, G. *et al.*, 'Social Justice in European Contract Law: A Manifesto', 10 *Eur. L. J.* 2004, p. 653 *et seq.*

Canaris, C.W., 'Grundrechte und Privatrecht', 184 *Archiv für die Civilistische Praxis*, 1984, p. 201 *et seq.*

Collins, H., 'Review', 10 *Eur. Rev. Cont. L.* 2014, pp. 466-472.

Derleder, P., 'Unterlegenenschutz im Vertragsrecht. Ein Modell für das Arbeitsrecht?', 28 *Kristische Justiz* 1995, p. 320 *et seq.*

Ecclesiastes 3:1-22 (King James Version).

Fabre-Magnan, M., 'Critique de la Notion de Contenu du Contrat', 3 *Revue des Contrats* 2015, p. 639 (II.C).

Gamillscheg, F., 'Zivilrechtliche Denkformen und die Entwicklung des Individualarbeitsrechts. Zum Verhältnis von Arbeitsrecht und BGB', *AcP* 1976, p. 197 *et seq.*

Gamillscheg, F., *Ausgewählte Schriften zu Arbeitsrecht und Rechtsvergleichung*, Baden-Baden: Nomos, 2006.

52 Collins, *supra* note 6.

Gitti, G., 'La Determinazione del Contenuto', *in* G. Villa (Ed.), *Il terzo contratto*, Bologna: Il Mulino, 2008, p. 110 *et seq.*

Graziadei, M., 'A Proposito di Life Time Contracts', 69 *Rivista Trimestrale di Diritto e Procedura Civile* 2015, p. 1317 *et seq.*

Grossi, P., *Locatio ad Longum Tempus: Locazione e Rapporti Reali di Godimento nella Problematica di Diritto Comune*, Napoli: Morano, 1963.

Hiez, D., 'À Propos de Life Time Contracts', 4 *Revue Trimestrelle de Droit Civil* 2014, pp. 817-827.

Höhn, G., *Kompensation Gestörter Vertragsparität*, München: Beck, 1982.

Hondius, E., 'Review', 37 *Nederlands Tijdschrift voor Burgerlijk Recht* 2014, pp. 308-309.

Kriz, J., Nohlen, D. & Schultze, R.-O. (Eds.), *Lexikon der Politik: Politikwissenschaftliche Methoden*, Vol. II, Munich: Springer.

Larenz, K., *Lehrbuch des Schuldrechts, I, Allgemeiner Teil*, München: Beck, 1987.

Lyon-Caen, G., 'Défense et Illustration du Contrat de Travail', *in* M. Villey (Ed.), *Archives de Philosophie du Droit*, Paris: Sirey, 1968, p. 69.

Mak, C., 'Book Review: Life Time Contracts: Social Long-term Contracts in Labour, Tenancy and Consumer Credit Law, *in* L. Nogler and U. Reifner' (Eds.), 2 *Eur. J. Comp. L. & Governance* 2015, p. 379 *et seq.*

Mengoni, L., *Diritto e valori*, Bologna: Il Mulino, 1985.

Micklitz, H.-W., 'Book Notes "Law"', 38 *J. Consumer Pol'y* 2015, p. 108.

Nogler, L., 'Die typologisch-funktionale Methode am Beispiel des Arbeitnehmerbegriffs', 11-12 *ZESAR* 2009, p. 465.

Nogler, L. & Reifner, U., 'The Principles of Life Time Contracts', *in* L. Nogler & U. Reifner (Eds.), *Life Time Contracts: Social Long-Term Contracts in Labour, Tenancy and Consumer Credit Law*, The Hague: Eleven International Publishing, 2014, pp. 5-10.

Nybergh, F., 'Access to Longterm Banking Services in the Nordic States', *in* L. Nogler & U. Reifner (Eds.), *Life Time Contracts: Social Long-Term Contracts in Labour, Tenancy and Consumer Credit Law*, The Hague: Eleven International Publishing, 2014, pp. 331-348.

Oppo, G., 'I Contratti di Durata', I *Rivista di Diritto Commerciale* 1943, p. 143 *et seq.*

Oppo, G., 'I Contratti di Durata', I *Rivista di Diritto Commerciale* 1944, p. 17 *et seq.*

Ortega Lozano, P.G., 'Recension', *Revista Española de Derecho del Trabajo* 2015, pp. 287-291.

Pinto-Oliveira, N.M., 'Uma Introducao aos Contratos Existenciais', *in* N.M. Pinto-Oliveira & B. MacCrorie (Eds.), *Em Torno de Life Time Contracts*, Braga, 2016, p. 43.

Pinto-Oliveira, N.M. & MacCrorie, B. (Eds.), *Em Torno de Life Time Contracts. Actas do colóquio internacional organizado pelo pelo grupo de investigação em Direito privado – phenómenos de constitucionalização, de materializaçãoe de socialização do Centro de Actas do colóquio internacional organizado pelo grupo de investigação interdisciplinar em Direito privado – fenómenos de constitucionalização, de materialização*, Braga: Direitos Humanos da Universidade do Minho, 2016.

Polanyi, K., *Una Società Umana, un'Umanità Sociale. Scritti 1918-1963*, Milano: Jaca Book, 1963.

Roppo, E., 'Parte Generale del Contratto, Contratti del Consumatore e Contratti Asimmetrici', 12 *Rivista di Diritto Privato* 2007, p. 669 *et seq.*

Ruffert, M., 'Die Rechtsprechung des Bundesverfassungsgerichts zum Privatrecht', 64 *Juristen Zeitung* 2009, pp. 389-390.

Sinzheimer, H., *Das Problem des Menschen im Recht*, Groningen: Batavia, 1933.

Sinzheimer, H., *Arbeitsrecht und Rechtssoziologie 2*, Frankfurt am Main: Europäische Verlagsanstalt, 1976.

Tamm, M., 'Buchbesprechung', 1 *Verbrauecher und Recht* 2015, pp. 39-40.

Vettori, G., 'Il Tempo dei Diritti', 68 *Riv. trim. dir. proc. civ.* 2014, p. 91.

Von Gierke, O., 'Dauernde Schuldverhältnisse', *in Jherings Jahrbücher für die Dogmatik des bürgerlichen Rechts* (Vol. 64), 1914, p. 24 *et seq.*

Weber, M., *Der Sozialismus*, Weinheim: Athenäum, 1995.

2 Life Time Contracts and General Contract Law in the EU: Pour un Droit Commun des Life Time Contracts

*Muriel Fabre-Magnan**

Quel est le projet des concepteurs de la notion de *Life Time Contracts* ? Ce travail a-t-il pour seule ambition de demeurer strictement doctrinal ?[1] De se limiter à analyser les règles techniques propres à certains contrats spéciaux et à comparer leurs évolutions respectives dans plusieurs systèmes juridiques ? Il est permis de penser, fût-ce contre l'avis de ses concepteurs mêmes, que la notion est plus fructueuse que cela. L'apparition, dans le contexte actuel, des Life Time Contracts n'est pas due au hasard. Il serait alors dommage de renoncer à lui faire produire des effets en droit commun des contrats (section 2.2). Il faudrait certes pour cela préciser auparavant le concept, et notamment sa traduction dans les langues continentales (section 2.1).

2.1 Le Concept de Life Time Contracts

La question est de savoir s'il est possible de trouver une unité conceptuelle aux Life Time Contracts, c'est-à-dire des traits communs justifiant une communauté – et aussi une particularité – de régime juridique. C'est en analysant les raisons de l'apparition des Life Time Contracts que l'on peut trouver les dénominations possibles, au moins dans les langues autres que l'anglais.

2.1.1 *Les Raisons de l'Apparition des Life Time Contracts*

Le droit des contrats se compose d'un droit commun des contrats (que l'on appelle parfois la théorie générale du droit des contrats),[2] et d'un droit spécial propre à chaque contrat. Comme l'explique le nouvel article 1105 du Code civil français issu d'une récente réforme du droit des contrats du 10 février 2016 (mais la règle est classique), "les contrats,

* Professeur à l'Université de Paris 1 (Panthéon-Sorbonne).

1 En ce sens, D. Hiez, "À propos des Life Time Contracts", *Revue trimestrielle de droit civil*, Vol. 4, 2014, p. 817: "C'est un travail donc strictement doctrinal. Une fois ce statut arrêté et l'éventuelle déception des praticiens assumée, il peut déployer tous ses effets."

2 Sur cette précision sémantique, *voir* la thèse classique de É. Savaux, *La théorie générale du contrat, mythe ou réalité?*, LGDJ, Paris, 1997.

qu'ils aient ou non une dénomination propre, sont soumis à des règles générales", qui "s'appliquent sous réserve" des "règles particulières à certains contrats [...] établies dans les dispositions propres à chacun d'eux".

En France, le droit commun des contrats n'avait guère été modifié depuis le Code civil de 1804, dont les historiens ont montré le caractère individualiste et centré sur la propriété. Les contractants y étaient représentés comme des individus abstraits et interchangeables, désancrés notamment de toute condition sociale. Ce sont alors les droits spéciaux (droit du travail, ou encore droit des contrats commerciaux) qui ont su innover et proposer des règles plus concrètes, adaptées aux situations de fait et notamment à l'inégalité des parties. On a alors pu constater une sorte de fuite vers ces contrats spéciaux, qui conduisait par là même à dessécher encore plus la théorie générale des contrats. Certains auteurs ont aussi essayé de renouveler l'étude des contrats en s'intéressant plus concrètement à l'objet de certaines clauses usuelles de la pratique contractuelle.[3]

La récente réforme française du droit des contrats introduit à son tour plusieurs mécanismes et notions permettant d'appréhender de façon beaucoup plus concrète et plus juste les situations contractuelles dans toute leur diversité. L'innovation se fait parfois – et c'est ce qui nous intéresse ici – par l'introduction de nouvelles catégories de contrats, lorsqu'il apparaît pertinent de réserver à certains types de contrats un régime juridique à part, fût-ce simplement sur une seule règle. C'est ainsi que, à l'occasion de la récente réforme du droit français des contrats, plusieurs types de contrats ont fait officiellement leur entrée dans le Code civil.

La principale illustration en est la notion de contrat d'adhésion, que la doctrine avait mis en avant depuis longtemps, mais à laquelle la jurisprudence n'avait jamais vraiment attaché de règle particulière. C'est à présent chose faite. La notion est également un très bon exemple de la perte de pensée[4] qui advient lorsqu'on fait un usage exclusif de l'anglais. Le contrat d'adhésion "est celui dont les conditions générales, soustraites à la négociation, sont déterminées à l'avance par l'une des parties", par opposition au contrat de gré à gré qui "est celui dont les stipulations sont librement négociées entre les parties" (nouvel article 1110 du Code civil). Il ne se confond donc pas avec la notion de *preformulated standard contract* par laquelle il est généralement traduit, par exemple dans la directive 93/13/CEE du Conseil du 5 avril 1993 concernant les clauses abusives dans les contrats conclus avec les consommateurs,[5] ou encore dans le Cadre commun de réfé-

---

3 *Voir* le précieux W. Dross, Clausier, *Dictionnaire des clauses ordinaires et extraordinaires des contrats de droit privé interne*, LexisNexis, Paris, 3ème éd., 2016, *ou encore*, J. Mestre & J.Ch. Roda (Eds.), *Les principales clauses des contrats d'affaires*, Lextenso, Paris, 2011; G. Helleringer, *Les clauses contractuelles. Essai de typologie*, LGDJ, Paris, 2012, préf. L. Aynès, postface F. Terré.

4 *Voir* H. Bruhns & F. Nies (Eds.), "La science pense en plusieurs langues" ("Wissenschaft denkt in mehreren Sprachen"), *Trivium*, No.15, 2013.

5 Selon l'article 3, 2. de cette directive, "Une clause est toujours considérée comme n'ayant pas fait l'objet d'une négociation individuelle lorsqu'elle a été rédigée préalablement et que le consommateur n'a, de ce fait, pas pu avoir d'influence sur son contenu, notamment dans le cadre d'un contrat d'adhésion. Le fait que certains éléments d'une clause ou qu'une clause isolée aient fait l'objet d'une négociation individuelle n'ex-

rence.[6] Un contrat d'adhésion est en effet celui qui, pour l'essentiel, n'est pas négociable (un voyageur en train pourra choisir son trajet, mais ni l'horaire, ni le tarif, ni les autres conditions générales du transport), mais il n'est pas nécessairement un contrat type (*standard contract*). Un contrat sur mesure proposé une seule fois à un seul partenaire peut très bien être un contrat d'adhésion. Quoi qu'il en soit, désormais, dans un tel contrat, "toute clause qui crée un déséquilibre significatif entre les droits et obligations des parties au contrat est réputée non écrite" (nouvel article 1171). La règle de principe selon laquelle le juge ne contrôle pas l'équivalence des prestations mais seulement l'absence totale de contrepartie trouve ainsi une exception dans les contrats d'adhésion. De même, le Code civil prévoit depuis la réforme que, "dans le doute, le contrat de gré à gré s'interprète contre le créancier et en faveur du débiteur, et le contrat d'adhésion contre celui qui l'a proposé" (nouvel article 1190). Le législateur a ainsi été convaincu qu'une catégorie jusque-là purement doctrinale méritait en réalité un traitement juridique différencié, et il en a donc fait un concept juridique. Autre catégorie nouvelle à faire son entrée dans le Code civil (nouvel article 1111): celle de contrat cadre, qui "est un accord par lequel les parties conviennent des caractéristiques générales de leurs relations contractuelles futures", par opposition aux contrats d'application qui "en précisent les modalités d'exécution". C'est cette fois-ci les juges qui avaient consacré la notion (seuls des juristes étrangers peuvent encore penser que la jurisprudence française n'est pas source de droit !) à l'occasion de la question de la détermination du prix dans les contrats. Entérinant la solution jurisprudentielle, la réforme du droit des contrats admet que, dans les contrats cadre, il peut être convenu que le prix sera fixé unilatéralement par l'une des parties, à charge pour elle d'en motiver le montant en cas de contestation. C'est seulement en cas d'abus dans la fixation du prix que le juge peut condamner cette partie à des dommages et intérêts et, le cas échéant, prononcer la résolution du contrat (nouvel article 1164 du Code civil).

Quelle est, dans cette ligne, la particularité propre aux Life Time Contracts ?

Ce n'est pas la nécessité de protection d'une partie faible. Le droit français des contrats contient désormais, comme la plupart des droits européens des contrats, des instruments permettant de compenser l'inégalité des parties. Le Code civil contient ainsi aujourd'hui des règles sur l'abus de dépendance, défini de façon plus large que la seule violence éco-

---

clut pas l'application du présent article au reste d'un contrat si l'appréciation globale permet de conclure qu'il s'agit malgré tout d'un contrat d'adhésion (en anglais: "A term shall always be regarded as not individually negotiated where it has been drafted in advance and the consumer has therefore not been able to influence the substance of the term, particularly in the context of a pre-formulated standard contract. The fact that certain aspects of a term or one specific term have been individually negotiated shall not exclude the application of this Article to the rest of a contract if an overall assessment of the contract indicates that it is nevertheless a pre-formulated standard contract").

6 *Voir* la section 4 sur les *unfair terms* qui vise l'hypothèse d'un "term forming part of standard terms supplied by one party".

nomique (*economic duress*), puisque toutes les formes potentielles de dépendance sont stigmatisées (par exemple la dépendance affective ou sociale). Le nouvel article 1143 du Code civil énonce ainsi qu' "il y a également violence lorsqu'une partie, abusant de l'état de dépendance dans lequel se trouve son cocontractant, obtient de lui un engagement qu'il n'aurait pas souscrit en l'absence d'une telle contrainte et en tire un avantage manifestement excessif". L'ordonnance consacre aussi la théorie de l'imprévision et admet la renégociation et même la révision forcée du contrat (à la demande d'une seule des parties) en cas de "changement de circonstances imprévisible lors de la conclusion du contrat" qui "rend l'exécution excessivement onéreuse pour une partie qui n'avait pas accepté d'en assumer le risque" (nouvel article 1195).

Les Life Time Contracts ont pour point commun une autre idée: celle de contrats importants pour la vie d'un des contractants (*Life*), et qui sont dès lors le plus souvent de longue durée (*Time*). Selon les premiers travaux du groupe, il s'agirait de regrouper les contrats de travail, de bail, et de crédit à la consommation.

Avant d'essayer d'élaborer un régime commun aux Life Time Contracts, et pour décider de l'opportunité d'un tel régime commun, il est intéressant d'essayer de comprendre pourquoi le besoin s'est fait sentir de créer une telle catégorie.

L'idée sous-jacente ne nous semble pas éloignée de celle qui avait présidé à l'invention de la notion française de service public. L'École éponyme menée par Léon Duguit [1859-1928] développa l'idée que l'État n'est pas fondé sur la souveraineté mais sur le service public, à savoir l'idée que certains biens fondamentaux devaient être garantis à tous, ce qui a ouvert la voie à l'idée d'État providence.

Dans un monde aujourd'hui dominé par le paradigme utilitariste et libéral, où tout est progressivement privatisé, l'idée est redécouverte d'un filet de sécurité ou d'un plancher qui doivent permettre à tous d'avoir le minimum nécessaire (le premier ouvrage sur les Life Time Contracts publié en 2014 évoque, sur la page intérieure de titre, l'idée de "services of first necessity"). La justice sociale ne peut se satisfaire de ce que tout soit laissé aux seules forces du marché. l'État doit donc intervenir, au minimum sur le mode de la "régulation", que l'anglais ne permet pas de distinguer de l'ancienne "réglementation" dont elle se distingue pourtant à maints égards. "Aux États-Unis, c'est la notion de *gouvernance* qui est le plus souvent utilisée à cet effet (par opposition à *government*), tandis qu'en Europe continentale on parle plus volontiers de régulation (*Regulierung, regolazione*) pour se démarquer de la simple réglementation (*Regelung, regolamentazione*)".[7] En mécanique, la régulation désigne l'ajustement spontané d'une machine aux objectifs qui lui sont assignés.[8] Plutôt que d'intervenir de façon autoritaire ou uniforme, on met en place des objectifs et des garde-fous en laissant une certaine marge de liberté aux agents pour naviguer entre les bornes définies. Les entreprises chargées d'un service d'intérêt économique général doivent alors se voir assigner des objectifs autres que la seule recher-

7 *Voir* A. Supiot, *Critique du droit du travail*, PUF, Paris, 2007, p. IX.
8 Id., p. X.

che du profit. C'est autour de cette idée qu'étaient apparues ce qu'on appelle les "autorités de régulation", chargées de veiller au bon fonctionnement d'un secteur considéré comme participant de l'intérêt général. Dans ce contexte, Marie-Anne Frison-Roche a introduit la notion très stimulante et très éclairante d'entreprise "cruciale", définie tout à la fois "d'une façon négative (l'entreprise dont la défaillance fait s'effondrer le secteur) et d'une façon positive (l'entreprise dont l'activité fait évoluer le secteur pour le bien public, notamment futur)".[9] Elle explique qu'il faut réguler les entreprises en situation de monopole (transport, communication), mais aussi les entreprises "ayant pour objectif de conquérir un espace crucial" (Google, par exemple). Plus récemment, elle montre que ces entreprises cruciales qu'il faut réguler ne se définissent plus seulement par des secteurs mais aussi par type d'entreprise.[10] L'idée est la même: lorsque l'intérêt général est en jeu, il n'est pas possible de laisser libre cours aux volontés des parties et un socle minimal de règles doit être imposé.

L'apparition des Life Time Contracts est liée à ce même mouvement. Certains services publics sont désormais fournis par des entreprises privées, et ils ne sont donc plus disponibles que par le biais de contrats privés. Ceux-ci deviennent dès lors cruciaux pour la personne.

2.1.2 *La Dénomination et la Traduction des Life Time Contracts*

Dans les langues latines, la notion de Life Time Contracts a été traduite par celle de contrats d'existence, en y ajoutant des références à l'idée de temps. En français cela donne: "contrats à temps essentiels à l'existence de la personne" ; en italien: "contratti di durata per l'esistenza della persona" ; enfin en espagnol: "contratos para la existencia", ou "contratos sociales a largo plazo" (contrats sociaux de long terme).

Autant le dire simplement, en français cela ne veut rien dire. Une lecture naturelle fait voir, dans un premier temps, d'un côté les "contrats" et, de l'autre, "à temps essentiels", comme si c'était les temps qui étaient essentiels, ce qui ne veut rien dire, surtout au pluriel. Si on avait voulu que le qualificatif "essentiels" se rapportât à "contrats", il eut fallu parler de "contrats essentiels à temps". Mais la notion de "contrat à temps" est également très maladroite, car en droit français elle fait plutôt penser à un contrat dont la durée est au contraire encadrée. Un célèbre article du Code civil datant de 1804, l'article 1780, énonce en effet, dans une formulation très connue, qu'on ne peut engager ses services "qu'à temps" ou "pour une entreprise déterminée". Un engagement ou un contrat "à temps" s'oppose ainsi à un engagement perpétuel. Il peut donc être à durée

9 M.A. Frison-Roche, '"Les entreprises 'cruciales' et leur régulation", *in* A. Supiot (Ed.), *L'entreprise dans un monde sans frontières. Perspectives économiques et juridiques*, Paris, Dalloz, 2015, p. 253; M.A. Frison-Roche, "Réguler les 'entreprises cruciales'", *Recueil Dalloz*, No. 27, 2014, p. 1556 *et seq.*

10 Frison-Roche, *supra* note 9, p. 1556 *et seq.*

indéterminée, mais non pas engager un contractant pour toute la durée de sa vie. Les Life Time Contracts ne sont certes pas des contrats perpétuels, qui seraient nuls, mais en même temps ils veulent au contraire indiquer l'idée que certains contrats seraient nécessaires durant toute la vie des personnes.

Une traduction littérale de la notion de Life Time Contracts ne serait pas plus satisfaisante. La formule *Life Time* fait penser à un contrat qui s'étale sur toute la durée de la vie, ce qu'on appelle en droit français des contrats viagers. La traduction serait cependant fort mal venue, car ces contrats renvoient à tout autre chose, et notamment aux ventes en viager, qui sont des contrats où une personne relativement âgée vend un bien immobilier au prix d'un capital fixe initial inférieur à la valeur réelle du bien (que l'on appelle en droit français un "bouquet"), auquel s'ajoute une rente viagère due donc jusqu'au décès du crédirentier. On parle d'ailleurs en anglais aussi, pour désigner ces contrats, de "Lifetime Sale Contracts". En Français l'analogie est cependant fort mal venue, car elle lie très explicitement ces contrats à l'idée de mort (on dit d'ailleurs souvent de ces contrats qu'ils favorisent le "vœu de mort", le "*votum mortis*", dans la mesure où le débirentier a intérêt à ce que son créancier meure rapidement), alors que les Life Time Contracts sont destinés à fournir les besoins de base nécessaires pour vivre.

La notion de contrat de dépendance ne serait pas plus appropriée, car elle renvoie trop à l'idée de partie faible qui n'est pas le point le plus original qu'introduit la notion de Life Time Contracts. La protection de la partie faible est une idée ancienne et à présent très ancrée en droit commun des contrats. La notion de Life Time Contracts renvoie, quant à elle, non pas tant à une notion procédurale ou à l'inégalité structurelle entre les parties qu'à la nécessité du contrat pour l'un des cocontractants. Elle oblige ainsi à regarder de plus près l'objet et la matière du contrat qui sont des points ayant toujours été délaissés dans la théorie générale du contrat. Le droit commun des contrats conçoit en effet principalement le contenu du contrat de façon abstraite et mesurable. Il suffit par exemple, comme on le sait, dans la plupart des droits, que la contrepartie ne soit pas dérisoire ou illusoire, mais un simple grain de poivre est une contrepartie valable ("*a pepper corn is a valid consideration*"). Cela montre précisément qu'on n'est pas très regardant sur le contenu du contrat...

La notion de contrat "d'existence" n'est pas non plus satisfaisante. Pour un Français, elle fait immanquablement penser à Sartre et à l'existentialisme... Il ne s'agit pourtant pas de philosophie mais bien de nécessités matérielles pour l'être humain. Certes, si l'on se tourne plutôt du côté de Heidegger, le vocabulaire convient davantage. On sait en effet que, chez le philosophe allemand, seuls les êtres humains existent, tandis que les animaux sont simplement là. Exister c'est avoir à être, et seul le *Dasein* a à être. En d'autres termes, l'essence du *Dasein* tient dans son existence, ce qui conviendrait mieux pour les besoins essentiels des personnes. On sait cependant que Heidegger utilise alors plutôt le néologisme d'"ek-sistence" ("*Die Ek-sistenz*") pour marquer que "exister" signifie assumer le *Dasein*, c'est-à-dire recevoir ou habiter le là.[11] Or le *ex* latin exprime la sortie, c'est-à-dire le passage d'un intérieur à un extérieur, tandis que le *ek* grec dit plutôt l'ouverture, l'espacement sans dehors ni dedans, qui est en réalité le monde.[12] L'ek-sistence conviendrait ainsi sans doute mieux en ce qu'elle marque le destin de notre être-au-monde. Il n'est pas certain cependant que le droit civil des contrats puisse reprendre un jour ce néologisme heideggérien...

On pourrait penser alors à qualifier les Life Time Contracts de contrats "de subsistance". Le radical "sto", du verbe latin "stare", est en effet commun avec le mot "existence", dont à nouveau l'idée générale rend assez bien celle des Life Time Contracts. "Stare" signifie "se dresser", "être debout", "être solide, inébranlable, fixe". Le préfixe "sub" renvoie alors à ce qui est en dessous, qui soutient, qui aide à (sup)porter. Les Life Time Contracts apportent aux êtres humains les biens minimums dont ils ont besoin, à savoir un filet de sécurité ou plutôt, pour garder l'image de ce qui est au-dessous, un plancher nécessaire à leur existence. Le mot se retrouve dans toutes les langues latines (en italien *sussistenza*, en espagnol *subsistencia*), et même en anglais (*subsistence*). Le mot allemand *unterhalt*, qui signifie "subsistance", renvoie exactement à la même idée, puisqu'il vient du mot *halt* qui signifie un appui. La notion contient ainsi l'idée sous-jacente au mot *life*, à savoir la nécessité d'assurer les besoins vitaux de la personne. C'est ainsi que, le 1er avril 2016 est entré en vigueur au Royaume-Uni un "*National Living Wage*" que l'on traduit précisément souvent par un salaire national "de subsistance".

La traduction la meilleure nous semble cependant être, dans la lignée de l'idée d' "entreprise cruciale" évoquée plus haut, celle de contrats "cruciaux". Ce qualificatif nous paraît être davantage adapté car il ne recouvre pas nécessairement un type donné de contrat. Tous les contrats de travail sont certes en général cruciaux, car même si la personne en cumule plusieurs, c'est qu'ils lui sont tous nécessaires pour vivre. Il n'en va cependant pas de même des autres types de contrats. Un contrat de bail n'est ainsi crucial que s'il est afférent au domicile de la personne. Le contrat de location d'une résidence secondaire n'aura pas le même statut, alors pourtant qu'il s'agit du même type de contrat, ayant le même objet et la même contrepartie. La qualification de contrat crucial permet en outre d'élargir ce que serait la notion de contrat de subsistance. Ainsi par exemple, un contrat d'accès à Internet ne pourrait pas vraiment être qualifié de contrat de subsistance, ou même d'existence, alors qu'il est clairement un contrat crucial dans le monde d'aujourd'hui. On pourrait dire à peu près la même chose par exemple du contrat d'ouverture d'un compte bancaire. La notion de contrat crucial montre également mieux que celle de contrat de subsistance que l'idée principale est l'importance du contrat pour la personne, plus que la protection d'une partie faible. Le qualificatif "crucial" marque enfin et surtout l'idée essentielle introduite et développée par Marie-Anne Frison-Roche, à savoir que certains secteurs/domaines/entreprises/contrats, bien que faisant partie du privé ont à voir avec l'intérêt général, et nécessitent donc une régulation particulière.

11 *Voir* P. Arjakovsky *et al.*, *Le Dictionnaire Martin Heidegger*, Cerf, Paris, 2013, p. 465 *et seq.*

12 Arjakovsky *et al.*, *supra* note 11, p. 467.

En l'occurrence, c'est parce qu'ils sont cruciaux pour la personne que ces contrats ont besoin d'être régulés d'une façon spéciale.

2.2 Le Régime des Life Time Contracts

Le droit commun des contrats contient déjà des règles suffisantes sur le processus de formation des contrats, les vices du consentement, ou même sur la consistance de la contrepartie. Ainsi, la récente réforme française du droit des contrats du 10 février 2016 introduit l'abus de dépendance, consolide le devoir d'information, ou encore propose de nombreux outils pour permettre aux juges, malgré l'interdiction de principe, de contrôler l'équilibre des prestations échangées.

Il existe cependant un certain nombre d'angles morts de la théorie générale du contrat, et qui, précisément, sont très bien mis en lumière dans les contrats réunis sous le vocable de Life Time Contracts. Ils correspondent à des types de règles auxquelles le droit commun des contrats pourrait aussi s'intéresser, à supposer qu'il consente à élargir son regard et à s'intéresser au contenu concret des contrats. Le grand intérêt des Life Time Contracts est en effet qu'ils s'attachent aux prestations fournies par le contrat et surtout, à travers les besoins que celui-ci permet d'assouvir, aux personnes concrètes qui contractent. Les contractants ne sont plus des particules élémentaires abstraites et interchangeables. On regarde leurs besoins concrets et la façon dont elles peuvent les assurer. La tendance lourde du droit des contrats contemporain est à l'inverse d'objectiver les contrats et de faire disparaître les personnes: il s'agit de voir l'obligation comme un bien et non plus comme un lien. La critique vaut particulièrement en matière financière. Si la crise des *subprimes* a fait reprendre conscience (l'espace d'un instant aujourd'hui dissipé) que les titres étaient composés d'engagements personnels reposant *in fine* sur la foi dans la parole, le mouvement de fond se poursuit à nouveau inexorablement: la financiarisation de l'économie exige de liquidifier tous les biens puis, *in fine*, d'objectiver et de "liquidifier" les personnes – pour ne pas dire les "liquider"[13] – car elles sont une source de viscosité du marché.

Une théorie globale des Life Time Contracts pourrait dès lors remettre les personnes concrètes au centre du droit des contrats.[14] Il en découlerait un certain nombre de règles nouvelles qui pourraient être intégrées dans une théorie renouvelée du droit commun des contrats.

13 *Voir* A. Supiot, "Contribution à une analyse juridique de la crise économique de 2008", *Revue internationale du travail*, Vol. 149, n°2, 2010, p. 165, qui dénonce "l'utopie d'un marché total, sous l'égide duquel les hommes, les signes et les choses ont tous vocation à être rendus commensurables et mobilisables dans une compétition devenue globale, c'est-à-dire à être 'liquidés' au sens juridique du terme."

14 *Voir* A. Hyde, *Les atteintes aux libertés individuelles par contrat. Contribution à la théorie de l'obligation*, IRJS Éditions, Paris, 2016, qui propose "une théorie de l'obligation contractuelle recentrée sur la personne physique au cœur du rapport d'obligations plutôt que sur un rapport d'obligations désincarné."

2.2.1 Accès aux Life Time Contracts

Le Principe 8 des Life Time Contracts évoque la question de l'accès aux contrats, mais pour la restreindre à un principe de non-discrimination bien réducteur. Le principe de non-discrimination est en outre commun à tous les contrats et non pas propre aux Life Time Contracts.

La particularité des Life Time Contracts est que ce sont des contrats permettant aux individus de pourvoir à leurs besoins essentiels. Ils permettent de se procurer des biens ou des services considérés comme cruciaux. La première garantie serait alors de consacrer un droit d'accès à ces biens ou services indispensables. En l'absence d'un service public garantissant à tous ces biens ou ces services, ces contrats sont en effet le seul moyen d'accès à des droits considérés comme fondamentaux: droit à la santé, à la culture, à l'éducation ou encore, dans le monde d'aujourd'hui, accès à Internet ou à des services bancaires.

On pourrait d'ailleurs à cet égard parler aussi de contrats fondamentaux, tout à la fois pour marquer que ces contrats sont essentiels pour la personne, et aussi qu'ils lui permettent de réaliser leurs droits fondamentaux économiques et sociaux. Ils sont nécessaires en particulier au respect de la dignité de la personne humaine, au sens notamment de la Convention universelle des droits de l'homme de 1948, à savoir le droit pour chaque individu de voir ses besoins de base assurés. Comme l'énonce l'article 22 de la Déclaration universelle des droits de l'homme de 1948, "toute personne, en tant que membre de la société, a droit à la sécurité sociale ; elle est fondée à obtenir la satisfaction des droits économiques, sociaux et culturels indispensables à sa dignité et au libre développement de sa personnalité, grâce à l'effort national et à la coopération internationale, compte tenu de l'organisation et des ressources de chaque pays".

Lorsque ce sont des contrats qui permettent la réalisation de ces droits économiques et sociaux fondamentaux, un droit d'accès doit être assuré à tous. Participent ainsi de la dignité humaine évoquée par la déclaration universelle, le droit à un travail décent et le droit à un logement décent, ou encore le droit à un revenu minimum de subsistance. On peut en revanche, du point de vue de la démarche générale, être sceptique sur l'idée de mettre le contrat de crédit dans la même catégorie que le contrat de travail ou encore le contrat de bail afférent au domicile. Les contrats de crédit participent en effet d'une politique consumériste et l'endettement des particuliers n'est sans doute pas un gage de leur libération.

L'accès aux Life Time Contracts suppose que le prix proposé pour les biens ou services cruciaux soit raisonnable. Il faudrait au demeurant en profiter pour dépasser l'analyse contractuelle classique qui demeure strictement interindividuelle. La notion de justice contractuelle et de juste prix doit être aujourd'hui appréhendée dans le cadre d'une juste répartition des richesses et des plus-values, notamment dans les chaînes de production et également dans les chaînes de distribution.

Enfin la notion de droit d'accès suppose un égal accès pour tous, effectivement sans discrimination, mais surtout au bénéfice de toutes les personnes et non pas seulement des plus faibles. Par définition même, les Life Time Contracts sont destinés aux besoins de base qui sont ceux de tous les êtres humains et non pas seulement d'une certaine catégorie d'entre eux. C'est d'ailleurs précisément pourquoi la catégorie est originale, et ne se limite pas au prisme habituel et aujourd'hui devenu classique de la protection de la partie faible.

2.2.2 *Continuité des Life Time Contracts*

Si l'on prend au sérieux la notion de Life Time Contracts, et donc l'idée de besoins de subsistance, l'accès aux biens et aux services de base ne doit pas être interrompu. Où l'on retrouve, une fois de plus, l'analogie avec la théorie des services publics dont un des principes essentiels est celui de la continuité du service public.

Il s'agit alors, comme par exemple dans le contrat de travail, de limiter les causes possibles de rupture du contrat. La résolution du contrat doit être limitée à des cas très particuliers de graves inexécutions, et requérir un préavis important (voir le Principe 11 des Life Time Contracts).

Le droit commun des Life Time Contracts pourrait aussi prévoir une obligation de motiver la rupture unilatérale de ces contrats cruciaux. Le droit commun des contrats – au moins le droit français – a toujours été réticent à admettre une telle obligation de motiver la rupture unilatérale des contrats,[15] sauf précisément dans les droits spéciaux comme le droit du travail. Que ce soit le droit général de chaque contractant de mettre fin de façon unilatérale à un contrat à durée indéterminée, ou le droit particulier à la résolution du contrat en cas d'inexécution par l'une des parties, la seule exigence traditionnellement posée par le droit français consiste à imposer, à la partie qui souhaite rompre, un préavis raisonnable. La récente réforme du droit des contrats français va un peu plus loin.

---

15 Certains arrêts ont pu laisser entrevoir un contrôle de la motivation de la rupture, ou tout au moins que celle-ci n'était pas entièrement discrétionnaire; la Cour de cassation a ainsi pu reprocher à une Cour d'appel d'avoir validé la rupture sans avoir constaté que le concessionnaire avait été informé des raisons qui la motivaient (Com., 20 janvier 1998, pourvoi n 96-18353; Recueil Dalloz 1998, p. 413 *et seq.*, note Ch. Jamin). D'autres arrêts en revanche semblent plus réticents, et retiennent "que le concédant peut résilier le contrat de concession sans donner de motifs, sous réserve de respecter le délai de préavis et sauf abus du droit de résiliation" (Com., 7 octobre 1997, n° 95-14158, l'attendu cité étant certes repris de la cour d'appel). On peut ajouter à ce tableau les arrêts relatifs à la question très similaire du non-renouvellement des contrats à durée déterminée. Là encore, la Cour de cassation a parfois retenu que lorsque "le refus de renouvellement du contrat était dépourvu de motif tandis qu'il causait préjudice à [l'agent commercial]", la cour d'appel avait pu caractériser "son caractère abusif" (Com., 27 octobre 1998, n° 96-11012) ; mais elle retient le plus souvent que "le concédant n'est pas tenu de motiver sa décision de ne pas conclure un nouveau contrat de concession" (Com., 4 janvier 1994, n° 91-18170), ou encore que l'auteur de la rupture "n'avait pas à donner de motifs au non-renouvellement du contrat" (Com., 25 avril 2001, *Recueil Dalloz* 2001, p. 3237, obs. D. Mazeaud; *Revue trimestrielle de droit civil* 2002, p. 99, obs. J. Mestre et B. Fages).

Elle entérine d'abord la solution d'un célèbre arrêt *Tocqueville*,[16] et prévoit ainsi (nouvel article 1126) que "le créancier peut, à ses risques et périls, résoudre le contrat par voie de notification." Le texte ajoute que, "sauf urgence, il doit préalablement mettre en demeure le débiteur défaillant de satisfaire à son engagement dans un délai raisonnable". Surtout, le nouvel article précise que "lorsque l'inexécution persiste, le créancier notifie au débiteur la résolution du contrat *et les raisons qui la motivent*". Une telle obligation de motiver la rupture est particulièrement opportune pour les contrats cruciaux.[17] Ces contrats sont fondamentaux pour la personne et seul un nombre limité de raisons, dont elle doit avoir l'explication, doivent pouvoir permettre de mettre fin à ces contrats.

Surtout, et c'est là où les mesures seraient plus originales, ces contrats pourraient s'accompagner de politiques publiques de soutien. C'est ainsi par exemple qu'en France, une loi du 24 mars 2014 dite loi ALUR (accès au logement et un urbanisme rénové) met en place une "garantie universelle des loyers". Il s'agit d'un dispositif "ayant pour objet de couvrir, sous la forme d'un système d'aides, les bailleurs contre les risques d'impayés de loyer, afin de favoriser l'accès au logement et de prévenir les risques d'expulsion". l'État ou les collectivités publiques peuvent ainsi se porter garants du paiement de certains loyers, et on pourrait étendre de telles garanties à tous les besoins de base du type gaz ou électricité, voire pour l'accès à Internet ou pour le maintien d'un compte bancaire, sachant que dans le monde d'aujourd'hui il est parfois difficile d'accéder à certains services sans passer par le réseau ou sans références bancaires. La continuité du contrat serait ainsi assurée sans que le cocontractant fournisseur de biens ou services cruciaux en soit trop désavantagé. Ce n'est pas, par exemple, à un bailleur personne privée de supporter le risque de non paiement pour que son locataire puisse jouir de son droit au logement. Ces risques peuvent être assumés de façon solidaire. Certaines entreprises ayant bénéficié de la privatisation de services publics pourraient être également tenues de prendre en charge une partie de ces risques, et se voir imposer des obligations de type service public.

2.2.3 Qualité des Biens et des Services Fournis par les Life Time Contracts

Un autre point obscur de la théorie générale du contrat est celui de la qualité des biens et des services fournis par contrat. Le droit commun des contrats se contente par exemple de vérifier que l'acheteur ne s'est pas trompé sur le produit qu'il achète, et qu'on lui

16 Civ. 1re, 13 octobre 1998, pourvoi n° 96-21485: "attendu que la gravité du comportement d'une partie à un contrat peut justifier que l'autre partie y mette fin de façon unilatérale à ses risques et périls, et que cette gravité, dont l'appréciation qui en est donnée par une autorité ordinale ne lie pas les tribunaux, n'est pas nécessairement exclusive d'un délai de préavis."

17 *Voir*, en ce sens, M. Fabre-Magnan, "L'obligation de motivation en droit des contrats", *in Études offertes à Jacques Ghestin, Le contrat au début du XXIe siècle*, Paris, LGDJ, 2001, p. 301 et *seq.*; M. Fabre-Magnan, "Pour la reconnaissance d'une obligation de motiver la rupture des contrats de dépendance économique", *Revue des contrats*, 2004, No. 2, p. 573 *et seq.*

délivre exactement le bien qu'il a acquis. S'agissant de biens ou services essentiels, le droit devrait s'intéresser davantage à leur qualité. Des normes et standards devraient être imposés pour empêcher que soient mis sur le marché des biens dont l'obsolescence est programmée, dont les composants ne sont pas remplaçables, ou encore indécents. Dans tous ces cas, la vérification de la conformité du bien ou du service fourni au bien ou au service promis – qui est la règle de base du droit des contrats – ne suffit pas. Il faut encore s'assurer et faire en sorte que le bien ou le service promis soit d'une qualité minimale. La règle devrait valoir toutes les fois où les contractants ne peuvent pas vraiment contrôler la qualité des biens ou des services qu'ils acquièrent, et elle vaut *a fortiori* pour les biens et services correspondant à des besoins de base.

La notion de Life Time Contracts a l'avantage de prêter attention aux besoins concrets des personnes et donc, nous l'avons vu, de transcender le cas échéant les types classiques de contrats. La notion de travail décent ou de logement décent doit ainsi, par exemple, être appréciée indépendamment de la dénomination et du type précis de contrat en cause. Les conditions de travail doivent être décentes que la personne soit engagée par un contrat de travail salarié ou par un contrat indépendant, dès lors que celui-ci est nécessaire pour sa subsistance. Il ne suffit pas d'utiliser le cadre du travail dit "indépendant" pour que la personne le soit réellement (comme le démontre chaque jour l' "uberisation" de la société).[18]

Les garanties légales devraient en outre être précisées, imposées dans davantage de contrats, et leur mise en œuvre facilitée (notamment par des actions de groupe).

2.3 Conclusion

Le droit commun des contrats a toujours été irrigué par les contrats spéciaux qui, plus ancrés sur les besoins concrets de la pratique, permettent de faire apparaître les évolutions nécessaires. La notion de Life Time Contracts a le grand mérite d'avoir mis le doigt à son tour sur de nouveaux points habituellement ignorés par ce droit commun. Le regroupement original de contrats qu'il opère a permis de comprendre les règles nécessaires, non pas seulement pour sauvegarder les intérêts d'une partie faible, mais pour garantir à chacun les biens et services cruciaux permettant d'assurer ses besoins de base. Ces règles mériteraient de se voir reconnaître une certaine transversalité, et même d'accéder au droit commun des contrats. Les concepteurs de la notion de Life Time Contracts ne devraient pas renoncer par avance à cette idée et à ce projet. Les difficultés de l'époque appellent à des ambitions fortes.

---

18 *Voir* la très stimulante *Proposition de Code du travail*, Dalloz, Paris, 2017, établie sous l'égide du Groupe de recherche pour un autre Code du travail (GR-PACT) dirigé par E. Dockès, et en particulier la section 1 du chapitre 1 sur la notion de contrat de travail.

Bibliography

Arjakovsky, P. *et al., Le Dictionnaire Martin Heidegger*, Paris: Cerf, 2013.

Bruhns, H., & Nies, F. (Eds.), "La Science Pense en Plusieurs Langues" ("Wissenschaft denkt in mehreren Sprachen"), *Trivium*, No.15, 2013.

Dockès, E. (Ed.), *Proposition de Code du Travail*, Paris: Dalloz, 2017.

Dross, W., *Clausier: Dictionnaire des Clauses Ordinaires Et Extraordinaires Des Contrats De Droit Privé Interne* (3ème éd), Paris: LexisNexis, 2016.

Fabre-Magnan, M., "L'obligation de Motivation en Droit des Contrats", *in Études Offertes à Jacques Ghestin, Le Contrat au Début du XXIe Siècle*, Paris: LGDJ, 2001, p. 301 et *seq.*

Fabre-Magnan, M., "Pour la Reconnaissance d'une Obligation de Motiver la Rupture des Contrats de Dépendance Economique", *Revue des Contrats*, 2004, No. 2, p. 573 *et seq.*

Frison-Roche, M.A., "Les Entreprises "Cruciales" et leur Régulation", *in* A. Supiot (Ed.), *L'entreprise dans un Monde sans Frontières. Perspectives Economiques et Juridiques*, Paris: Dalloz, 2015, p. 253.

Frison-Roche, M.A., "Réguler les "Entreprises Cruciales"", *Recueil Dalloz*, No. 27, 2014, p. 1556 *et seq.*

Helleringer, G., *Les Clauses Contractuelles. Essai de Typologie*, Paris: LGDJ, 2012.

Hiez, D., "À Propos des Life Time Contracts", *Revue Trimestrielle de Droit civil*, Vol. 4, 2014, p. 817.

Hyde, A., *Les Atteintes aux Libertés Individuelles par Contrat. Contribution à la Théorie de l'Obligation*, Paris: IRJS Éditions, 2016.

Mestre, J. & Roda, J.Ch. (Eds.), *Les Principales Clauses des Contrats d'Affaires*, Paris: Lextenso, 2011.

Savaux, É., *La Théorie Générale Du Contrat, Mythe Ou Réalité?*, Paris: LGDJ, 1997.

Supiot, A., "Contribution à une Analyse Juridique de la Crise Économique de 2008", *Revue Internationale du Travail*, Vol. 149, n°2, 2010, p. 165.

Supiot, A., *Critique du Droit du Travail*, Paris: PUF, 2007.

3 Life Time Contracts and Contracts in General: Fundamental Rights of the Person and Their Family, Fair Price, Termination

Andrea Nicolussi[*]

3.1 Contracts, Legal Values, and Morals

In the confused times in which we live nowadays, a re-ignited interest in the studying of the relationship between contract and ethics is a significant development and to be welcomed. Moreover, from the perspective of private law, the wall that was built in the Modern Ages to rigidly separate, not simply distinguish, law from morals finally shows some cracks. The reference to ethics cannot only be considered as an obvious consequence of the chasm deriving from the economic crisis, but also as a recognition of the fact that pure normativism and state sovereignty have decreased in effectiveness. That leads, inevitably, to an increase in judge-made law, and judges are obliged to refer their judgments, implicitly or explicitly, to a set of values. From a correct juridical perspective in civil law countries, this occurs through those bridges spanning law and ethics, such as general values, including good faith or constitutional values. Life Time Contracts may also be considered, from this point of view, as an attempt to provide the courts and legislatures with a set of principles to be taken into account when dealing with contracts that have a strong impact on people's lives. Since the frame of reference must be legal ethics, not ethics *tout court*, this implies a coherent match between the perspective of values and the perspective of contractual dogmatics.[1]

Exploring this path, one author compared the recent attempts to create a European private law with the main philosophical points of view explicitly dealing with the problem relating to a reasonable and tolerant integration of morals into contract law.[2] He chal-

* Professor of Civil Law, Università cattolica del Sacro Cuore di Milano.

1 *See* C. Castronovo, A. Nicolussi & A. Albanese (Eds.), *Luigi Mengoni, Scritti I, Metodo e teoria giuridica*, Milano, Giuffrè Editore, 2011.

2 M.W. Hesselink, *Unconscionability, Unfair Exploitation and the Nature of Contract Theory, Comments on Melvin Eisemberg's Foundational Principles of Contract Law*, Amsterdam Law School Legal Studies Research Paper No. 2013-07, Retrieved on 16 February 2017 from <http://ssrn.com/abstract=2209752>; M.W. Hesselink, 'Five Political Ideas of European Contract Law', 7 *Eur. Rev. Contract L.* 2011, pp. 295-313.

lenged the concept of unconscionability by declaring his favour for a subordination of market efficiency to the principle of human dignity.

His position that, in contract law, there is no place for either ethical fundamentalism or ethical relativism seems to be not only agreeable, but also a fruitful approach. Pluralism forces us to look for inclusive points of view, not to pursue pointless attempts to impose unilateral visions.

This approach presupposes the complexity and the social dimension of the market, denouncing reductionism that characterizes the typical doctrine of the protection of the weak party as a remedy for market failure. In particular, according to certain authors, voluntariness cannot play the role of the sole foundational value of justice in market exchanges. This critique accompanies a critique advanced against the equation that market price equals just price.

The argument is that the market is not the natural way, but only one of the many, equally legitimate ways, through which the opinion of the majority can be collected and, moreover, is a way prone to be affected by the different possible regulations to which it may be subjected.[3] Consequently, identifying the just price with the market price may mean a legitimation of the most influential powers in the market. Moreover, an institutional conception of the market as a social structure implies ground rules and, consequently, the recognition of values according to which relationships are being oriented towards positive ends.

In these few notes, some elements of contractual theory are challenged from the perspective of Life Time Contracts, which are contracts that establish social, long-term relationships that, with regard to the entire or certain periods of the lifetime of individuals, provide essential goods, services, labour, and income opportunities for self-realization and participation.[4] Reference has been made to the object of contracts, either from the point of view of the justice of the exchange or from the point of view of the limit of the burden imposed on the party, who needs a service or a good of primary importance for their life. Moreover, a long-term contract indisputably reveals certain particularities regarding its termination. However, as a starting point, a general premise may be of use.

3 F. Denozza, *Law and Power in a World with no Transaction Costs: An Essay on the Legitimating Function of the Coasian Narrative*, Retrieved on 16 February 2017 from <http://ssrn.com/abstract=1361613>.

4 *See* Principle 1 of Principles of Life Time Contracts. The principle of substantive equality, as demonstrated explicitly by Art. 3 of the Italian Constitution, implies the idea of participation of people which the law must favour, eliminating some obstacles that prevent people from developing their personality. Correspondingly Art. 41 prescribes that the freedom of enterprise and thus freedom of contract shall only be exerted if it is not contrary to human dignity.

3.2 Contracts and Relational Autonomy

From the perspective of contract law, voluntariness is traditionally a fundamental value of the justice of the contract, 'justice' meaning, in this context, not the fairness of the exchange, but the set of values which contracts are designed to pursue.

From this point derives an issue of juridical logic or, as we say traditionally, of juridical dogmatics. How much flexibility does the concept of contract have?

European legal tradition has delivered an idea of the contract as an act of autonomy, but not necessarily in the sense used in English legal literature when it refers to 'classical doctrine of contract'.[5] Probably, more precisely, a contract is an act of relational, not simply individual, autonomy and, thus, is bound to the rule of good faith, which is based on the concept of reliance.[6] This idea proves to be of particular significance when contracts are not transactions, but long-term relationships in which, as one author put it, "the parties may imperceptibly slide into a situation from which they would feel it impossible to withdraw".[7] In these cases also, an English academic theorist recognised that "a concept of 'good faith', or fidelity to the relationship, becomes important" and that "commercial and even ethical norms arising out of long-term relations have an impact on lawyers and judges who may be called upon to apply classical principles to situations which they do not seem to fit".[8] Moreover, contracts are not immune from interventions in order to protect certain basic interests of the parties. Certainly, interventions must be respectful and balanced, though they are common, especially, with regard to long-term contracts.

Unfortunately, a legacy of the last century is a kind of taboo, called paternalism, which often prevents a serious discussion about the idea of providing rules in order to protect important rights or interests of a party of a contract.[9] Given that any dissertation must avoid being too abstract or ideological, but instead must take into consideration actual circumstances, it is of particular importance to underline the fact that the need for intervention in contracts is greater when, as happens today, the role of the State is shrinking, on one hand, while the rise of the corporate colossus is at the heart of the global economy, on the other. Moreover, the protection of employees has been restricted in recent decades

5 *See, inter alia*, P.S. Atiyah, *An Introduction to the Law of Contract*, 5th edn, Oxford University Press, New York, 1995, p. 7.

6 *See* C. Castronovo, 'Autonomia Privata e Costituzione Europea', 1 *Europa dir. priv.* 2005, p. 39. The expression 'relational autonomy' is more common in the context of physician-patient relationships: *see, e.g.*, C. Ells *et al.*, 'Relational Autonomy as an Essential Component of Patient-Centered Care', 4 *Int'l J. Feminist Approaches Bioethics* Fall 2011, pp. 79-101.

7 Atiyah, *supra* note 5, p. 52; O.E. Williamson, 'Transaction Cost Economics: The Governance of Contractual Relations', 22 *J. L. Econ.* 1979, p. 233, emphasized and developed the issue as an economic insight. According to E. McKendrick, 'The Regulation of Long-Term Contracts in English Law', *in* J. Beatson & D. Friedman (Eds.), *Good Faith and Fault in Contract Law*, Oxford, 1995, p. 310, the parties invest "so heavily in the relationship that they are effectively locked into each other".

8 Atiyah, *supra* note 5, p. 53.

9 *See* among others, J. Gordley, 'Morality and Contract: The Question of Paternalism', 8 *Will. Mary L. Rev.* 2007, p. 1733; A.T. Kronman, 'Paternalism and the Law of Contract', 92 *Yale L. J.* 1983, p. 763.

through what liberals and libertarians call reforms, so that the need for rethinking general Life Time Contracts becomes more pressing. The reduction of protection of the main means for a living must be balanced by an extension of protection within contracts that provide goods or services to satisfy basic needs.[10]

3.3 Spot Contracts and Life Time Contracts from the Perspective of European Contract Law

However, more than three decades of studies conducted by eminent experts in Europe on a European contract law seem to have finally ended in a proposal that was, in the end, discarded: The Common European Sales Law (CESL Optional Code) (i.e., the traditional spot contract). Since spot contracts cannot be assumed to be a paradigm of the most important types of contract affecting people's lives over a long period,[11] they were not taken into account and integrated, even in the *acquis* principle or in the Draft Common Frame of reference (DCFR).[12]

This remark is not meant to deny that a step towards a more-integrated, European contract law is welcome, especially regarding the digital single market, which is, in effect and by definition, cross-border, but it seems to be reductive to draw general rules of contract law from only sales law. Significant is the justification[13] of the amendment of the aforementioned discarded proposal extending unfairness control to 'core terms' or 'main terms' including price, by deleting Paragraph 2 of Article 80 CESL[14] referred, be-

10 *See* I. Ramsay, 'Consumer Credit Law, Distributive Justice and the Welfare State', 15 *Oxford J. Legal Stud.* 1995, p. 179.

11 These types of contracts evidence, in a particular way, the requirement for an ethical dimension of the contract that spot contracts tend to obscure due to the heightened level of depersonalization.

12 *See* B. Lurger, 'Old and New Insights for the Protection of Consumers in European Private Law in the Wake of the Global Economic Crisis', *in* R. Brownsword *et al.*(Eds.), *The Foundations of European Private Law*, Hart Publishing, Portland, 2011, p. 92. According to Y. Adar & M. Gelbard, 'Contract Remedies – A Relational Perspective', *in* S. Grundmann, F. Cafaggi & G. Vettori (Eds.), *The Organizational Contract*, Farnham Surrey, Burlington, 2013, p. 289, "while the DCFR does not explicitly relate to the relational contract theory, the document as a whole employs a number of relational notions, such as solidarity, cooperation, and the contractual validation of consensual norms of conduct. This is expressed both in the general principle of good faith interspersed among its various sections and in other contexts, such as contractually validating practices endorsed by the parties in the course of contract and imposing the obligation of cooperation between the parties to the contract."

13 The aim of deleting Paragraph 2 of Art. 80 was to extend unfairness review to 'core terms' (or 'main terms'). This would have been the most far reaching improvement of consumer protection. In most Member States, the courts cannot control the fairness of 'core' terms (including price), but in some Member States they can, generally (*see* the "big general clause", Art. 36 of the Scandinavian contract law act) or in specific contexts, like for mortgage contracts in Spain (*see Caja de Ahorros y Monte de Piedad de Madrid*, C-484/08, Judgment, EU:C:2010:309).

14 The amendment deleted Paragraph 2. Section 2 does not apply to the definition of the main subject matter of the contract, or to the appropriateness of the price to be paid in so far as the trader has complied with the duty of transparency set out in Art. 82.

sides the example of Scandinavian Contract Law, to mortgage contracts that reveal the importance of taking into consideration also other types of contract that present different elements like duration and have more impact on people's lives.[15]

This insight has been deepened by economists and other academic theorists, who distinguish between contracts that are transactions, called also spot contracts, and are typically sales or sales-related contracts, and contracts that are actually relationships – that is, relational, long-term contracts – where the definitions and rules provided in the initial phase of the conclusion of the contract are less important than institutional arrangements for unforeseen events and conflicts during the life of such long-term contracts.[16]

Therefore, in the proposal to extend the debate on contract law adding to the sales-oriented contract law on which the focus seems to be restricted currently in Europe, the so-called Life Time Contracts[17] is important.

Life Time Contracts can benefit from a tradition of distributive interventions. For example, if we think of a contract of labour, the principle that an employer is obliged to pay a salary necessary to ensure that the employee and his family enjoy a dignified existence is expressed in the Italian Constitution. Furthermore, as is well known, many safeguards are provided in favour of the employee during the employment relationship and about his or her dismissal. In addition, mortgage contracts, as in other countries, are submitted to a particular control regarding the appropriateness of the price. Virtually no one would say, nowadays, that lending money to earn interest is like selling the time that belongs to God alone,[18] but some part of that medieval idea about non-commodificability of time that ultimately corresponds to life, although in a secular way, is retained. Moreover, a tenancy for housing is not completely left to the bargain principle. From this perspective, Article 9 of the Principles of Life Time Contracts provides "the mutual obligations of Life Time Contracts shall not be grossly disproportionate."

However, a general control of prices relative to every contract, of whatever type, has been controversial since the topic was first discussed. In the Middle Ages, contrary to the chancellor at the University of Paris (Jean Gerson),[19] who had previously suggested that

15 This confirms, anyway, that justice is not detached from contract law, neither if one considers those types of contract that are less effected by their duration, and on the other hand, it is necessary to focus also on other types of contracts that are different to spot contracts in order to acquire a more complete vision of the concept of the contract in its entirety.

16 The distinction between contracts which are transaction and contracts which are actually relations is made by Atiyah, *supra* note 5, p. 50 according whom this idea owes its origins and development to Ian MacNeil; *see e.g.*, I.R. MacNeil, 'Relational Contracts: What We Do and Do Not Know', *Wisconsin L. Rev.* 1985, p. 483.

17 Or as expressed in the Romance languages: *contratti di durata per l'esistenza della persona. See* L. Nogler & U. Reifner, 'Introduction: The New Dimension of Life Time in the Law of Contracts and Obligations', *in* L. Nogler & U. Reifner (Eds.), *Life Time Contracts*, Eleven International Publishing, The Hague, 2014, p. 3.

18 *See* J. Le Goff, 'Church Time and Merchant Time in the Middle Ages', 9 *Inf. Int. Soc. Sci. Counc* 1970, p. 151.

19 *See* R. De Roover, 'The Concept of the Just Price: Theory and Economic Policy', 18 *J. Econ. Hist.* 1958, p. 425.

setting prices was to be extended to all products on the basis that no one should presume to be wiser than the legislature, scholars of the famous school of Salamanca opposed any price control because it was pointless in times of abundance and ineffective or harmful in times of shortage.[20] It should also be noted that, even the recent attempt to introduce a provision in the CESL concerning judicial review of the appropriateness of prices, as usual regarding unfair terms, is subjected to the requirement of a lack of individual negotiation. So, the question that might arise shifts to that of the certainty of contract, which can be put in doubt by the uncertainty of the criteria that judges must follow.

Referring back to Life Time Contracts, price controls or, more generally speaking, control over the fairness of the exchange, may involve an adaptation related to changes of circumstances that are likely in a long-term relationship. Therefore, Principle 10 of Life Time Contracts provides the following rule regarding adaptation:

> If the social and economic circumstances upon which a Life Time Contract is based have changed significantly since the contract was entered into, or if material circumstances from which the parties derived have arisen that are found to be at variance with its original situation to such an extent that the social nature of the contract is jeopardized, and if the parties would not have entered into the contract or would have entered into it on different terms had they foreseen this change, adaptation of the contract may be required if, taking into account all the circumstances of the specific case, and in particular the contractual or statutory allocation of risk and the fundamental obligation of a human being, one of the parties cannot reasonably be expected to continue to comply with the contract without variation of its terms. Collective regulation shall take precedence over individual adaptation.

The difference between this rule and Article 6:111 of the Principles of European Contract Law (Change of circumstances) may, to a significant degree, be explained by referring to the fact that Principles of European Contract Law do not take into full consideration Life Time Contracts.[21] While determining the price is quite obvious in spot contracts, in long-term relationships, price determination at the beginning is more difficult, depending on the likelihood of changes of circumstances. In a Life Time Contract, this factor may aggravate the asymmetry between the parties because of the difference in capacity to foresee the future and some unpredictable events in the life of a person. Although a rigid determination is common and a result of the principle of voluntariness and is also consistent with the dominant model of a sale contract, in Life Time Contracts, the price should be viewed from a more dynamic perspective, so that a principle of adaptation

20 Id., p. 426.

21 *See* O. Lando & H. Beale (Eds.), *Principles of European Contract Law, Part I and II*, Kluwer Law International, Dordrecht, 2000, p. 322 *et seq.*

not necessarily made by the courts can be deemed to be essentially needed.[22] It is an integral part of the reference framework within which these kinds of contracts must be conceived.[23]

3.4 Contracts and Basic Needs

There are several reasons, apart from the question of price, for taking into account Life Time Contracts in order to develop a more-complex and better-defined framework for contracts in comparison with that of a sales-oriented contract law, which can lead to more unilateral, or sometimes a more generic, set of rules.

Interventions in Life Time Contracts are easier to explain and justify, even if they deal with core-term contracts. It is even easier when the object of long-term contracts is a primary good, provided that contemporary culture does not lose the capacity to share a common vision about what is fundamental and does not fall in despairing relativism.[24] Self-determination within a solidarity-based system cannot be the unique criterion for evaluating the value of goods. As a matter of fact, if contracts are reduced to the absolute idea of contractual self-determination, it will be very difficult to determine a good reason

22 However, there is no common consensus to this point in Europe. As stated in *Anston's Contract Law* (J. Beatson, H. A. Burrows, & J. Cartwright (Eds.), Oxford/New York, Oxford University Press, 2010, p. 473): "Some legal systems accept that changes of circumstances may justify modifying a contract where to maintain the original contract would produce intolerable results incompatible with justice. But many legal systems, including English law, concerned that modification would undermine certainty and alter the risks allocated by the contract, make provisions for the discharge of the contract only where, after its formation, a change of circumstances makes contractual performance illegal or impossible."

23 According to Adar & Gelbard (*supra* note 12, pp. 289-290), "sub-section (1) DCFR lays down the basic principle of the duty of fulfilling contractual obligations even in the face of changing circumstances. Notwithstanding sub-section (2) specifically addresses situations, in which the performance of the original obligation would be unjust due to a change of circumstances. In those situations, the court is authorized to change the substance of the obligation in order to render it reasonable and fair, or, under certain circumstances, to terminate the contract subject to the conditions set forth by the court. Without a doubt, this section reflects insights based on the theory of relational contracts."

24 Atiyah, *supra* note 5, pp. 35-36: "There is a tendency (as we have seen) to treat contractual obligations as self-imposed, and therefore to think that the role of contract law is the relatively minor one of deciding which promises to enforce and how to enforce them. Community ideas of fairness and justice are then seen as having little role in contract law. There is a basis of truth in this with regard to the first of contract law's three main purposes, but even with regard to this purpose the point is often greatly exaggerated. While many contractual obligations are self-imposed, others are not; it is, for instance, the law and not the parties which must decide what kind of expectations are reasonable and should be protected. And in any event the whole of the law's remedial system – deciding what kind of remedy to award a party for a breach of contract – is largely imposed by the law, and not decided by the parties themselves. And as regards the second and third purposes of contract law it is anyhow evident that they require a substantial infusion of community values. Deciding what kind of enrichment is unjust, and what kind of reliance is reasonable, which are essential elements in the second and third of contract law's three main purposes, are matters which must be done by reference to the community's ideas of justice and reasonableness."

for certain interventions, since this idea constitutes a sort of Great Wall of China against intervention.[25]

A good example of the fact that self-determination within a solidarity-based system cannot be the unique criterion for evaluating the value of goods can be drawn from the recent case law of the United States' Supreme Court. As is well known, this is a country that is experiencing a difficult attempt to introduce mandatory rules in contract law regarding healthcare insurance. How difficult this attempt is, in the absence of a precise constitutional reference, is also proven by the fact that recent political changes could reverse this policy.

The reference is to the Patient Protection and Affordable Care Act of 2010 (commonly called Obamacare), which obliged individuals to obtain medical insurance coverage, and imposed a penalty for failure to do so. For individuals who are not exempt and who do not receive health insurance through an employer or government program, the means of satisfying the requirement is to purchase insurance from a private company. The Act was subjected to the judgment of the US Supreme Court, which, as far as we are concerned, substantially justified the violation of freedom of contract by those mandatory rules.[26] From the libertarian perspective, the Act discriminates against young and healthy people who are less likely to be in need of immediate medical treatment or who do not choose to make allowances for it, but instead favours the elderly and the unhealthy, who can obtain better insurance coverage as a result of the general coverage provided by health insurance. According to the US Supreme Court, such discrimination is legitimate because health is to be acknowledged as a particular value that is completely different from other goods, since it concerns everybody and for their entire lifetime.[27]

In Italy, according to Article 32 of its Constitution, the Republic safeguards health as a fundamental right and as a collective interest, and guarantees free medical care to the indigent. So, the importance of healthcare is beyond discussion and it could be considered surprising that, in the opinion of the US Supreme Court, one finds that at least some

25 A poignant example can be drawn from W. Block, 'Toward a Libertarian Theory of Inalienability: A Critique of Rothbard, Barnett, Smith, Kinsella, Gordon, and Epstein', 17 *J. Libertarian Stud.* 2003, p. 39. The example regards a poor man whose child has fallen ill with a dreaded disease. The cure will cost one million dollars. A rich man is willing to pay him this amount if he signs himself over to him as a slave. The poor man is very willing to do it since his child's life is vastly more important to him than his own liberty, or even his own life. According to the libertarian author (who believes it to be unfortunate!) this would be illegal, at least if the doctrine of inalienability (non-transferability) is valid. Therefore, the protection provided by the law, which protects the dignity of the weaker party, would be unacceptable, because it actually ended in the privation of the only chance the poor father had to save his son. Many libertarians would not share the opinion held by Block, but this example relates, at the same time, both to the justice of an exchange and the principle of human dignity. Moreover, it can explain the usefulness of the view that contract law and social justice are not separate fields, and protection of weaker party should not be undertaken in a generic way, but rather by taking into consideration some significant aspects like the type of good involved.

26 Here it is not necessary to consider the question whether Section 5000A of the law provides for a command to buy insurance or the penalty provided by Section 5000A for those who do not buy it is a tax.

27 *Nat'l Fed'n of Indep. Bus. v. Sebelius*, 567 U.S. 519 (2012).

Justices deemed it necessary to state it.[28] But, the lessons from the United States are clear about the consequences of the radicalization of the idea of contractual self-determination. It is also remarkable that Article 32 of the Italian Constitution is laid down in the section on ethical and social relations, directly after the three articles devoted to the family.

This frame of reference favours the idea of reasonableness in the price of services and goods in the field of health,[29] where, in the case of the shrinking role of the State in terms of the welfare state, a new conceptualization is required with respect to the ground rules for the contracts people must agree to in order to ensure their health. In general, controlling the price of basic commodities has had a long history. Although certain critiques have been expressed by some economists against price controls, the invisible hand of the market must not only be rendered visible, but also governed, at least when basic necessities are at stake.

3.5 Contracts and Familial Relationships

Free from the obstacle of reductionism implicit in the idea that freedom of contract is the sole value in contracts, the principle of good faith combined with fundamental rights or fundamental duties can play an important role and also provide for substantive fairness.[30] For instance, the development of a doctrine that limits the creditor's claim when the performance of an obligation conflicts with another duty that is more important, from a constitutional perspective, is highly significant (the German doctrine of *Unzumutbarkeit*, corresponding to the Italian doctrine of *inesigibilità*).[31] This is of particular interest within the context of the duration of contracts that may infringe upon the debtor's relationships, especially in familial relationships. Principle 2 of the Principles of Life Time Contracts establishes that the role of the law governing them is to frame the power relationships of those contracts in terms of human development, so that on-going cooperation, rather than the formation of the contract, lies at the heart of the contractual relationship. Personal relationships, such as the family, have to be taken into account.[32]

---

28 *See* id., Opinion of Ginsburg, J., p. 21: "Nor is it accurate to say that the minimum coverage provision 'compel[s] individuals...to purchase an unwanted product' [...]. If unwanted today, medical services secured by insurance may be desperately needed tomorrow. Virtually everyone, I reiterate, consumes health care at some point of his or her life".

29 An actual example may be the question about the price of a breakthrough Hepatitis C drug that offers a cure for the chronic liver infection (HCV) at a US dollar price approaching six figures.

30 For an analysis of the law relating to good faith in the Member States of the European Union, *see* R. Zimmermann & S. Whittaker, *Good Faith in European Contract Law*, Cambridge University Press, Cambridge, 2000.

31 *See* L. Mengoni, 'Responsabilità contrattuale (dir. vig.)', *in Enc. Dir.*, XXXIX, 1988, p. 1089.

32 Duration is the framework in which an ethical approach is more appropriate, and we should note three points. One is that when a relationship lasts for an extended period, it creates reliance and proximity. This is valid, although one party is an enterprise, otherwise we create a moral shield in favour of people who take advantage of the enterprise and conceive the enterprise as a machine in which people are mere cogs to be

Moreover, this point is consistent with Article 33 of the Charter of the Fundamental Rights of the European Union, which provides the principle of reconciliation between family and professional life.

From this perspective, the contract of labour ensures the sanctity of maternity. Evidently, the duty to the family, in this case the child, is more important than the duty to perform. The law restricts the landlord's right to withdraw the leased property from tenancy in order to protect not only the tenant's right to housing, but also that of his or her family or cohabitants with children.[33] We can also imagine a right to suspend payment of instalments on a loan in the case of redundancy, through no fault of the debtor, when the worker has to provide for him or herself, or a member of his or her family (e.g., to pay school fees or medical bills).[34] More generally, outside the logic of conflicting duties, certain authors support the possibility of providing a legal entitlement to reschedule the repayment of debts when a debtor is unable, due to illness, unanticipated unemployment, or other reasonable cause to meet his or her obligations under a credit contract.[35] This contract excuse for non-performance might evoke the contract excuse developed by Wilhelmsson as a general principle of social *force majeure*.[36] However, it seems to be more persuasively explained by referring to a conflict between the creditor's right and the debtor's fundamental rights, if, and to the extent to which, a conflict arises, otherwise the rule may result in being unmanageable and unsustainable in private law. This explanation remains tied to the particular case and, therefore, avoids opportunism that is possible when referring to the principle of social *force majeure*.

---

exploited. Moreover, the extended period tends to aggravate the differences between a professional party (enterprise) and a person who contracts for personal purposes (labour, loans for the purchase of a house, guarantees in favour of a family member, tenancy for housing), especially in case of change of circumstances given that an enterprise is more able to calculate risks and administer their costs than non-professionals. Finally, the different relationships may be inextricably unresolvable and in certain cases we can speak about a sort of contractual links (in Italian *collegamento negoziale*, in German *Verbundene Verträge* in a broad sense), e.g., labour, tenancy, loans, and familial relationships.

33 For a broader discussion, *see* C. Schmidt & J. Dinse, 'Towards a Common Core of Residential Tenancy Law in Europe: The Impact of the European Court of Human Rights on Tenancy Law', *in* Nogler & Reifner (Eds.), *supra* note 17, p. 605 *et seq*.

34 In case of a guarantee by a non-professional person in favour of a member of the family, the bank has, at least, the duty to keep the guarantor regularly updated regarding the economic conditions of the debtor and the consequences the guarantee would have to face in order to allow the guarantor to terminate the contract before default proceedings have been initiated, when circumstances have varied too greatly with respect to the initial contractual obligations.

35 *See* Ramsay, *supra* note 10, p. 191, who refers to Sec. 66 Australian Draft Uniform Consumer Credit Laws 1993 from which the formula in the text, above, is taken.

36 T. Wilhelmsson, *Critical Studies in Private Law. A Treatise on Need-Rational Principles in Modern Law*, Springer, Dordrecht, 1992, pp. 43, 185.

3.6 Termination

An integral element of the legal governance of long-term relationships is termination, particularly early termination. Special regard must be used with respect to the different positions of the parties relating to the right to early termination of a Life Time Contract. Principle 11 of Life Time Contracts refers to such termination when "it is in the interest of that party which has developed the contract and organised the service".[37] Apart from the rule that "early termination against the will of the consumer, tenant or worker must be a measure of last resort",[38] two rules deserve particular attention. Firstly, the provision for a general rule of 'a reasonable period before termination comes into effect' is important. Although one may consider it as not mandatory, the rule may imply that if the party who developed the contract wishes to derogate from the rule, he or she has to provide an alternative proposal in order to counterbalance the contract in favour of the other party who waives this protection. Secondly, the rule as per Principle 11 ("as far as the termination is in the interest of that party which has developed the contract and organised the service it has to consider the interest of the other party with due diligence"), may be considered as being integral to a similar rational, which, in turn, could be considered as corresponding to a principle of good faith. Good faith is a basis for duties of protection, from which emerges the duty to protect the other party of a Life Time Contract when the right of termination is enjoyed. This rule, generally, does not have a practical impact on sales contracts with consumers. However, it may have a practical impact in the case of a tenancy, if a reasonable period before termination, which comes into effect, is not provided for. In Italy, a very particular application of this principle has been proposed by an author regarding cases of interruption of a period of living together.[39] The party who has control of the house must allow the other party to stay for a reasonable period of time in order to find, at least, a temporary alternative solution; otherwise, he must pay damages for the unreasonably precipitous eviction. The duty of protection may have more impact

37 Principle 11 of Life Time Contracts establishes: "Termination: Termination of life time contracts imposed on workers and consumers must be transparent, accountable and socially responsible. Early termination against the will of the consumer, tenant or worker must be a measure of last resort. Disclosure of true and fair grounds for termination must be non-discriminatory and be provided a reasonable period before termination comes into effect. The only grounds for termination are personal behaviour of such significance as to merit termination, or financial circumstances or interests on the part of the provider which materially affect the viability of the subject matter of the contract. Where the reasons for termination are financial in nature, users are entitled to have recourse to mechanisms of collective redress, including the right of the individual to be heard or represented. This procedure must allow sufficient time for users to put forward measures preventing termination and/or its consequences. As far as the termination is in the interest of that party which has developed the contract and organised the service it has to consider the interest of the other party with due diligence."

38 Id.

39 L. Mengoni, 'La famiglia in una Società Complessa', *Iustitia*, 1990, p. 7.

in the field of contracts of labour, *lato sensu*, when there is a need for a similar protection of the party, who, while not formally an employee, in reality, is.[40]

As for the effect of termination, the rule ought to be differentiated according to the different types of long-term relationships involved. For instance, if the termination of a contract of hire purchase has only a future effect, this rule could cause an unjustified enrichment at the expense of the customer, who loses the entire amount of the instalments paid, even though they were calculated taking into account a sum for the acquisition of the object of the contract. On the contrary, termination of a tenancy with only future effect may favour the tenant, who does not have to pay for the enjoyment of the house over and above that which he or she has already paid. These examples illustrate that a revision of Principle 3 of Life Time Contracts may be opportune in order to render that Principle more flexible and more appropriate and, thus, avoid the rigidity of the rule which provides: "early termination must have only future effect, having no bearing on the contract prior to that point."[41]

3.7 CONTRACTS AND BIOTECHNOLOGY

There is a field of contracts that is not directly taken into consideration in the Principles of Life Time Contracts, although they are of increasing importance in people's life. In fact, they are contracts that are not necessarily made in order to provide goods or services for a person, but they relate to personal rights of 'biolaw' interest. From this point of view, contracts relating to biological samples can be considered a sector of significant impact. It is increasingly common for people to give biological samples, especially to biobanks, for the purposes of scientific research, healthcare, or both. The problems posed by this practice refer not only to the property of this separate part or parts of the body of a person, but also to the limitations of use that are established for researchers. Biological samples can provide many sensitive pieces of information about the person they come from. They can reveal predispositions to particular illnesses, and also give information about ancestors and other familial relationships. Another problem may arise from certain uses of the samples, for instance, the use of gametes for the purpose of creating embryos for scientific research. Since the biological samples can be stored for the entire life of the person, and beyond, the contract with which the person expresses their informed consent to allow the use of the biological samples is a lifetime contract, although not a Life Time Contract in the term's strictest sense.

As a result of the particularity of the content of this contract and its long-term duration, many problems arise, which also make clear that referring only to the principle of

40 The solution found by the Italian Court of Cassazione, III, 18 September 2009, n. 20106, is similar, but the case regarded firms that cannot be compared with a de facto employee.

41 *Cf.* Arts. 9:305, 9:306, 9:307, 9:308 and 9:309 of Principles of European Contract Law.

autonomy may, in essence, be insufficient and illusory. First of all, one might ask what the object of the informed consent is. The scientific reason for, and meaning of certain scientific investigations, are often difficult to explain to a layman. Moreover, the need and the opportunity for such research may emerge at a later time, after the moment at which the so-called informed consent was given. Therefore, the consent must be related to practical consequences for the person giving their consent and that person's life, such as any information about their state of health, their origins, or the fact that certain uses could be contrary to or incompatible with their values.

Moreover, a particular issue raised, from the contractual perspective, is the right to withdraw consent at any time the person chooses to do so and terminate the contract. Generally, denying this option is difficult, given the tight relation between samples and fundamental rights of the person in question. However, the purpose to favour or at least not to hinder research may suggest allowing the person to renounce the right of withdrawing when his or her fundamental rights are secured and a remuneration is provided.

But, returning to the possible link between contracts and familiar relationships, information about health could be of interest not only to the person from whom the sample derives, but also to the entire group of the family. In this case, the conflict between privacy of the person and the right to health of the members of the family could be resolved in favour of the members of the family. Solidarity within the family can explain not only why a person is justified in not performing, as we discussed above, but also why they cannot claim that their privacy takes precedence over the health of family members.

Bibliography

Adar, Y. & Gelbard, M., 'Contract Remedies – A Relational Perspective', *in* S. Grundmann, F. Cafaggi & G. Vettori (Eds.), *The Organizational Contract*, Farnham, Surrey: Ashgate Publishing, 2013, p. 289.

Atiyah, P.S., *An Introduction to the Law of Contract* (5th ed.), New York: Oxford University Press, 1995.

Beatson, J., Burrows, H.A. & Cartwright, J. (Eds.), *Anston's Contract Law*, Oxford/New York: Oxford University Press, 2010.

Block, W., 'Toward a Libertarian Theory of Inalienability: A Critique of Rothbard, Barnett, Smith, Kinsella, Gordon, and Epstein', 17 *J. Libertarian Stud.*, 2003, p. 39.

Castronovo, C., 'Autonomia Privata e Costituzione Europea', 1 *Europa Dir. Priv.* 2005, p. 39.

Castronovo, C., Nicolussi, A. & Albanese, A. (Eds.), *Luigi Mengoni, Scritti I, Metodo e Teoria Giuridica*, Milano: Giuffrè Editore, 2011.

Denozza, F., *Law and Power in a World with no Transaction Costs: An Essay on the Legitimating Function of the Coasian Narrative*, Retrieved on 16 February 2017 from <http://ssrn.com/abstract=1361613>.

De Roover, R., 'The Concept of the Just Price: Theory and Economic Policy', 18 *J. Econ. History* 1958, p. 425.

Ells, C., *et al.*, 'Relational Autonomy as an Essential Component of Patient-Centered Care', 4 *Int'l J. Feminist Approaches to Bioethics* Fall 2011, pp. 79-101.

Gordley, J. 'Morality and Contract: The Question of Paternalism', 48 *Will. Mary L. Rev.* 2007, p. 1733.

Hesselink, M.W., 'Five Political Ideas of European Contract Law', 7 *Eur. Rev. Contract L.* 2011, pp. 295-313.

Hesselink, M.W., *Unconscionability, Unfair Exploitation and the Nature of Contract Theory, Comments on Melvin Eisemberg's Foundational Principles of Contract Law*, Amsterdam Law School Legal Studies Research Paper No. 2013-07, Retrieved on 16 February 2017 from <http://ssrn.com/abstract=2209752>.

Kronman, A.T., 'Paternalism and the Law of Contract', 92 *Yale L. J.* 1983, p. 763.

Lando, O. & Beale, H. (Eds.), *Principles of European Contract Law, Part I and II*, Dordrecht: Kluwer Law International, 2000.

Le Goff, J., 'Church Time and Merchant Time in the Middle Ages', 9 *Inf. Int. Soc. Sci. Counc.* 1970, p. 151.

Lurger, B., 'Old and New Insights for the Protection of Consumers in European Private Law in the Wake of the Global Economic Crisis', *in* R. Brownsword *et al.* (Eds.), *The Foundations of European Private Law*, Portland: Hart Publishing, 2011, p. 92.

MacNeil, I.R., 'Relational Contracts: What We Do and Do Not Know', *Wisconsin L. Rev.* 1985, pp. 483-525.

McKendrick, E., 'The Regulation of Long-Term Contracts in English Law', *in* J. Beatson & D. Friedman (Eds.), *Good Faith and Fault in Contract law*, Clarendon, Oxford, 1995.

Mengoni, L., 'La famiglia in una Società Complessa', *Iustitia* 1990, p. 7.

Mengoni, L., 'Responsabilità Contrattuale (dir. vig.)', XXXIX *Enc. Dir.* 1988, p. 1089.

Nogler, L. & Reifner, U., 'Introduction: The New Dimension of Life Time in the Law of Contracts and Obligations', *in* L. Nogler & U. Reifner (Eds.), *Life Time Contracts*, The Hague: Eleven International Publishing, 2014, p. 3.

Ramsay, I., 'Consumer Credit Law, Distributive Justice and the Welfare State', 15 *Oxford J. Legal Stud.* 1995, p. 179.

Schmidt, C. & Dinse, J., 'Towards a Common Core of Residential Tenancy Law in Europe: The Impact of the European Court of Human Rights on Tenancy Law', *in* L. Nogler & U. Reifner (Eds.), *Life Time Contracts*, The Hague: Eleven International Publishing, 2014, p. 605 *et seq.*

Wilhelmsson, T., *Critical Studies in Private Law. A Treatise on Need-Rational Principles in Modern Law*, Dordrecht: Springer, 1992.

Williamson, O.E., 'Transaction Cost Economics: The Governance of Contractual Relations', 22 *J. L. Econ.* 1979, p. 233.

Zimmermann, R. & Whittaker, S., *Good Faith in European Contract Law*, Cambridge: Cambridge University Press, 2000.

4 Do Some Business Relationships Fall within the Scope of the Principles of Life Time Contracts?

*Antonio Albanese**

4.1 Continuative Collaboration Relationships between Firms in the Modern, Decentralized-industrial System

Given that, in EU contract law, there is a fundamental distinction between consumer contracts and business contracts, it makes sense to question whether the Principles of Life Time Contracts could, or even should, be extended to business relationships.

Under Principle 1, "*Life Time Contracts* are long-term social relationship providing goods, services and opportunities for work and income creation. They are essential for the self-realization of individuals and their participation in society at various stages in their life".[1]

It is, therefore, time to check whether this definition covers also business contracts which do not lead to a simple spot-market exchange of instant execution, but rather establish long-term relationships between firms, instrumental to the ongoing needs of their respective economic activity.

This happens primarily in cases in which the contract is the means by which one firm (usually, but not always, small)[2] is integrated in the business organization of a bigger company, on whose behalf the former carries out a step of the economic activity of the latter, adjusting its own work process in relationship to the latter's needs.

The spread of decentralized production and outsourcing is the consequence of some economic changes that have led to the downfall of the Fordist model, which was characterized by a business organization that incorporates all the productive factors.[3] That

* Professor of Civil Law, Università cattolica del Sacro Cuore di Milano.

1 'Principles of Life Tome Contracts', *in* L. Nogler & U. Reifner (Eds.), *Life Time Contracts: Social Longterm Contracts in Labour, Tenancy and Consumer Credit Law*, The Hague, Eleven International Publishing, 2014, p. xvii.

2 There are also forms of productive decentralization involving only medium and large firms: A. Bertolotti, *Il Contratto di Subfornitura*, Utet, Torino, 2000, p. 3. In these cases, however, does not occur the conditions of monopsony, which, as we shall see, normally characterize the relationship between companies that have significantly different dimensions.

3 E. Rullani & L. Romano (Eds.), *Il Postfordism. Idee per il Capitalismo Prossimo Venturo*, Etas Libri, Milano, 1998.

model, in fact, functioned to minimize the transaction costs associated with establishing and administering an ongoing-business relationship, through which companies purchased, on the market, the resources for their economic activities,[4] but has been losing relevance, insofar as new technologies and media development[5] have improved the efficiency of the supply of products and services from external providers.[6] By means of long-term contractual relationships, a company can more efficiently retain control over different stages of its activity, entrusting some of them to other firms, because of their specific expertise. Such coordination between companies is called 'vertical quasi-integration' and is different from cases of vertical integration in the strict sense, in which the same processing or distribution firms internalize all the production stages, so as to conform them to their specific needs, but at the same time assuming the related risks.[7]

In the present case, instead, such risks are transferred to the other party, who agrees to provide services or goods required for the purchaser's business in return for certainty in allocating all of its own production. Ultimately, each party, by exercising his contractual freedom, assumes the risks that it can manage more efficiently than the other party.[8]

Such vertical quasi-integration does not imply a contract for instant execution, but rather a long-term relationship, in which time plays a crucial role, since that the satisfaction of both parties' interests requires an ongoing relationship, on the one hand, ensuring the purchaser a continuous supply of goods and/or services with certain qualities and, on the other hand, providing the supplier a consistent source of revenue for its activity.

Actually, mere exchange contracts assume a nonstrategic role in transactions between traders, as they are merely instrumental to the acquisition of standard goods, without specific qualitative connotations (i.e., commodities), while business development is entrusted to continuing collaboration contracts, which concern nonfungible performance. The duration, therefore, does not depend on a contingent agreement about how to perform, but is an essential feature of the parties' mutual obligations, since the continuing performance – that is, meeting enduring interests of both parties – is the basis of achiev-

4 The choice to internalize all production factors, is reflected from the point of view of economic science, in the theory of 'transaction costs'. R. Coase, 'The Nature of the Firm: Origin, Meaning, Influence', 4 *J.L. Econ. & Org.* 1988, p. 33, *reprinted in* O.E. Williamson, *The Economic Institutions of Capitalism: Firms, Markets, Relational Contracting*, Free Press, New York, 1985.

5 P. Milgrom & J. Roberts, 'The Economic of Modern Manufacturing: Technology, Strategy and Organization', 80 *Am. Econ. Rev.* 1990, p. 511 *et seq.*

6 A. Giunta & D. Scalera, 'Dal Decentramento alle Catene Globali del Valore: la Subfornitura Industriale in Italia', *Analisi Giur. Economia* 2011, p. 195 *et seq.;* and A. Ferruggia, 'Le Esternalizzazioni "Relazionali" nel Decentramento di Attività d'Impresa', *Riv. giur. lav. prev. soc.*, 2013, p. 811.

7 These long-term contracts are in fact vertical integration forms alternative to the ownership integration by stock or asset acquisition: *see* F. Kessler & R.H. Stern, 'Competition, Contract, and Vertical Integration', 69 *Yale L.J.* 1959, p. 1 *et seq.*

8 In this sense, especially in the agricultural sector, a family-owned enterprise is "the most efficient unit of production", since "economics of scale are not substantial and individual ownership provides strong incentives for working when and how it is most effective". H. Hansmann, *The Ownership of Enterprise*, The Belknap Press of Harvard University Press, Cambridge, MA /London, 1996, p. 141.

ing the purpose of the contract[9] and "the performance in its entirety depends on the duration (*Länge*)".[10]

Such contractual relationships should, therefore, be included in the category of Life Time Contracts, not only in consideration of mere continuous performance of obligations, but also because at least one of the fundamental interests pursued by parties requires ongoing satisfaction throughout the contract's term.[11]

This approach not only benefits individual parties, but also increases the efficiency of the whole economic system,[12] both in terms of improving the quality of production, which can comply better with the needs of the end markets,[13] and in terms of harmonizing supply and demand quantity thus, avoiding the risk of *surplus* items that remain unsold.[14] The development of integration contracts, in fact, makes it possible to overcome the connatural difficulty of the market to ensure, without disproportionately high information costs, the correspondence between supply and demand from the processing and distribution sectors.[15]

But, at the same time, the purpose underlying the contract may give rise to a situation of monopsony between the parties, since one of them provides goods and services exclusively for the benefit of the other, while the latter purchases them also from other suppliers. Normally, this is not the legal effect of an exclusivity clause; rather, it results from the fact that the activities of the supplier, being designed according to the customer requests, are not adjustable to other buyers' needs.

For these reasons, this form of contractual integration to one party is not a sole instrument to make a profit, but is also the way of self-realization through its professional activities.[16]

---

9 *Cf.* G. Oppo, 'I Contratti di Durata', *Riv. dir. comm.*, 1943, I, pp. 219-220 and 246-249.

10 K. Larenz, *Lehrbuch des Schuldrechts. Band I: Allgemeineir Teil*, C.H. Beck, München, 1987, p. 30; and D. Medicus, *Schuldrecht I. Allgemeineir Teil: ein Studienbuch*, C.H. Beck, München, 2005, p. 5.

11 This is a requirement for a contractual relationship to be included in the category of life-time contract, according to the notion outlined by L. Nogler & U. Reifner, 'Introduction: The New Dimension of Life Time in the Law of Contracts and Obligations', *in* Nogler & Reifner (Eds.), *supra* note 1, pp. 6-7.

12 With regard to vertical integration by contract farming *see* H.S. James Jr., *et al.*, 'The Adoption, Diffusion and Evolution of Organizational Forms: Insights from the Agrifood Sector', 32 *Manage. Decis. Econ.* 2011, pp. 243-259.

13 *See*, in this sense, M. Maugeri & V. Falce, 'Indotto, Concorrenza e Mercato: il Caso della Subfornitura', *Analisi Giur. Economia* 2011, p. 275, who point out that supply relationships, through specialization of labour, improve the supply capacity to meet the new needs of demand, stimulating the dynamic competition.

14 This risk arises in particular in the food chain: *see* A. Albanese, 'Contractual Justice and Market Efficiency in the Supply Relationships within the Agro-Food Chain', *Riv. Reg. Mercati* 2016, p. 82 *et seq.*

15 Hansmann, *supra* note 8, p. 161.

16 The guarantee of economic freedom and the development of the human person through self-employment or business, with special reference to micro-, small-, and medium-sized firms, are the aims of l. 11.11.2011, no. 18 'Statute of business', by which the Italian legal system has implemented the European Commission Communication 'Small Business Act', no. 394/2008.

The contract, in fact, is the only or the main source of economic revenue for this one, necessary to ensure the lasting sustainability of its business as well as the income of the people working for it. From this perspective, these contractual relationships are not merely a business, as they are essential for the human development of the people involved, both as individuals and in their social life. A firm, in fact, is not just a 'technical' organization that can be rationally optimized, based on a fixed objective (for example, the maximization of profits), but it is also a 'human' construct, in which individuals pursue their various personal goals.[17] Therefore, in these cases, too, parties enter into a lifetime contract, which, unlike other long-term contracts, offers one of them opportunities to work and earn money to satisfy material needs and aspire to self-realization.[18]

4.2 Long-term Contracts and the Need to Protect the Economically Dependent Enterprise

At the same time, this ongoing cooperation leads to economic dependence, comparable with that of an employed worker,[19] increasing the risk of abuse and unfair conduct by the stronger party. This can happen especially in cases of vertical quasi-integration in agriculture through contract farming, which requires producers to comply with specific criteria and techniques for cultivation and breeding, and to sell all of their products to the other party, who, in turn, must purchase the products after having verified compliance with all the agreed standards.

The example also makes clear that these contractual relationships between companies integrated in a supply chain are not mere exchanges of products or services for a price. They provide, in fact, for further service obligations, requiring producers to adapt their activities and, sometimes (as a consequence), their family life in accordance with a program that accords with their industrial or commercial partner. All this involves a social relationship between the contracting parties quite apart from a simple spot exchange.

The relationship between customer (i.e., the industrial or commercial partner) and the supplier implies certain common objectives,[20] to be achieved through a lasting partner-

17 S. Urban, 'The Firm and the Fulfilment of a New Humanism: Critical Reflections', 18 *Eur. Bus. L. Rev.* 2007, p. 348.

18 *Cf.* Nogler & Reifner, *supra* note 11, p. 6.

19 With reference to the economic dependence of self-employed workers, *see* O. Razzolini, 'Self-Employment and Economic Dependency in the Light of the Social Contract Law', *in* Nogler & Reifner (Eds.), *supra* note 1, p. 387 *et seq.*

20 About that M. Wellenhofer-Klein, *Zulieferverträge im Privat - und Wirtschaftsrecht*, Beck Verlag, München, 1999, p. 177 *et seq.* utilizes the concepts of '*Interessenverschmelzung, Interessenberührung und Interessenverknüpfung*'.

ship;[21] one that cannot be reduced to an isolated synallagmatic contract, but one that is, partly, comparable with a membership.[22]

Moreover, these contracts have another feature of the Life Time Contracts:[23] they play an essential role in the organization of a whole community of people,[24] all of whom work toward both common and individual objectives, particularly the means by which the supplier, its dependent workers, and their families satisfy their life needs.

However, this vertical quasi-integrated system of production exposes such external suppliers to the risk of abuse, due to their economic dependence on the other party,[25] especially when, in order to adjust their production to the other party's demands, they make specific investments that are difficult to change.[26] Indeed, the fear that the contractor will refuse to renew the contract may subject the provider to the other party's abuses,[27] such as late payments,[28] discriminatory treatment, or claims for undue benefits. Besides, when the contract expires, the buyer can take advantage of the renegotiation, imposing unfair contractual terms.

The supplier, in fact, 'to keep his job' can accept unfair conditions, justified on the basis of a purely economic assessment, compromising values such as contractual justice, personal freedom, and human dignity.

Actually, economic dependence may result from other circumstances that limit the contractual freedom of a contracting party, regardless of the existence of previous supply relationships.[29] However, in a decentralized system of production or distribution, the need to protect the firm integrated in another's organization arises precisely from its ongoing relationship, which makes it economically dependent on the other.

---

21 R.J. Gilson *et al.*, 'Contracting of Innovation: Vertical Disintegration and Interfirm Collaboration', 109 *Columbia L. Rev.* 2009, p. 431 *et seq.*

22 Maugeri & Falce, *supra* note 13, p. 276.

23 Nogler & Reifner, *supra* note 11, p. 6.

24 With regard to this category, *see* P. Grossi, *Locatio ad Longus Tempus*, Morano, Napoli, 1963, p. 26.

25 Wellenhofer-Klein, *supra* note 20, p. 58, points out the situation of the supplier, who remains isolated from the final-good market, depending structurally from the organizational choices made by the customer. Even in cases of integration through network contracts, A. Barba, 'Reti di Impresa e Abuso di Dipendenza Economica', *Contratto e impresa* 2015, p. 1264 *et seq.*, highlights the risk of abuse of economic dependence.

26 P.L. Joskow, 'Asset Specificity and Vertical Integration', *in* P. Neuman (Ed.), *The New Palgrave Dictionary of Law and Economics*, MacMillan, Oxford, 1998, pp. 107-108.

27 B. Klein *et al.*, 'Vertical Integration, Appropriable Rents and the Competitive Contracting Process', 21 *J.L. Econ.* 1978, pp. 297-326. About the supply relationship as a general criterion for identifying the economic dependence, *see* O. Razzolini, 'Perchè Avviare una Riflessione su Piccolo Imprenditore e Lavoro Prevalentemente Personale', 4 *Diritto delle Relazioni Industriali* 2013, p. 1095 *et seq.*

28 About combatting late payment in commercial transactions, *see* Directive 2000/35/EC.

29 A. Albanese, 'Abuso di Dipendenza Economica: Nullità del Contratto e Riequilibrio del Rapporto', 1 *Europa Dir. Priv.* 1999, p. 1182, and A. Albanese, *Contratto Mercato Responsabilità*, Giuffré, Milano, 2008, p. 120. *But cf.*, C. Castronovo, *Eclissi del diritto civile*, Giuffré, Milano, 2015, p. 103 *et seq.*

The inequality of bargaining power is, therefore, closely related to the need for a long-term contract, as a means to satisfy a supplier's personal interests; the two aspects cannot be considered logically opposite.[30]

In all such cases, the inequality of bargaining power, also typical of other Life Time Contracts, can prevent the fair allocation of the revenue of the entire market among the people that are involved in it. At the same time, outsourcing is no longer able to efficiently allocate business risk, as it tends to transfer that risk to the weaker party, even when the other one is likely better able to handle it.

For this reason, the law, without generally prohibiting any form of vertical integration by contract, given the social utility that can result from it, should provide adequate protection for the company integrated into the main firm organization and for its employees, in order to prevent, or correct, possible abuses. So, a special regulation, inspired by social values, should prevent opportunistic behaviors to the detriment of the supplier,[31] as well as fake forms of labor division among related companies, aimed exclusively to circumvent legislation ensuring the rights of workers.[32]

In this sense, the rules improving contractual justice in supply relationships safeguard not only the supplier, but also its employees, and, thereby, indirectly assures them against the risk of losing their jobs because of early termination of the supply relationship or the bankruptcy of their employer.

In addition, direct protection of employees can be assumed when the organizational autonomy of the supplier is excluded by a lack of satisfactory alternatives in the market, such that its workers should be allowed to enforce their rights against the company that has actually exercised its hierarchical power over them.[33]

This perspective makes it also clear that it is not in every case of economic dependence or unequal bargaining power arising from a long-term contract that there are the conditions laid down by the Principles of Life Time Contracts. But, they do appear when a long-running contract is essential to the enterprise's freedom and/or to the economic survival of one of the parties.

30 For a different perspective, with regard to labor relations, *see* Razzolini, *supra* note 19, p. 390 *et seq.*, according to whom the need for social contractual protection has to be founded not on workers' economic dependence, but on personal character of their performance.

31 O.E. Williamson, 'Transaction Cost Economics: The Governance of Contractual Relations', 22 *J.L. Econ.* 1979, p. 233 *et seq.*

32 Ferruggia, *supra* note 6, p. 819 *et seq.*

33 *See* O. Mazzotta, *Rapporti Interpositori e Contratto di Lavoro*, Giuffrè, Milano, 1979, p. 412 and F. Scarpelli, 'Interposizione e Appalto nel Settore dei Servizi Informatici', *in* O. Mazzotta (Ed.), *Nuove Tecnologie e Rapporti Fra Imprese: Profili Giuslavoristici degli Appalti di Opere e Servizi Informatici*, Milano, Giuffrè, 1990, p. 69.

4.3 Rebalancing Unequal Bargaining Power in Business Contracts

In achieving these objectives, mandatory rules play a key role, since they can minimize the risk that, while free trade may comply with economic criteria, a transaction can still violate fundamental human interests.[34] The protection of these interests cannot be left to the spontaneous functioning of the market, which calls, instead, for a choice of legal policy resulting in a regulation of contractual relationships, coherent with the ethical function of the market, as an expression of human freedom.

Indeed, recognizing the artificiality of the market – as an institution governed by legal rules – does not necessarily mean agreement with a merely positivistic model of law, based on the arbitrary will of a political majority.[35] The positive law, instead, should be legitimated in terms of compliance with values, recognized by social consensus, as the basis of the legal system.[36] Public intervention, however, although necessary, cannot adopt authoritarian forms of government control, but should respect the market as a social institution[37] and ensure that its functioning is not only efficient, but also fair.[38]

Freedom of economic initiative grounds, in fact, its legitimacy on the idea that human well-being is a part of human dignity, on the condition that the allocation of resources may be considered as 'correct'.[39] In this logic, the rules concerning contracts should aim not only at increasing the quantity and quality of products, in order to offer consumers better goods at lower prices, but also at providing a more equitable distribution of the profits in the market among those active in it.[40]

Therefore, the full development of the human personality has to be combined with an economic system that favors social progress through the meeting of supply and de-

34 Albanese, *supra* note 29, p. 51.

35 This point of view, criticized here, has been expressed by N. Irti, *L'ordine Giuridico del Mercato*, Laterza, Roma, 2004, p. 10 *et seq.*

36 L. Mengoni, 'La Questione del Diritto Giusto nella Società Post-Liberale', *in* C. Castronovo *et al.* (Eds.), *Metodo e Teoria Giuridica*, Milano, Giuffré, 2011, pp. 55-71.

37 In this regard R.H. Thaler & C.R. Sustein, *Nudge. Improving Decisions about Health, Wealth and Happiness*, New Haven, CT/London, Yale University Press, 2008, speak of 'libertarian paternalism'. This idea is opposed to the concept of 'coercive paternalism', sustained by S. Conly, *Against Autonomy. Justifying Coercive Paternalism*, Cambridge University Press, Cambridge, 2012.

38 G. Brennan & J.M. Buchanan, *The Reason of Rules: Constitutional Political Economy*, Cambridge University Press, Cambridge, 2008, p. 168. Similarly, R.S. Summers, 'Economics and the Autonomy of Law. Legal Analysis and Legal Theory', *in* T. Eckhoff *et al.*(Eds.), *Rechtstheorie, Beiheft 10, Vernuft und Erfahrung im Rechtsdenken der Gegenwart*, Berlin, Duncker & Humblot, 1986, p. 399 *et seq.*, argues that regulatory decisions cannot be based solely on an economic assessment of efficiency. Even R. Posner, 'The Ethical and Political Basis of The Efficiency Norm in Common Law Adjudication', 8 *Hofstra L. Rev.* 1980, p. 846, recognizes that overall usefulness is an ethical criterion of the common law that does not necessarily apply to other legal systems.

39 *See* Council of Europe, Concerted Development of Social Cohesion Indicators. Methodological Guide, Council of Europe Publishing, Strasbourg, 2005, p. 54 *et seq.*

40 About the purposes of the rules governing contracts, *cf.* M.J. Trebilcock, *The Limits of Freedom of Contract*, Harvard University Press, Cambridge, MA/London, 1993, p. 310, and A.M. Polinsky, *An Introduction to Law and Economics*, Wolters Kluwer, New York, 2011, p. 195.

mand.[41] In fact, the legal protection does not aim to keep alive inefficient economic activities, but to prevent that unequal bargaining power which pushes out of the market even those who are able to produce income and social welfare.

From this point of view, determining the content of negotiation should not be the goal of the law, but rather that of free bargaining between private parties. Fair business relationships, in fact, should be achieved by ensuring effective contractual freedom to each party and not by imposing on them a predetermined contractual settlement.[42]

This logic does not require complete regulation of individual business contracts, being sufficient rules and principles, applicable to an indefinite number of different kinds of agreements,[43] in order to restore balance in specific situations of unequal bargaining power.

So, EU Regulation, which derogates from the general prohibition of agreements restricting competition, allows joint activities by agricultural producers in order to strengthen their position toward their commercial partners, not preventing – but promoting – proper market functioning;[44] and, even in the United States, farmers' cooperatives have been given a partial exemption from the antitrust laws.[45]

In this way, the bargaining power of the company that coordinates the integrated system of production is rebalanced by forms of horizontal integration between suppliers. As a result, on the one hand, producer organizations are able to concentrate supply, selling products supplied by their members[46] and, on the other hand, they may balance the bargaining power of stronger parties entering into Framework Agreements with opposing companies or with their representative organizations, in order to determine the content of individual farming contracts.[47] Therefore, the contractual settlement is not predefined by the law, but is determined by collective autonomy through a standard model, designed

41 W.H. Balekjian, 'Legal Reasoning and Economic Reasoning', *in* Eckhoff *et al.* (Eds.), *supra* note 38, pp. 375-377.

42 More in Albanese, *supra* note 29, p. 7 *et seq.*

43 Decentralization of productive activities and outsourcing are implemented through a number of different agreements, not referable to a single typical or atypical figure. *See*, in this sense, with respect to subcontracting regulated by Italian law Art.1, l. 192/1998, G. Tucci & C. Calia, 'La Subfornitura in Italia: Sette Anni di Applicazione Della Legge 18 Giugno 1998 no. 192', *Riv. dir. priv.* 2006, p. 105.

44 The Treaty on the Functioning of the European Union (TFEU) provides a specific status for the agricultural sector with regard to competition rules and Art. 42 gives unique powers to the EU legislator to decide to what extent the competition rules apply to this sector. This principle is laid out in the basic act for agricultural markets, the Common Organization of the Market (CMO) Regulation no. 1308/2013 of the European Parliament and of the Council of 17 December 2013. In particular Art. 209, by derogating from the general prohibition of agreements restricting competition under Art. 101(1) TFEU, allows joint activities by agricultural producers.

45 *See* Hansmann, *supra* note 8, p. 125 *et seq.*

46 The cooperatives may simply sell the products on behalf of their members or purchase the goods and then resell them. Sometimes they process their members' commodities into finished products and even market these to consumers.

47 H.L. Moore, 'Ensuring Contract Producers' Interests are Protected', *in Am-Coop*, National Council of Farmer Cooperatives, Washington DC, 1994, p. 28 *et seq.*

to regulate future relationships between individual parties. Even for contracts in the food supply chain, similarly to employment contracts,[48] collective agreements are functional to balance unequal bargaining power.

However, in compliance with the antitrust law, Framework Agreements in agriculture, unlike employment contracts, cannot intervene on the supply's prices,[49] which can only be agreed upon by the individual parties.[50]

Anyhow, regardless of the signing of collective contracts, a regulation is also appropriate at the level of individual bargaining.[51] For this purpose, most European legal systems focus on the protection of agricultural producers primarily on the end runtime of the farming contract, when they sell their products to wholesalers, supermarket chains, or the processing industry.[52] This choice of legal policy can largely be explained as an expression of a more general trend in European law toward shaping legislation on contracts to the liberal model of a commercial sale, by transforming long-term partnerships into synallagmatic spot relationships.[53] But, it is also based on the empirical finding that the imbalance of bargaining power between producers and buyers, even in vertical integration relationships, is, typically, crystallized in the sale of goods.[54]

4.4 The Contractual Justice in Business Relationships: Judicial Review and Minimum Mandatory Content of the Agreement

Broadly speaking, protection of the weaker party has been gradually extended by the law, from consumer contracts to businesses relations.

According to some scholars, these cases fall within the scope of the regulation of 'contracts with asymmetry of bargaining power', a basically unitary category clearly dif-

48 L. Nogler, *Saggio sull'Efficacia Regolativa del Contratto Collettivo*, CEDAM, Padova, 1997, p. 251 *et seq.*

49 However, in the United States, bargaining cooperatives are allowed to negotiate a common price for their members' commodity, leaving purchaser to deal directly with individual farmers to arrange delivery at that price. *Cf.* Hansmann, *supra* note 8, pp. 121, 125 *et seq.*, who highlights the risk that this marketing power is used not just to counter monopsony, but further to extract monopoly profits for their members from ultimate consumers.

50 In this way, *see* Art. 209, co. 1, reg. No. 1308/2013. It is indeed an exception to Art. 149 reg. No. 1308/2013, that, by derogating from competition rules, allows producer organizations to negotiate, under certain conditions and within certain limits, the price of milk with the processing industry. This provision is explicitly aimed to 'ensure the viable development of production and a resulting fair standard of living for dairy farmers', so that 'their bargaining power *vis-à-vis* processors' could 'be strengthened, which should result in a fairer distribution of added value along the supply chain' (Recital 128).

51 *Cf.* A. Schwartz & R.E. Scott, 'Contract Theory and Limits of Contract Law', 113 *Yale L.J.* 2003, pp. 541-620.

52 In this sense, *see* Italian law, Art. 62, co. 2, d. l. 1/2012.

53 Point 5, EuSoCo Declaration, *in* Nogler & Reifner (Eds.), *supra* note 1, p. 22.

54 C. Del Cont, *Filiéres Agroalimentaires et Contrat: L'expérience de Contracualisation des Relations Commerciales Agricoles*, Retrieved on 9 February 2017 from <www.rivistadirittoalimentare.it>, p. 3.

ferent from the traditional figure of contract law.[55] On the contrary, according to others, there is an autonomous category, the so-called third contract, with its own distinct discipline.[56] Indeed, without a specific provision of law, judges can neither automatically apply consumer protection rules to businesses who are in a weak bargaining position (and vice versa),[57] nor rule out such an extension on the basis of a difference between the two situations, always considered essential. Instead, they have to extend – by analogy – the rules governing certain contracts to other contracts, where there are the required conditions (*casus omissus* and same legal reasoning).[58]

Only in these cases may judges carry out an *ex post* review of the fairness of the exchange in order to ensure effective freedom of contract for the weaker party, avoiding those terms that are not an authentic expression of both parties' autonomy, but are, instead, the consequence of an abuse of bargaining power by one of them.[59] In this approach, both formal and substantive justice is involved.[60] According to the idea of procedural justice,[61] the law does not authoritatively impose a contractual settlement, considered an *a priori* right; rather, it corrects the imbalances generated by abuses of bargaining power that would otherwise limit the freedom of the economically weaker party, forcing it to accept unfair conditions.[62]

Moreover, the long duration of these relationships also makes it necessary to protect this party not only with regard to the formation of the contractual settlement, but also throughout its execution. Using this logic, it can be appropriate to impose some formal requirements and a minimum mandatory content for the agreement, in order to establish more transparent contractual terms and prevent claims for undue benefits by the stronger party. For example, obliging it to determine the price of products at the time of signing the contract combats a common practice of setting the consideration for the sale by

55 In favour of a single contractual category governed by common rules, *see* V. Roppo, *Il Contratto del Duemila*, Giappichelli, Torino, 2011, p. 141.

56 On the different opinions, which separate cases of contractual weakness in business relationships from those in consumer contracts, *see* A.M. Benedetti, 'Contratto Asimmetrico', *Enc. Dir. Annali* V, Giuffré, Milano, 2012, p. 370 *et seq.*

57 In this sense C. Castronovo, 'Diritto Privato Generale e Diritti Secondi. La Ripresa di un Tema', *Europa Dir. Priv.* 2006, pp. 421-422.

58 *See* A. Albanese, 'I Contratti dei Consumatori Tra Diritto Privato Generale e Diritti Secondi', *Jus* 2009, pp. 347-358, 352, 355 (noting that the protection of the weaker party does not exclude the application of general contract law, not only to fill the legislative gaps, but also to make the interpretation of special rules coherent with the entire system). On this point *see also* L. Mengoni, 'Istituzioni di Diritto Privato e Discipline Speciali', *in* Castronovo *et al.* (Eds.), *supra* note 36, p. 282 *et seq.*

59 *See* A. Albanese, 'I Contratti Della Filiera Agroalimentare Tra Efficienza del Mercato e Giustizia Dello Scambio', *in* A. D'Angelo & V. Roppo (Eds.), *Annuario del contratto 2015*, Torino, Giappichelli, 2016, p. 25 *et seq.*

60 C. Castronovo, 'Autonomia Privata e Costituzione Europea', *Europa Dir. Priv.* 2005, pp. 29-50.

61 R.M. Unger, *Law in Modern Society. Toward a Criticism of Social Theory*, Free Press, New York, 1976, p. 315. *But cf.* Castronovo, *supra* note 60, p. 47 *et seq.*, who speaks of 'corrective justice', as such commutative in form, but distributive in substance.

62 H. Collins, *The Law of Contract*, Butterworths, London, 1993, p. 260 *et seq.*

reference to mercurial price lists at the moment the goods or services are provided. In this way, the law does not impose specific contractual terms or determined prices, but it requires the stronger party to make the content of the exchange more reliable and transparent.[63]

Besides, the contract's execution cannot be reduced to the formalistic fulfilment of the obligations expressly agreed, as it also requires each party to comply with a fairness rule, in order to meet those personal needs of the other party, which are the purpose of the contract. In long-term relationships, in fact, it is impossible to provide for every possible contingency, in which the parties shall fulfil the contract[64] or to specify, in advance, the means by which their interests can be adequately satisfied.[65] Therefore, the unavoidable shortcomings of the contract require integration with the general principle of good faith and fair dealing, which is even more true in the case of relational contracts,[66] based on a relationship of trust between the parties, whose behavior is not entirely regulated by the contract's express terms, but also conforms to implicit terms and understandings.[67]

It is also important to protect the dependent party's interest in continuing the relationship, not only on account of specific investments that party has made,[68] but also because of the impossibility of ensuring its survival after the conversion of its business model. Unlike the labor regulation,[69] in this case, it does not seem adequate to provide an indeterminate-length contract and just prevent the stronger party to withdraw therefrom, outside of certain circumstances. Judicial review of the proper exercise of the buyer's right to terminate, in fact, would not satisfy the certainty needs of the provider. Rather, this party ought to be able to rely, anyhow, on a fixed-term contract, one that allows him to recoup his initial investments and support any switching costs necessary to permit it to continue its work with another partner, ensuring its own interest in the long-term sustainability of its business. But, for this purpose, a minimum period cannot be established by law, because of the insufficient cognitive competence of the legislative bodies.[70] The

---

63 About legal remedies for the lack of formal requirements and mandatory minimum content, *see* Albanese, *supra* note 59, p. 20 *et seq.*

64 This problem arises especially where "the transactions are likely to extend over such a long period of time, and are sufficiently complex and unpredictable, that important aspects of future transactions cannot be reduced to contract in advance but rather must be dealt with over time according to experience": Hansmann, *supra* note 8, p. 25.

65 The incomplete contracting theory was pioneered by S.J. Grossman & O.D. Hart, 'The Costs and Benefits of Ownership: A Theory of Vertical and Lateral Integration', 94 *J. Pol. Econ.* 1986, pp. 691-719.

66 For the partial matching of Life Time Contracts and Relational Contracts, *see* Nogler & Reifner, *supra* note 11, p. 5.

67 On this category, *see* I.R. MacNeil, 'Reflection on Relational Contract Theory after a Neoclassical Seminar', *in* H. Collins *et al.* (Eds.), *The Implicit Dimensions of Contract*, Oxford, Hart, 2003.

68 *See, e.g.*, R. Caso, 'Subfornitura Industriale: Analisi Giuseconomica delle Situazioni di Disparità Contrattuale', *Riv. Crit. Dir. Priv.* 1998, p. 248.

69 Nogler & Reifner, *supra* note 11, p. 11.

70 About the general question, *see* Mengoni, *supra* note 36, p. 65.

law may, instead, require the parties to determine the contract duration at the moment of its formation, leaving it to the judge to correct, *ex post*, an ultimately unfair agreement.

In conclusion, such a regulatory measure, as well as the others previously examined, following a typical demand for contractual justice in the postliberal society, can counteract the economic limits of the freedom and equality of the parties that would prevent the full development of the human person, even in the context of business relationships. In this sense, the regulation of supply contracts should not follow a purely commutative justice, regardless of the specific situation of a single party, but had rather take as its reference a human being in the context of social relationships that also affect the supplier's contractual choices.[71]

This neo-institutional view of contract law, while recognizing both market and private autonomy as self-regulatory instruments, does not adopt a liberal model, since legal intervention, from this perspective, is not limited to establishing organizational and procedural rules in compliance with a principle of formal equality; rather, it aims at removing social and economic barriers to substantial equality of the contracting parties.[72]

BIBLIOGRAPHY

Albanese, A., 'Abuso di Dipendenza Economica: Nullità del Contratto e Riequilibrio del Rapporto', 1 *Europa dir. priv.* 1999, p. 1182.

Albanese, A., *Contratto Mercato Responsabilità*, Milano: Giuffré, 2008.

Albanese, A., 'I Contratti dei Consumatori Tra Diritto Privato Generale e Diritti Secondi', *Jus* 2009, pp. 347-358.

Albanese, A., 'Contractual Justice and Market Efficiency in the Supply Relationships within the Agro-Food Chain', *Riv. Reg. Mercati* 2016, p. 82 *et seq.*

Albanese, A., 'I Contratti Della Filiera Agroalimentare Tra Efficienza del Mercato e Giustizia Dello Scambio', *in* A. D'angelo & V. Roppo (Eds.), *Annuario del contratto 2015*, Torino: Giappichelli, 2016, p. 25 *et seq.*

71 On justice, as a criterion to correct the depersonalizing effects of spot market trading, *see* A. Nicolussi, 'Etica del contratto e "Contratti 'di Durata' per l'Esistenza della Persona"', *in* Nogler & Reifner (Eds.), *supra* note 1, p. 128 *et seq.*

72 L. Raiser, *Die Aufgabe des Privatrechts*, Athenäum-Verlag, Regensburg, 1977, p. 263.

Balekjian, W.H., 'Legal Reasoning and Economic Reasoning', *in* T. Eckhoff *et al.* (Eds.), *Rechtstheorie, Beiheft 10, Vernuft und Erfahrung im Rechtsdenken der Gegenwart*, Berlin: Duncker & Humblot, 1986.

Barba, A., 'Reti di Impresa e Abuso di Dipendenza Economica', 31 *Contratto e Impresa* 2015, p. 1264 *et seq.*

Benedetti, A.M., 'Contratto Asimmetrico', *Enc. Dir. Annali* V, Milano: Giuffré, 2012, p. 370 *et seq.*

Bertolotti, A., *Il Contratto di Subfornitura*, Torino: Utet, 2000.

Brennan, G. & Buchanan, J.M., *The Reason of Rules: Constitutional Political Economy*, Cambridge: Cambridge University Press, 2008.

Caso, R., 'Subfornitura Industriale: Analisi Giuseconomica delle Situazioni di Disparità Contrattuale', *Riv. Crit. Dir. Priv.* 1998, p. 248.

Castronovo, C., 'Autonomia Privata e Costituzione Europea', *Europa Dir. Priv.* 2005, pp. 29-50.

Castronovo, C., 'Diritto Privato Generale e Diritti Secondi. La Ripresa di un Tema', *Europa Dir. Priv.* 2006, pp. 397-423.

Castronovo, C., *Eclissi del diritto civile*, Milano: Giuffré, 2015.

Coase, R., 'The Nature of the Firm: Origin, Meaning, Influence', 4 *J.L. Econ. Org.* 1988, p. 33, *reprinted in* O.E. Williamson, *The Economic Institutions of Capitalism: Firms, Markets, Relational Contracting*, Free Press, New York, 1985.

Collins, H., *The Law of Contract*, London: Butterworths, 1993.

Conly, S., *Against Autonomy. Justifying Coercive Paternalism*, Cambridge: Cambridge University Press, 2012.

Council of Europe, *Concerted Development of Social Cohesion Indicators. Methodological Guide*, Strasbourg: Council of Europe Publishing, 2005.

Del Cont, C., *Filiéres Agroalimentaires et Contrat: L'expérience de Contracualisation des Relations Commerciales Agricoles*, Retrieved on 9 February 2017 from <www.-rivistadirittoalimentare.it>.

Ferruggia, A., 'Le Esternalizzazioni «Relazionali» nel Decentramento di Attività d'Impresa', *Riv. Giur. Lav. Prev. Soc.* 2013, p. 811.

Gilson, R.J. *et al.*, 'Contracting of Innovation: Vertical Disintegration and Interfirm Collaboration', 109 *Columbia L. Rev.* 2009, p. 431 *et seq.*

Giunta, A. & Scalera, D., 'Dal Decentramento alle Catene Globali del Valore: la Subfornitura Industriale in Italia', *Analisi Giur. Economia* 2011, p. 195 *et seq.*

Grossi, P., *Locatio ad Longus Tempus*, Napoli: Morano, 1963.

Grossman, S.J. & Hart, O.D., 'The Costs and Benefits of Ownership: A Theory of Vertical and Lateral Integration', 94 *J. Pol. Econ.* 1986, pp. 691-719.

Hansmann, H., *The Ownership of Enterprise*, Cambridge, MA/London: The Belknap Press of Harvard University Press, 1996.

Irti, N., *L'ordine Giuridico del Mercato*, Roma: Laterza, 2004.

James Jr., H.S., *et al.* 'The Adoption, Diffusion and Evolution of Organizational Forms: Insights from the Agrifood Sector', 32 *Manage. Decis. Econ.* 2011, pp. 243-259.

Joskow, P.L., 'Asset Specificity and Vertical Integration', *in* P. Neuman (Ed.), *The New Palgrave Dictionary of Law and Economics*, Oxford: MacMillan, 1998.

Kessler, F. & Stern, R.H., 'Competition, Contract, and Vertical Integration', 69 *Yale L.J.* 1959, p. 1 *et seq.*

Klein, B., *et al.*, 'Vertical Integration, Appropriable Rents and the Competitive Contracting Process', 21 *J.L. Econ.* 1978, pp. 297-326.

Larenz, K., *Lehrbuch des Schuldrechts. Band I: Allgemeineir Teil*, München: C.H. Beck, 1987.

MacNeil, I.R., 'Reflection on Relational Contract Theory after a Neoclassical Seminar', *in* H. Collins *et al.* (Eds.), *The Implicit Dimensions of Contract*, Oxford: Hart, 2003.

Maugeri, M. & Falce, V., 'Indotto, Concorrenza e Mercato: il Caso della Subfornitura', *Analisi Giur. Economia* 2011, p. 275.

Mazzotta, O., *Rapporti Interpositori e Contratto di Lavoro*, Milano: Giuffré, 1979.

Medicus, D., *Schuldrecht I. Allgemeineir Teil: ein Studienbuch*, München: C.H. Beck, 2005.

Mengoni, L., 'Istituzioni di Diritto Privato e Discipline Speciali', *in* C. Castronovo *et al.* (Eds.), *Metodo e Teoria Giuridica*, Milano: Giuffré, 2011, p. 282 *et seq.*

Mengoni, L., 'La Questione del Diritto Giusto nella Società Post-Liberale', *in* C. Castronovo *et al.* (Eds.), *Metodo e Teoria Giuridica*, Milano: Giuffré, 2011, pp. 55-71.

Milgrom, P. & Roberts, J., 'The Economic of Modern Manufacturing: Technology, Strategy and Organization', 80 *Am. Econ. Rev.* 1990, p. 511 *et seq.*

Moore, H.L., 'Ensuring Contract Producers' Interests are Protected', *Am-Coop*, National Council of Farmer Cooperatives, Washington DC, 1994, pp. 28-32.

Nicolussi, A., 'Etica del contratto e "Contratti 'di Durata' per l'Esistenza della Persona"', *in* L. Nogler (Ed.), *Saggio sull'Efficacia Regolativa del Contratto Collettivo*, Padova: CEDAM, 1997.

Nogler, L. & Reifner, U., 'Introduction: The New Dimension of Life Time in the Law of Contracts and Obligations', *in* L. Nogler, & U. Reifner, (Eds.), *Life Time Contracts: Social Longterm Contracts in Labour, Tenancy and Consumer Credit Law*, The Hague: Eleven International Publishing, 2014.

Nogler, L. & Reifner, U. (Eds.), *Life Time Contracts: Social Longterm Contracts in Labour, Tenancy and Consumer Credit Law*, The Hague: Eleven International Publishing, 2014, p. 128 *et seq.*

Oppo, G., 'I Contratti di Durata', *Riv. Dir. Comm.* 1943, I.

Polinsky, A.M., *An Introduction to Law and Economics*, New York: Wolters Kluwer, 2011.

Posner, R., 'The Ethical and Political Basis of the Efficiency Norm in Common Law Adjudication', 8 *Hofstra L. Rev.* 1980, p. 846.

Raiser, L., *Die Aufgabe des Privatrechts*, Regensburg: Athenäum-Verlag, 1977.

Razzolini, O., 'Perchè Avviare una Riflessione su Piccolo Imprenditore e Lavoro Prevalentemente Personale', 4 *Diritto delle Relazioni Industriali* 2013, p. 1095 *et seq.*

Razzolini, O., 'Self-Employment and Economic Dependency in the Light of the Social Contract Law', *in* L. Nogler & U. Reifner (Eds.), *Life Time Contracts: Social Longterm Contracts in Labour, Tenancy and Consumer Credit Law*, The Hague: Eleven International Publishing, 2014, p. 387 *et seq.*

Roppo, V., *Il Contratto del Duemila*, Torino: Giappichelli, 2011.

Rullani, E. & Romano, L. (Eds.), *Il Postfordism. Idee per il Capitalismo Prossimo Venturo*, Milano: Etas Libri, 1998.

Scarpelli, F., 'Interposizione e Appalto nel Settore dei Servizi Informatici', *in* O. Mazzotta (Ed.), *Nuove Tecnologie e Rapporti Fra Imprese: Profili Giuslavoristici degli Appalti di Opere e Servizi Informatici*, Milano: Giuffré, 1990.

Schwartz, A. & Scott, R.E., 'Contract Theory and Limits of Contract Law', 113 *Yale L.J.* 2003, pp. 541-620.

Summers, R.S., 'Economics and the Autonomy of Law. Legal Analysis and Legal Theory', *in* T. Eckhoff *et al.* (Eds.), *Rechtstheorie, Beiheft 10, Vernuft und Erfahrung im Rechtsdenken der Gegenwart*, Berlin: Duncker & Humblot, 1986, p. 399 *et seq.*

Thaler, R.H. & Sustein, C.R., *Nudge. Improving Decisions about Health, Wealth and Happiness*, New Haven, CT/London: Yale University Press, 2008.

Trebilcock, M.J., *The Limits of Freedom of Contract*, Cambridge, MA/London: Harvard University Press, 1993.

Tucci, G. & Calia, C., 'La Subfornitura in Italia: Sette Anni di Applicazione Della Legge 18 Giugno 1998, no. 192', 11 *Riv. Dir. Priv.* 2006, p. 105.

Unger, R.M., *Law in Modern Society. Toward a Criticism of Social Theory*, New York: Free Press, 1976.

Urban, S., 'The Firm and the Fulfilment of a New Humanism: Critical Reflections', 18 *Eur. Bus. L. Rev.* 2007, p. 348.

Wellenhofer-Klein, M., *Zulieferverträge im Privat - und Wirtschaftsrecht*, München: Beck Verlag, 1999, p. 177 *et seq.*

Williamson, O.E., 'Transaction Cost Economics: The Governance of Contractual Relations', 22 *J.L. Econ.* 1979, p. 233 *et seq.*

5 Comparing Rules on Change of Circumstances with the Principles of Life Time Contracts

*Nuno Manuel Pinto Oliveira**

5.1 Introduction: From Alternative Legal Dogmatics to the Principles of Life Time Contracts

In the late 1980s, Professor Thomas Wilhelmsson wrote an important and influential book.[1] It aimed at establishing the foundations for alternative or critical legal dogmatics. Whereas 'mainstream' or 'traditional' legal dogmatics were conservative, for they were 'based on conservative social values',[2] he argued that alternative legal dogmatics should be based on progressive social values – that they should be 'future-directed' or 'future-oriented'.[3] Whereas 'mainstream' or 'traditional' legal dogmatics were '*bourgeois*' (i.e., liberal), he suggested that alternative legal dogmatics should be social.[4] It should be stressed that, among the many (possible) futures of contract law,[5] he argued a line was to be drawn between those possible futures inspired by socially conservative ideals and those possible futures inspired by socially progressive, emancipatory ideals. In such a subject matter, as probably in any other subject matter relating to the law, it would all come down to *substantive values*. "If one does not wish to subsume under alternative legal dogmatics all forms of legal dogmatics that question *communis opinio*", the term 'alternative legal dogmatics' is to be reserved to the forms of legal dogmatics based upon a specific set of substantive *values*, of substantive *ideals* and *attitudes*. In fact, "[w]hat is of interest is ultimately *what one defines* as those *emancipatory ideals* that are typical of [an] alternative legal dogmatics".[6]

---

* Professor at the University of Minho, Portugal. The following chapter was originally presented at the conference entitled 'Life Time Contracts: Rethinking Contract Law', held at the University of Luxembourg on Friday, 30 September 2016. I would like to thank the University of Luxembourg and the organizers of the conference, Professors Ratti, Reifner, and Nogler for their kind invitation.

1 T. Wilhelmsson, *Critical Studies in Private Law: A Treatise on Need-Rational Principles in Modern Law*, Springer, Dordrecht, 1992. While the English translation was initially published in the early 1990s, the original Finnish publication occurred in the late 1980s.

2 Id., p. 4.

3 Id., p. 46.

4 Id., p. 47.

5 *See* for a similar expression, I. MacNeil, 'The Many Futures of Contracts', 47 *S. Cal. L. Rev.* 1973-1974, p. 691.

6 Wilhelmsson, *supra* note 1, p. 48 (emphasis added).

In referring to Habermas' distinction between three paradigms of law, it could perhaps be argued that the concept of 'mainstream' or 'traditional' legal dogmatics referred to the old, liberal model of formal private law and alternative legal dogmatics to the new, social-welfare model of materialized private law.[7] In a sense, it could be argued that alternative legal dogmatics are but a reflection of the so-called materialization of private law.[8]

Professor Wilhelmsson further stressed two or three topics common to all forms of alternative dogmatics relating to contract law. First, contract law should consider the parties' concrete, material, and moral needs – it should be 'need-directed', 'need-oriented', or 'need-rational'. Even though concepts such as *need-directed* or *need-rational* are somewhat vague,[9] they could be supplemented by referring to particular, specific needs of the contractual partners – such as 'the parties' need for protection', at least 'when hit by special events, such as illness, unemployment and old age,'[10] and, generally, 'the parties' need for a certain minimum subsistence.'[11]

I suppose it is apparent that there is a close connection between the concepts of *alternative legal dogmatics*, as described by Professor Wilhelmsson, and the *Principles* of *Life Time Contracts*. In arguing that the connection is apparent, I am taking no risk at all, for Professors Reifner and Nogler acknowledge such a relationship.[12] In fact, the basic question of all alternative or critical legal dogmatics, including critical legal dogmatics referring to 'Life Time Contracts', could be phrased as follows: "How can human needs, the human personality, the social dimension of economic action and the aspiration of social justice adequately be reflected in contract law?"[13]

In the first place, both approaches share a common concern for the concept of contractual freedom, aimed at contextualizing freedom, by referring to 'social interests'. Contractual freedom, so the EuSoCo Declaration says, "should be complemented with the freedom of social interests to be sheltered from the three social dangers of our time: unemployment, over-indebtedness, and homelessness."[14]

Secondly, both approaches share a common concern for the concept of social justice. Professors Reifner and Nogler define the concept of *social justice* as related to human

---

7 J. Habermas, *Between Facts and Norms. Contributions to a Discourse Theory of Law and Democracy*, MIT University Press, Cambridge, MA, 1996, pp. 388-409.

8 Id., p. 392 *et seq.*

9 Wilhelmsson, *supra* note 1, p. 72 (emphasis added).

10 Id., p. 55.

11 Id.

12 L. Nogler & U. Reifner, *Lifetime Contracts – Rediscovering the Social Dimension of the Sales Contract Mode*, Retrieved on 24 January 2017 from <http://eusoco.eu/wp-content/uploads/2009/12/reifnernoglerfswilehmensson_lifetime-contracts_rediscovering-the-social-dimension1.pdf>.

13 Id., p. 2.

14 Point 8, EuSoCo Declaration, *in* L. Nogler & U. Reifner (Eds.), *Life Time Contracts: Social Long-Term Contracts in Labour, Tenancy and Consumer Credit Law*, The Hague, Eleven International Publishing, 2014. p. 23.

needs[15] and Professor Wilhelmsson characterizes it as 'need-directed' or 'need-oriented'.[16]

Thirdly, in elaborating the values of freedom and justice, both approaches share a common concern for principles. Professor Wilhelmsson defines general principles as 'integrative elements within each branch of law'.[17] From the definition of general principles of contract law as 'integrative elements within each branch of law', two consequences follow. On the one hand, the concept of general principles of law is a broad concept, for it is defined so as to comprehend all "concepts and [...] principles developed by legal science [that] hold together both private law in general and its particular sub-areas."[18] On the other hand, the concept of general principles is a broad concept for it is defined by the function of transforming the legal order into a legal system. "Using the concepts and principles, the individual fragments of law are connected together: through them is created a system of law."[19]

Fourthly, in applying the general principles of law to individual, concrete, and specific situations, so that the substantive values of freedom and justice become a part of economic and social relationships, both approaches share a common concern for the interpretation of existing private law, especially the interpretation of existing contract law. In a sense, they are both inspired by Professor Reifner's concept of *social interpretation*.[20] It could be argued, however, that the approaches differ with respect to such interpretation in the following way: Professor Wilhelmsson's approach aims at transforming contract law from the inside and it focuses on the interpretation both statutes and contracts.

Inasmuch as the interpretation of statutes is concerned, Wilhelmsson stresses that general standards of contract law "leave the courts a fairly wide discretion"[21] thus, allowing them to "to take into account need-oriented viewpoints".[22] Furthermore, inasmuch as the interpretation of contracts is concerned, he suggests that both negotiated and non-negotiated terms allow the courts to pay 'explicit attention' to the needs of the parties.[23] In the case of the former (negotiated terms), the argument applies, at least, to open contracts and open terms in 'closed contracts', and in the latter case (i.e., non-negotiated, standard clauses), it might even apply to 'closed terms'.

---

15 Id., Art. 5.

16 Wilhelmsson, *supra* note 1, p. 97. Professor Wilhelmsson thus stresses that alternative legal dogmatics is to investigate "*the occurrence of traces of need-oriented concepts* and as far as possible to develop these" (emphasis added).

17 Id., p. 22.

18 Id., p. 22 *et seq.* (confirming that the concept of general principles is a broad concept, by explaining that the term "general principles is used to refer to the content of the system-building elements – both legal concepts and legal principles – which form part of the 'general doctrines of civil law'").

19 Id., p. 22.

20 *See, generally,* U. Reifner, *Alternatives Wirtschaftsrecht am Beispiel der Verbraucherverschuldung. Realitätsverleugnung und soziale Auslegung im Zivilrecht*, Luchterhand, Neuwied, 1979.

21 Wilhelmsson, *supra* note 1, p. 75.

22 Id., p. 144.

23 Id. ("In interpretation and supplementation of contracts, too, one can conceive of paying explicit attention to the needs of the parties").

Whereas Professor Wilhelmsson's approach aims at transforming law from the inside, by focusing on the interpretation of statutes and contracts, Professors Reifner and Nogler's approach aims to transform contract law both from the inside and from the outside: from the inside, because it is a dogmatic, scientific approach, and from the outside, because it is also a political approach. The EuSoCo Declaration clearly refers 'to the legislative process[es]'.

Despite these superficial differences, I submit that there is a deep convergence between both perspectives. In referring to the 'number of possible answers' to the question of *social contract law*, Professors Reifner and Nogler express their conviction that "the time has now come for legal theory to take the notion fully on board that time is not alien to contract law."[24] The concept of Life Time Contracts proposes to contribute to the reframing of the problem of *social law*; by considering Life Time Contracts, the case for a *social contract law* is expected to develop into a stronger case.

5.2 Commutative and Distributive Elements in Contract Law

Despite my general sympathy toward context-sensitive (and, thus, social) concepts of contractual freedom and contractual justice, I confess I do have a few doubts about the distinction between alternative and traditional legal dogmatics. Professor Wilhelmsson recognized that "[n]o clear demarcation can be made between alternative forms of legal dogmatics and progressive variants of traditional dogmatics."[25] I suggest, however, that such a statement is better divided into two parts. I am convinced that no demarcation at all can be made on the basis of formal values – such as coherence – and that no clear demarcation can be made on the basis of substantive values.

I suppose it is apparent that no demarcation can be made on the basis that traditional legal dogmatics aims at interpreting the law and alternative legal dogmatics aims at transforming it. In defining legal dogmatics, it must be stressed that all forms of legal dogmatics attempt to determine the content of the law[26] by means of interpretation and systematization of the norms.[27]

I also suppose it is apparent that no demarcation can be made on the basis of formal values, such as coherence. For all forms of legal dogmatics aim at determining the content of the law, by means of interpretation and systematization, and all forms of legal dogmatics concentrate on general principles.[28] In keeping with Professor Canaris, for in-

24 Nogler & Reifner, *supra* note 12, p. 3.
25 Wilhelmsson, *supra* note 1, pp. 11-12.
26 Id., p. 4.
27 Id., p. 4.
28 Id., p. 6.

stance, the legal system itself can be properly defined as an 'order of general principles of law'.[29]

I finally suppose it is apparent that no clear demarcation can be made on the basis of substantive values, such as "commutative justice"[30] or 'corrective justice'.[31] With the (possible) exception of Ernest Weinrib,[32] I am convinced that most, if not all, contract lawyers would accept a system based on combination of commutative and distributive elements.

In fact, every legal system must consider the question of justice. If contractual freedom is to be recognized, it is to be recognized under the condition that the results of their exercise do not contradict the requirements of justice.[33] In referring to the requirements of *justice, sic et simpliciter*, both the requirements of *commutative justice* and *distributive justice* are at stake.

It can be accepted that the very concept of a contract, by requiring the agreement of the parties, provides for a certain guarantee that – for *eine gewisse Gewähr* – the result will not contradict the basic requirements of commutative justice.[34] Despite that, the guarantee provided by the concept of 'contract' is subject to limits. In the first place, inasmuch as commutative justice is concerned, it is not sufficient, and, secondly, inasmuch as distributive justice is concerned, it is neither sufficient nor appropriate.

It may be argued that a demarcation could be made on the basis of the different weighing of the two forms of justice. Within the framework of conservative, traditional legal dogmatics, there would be a hierarchy – commutative justice would outrank distributive justice. Commutative justice would be the rule and distributive justice the exception.[35] Within the framework of alternative, progressive legal dogmatics, however, things could be significantly different – there would be no hierarchy at all.

Professor Stefan Arnold convincingly argued that the concept of justice is a part of the objective concept, or idea, of law – of the *objektive Rechtsidee*.[36] Furthermore, he argued

29 *See* C.W. Canaris, 'Systemdenken und Systembegriff in der Jurisprudenz', *in* C.W. Canaris (Ed.), *Gesammelte Schriften. I – Rechtstheorie*, Berlin, de Gruyter, 2012, pp. 191-346, p. 230 *et seq.*: *System als Ordnung 'allgemeiner Rechtsprinzipien.*

30 On the concepts of commutative justice and distributive justice, *see, e.g.*, A.T. Kronman, 'Contract Law and Distributive Justice', 89 *Yale L.J.* 1979-1980, pp. 472-511; C.W. Canaris, 'Die Bedeutung der iustitia distributiva in deutschen Vertragsrecht', *in* C.W. Canaris (Ed.), *Gesammelte Schriften* III – *Privatrecht*, Berlin, de Gruyter, 2012, pp. 35-137; S. Arnold, *Vertrag und Verteilung. Die Bedeutung der iustitia distributiva im Privatrecht*, Mohr Siebeck, Tübingen, 2014.

31 On the concept of corrective justice, *see* E.J. Weinrib, *The Idea of Private Law*, Harvard University Press, Cambridge, MA, 1995; and E.J. Weinrib, *Corrective Justice*, Oxford University Press, Oxford, 2012.

32 *See* Weinrib 1995, *supra* note 31, p. 204 *et seq.*

33 *See, e.g.*, C.W. Canaris, 'Verfassungs- und europarechtliche Aspekte der Vertragsfeiheit in der Privatrechtsgesellchaft', *in* Canaris (Ed.), *supra* note 29, pp. 871-890.

34 *See, e.g.*, Canaris, *supra* note 33, p. 883.

35 *See, e.g.*, Canaris, *supra* note 30, p. 126.

36 Arnold, *supra* note 30, p. 11 *et seq.*

that, since both *commutative, corrective justice* and *distributive justice* are two forms of justice, they are both essential.[37]

Within the framework of conservative, traditional legal dogmatics, there would be a relationship of *normative precedence* between the two basic forms of justice. *Commutative justice*, for it is the rule, would have *normative precedence* over *distributive justice*, for distributive justice is the exception. Within the framework of progressive, alternative legal dogmatics, there would be no relationship of *normative precedence* at all.

In abstract and general terms, no hierarchies, no precedence, and no priorities could be established between the two basic, fundamental forms of justice: on the one hand, it would be wrong to assume a normative precedence or a normative priority of commutative justice over distributive justice[38] but, on the other hand, it would be wrong to assume a normative priority of distributive justice over commutative, corrective justice.[39]

Even though a demarcation could be made on the basis of the different weighing of the two forms of justice, I suppose it is apparent that it could never be a clear demarcation. The concepts of *contractual solidarity*[40] and *contractual solidarism*[41] and of *socially responsible private law* are common topics in all forms of legal dogmatics. "If you want a private law society", Professor Neuner says, "you must respect its social responsibility."[42]

I do think that, in a social, welfare state, a certain concept of justice is only to be acknowledged as appropriate in contract law in the case when it refers both to commutative justice and distributive justice. If the idea of justice underlying the social, welfare state "approves forced redistribution of wealth, at least up to a point, as a means of achieving a fair division of material resources among the members of society,"[43] then it requires some degree of state control over the distributive effects of contract law.

Despite the fact the Principles of Life Time Contracts make a rather short reference to the idea of social, distributive justice,[44] I suppose distributive, social justice is the basic concept underlying all the Principles – to say that "[t]he contractual freedom of suppliers

---

37 Id., p. 11 *et seq.*

38 Id., p. 181 *et seq.*

39 Id., p. 186 *et seq.*

40 *See, e.g.*, C. Thibierge-Guelfucci, 'Libres-Propos sur la Transformation du Droit des Contrats', *Rev. Trimestrielle de droit civil*, 1997, p. 357 *et seq.*; B. Lurger, *Vertragliche Solidarität*, Nomos, Baden-Baden, 1998; D. Mazeaud, 'Loyauté, Solidarité, Fraternité: La Nouvelle Devise Contractuelle ?', *in L'avenir du Droit, Mélanges en l'Honneur de François Terré*, PUF / Dalloz / Jurisclasseur, Paris, 1999, p. 617 *et seq.*

41 *See, e.g.*, C. Jamin, 'Plaidoyer pour le Solidarisme Contractuel', *in Mélanges en Honneur de Jacques Ghestin*, Paris, LGDJ, 2001, p. 441 *et seq.*; D. Mazeaud, *La bataille du solidarisme contractuel : du feu, des cendres, des braises…*, Retrieved on 18 April 2017 from <http://ddata.over-blog.com/xxxyyy/3/61/42/26/civil-II/Denis-Mazeaud-melanges-Jean-Hauser.pdf>; *but see* Y. Lequette, 'Bilan des Solidarismes Contractuels', *in Mélanges Offerts à Paul Didier. Etudes de Droit Privé*, Economica, Paris, 2008, p. 247 *et seq.*

42 J. Neuner, *Privatrecht und Sozialstaat*, C. H. Beck, München, 1998, p. 291 ("wer die Privatrechtsgesellschaft postuliert, muß deren soziale Verantwortung respektieren").

43 *See* Kronman, *supra* note 30, p. 485 (referring to "[a] liberal theory of society").

44 *See* Principle 8, Access:"The importance of life time contracts in meeting the basic human needs of subsistence, employment and participation in economic life gives access to these goods, services and income opportunities the status of fundamental human right (distributive justice)."

and employers in the traditional sales-based contract model should be complemented with the freedom of social interests to be sheltered from the three dangers of our time", such dangers being "unemployment, over-indebtedness and homelessness"[45] – as the EuSoCo Declaration does – is roughly equivalent to saying that *commutative, corrective justice should be complemented with distributive, social justice.*[46]

In fact, the influence of distributive, social justice in contract law results from two simple, consensual ideas: it results from the recognition of the fact that, first, a social, welfare state requires (some) distribution and redistribution of wealth among private persons[47] and, second, the principles and rules that form a system of contract law have an impact in the distribution and redistribution of wealth among private persons.[48] In acknowledging that the system of contract law has distributive and redistributive effects, the concept of a social, welfare state requires– *at the very least* – that they are not *intolerably unfair.*[49]

I do not think, however, that, for a certain concept of justice to be recognized as appropriate to contract law in the case, it rejects all kinds of precedence or priority of *commutative justice* over *distributive justice. Commutative justice* is immanent in the concept of a contract – *distributive justice* is not. I do think *immanence* is a rather good argument to justify *precedence*,[50] and I do think the normative precedence of *commutative* over *distributive justice* has the effect of imposing on a legislature a particular, specific burden of argument. In the event the legislature decides to intervene in contract law, so as to make it perform a distributive or redistributive function in order to achieve a *fair distribution* or to correct an *unfair distribution* of wealth, that legislature must give strong, compelling reasons for such an intervention.[51]

---

45 EuSoCo Declaration (8), *supra* note 14.

46 I could perhaps complement the objective argument, stated in the text, with a couple of subjective, personal references. When I first read Professors Reifner and Nogler's *Principles of Life Time Contracts*, I could not fully acknowledge the importance of drawing general provisions, valid to general contract law, from specific provisions of consumer, labor, and tenancy law. In preparing this paper, I realized that the very concept of contractual justice was at stake and, in the course of the Luxembourg conference, I had my impression confirmed by talking with Professor Nicolussi. General contract law and specific areas of contract law, such as consumer law, labor law, and tenancy law refer to different concepts of justice. General contract law seems to be entangled by the concept of commutative justice. It seems to be impoverished by the absence of distributive elements. Specific areas of contract law, such as consumer law, labor law, and tenancy law, seem to be impoverished by the absence of commutative elements, such as contractual freedom. I do think the gap is to be bridged. Therefore, I can only agree with Professor Nicolussi's idea that one of the most important things, and perhaps the most important thing about the Principles of Life Time Contracts is that they widen up the horizon of principles and values relevant to *general contract law*.

47 Arnold, *supra* note 30, p. 406.

48 Id., p. 90.

49 Id.

50 *See* N.M. Pinto Oliveira, 'The Private Law Society and Contract Law Application', 5 *Eur. Rev. Cont. L.* 2009, pp. 29, 38 *et seq.*

51 *See, e.g.*, Canaris, *supra* note 30, p. 126.

5.3 THE CASE FOR SOCIAL FORCE MAJEURE

The reference to distributive justice is evident, for example, in the case of social *force majeure*. In referring, extensively, to Professor Reifner's work on consumer insolvency,[52] Professor Wilhelmsson argued that the classic concept of *force majeure* was to be interpreted so as to comprehend 'social *force majeure*'.[53] In the case of consumers, the problem of delays in payment[54] could not be resolved on the basis of traditional principles, such as the principle according to which "[*e*]*ach person is responsible for his ability to pay*."[55] In this respect, the German legal doctrine is rather clear: '*Geld muss man haben*' – you've got to have money.[56] In softening such a principle, Professor Wilhelmsson argued that the debtor's liability should be softened, by allowing him to invoke 'social *force majeure*': "[S]ocial force majeure [might] be conceived as leading to the mitigation of *all* sanctions that [might] be aimed against the debtor because of the delay."[57]

The prerequisites of such social *force majeure* could be summarized as follows: in the first place, social *force majeure* should apply only to cases of relevant occurrences, including changes in the debtor's state of health,[58] changes in the debtor's work situation,[59] changes in the debtor's housing situation,[60] changes in the debtor's family circumstances[61] (such as divorce), and changes in the debtor's property circumstances;[62] secondly, social *force majeure* should only apply to cases in which the delay in payment was caused by the relevant occurrence;[63] thirdly, it should only apply only to cases in which the occurrence was unforeseeable;[64] and fourthly, it should only apply to cases in which the occurrence was not due to the debtor's fault.[65] In the event all of the prerequisites of social *force majeure* have been met, contract law should react by allowing the debtor to either force an adaptation or modification of the contractual terms or to terminate the (long-term) contractual relationship.[66]

Despite the fact that the concept of social *force majeure* is far from consensual, it should at least contribute to a re-examination of conservative, traditional principles,

52 *See, e.g.*, Wilhelmsson, *supra* note 1, pp. 185-188.
53 T. Wilhelmsson, 'Social Force Majeure – A New Concept in Nordic Consumer Law', 13 *J. Consumer Pol.* 1990, p. 1; Wilhelmsson, *supra* note 1, p. 180 *et seq.*
54 Wilhelmsson, *supra* note 1, p. 130 *et seq.*
55 Id., p. 130.
56 Id.
57 Id., p. 207.
58 Id., p. 198.
59 Id., p. 199.
60 Id., pp. 199-200.
61 Id., p. 200.
62 Id., pp. 200-201.
63 Id., p. 201 *et seq.*: 'causal connection'.
64 Id., p. 204.
65 Id., p. 204 *et seq.*: 'absence of fault'.
66 Id., p. 206 *et seq.*

such as '*Geld muss man haben*' – "you've got to have money.[67] The Principles of Life Time Contracts reflect a set of principles and rules intended to regulate *changes of circumstances* and suggest that the standards applying to *change of circumstances* are sufficient to tackle the issue of *social force majeure.* In keeping with my conviction that the appropriateness of the Principles of Life Time Contracts to interpret and, if necessary, to fill the gaps in (existing) contract law is to be assessed by considering concrete, specific cases, I will concentrate on Principles 10 and 11 thereof.

5.4 Change of Circumstances in the Principles of Life Time Contracts

From a rather formal, strictly dogmatic perspective, I find it rather remarkable that the Principles of Life Time Contracts represent change of circumstances as a *disturbance of the foundation of the transaction.*[68] It follows from such a representation that initial and subsequent disturbances are to be treated equally – principles and rules applying to initial disturbances (such as, for instance, the principles and rules on common mistake) are also to apply to subsequent disturbances and vice-versa. Therefore, strictly speaking, Principle 10 is not a principle on change of circumstances, for it applies both to cases in which the relevant circumstances changed *and* to cases in which the relevant circumstances did not change at all, but the contractual parties simply failed to properly and accurately understand them.

In fact, Principle 10 clearly contemplates two types of situations. It first refers to cases in which there is change of circumstances, for the disturbance of the foundation of the transaction materializes after the contract has been concluded; it applies to cases in which "the social and economic circumstances upon which a life time contract is based have changed significantly since the contract was entered into". Further, it then refers to cases in which there is no change of circumstances at all, for the disturbance materialized before the contract had been concluded: it applies to cases in which "material circumstances from which the parties derived have arisen that are found to be at variance with its original situation to such an extent that the social nature of the [life time] contract is jeopardized".[69]

I suppose the requirement that the relevant circumstances be *material*, as well as the requirement that the 'social nature of the contract is jeopardized', apply to both the first and second situations. In saying this, I am saying two things. I am saying, first, that I think that, even in the first situation, "the social and economic circumstances upon which the contract is based" are only to be considered if they are *material circumstances.* I am

67 For a more thorough discussion, *see* Arnold, *supra* note 30, p. 407 *et seq.*

68 For a thorough critique, *see* H. Sousa Antunes, 'A Alteração das Circunstâncias e os *Life Time Contracts*', *in* N.M. Pinto Oliveira & B. MacCrorie (Eds.), *Em Torno de* Life Time Contracts, Retrieved on 2 February 2017 from <https://issuu.com/direitoprivado/docs/em_torno_de_life_time_contracts>, p. 119 *et seq.*

69 *See* Principle 10, Adaptation.

also saying that, second, I think that, even in the first situation, a change of the material economic and social circumstances upon which the contract is based is only to be considered if it jeopardizes 'the social nature of the contract'.

In addition, moving from a formal, dogmatic perspective to a substantive, value-oriented perspective, I find it rather remarkable that the Principles of Life Time Contracts assume that the human dimension of contracts has a double meaning: on the one hand, it means fidelity to the contract and, on the other hand, it means that fidelity to the contract has a different value, or at least a different weight, for each of the parties to a Life Time Contract.

Principle 3 refers to *fidelity to the contract* (*Vertragstreue*) as a value for both parties. Fidelity to the contract is to be bilateral or reciprocal.[70, 71] Principle 11 refers to the *exceptions* to fidelity to the contract. In accordance with Principle 11, fidelity has a different value for each of the parties. If one considers the human dimension of Life Time Contracts, the difference is apparent. In many, if not in most cases, performance of contracts by the professional is more important for the consumer than performance of contracts by the consumer for the professional. It is more important for the lessee than for the lessor. It is more important for the worker than for the employer. – *If the professional, lessor, or employer fails to perform its contractual obligations, the social existence of the consumer, lessee, or employee is at risk.*

In departing from the principle of *fidelity to the contract* as a *value*, Principles 10 and 11 distinguish *general requirements* for the disturbance of the foundation of the transaction to be significant and *specific requirements*, for the disturbance to be so significant that the disadvantaged party is entitled to terminate the contractual relationship. Principle 10 refers to the general requirements of significance – if the disturbance of the foundation of the transaction fails to meet them, it is *immaterial*. Principle 11 refers to additional, specific significance requirements for the termination of the contractual relationship – unless the disturbance meets such additional, specific requirements, the disadvantaged party is not entitled to terminate the contractual relationship. Even if the disturbance is material – even if it is significant – it is not sufficient for termination.

If all of the *general requirements* are met, the disadvantaged party, overburdened by the consequences of the disturbance, is entitled to seek a renegotiation of the contract and, if renegotiation fails, he is entitled to an adaptation or modification of the contractual terms. The right to require a renegotiation of the contract results from both Principles 10 and 12. Principle 10 refers to adaptation of the contract, distinguishing collective and individual adaptation, and expressing a preference for collective over individual

70 For a more thorough discussion, *see* M.P. Weller, *Die Vertragstreue. Vertragsbindung – Naturalerfüllungsgrundsatz – Vertragstreue*, Mohr Siebeck,Tübingen, 2009.

71 Stressing the value of *fidelity to the contract*, even in the case of *insolvency*, and even if the requirements for *discharge* are met, *see* C. Serra, 'As Funções do Direito da Insolvência no Ambito de *Life Time Contracts* (Breve reflexão)', *in* Pinto Oliveira & MacCrorie (Eds.), *supra* note 68, p. 95 *et seq.*, especially p. 101 *et seq.*

modification of the contractual terms, while Principle 12 requires that adaptation or modification of the contractual terms results from a "continuing and co-operative dialogue [...] with regard to fulfilling the purpose of the contract". If, however, renegotiation fails, the right to require adaptation or modification of the contractual terms results, exclusively, from Principle 10.

Furthermore, in the event the *specific requirements* stated in Principle 11 are met, the disadvantaged party may terminate the contract.

5.4.1 *General Requirements for the Disturbance of the Foundation of the Transaction to be Significant*

General requirements, which are *necessary to the disturbance to the foundation of the transaction to be significant at all,* are basically two: first, the disturbance must be material and, second, the disturbance must be so material that the disadvantaged party "*cannot be reasonably expected to continue to comply with the contract without variation of its terms*".

Principle 10 proposes two cumulative criteria for assessing whether the disturbance is so material, so serious that the disadvantaged party is entitled to adaptation or modification of the contractual terms. The first criterion is *subjective,* in the sense that it refers to the parties' will (that is, it refers to the parties' hypothetical will). The disturbance is to be taken into account if, and only if, "the parties would not have entered into the contract or would have entered into it on different terms had they foreseen this change". The second criterion is objective, in the sense that it refers to the content, to the nature, or purpose of the contract. The disturbance is to be taken into account if, and only if, it jeopardizes either the economic and social content, or the nature, or the purpose of the contract.

5.4.2 *Specific Requirements for the Disturbance of the Foundation of the Transaction to Be So Significant that the Disadvantaged Party Is Entitled to Terminate the Contractual Relationship*

Principle 11 distinguishes between formal and substantive requirements and, within both formal and substantive requirements, it further distinguishes between (i) termination on the initiative of the professional, employer, or lessor, and (ii) termination on the initiative of the consumer, employee, or lessee.

I will start with the *formal requirements.* If early termination of a Life Time Contract conforms to the will of the consumer, employee, or lessee, the formal requirements of termination are rather simple – it all comes at giving the true reasons for the termination. If, however, early termination does not conform to the will of the lessee, employee, or worker, the formal requirements of termination are rather complex. First, professionals, lessors, and employers are under a duty to inform the consumer, lessee, or worker of the circumstances underlying their attempt to terminate the contract. Secondly, professionals, lessors, and employers are under a duty to propose the renegotiation of the contractual terms. Principle 10 distinguishes collective and individual renegotiation, preferring 'collective regulation', which Principle 10 says, "shall take precedence over individual adaptation". Professionals, lessors, and employers are, therefore, under a duty to propose collective renegotiation and, if collective renegotiation is impossible, or fails, they are under a duty to propose individual adaptation of the contractual terms. Thirdly, and finally, if both collective and individual renegotiation fail, professionals, lessors, and employers are under a duty to give the true reasons for termination.

I will now move into the *substantive requirements.* If early termination does not conform to the will of the worker, lessee, or employee, Principle 11 refers to five substantive requirements. In the first place, Principle 11 requires termination of the contractual relationship imposed on, or against the will of, a worker, tenant, or consumer to be "transparent, accountable and socially responsible". Secondly, it requires the reasons for termination to be recognized by the law as appropriate and sufficient. The English and the French versions of the Principles of Life Time Contracts refer exclusively to two types of reasons. The first relates to the behavior of the consumer, lessee, or employee, in requiring that it be "personal behavior of such significance as to merit termination". The second relates to the financial situation or interest of the professional, lessor, or employer. The German and Italian versions go further, adding a third type of reasons for termination – reasons relating to the person of the consumer or to the person of the employee (= to the person of the debtor): the German version refers to '*Gründen in die Person... des Nutzenden*' and the Italian version, to '*condizione fisiche del debitore*'.[72]

It should be stressed that, in the event of adaptation or termination of the contract on the grounds of change of circumstances, the problem will relate, in many cases, to the economic and the financial circumstances of the lessor, employer, or professional. It should also be stressed that 'financial circumstances or interests' of the lessor, employer, or professional are only relevant if they qualify as fundamental to the equilibrium of interests within the contractual relationship. The criterion for such a qualification is as follows: financial circumstances or interests are to be taken into account if – *but only if* – they have a significant impact on the viability of the subject matter of the contract.

Thirdly, Principle 11 requires that the economic and financial circumstances of the professional, lessor, or employer be so serious that the costs and efforts required to continue the contractual relationship are *disproportionate* and *excessive* – that is, they are so disproportionate and so excessive that the economic and social significance of the consumer transaction, lease relationship, or labor relationship would be distorted.

72 In considering the Italian version, I have to admit I face a few doubts as to the scope of the term '*condizione fisiche*': are physical circumstances – that is, '*condizione fisiche*' – to be treated differently from psychological circumstances, for instance?

Fourthly, Principle 11 requires the professional, lessor, or employer to consider carefully (that is, with due diligence) the *rights*, the material and moral interests, and the material and moral needs of the consumer, lessee, or employee (for example, by giving them an appropriate period of time to prevent termination, or to prepare for their consequences).

Fifthly, and finally, Principle 11 requires that termination of the contract (against the will of the consumer, lessee, or employee) as a measure of last resort. It is to be taken as *extrema ratio* or *ultima ratio*.

5.5 The Principles of Life Time Contracts and the Interpretation of Contract Law

I would dare to suggest the principles and rules on *change of circumstances* in the Principles of Life Time Contracts are of interest for the interpretation of and, whenever necessary, for the filling of the gaps existing in, general contract law, at both the European and national levels.

First, the Principles of Life Time Contracts emphasize that adaptation of contractual terms and termination of the contractual relationship should depend on the human and social dimensions of the contract. Secondly, they emphasize that there should be a difference between the *general requirement* that the disturbance of the foundation of the transaction to be significant for any adaptation or modification and the *specific requirement* that the disturbance to be so significant that the disadvantaged party is entitled to terminate the contract. Thirdly, by stating a principle of precedence of collective over individual adaptation, they emphasize an important consequence of distributive justice in general contract law – in the event of major disturbances of the foundation of the transaction, adaptation of contracts is to conform to the requirements of coherence, equality, and proportionality.

5.6 On the Interpretation of the General Requirements for the Disturbance of the Foundation of the Transaction to Be Significant

In what concerns the general requirement for the disturbance of the foundation of the transaction to be significant, Principle 10 is quite close to German, Italian, Portuguese, and French law. It corresponds, almost word for word, to § 313 of the German Civil Code. It is both a formal and functional equivalent to the principles and to the rules in § 313 (1) and (2) of the German Civil Code.[73] It is also a functional equivalent to Article

73 According to the official translation (Retrieved on 3 February from <www.gesetze-im-internet.de/englisch_bgb/>), § 313 of the German Civil Code reads as follows:

1. If circumstances which became the basis of a contract have significantly changed since the contract was

1467 of the Italian Civil Code,[74] to Articles 252(2) and 437 of the Portuguese Civil Code,[75] and to new Article 1195 of the French Civil Code.[76, 77]

Section 313 of the German Civil Code, as well as Principles 10 and 11 of the Principles of Life Time Contracts, are drafted in rather complex terms. The reason for this is probably that they aim at a higher degree of precision. Article 1195 of the French Civil Code is drafted in somewhat simpler words. The requirement that the circumstances that have changed must constitute the foundation of the transaction, such that they are so fundamental that the "the parties would not have entered into the contract or would have entered into it on different terms had they foreseen this change", that they must be so fundamental that change or modification jeopardizes the nature and the purpose of the

---

entered into and if the parties would not have entered into the contract or would have entered into it with different contents if they had foreseen this change, adaptation of the contract may be demanded to the extent that, taking account of all the circumstances of the specific case, in particular the contractual or statutory distribution of risk, one of the parties cannot reasonably be expected to uphold the contract without alteration.

2. It is equivalent to a change of circumstances if material conceptions that have become the basis of the contract are found to be incorrect.

74 Art. 1467 of the Italian Civil Code reads as follows:
In contracts with continuous or periodical execution or adjourned execution and in case that the obligation of one of the parties has become excessively onerous due to extraordinary and unpredictable events, the party who is obliged to such performance can demand the dissolution of the contract with the effects laid down in art. 1458. The dissolution cannot be demanded if the supervening onerosity is part of the normal risk of the contract. The party against which the dissolution is demanded can prevent this by offering to modify equitably the conditions of the contract. Retrieved on 3 February 2017 from <www.trans-lex.org/601300>.

75 Art. 437 of the Portuguese Civil Code reads as follows:
1. If the circumstances on which the parties founded the decision of contracting have suffered an abnormal change, the injured party has the right to terminate the contract or amend it according to equity criteria, provided the demands of the obligations undertaken seriously affect the principles of good faith and are not included in the set of risks inherent to the contract.
2. Should termination be requested, the other party may object to the request, stating to accept the amendment to the contract under the preceding paragraph".

I follow the translation by M. Carnneiro da Frada & M. Fontes da Costa, 'Discussing the *(Ab)Normality* of Financial Crises as a Relevant Change of Circumstances Under Portuguese La', *in* B. Basoglu (Ed.), *The Effects of Financial Crises on the Binding Force of Contracts – Renegotiation, Rescission or Revision*, Springer, Cham / Heidelberg/New York/Dordrecht/London, 2016, p. 222.

76 The new Art. 1195 of the French Civil Code reads as follows:
1. Where a change of circumstances that was unforeseeable at the time of the contract's conclusion renders performance exceedingly burdensome for a party that had not accepted to assume such a risk, the disadvantaged party may ask the other party to renegotiate the contract. It shall continue to perform all its obligations during renegotiation.
2. In the event of refusal or failure of the renegotiation, the parties may agree to terminate the contract, on a date and on terms determined by them, or they may jointly apply to a judge to proceed with its adaptation. Failing agreement within a reasonable period of time, the judge may, upon a party's request, revise the contract or terminate it, on the date and terms he decides.

77 For a comparison between German law, prior to 2001, Italian law, Portuguese law, and French law, prior to 2006, *see* A.M. Cordeiro, *Da Boa fé no Direito Civil*, Livraria Almedina, Coimbra, 1997, p. 903 *et seq.*

contract, that the disadvantaged party "cannot be reasonably expected to continue to comply with the contract without variation of its terms" are replaced by a single requirement – that performance must be *excessively burdensome* or *exceedingly onerous*. The reason for this is probably that French legislature prefers *clarity* to *precision*.

Despite the fact that it is quite close to § 313 of the German Civil Code, Principle 10 goes beyond the German, French, Italian, and Portuguese law, by referring to two further criteria: first, to the *purpose of the contract* and, second, to the *fundamental duties and obligations of the human being*.

Section 313 (1) of the German Civil Code, Articles 1467 and 1469 of the Italian Civil Code, and Article 437 of the Portuguese Civil Code require the judge to take into account the contractual and statutory distribution of risk. Article 1195 of the French Civil Code requires the judge to take the contractual distribution of risk into account by ruling that, in the case of a change of circumstances, the disadvantaged party has no right to require adaptation or termination if he has assumed the risk of such a change. In contrast with the German, Italian, French, and Portuguese law, Principle 10 requires the judge to consider three elements: first, the contractual and statutory allocation or distribution of risk; second, the content, nature, and purpose of the contract; and third, the fundamental duties and obligations of the human being.

Even if Principle 10 says 'fundamental obligation of the human being', I suppose it is to be interpreted broadly. In stressing that the judge is to consider the *fundamental duties* and *fundamental obligations* of the human being, Principle 10 aims at referring, globally, to the human and social dimensions of the contract. Therefore, the reference to the fundamental duties and obligations of the human being should be read as referring, at one and the same time, to the three aspects or three elements of the human and social dimensions of the contract. It should be read as referring, at one and the same time, to the fundamental rights, duties, and obligations of the individual to himself, his or her family relationships, and to his or her social relationships.

I would dare to suggest there are even two additional, supplementary criteria stated in Principle 10 that should be recognized as a contribution to a harmonized, human, and social interpretation of the principles and rules in general contract law. I think that the reference to the content, nature, or purpose of the contract is consensual and that the reference to the human and social dimensions thereof is fully warranted. Even if it is not, it should be consensual: it should inspire the interpretation of German and French, of Italian and Portuguese law on change of circumstances.

5.7 On the Interpretation of the Specific Requirements for the Disturbance of the Foundation of the Transaction to Be So Significant That the Disadvantaged Party Is Entitled to Terminate the Contractual Relationship

Principles 10 and 11 of the Principles of Life Time Contracts distinguish the requirements for adaptation or modification of the contractual terms from the requirements for termination of the contractual relationship. It follows from such a distinction that adaptation or modification of the contractual terms is to be preferred to the termination of the contractual relationship.

German law makes that supposition explicit: § 313 (3) of the German Civil Code states "if adaptation of the contract is not possible or one party cannot reasonably be expected to accept it, the disadvantaged party may revoke the contract. In the case of continuing obligations, the right to terminate takes the place of the right to revoke". French, Italian, and Portuguese law do not.

In the case of Italian and Portuguese law, some submit that the precedence of adaptation over termination can be construed as implicit; in the case of French law, many submit that it cannot be construed as such.[78]

New Article 1195 of the French Civil Code simply says that the judge may adapt the contractual terms or terminate the contractual relationship: "A défaut d'accord dans un délai raisonnable, le juge peut, à la demande d'une partie, réviser le contrat ou y mettre fin, à la date et aux conditions qu'il fixe". Despite the fact it refers to both remedies – to adaptation and to termination – new Article 1195 of the French Civil Code says nothing about their hierarchy.

It is submitted that both Principles 10 and 11 provide a strong argument in favor of a general principle that, as a general rule, adaptation is to be preferred to termination. In general terms, the argument is that such a rule of precedence or priority is grounded in the general principle of fidelity to the contract (*Vertragstreue*).[79] If the confidence of both parties in the continuation of the contractual relationship is to be taken seriously, then continuation of the contractual relationship, albeit adapted or modified, it is to be preferred to (early) termination. In the specific context of Life Time Contracts, the general

78 In fact, the history of new Art. 1195 of the French Civil Code suggests that the legislature preferred termination to adaptation! *See* N. Molfessis, 'Le Rôle du Juge en Cas d'Imprévision dans la Réforme du Droit des Contrats', *La semaine juridique*, No. 52, 2015, p. 2390 *et seq.* In general terms, considering, in particular, the provisions of the French Civil Code that tackle the issue of economic duress, *see* P. Ancel, 'Art. 1142: Violence Économique', *Rev. des contrats*, No. 3, 2015, p. 747 *et seq.*, p. 748: "Là aussi, on peut reconnaître l'influence d'une certaine doctrine qui, plus encore que la sanction des déséquilibres contractuels, redoute plus que tout l'immixtion du juge dans le contrat."

79 *See, generally*, M.P. Weller, *Die Vertragstreue. Vertragsbindung – Naturalerfüllungsgrundsatz – Vertragstreue*, Mohr Siebeck, Tübingen, 2009, p. 297 *et seq.*

argument is supplemented by a special one, deduced from the distinction between two forms of contractual ethics.

In saying this, I am referring to Professor Nicolussi's distinction between ethics applying to the relationship between "moral neighbors" (in German: *Nähbereichsmoral*) and ethics applying to the relationship between "moral strangers" (in German: *Fernbereichsmoral*). Parties to short-term, spot contracts are typically moral strangers and they should conform to the dictates of the *Fernbereichsmoral*, and of the *Fernbereichsmoral* only: parties to long-term contracts are typically moral neighbors and they are to conform to the dictates of a *Nähbereichsmoral*.[80] It is submitted that, within the context of a *Nähbereichsmoral*, termination of a contractual relationship is to be used only in exceptional circumstances (as *extrema ratio*).[81]

5.8 On the Preference for Collective over Individual Adaptation

The final sentence of Principle 10 reads as follows: "Collective regulation shall take precedence over individual adaptation." In affirming the precedence of *collective*-over-*individual* adaptation, Principle 10 raises a highly controversial issue:[82] of all issues addressed by Principles 10 and 11, this one is probably the most controversial.

It could be asked – and it has, indeed, been asked[83] – whether the principle of precedence of collective-over-individual adaptation of contractual terms could ever be of some interest for general contract law. In general contract law (at least in contemporary contract law, *as we know it*), there is no place for a collective negotiation or renegotiation of contractual terms. I would, however, still like to propose an answer to such a question, by suggesting that the precedence of collective-over-individual adaptation of contractual terms is but a *procedural reflection* of *substantive principles* and *substantive values*.

In the first place, I think that the principle of precedence of collective-over-individual adaptation cannot be considered an argument for the *interpretation* of general contract law. Secondly, I suppose that the principle of precedence of collective-over-individual adaptation should only apply to disturbances of the 'major' foundation of the transaction. Thirdly, and finally, if the principle of precedence of collective-over-individual adapta-

80 A. Nicolussi, 'Etica del Contratto e 'Contratti di Durata per l'Esistenza della Persona", *in* Nogler & Reifner (Eds.), *supra* note 14, p. 123 *et seq.*

81 In the course of the Luxembourg conference, Dr. Schiavon criticized new Art. 1195 of the French Civil Code for failing to state a general principle of precedence of adaptation over termination. I fully agree with him. I would even go a step further, emphasizing that, under such a technical question, there is a reference to the philosophy of contract law, to the very concept of justice upon which contract law is based. In a sense, the precedence of adaptation or modification over termination is the precedence, albeit limited in scope, of distributive justice over commutative justice in contract law.

82 For a critique on the precedence of collective-over-individual adaptation, *see*, thoroughly, A.A. Cardoso Guedes 'Será a Negociação Coletiva Desejável no Contexto dos Life Time Contracts?' *in* Pinto Oliveira & MacCrorie (Eds.), *supra* note 68, p. 55 *et seq.*

83 *See*, *e.g.*, Cardoso Guedes, *supra* note 82, p. 57 *et seq.*

tion is only to apply to disturbances of the 'major' foundation of the transaction, I suppose it is a good principle, based upon acceptable arguments.

In order to understand the scope of priority of collective-over-individual adaptation, I think there might be some use for the old concepts of the 'major' and 'minor' foundations of a transaction – that is, for the old concepts of *grosse Geschäftsgrundlage* and *kleine Geschäftsgrundlage*. In simple – perhaps much too simple – terms, disturbances of the 'minor' foundation of the transaction affect only a few contracts (in some cases, they affect only a single contract, and no more than that single contract); disturbances of the 'major' foundation of the transaction affect many contracts.[84] In fact, they consist of disturbances to the social existence according to Flume[85] and in global changes in the conditions of social existence according to Carneiro da Frada.[86] They result from 'mass calamities', as Wieacker referred to them (such as natural catastrophes); from major legislative changes; from major economic and financial events (such as the depreciation of currency, deflation, and inflation); and from major political events (such as *wars* and situations similar to war).[87]

The principle according to which changes of circumstances fall within the debtor's sphere of risk cannot apply to cases of disturbance of the 'major' foundation of the transaction – *global changes in the conditions of social existence are at everyone's risk*. It follows from such a principle that losses are to be divided, so that no one party is to be awarded all the gains and no one is exempted from all the losses, and that they are to be divided according to criteria of coherence, equality, proportionality, and fairness.[88]

In the event of disturbances of the 'major' foundation of the transaction, the principle of precedence of collective-over-individual adaptation is the consequence of three elements: first, change of circumstances is a collective problem; second, such collective problems are to be resolved through renegotiation; and, third, the results of renegotiation are to conform to the principles of coherence, equality, and proportionality.[89]

Even if it cannot be used as an interpretive criterion, the procedural principle of *precedence of collective-over-individual adaptation of contractual terms* can be used as a heuristic method, as it stresses that substantive values (such as coherence, equality, and proportionality), also apply to *(general) contract law*, because they reflect *basic requirements of distributive, social justice*.

---

84 For the distinction between both concepts, *see* K. Larenz, M. Wolf & J. Neuner, *Allgemeiner Teil der Bürgerlichen Rechts*, 10th edn, C. H. Beck, München, 2014, p. 498.

85 W. Flume, *Allgemeiner Teil des Bürgerlichen Rechts* II – *Das Rechtsgeschäft*, 4th edn, Springer, Berlin/New York, 1992, p. 518.

86 M. Carneiro da Frada, 'Crise Financeira Mundial e Alteração das Circunstâncias: Contratos de Depósito vs. Contratos de Gestão de Carteiras', 69 (III/IV) *Rev. da Ordem dos Advogados* 2009, pp. 633-695; M. Carneiro da Frada, *Forjar o Direito*, Livraria Almedina, Coimbra, 2015, p. 28 *et seq*.

87 Flume, *supra* note 85, p. 518.

88 Carneiro da Frada, *supra* note 86, p. 680 *et seq*.

89 In accordance with Principle 8, "[p]roviders of life time contracts must refrain from discrimination in terms of the personal and social characteristics of consumers at all stages of the contract."

Bibliography

Ancel, P., 'Article 1142: Violence Economique', 3 *Revue des Contrats* 2015, p. 747 *et seq.*

Arnold, S., *Vertrag und Verteilung. Die Bedeutung der Iustitia Distributiva im Privatrecht*, Tübingen: Mohr Siebeck, 2014.

Basoglu, B. (Ed.), *The Effects of Financial Crises on the Binding Force of Contracts – Renegotiation, Rescission or Revision*, Cham/Heidelberg/New York/Dordrecht/London: Springer, 2016.

Canaris, C.W., 'Die Bedeutung der Iustitia Distributiva in Deutschen Vertragsrecht', *in* C.W. Canaris (Ed.), *Gesammelte Schriften III – Privatrecht*, Berlin: de Gruyter, 2012.

Canaris, C.W., 'Systemdenken und Systembegriff in der Jurisprudenz', *in* C.W. Canaris (Ed.), *Gesammelte Schriften. I – Rechtstheorie*, Berlin: de Gruyter, 2012.

Canaris, C.W., 'Verfassungs- und Europarechtliche Aspekte der Vertragsfeiheit in der Privatrechtsgesellchaft', *in* C.W. Canaris (Ed.), *Gesammelte Schriften I – Rechtstheorie*, Berlin: de Gruyter, 2012.

Cardoso Guedes, A.A., 'Será a Negociação Coletiva Desejável no Contexto dos Life Time Contracts?', *in* N.M. Pinto Oliveira & B. MacCrorie (Eds.), *Em torno de Life Time Contracts*, Retrieved on 2 February 2017 from <https://issuu.com/direitoprivado/docs/em_torno_de_life_time_contracts>.

Carneiro da Frada, M., 'Crise Financeira Mundial e Alteração das Circunstâncias: Contratos de Depósito vs. Contratos de Gestão de Carteiras', 69 (III/IV) *Revista da Ordem dos Advogados* 2009, pp. 453-503.

Carnneiro da Frada, M., *Forjar oDireito*, Coimbra: Livraria Almedina, 2015.

Carnneiro da Frada, M. & Fontes da Costa, M., 'Discussing the (Ab)Normality of Financial Crises as a Relevant Change of Circumstances Under Portuguese La', *in* B. Basoglu (Ed.), *The Effects of Financial Crises on the Binding Force of Contracts – Renegotiation, Rescission or Revision*, Cham/Heidelberg/New York/Dordrecht/London: Springer, 2016.

Cordeiro, A.M., *Da Boa fé no Direito Civil*, Coimbra: Livraria Almedina, 1997.

Flume, W., *Allgemeiner Teil des Bürgerlichen Rechts II – Das Rechtsgeschäft* (4th ed.), Berlin/New York: Springer, 1992.

Habermas, J., *Between Facts and Norms. Contributions to a Discourse Theory of Law and Democracy*, Cambridge, MA: The MIT University Press, 1996.

Jamin, C., 'Plaidoyer pour le Solidarisme Contractuel', *in Mélanges en Honneur de Jacques Ghestin*, Paris: LGDJ, 2001.

Kronman, A.T., 'Contract Law and Distributive Justice', 89 *Yale L.J.* 1979-1980, pp. 472-511.

Larenz, K., Wolf, M. & Neuner, J., *Allgemeiner Teil der Bürgerlichen Rechts* (10th ed.), München: C. H. Beck, 2014.

Lequette, Y., 'Bilan des Solidarismes Contractuels', *in Mélanges Offerts à Paul Didier. Etudes de Droit Privé*, Paris: Economica, 2008.

Lurger, B., *Vertragliche Solidarität*, Baden-Baden: Nomos, 1998.

MacNeil, I., 'The Many Futures of Contracts', 47 *S. Cal. L. Rev.* 1973-1974, p. 323.

Markesinis, B.S., Unberath, H. & Johnston, A., *The German Law of Contract* (2nd ed.), Oxford/Portland, OR: Hart Publishing, 2006.

Mazeaud, D., 'Loyauté, Solidarité, Fraternité : la Nouvelle Devise Contractuelle ?', *in L'avenir du droit, Mélanges en l'Honneur de François Terré*, Paris: PUF, Dalloz, Jurisclasseur, 1999.

Mazeaud, D., 'La Bataille du Solidarisme Contractuel: du Feu, des Cendres, des Braises…', Retrieved on 18 April 2017 from <http://ddata.over-blog.com/xxxyyy/3/61/42/26/civil-II/Denis-Mazeaud-melanges-Jean-Hauser.pdf>.

Molfessis, N., 'Le Rôle du Juge en cas d'Imprévision dans la Réforme du Droit des Contrats', 52 *La Semaine Juridique*, 2015, p. 1415.

Neuner, J., *Privatrecht und Sozialstaat*, München: C. H. Beck, 1998.

Nicolussi, A., 'Etica del Contratto e 'Contratti di Durata per l'Esistenza della Persona'', *in* L. Nogler & U. Reifner (Eds.), *Life Time Contracts: Social Long-term Contracts in Labour, Tenancy and Consumer Credit Law*, The Hague: Eleven International Publishing, 2014.

Nogler, L. & Reifner, U. (Eds.), *Life Time Contracts: Social Long-term Contracts in Labour, Tenancy and Consumer Credit Law*, The Hague: Eleven International Publishing, 2014.

Nogler, L. & Reifner, U., *Lifetime Contracts – Rediscovering the Social Dimension of the Sales Contract Mode*, Retrieved on 24 January 2017 from <http://eusoco.eu/wp-content/uploads/2009/12/reifnernoglerfswilehmensson_lifetime-contracts_rediscovering-the-social-dimension1.pdf>.

Pinto Oliveira, N.M., 'The Private Law Society and Contract Law Application', 5 *Eur. Rev. Cont. L.* 2009, pp. 29-40.

Pinto Oliveira, N.M. & MacCrorie, B. (Eds.), *Em torno de Life Time Contracts*, Retrieved on 2 February 2017 from <https://issuu.com/direitoprivado/docs/em_torno_de_life_time_contracts>.

Reifner, U., *Alternatives Wirtschaftsrecht am Beispiel der Verbraucherverschuldung. Realitätsverleugnung und soziale Auslegung im Zivilrecht*, Neuwied: Luchterhand, 1979.

Serra, C., 'As funções do direito da insolvência no âmbito de *life time contracts* (Breve reflexão)', *in* N.M. Pinto Oliveira & B. MacCrorie (Eds.), *Em torno de Life Time Contracts*, Retrieved on 2 February 2017 from <https://issuu.com/direitoprivado/docs/em_torno_de_life_time_contracts>.

Sousa Antunes, H., 'A Alteração das Circunstâncias e os Life Time Contracts', *in* N.M. Pinto Oliveira & B. MacCrorie (Eds.), *Em torno de Life Time Contracts*, Retrieved on 2 February 2017 from <https://issuu.com/direitoprivado/docs/em_torno_de_life_time_contracts>.

Thibierge-Guelfucci, C., 'Libres-Propos sur la Transformation du Droit des Contrats', 96 *Revue Trimestrielle de Droit Civil* 1997, p. 357.

Weinrib, E.J., *The Idea of Private Law*, Cambridge, MA: Harvard University Press, 1995.

Weinrib, E.J., *Corrective Justice*, Oxford: Oxford University Press, 2012.

Weller, M.P., *Die Vertragstreue. Vertragsbindung – Naturalerfüllungsgrundsatz – Vertragstreue*, Tübingen: Mohr Siebeck, 2009.

Wilhelmsson, T., 'Social *Force Majeure* – A New Concept in Nordic Consumer Law', 13 *J. Consumer Pol.*, 1990, p. 1.

Wilhelmsson, T., *Critical Studies in Private Law. A Treatise on Need-Rational Principles in Modern Law*, Dordrecht: Springer, 1992.

6 Regulating 'Imprévision' in the New French Contract Law Reform and Life Time Contracts

*Alvise Schiavon**

6.1 Introduction

The *Ordonnance*[1] adopting major amendments to the French *Code Civil* as well as a global reform of the general part of the French *droit des obligations* (the 'Law of Obligations') was published on 11 February 2016, almost eleven years after its antecedent, the so-called Catala *Avant-Projet*,[2] was first published.

The Catala *Avant-Projet* was conceived after a colloquium on a comparison of French contract law with the principles of European contract law,[3] which was held in concurrence with the 200th anniversary of the enactment of Napoleon's *Code civil* in 1804. As we will see, the circumstances of this renewed interest in a major reform of French contract law reveal both the reasons and the goals of this legislative reform initiative.[4]

The project to reform the French 'law of obligations' (the 'Reform Project') was led, and moved forward, by some of the most distinguished and influential scholars in French private law, particularly Pierre Catala (with the *Association Henri Capitant des Amis de la*

---

* Alvise Schiavon holds a PhD in Comparative and European Legal Studies from the University of Trento and is currently postdoctoral researcher at the Faculty of Law of the University of Bologna.

1 Ordonnance n° 2016-131 du 10 février 2016 Portant Réforme du Droit des Contrats, du Régime Général et de la Preuve des Obligations, JO 11 February 2016, Textes 26 sur 113, NOR: JUSC1522466R [hereinafter the 'Ordonnance'].

2 The Avant-Projet de Reforme du Droit des Obligations (Articles 1101 À 1386 Du Code Civil) et du Droit de la Prescription (Articles 2234 À 2281 Du Code Civil), Rapport à Monsieur Pascal Clément Garde des Sceaux, Ministre de la Justice 22 Septembre 2005, incorporated the Pierre Catala's Présentation Générale de l'Avant-Projet (Retrieved on 8 June 2017, from <www.justice.gouv.fr/art_pix/RAPPORTCATALASEPTEMBRE2005.pdf>) [hereinafter, the 'Catala Avant-Projet']. *See* S. Vogenauer, 'The Avant-Projet de Reforme: An Overview', *in* J. Cartwright, S. Vogenauer, & S. Whittaker (Eds.), *Reforming the French Law of Obligations*, Oxford-Portland, Hart, 2009, pp. 3-28, p. 3.

3 P. Rémy-Corlay & D. Fenouillet (Eds.), *Les concepts contractuels français à l'heure des principes du droit européen des contrats*, Paris, Dalloz, 2003.

4 *See* Introduction, *in* O. Deshayes, *et al.* (Eds.), *Réforme du droit des contrats, du régime général et de la preuve des obligations: commentaire article par article*, Paris, Lexis-Nexis, 2016, p. IX.

Culture Juridique Française) and Francois Terré (with the *Institut de France*),[5] and was publicly discussed among scholars[6] as well as lawyers and professionals.

Catala's and Terré's clearly different views of contract law emerged during the Reform Project's preparatory work. The Catala *Avant-Projet* was perceived as too conservative[7] thus, confirming the inclination of French scholars to preserve the identity of French *Code Civil* despite the new challenges arising from economic globalization and the Europeanization of private law; the Terré project, on the contrary, more clearly pursued the political goals of the French Government. The shift of perspective from the Catala *Avant-Projet* to the final text of the *Ordonnance* is also evident, particularly with reference to the role of *imprévision*, as will be evident at the conclusion of this chapter.

6.2 The Reform Project's Political Goals

The political goals of the desire to reform and recodify the general part of the Law of Obligations were clearly stated in the 2016 President's Report attached to the *Ordonnance*.[8] It was particularly evident that the legislature's main aim was to adjust the *Code Civil* to respond to the demands arising from the international business community and, thus, to make it more economically attractive (from the point of view of 'forum shopping') to business and international trade.[9] It is no coincidence that the Reform Project

5 The sequence of events is summarized in the *Rapport au Président de la République relatif à l'ordonnance n° 2016-131 du 10 février 2016 portant réforme du droit des contrats, du régime général et de la preuve des obligations* (Retrieved on 07 June 2017 from <www.legifrance.gouv.fr/eli/rapport/2016/2/11/JUSC1522466P/jo/texte>, (the text to which I refer for quotations) [hereinafter the '2016 President's Report']: "Plusieurs projets académiques ont ainsi été élaborés ces dernières années: celui du groupe de travail réuni autour de Pierre Catala puis celui du groupe de travail de l'académie des sciences morales et politiques sous l'égide de François Terré. Par la publicité donnée à ces projets, les acteurs de la vie économique et juridique ont été mis en mesure d'émettre des observations. La Chancellerie, a également préparé des avant-projets qui ont été largement diffusés et commentés. Enfin, à la suite de l'habilitation accordée au Gouvernement pour procéder à cette réforme par voie d'ordonnance, un nouveau texte, nourri de l'ensemble de ces travaux, a été soumis à consultation publique. Celle-ci a permis de recueillir les observations des professionnels du droit et des acteurs du monde économique qui, complétées par les nombreux articles de doctrine publiés sur le sujet, ont permis au Gouvernement d'aboutir à un texte répondant aux objectifs fixés de modernisation, de simplification, d'accessibilité et d'efficacité du droit commun des contrats et du régime des obligations, et susceptible de répondre aux attentes des praticiens." p. 2.

6 *See* 'Colloque La Réforme du Droit des Contrats: Projet et Perspectives', 1 *Revue des contrats* 2006.

7 Indeed, Professor Catala, in his *Présentation Générale de l'Avant-Projet* in the Catala *Avant-Projet*, at p. 13, explicitly stated that "l'avant-projet ne propose pas un code de rupture, mais d'ajustement". *See also* the observations put forward by P. Stoffel-Munk, *Réforme du Droit des Obligations: la Force Obligatoire du Contrat en Danger* (Retrieved on 07 June 2017 from <www.dalloz-actualite.fr/interview/reforme-du-droit-des-obligations-force-obligatoire-du-contrat-en-danger#.VoF_waTZg-8>).

8 2016 President's Report, *supra* note 5.

9 Id., p. 2: "Dans une économie mondialisée où les droits eux-mêmes sont mis en concurrence, l'absence d'évolution du droit des contrats et des obligations pénalisait la France sur la scène internationale" and it goes further stating that "en dehors même de cette dimension politique, l'enjeu au niveau international d'une telle réforme du droit français est économique: les rapports "Doing business" publiés par la Banque

began after the World Bank released its 2004 'Doing Business' Report,[10] according to which countries with a French legal heritage "were lagging behind".[11]

From this point of view, and by pursuing a new hegemonic role for French law in the context of international trade, the Reform Project implicitly rejected the common European Civil Code project as a means for European legal systems to regain efficiency within a globalized economy[12] and, instead, endorsed the rather hostile attitude of many French jurists toward a potential *Eurocode* on contract law.[13]

This major goal of the Reform Project was pursued through substantial changes affecting several parts of France's general discipline of the law of contracts. Among the different substantive issues in the Law of Obligations affected by the Reform Project, two issues directly assume crucial significance in light of research on the role of long-term contractual relationships in the new European contract law: the introduction of *imprévision contractuelle*[14] and the abolition of *cause contractuelle*. The latter, venerable concept, in particular, was perceived as a source of concern in connection with legal certainty, and thus, negatively impacting on the attractiveness of French contract law.[15]

---

mondiale, mettant régulièrement en valeur les systèmes juridiques de Common law, ont notamment contribué à développer l'image d'un droit français complexe, imprévisible, et peu attractif. Dans ce contexte, se doter d'un droit écrit des contrats plus lisible et prévisible, en s'attachant à adopter une rédaction dans un style simple ainsi qu'une présentation plus claire et didactique, constitue un facteur susceptible d'attirer les investisseurs étrangers et les opérateurs souhaitant rattacher leur contrat au droit français."

10 World Bank, *Doing Business in 2004: Understanding Regulations*, Washington D.C., 2004. *See* discussions on this report by French jurists *in* (a) B. Fauvarque-Cosson & S. Patris-Godechot (Eds.), *Le Code Civil Face à Son Destin, la Documentation Française*, Paris, La Documentation Française, 2006 and (b) Association Henri Capitant, *Les Droits de Tradition Civiliste en Question. À Propos des Rapports* Doing Business *de la Banque Mondiale, Contributions des Groupes Autres que le Groupe Français de l'Association Henri Capitant des Amis de la Culture Juridique Française*, Paris, *Société de Législation Comparée*, 2006.

11 *See* Vogenauer, *supra* note 2, p. 7.

12 2016 President's Report, *supra* note 5, p. 2: "Dans le même temps, au cours de ces vingt dernières années, les projets européens et internationaux d'harmonisation du droit des contrats se sont multipliés: les principes UNIDROIT relatifs aux contrats du commerce international publiés en 1994 et complétés en 2004, les principes du droit européen des contrats (PDEC) élaborés par la commission dite Lando, publiés entre 1995 et 2003, le projet de code européen des contrats ou code Gandolfi, publié en 2000, le projet de cadre commun de référence (DCFR), qui couvre tout le droit Privé et a été remis officiellement au Parlement européen le 21 janvier 2008, et enfin les travaux menés par la société de législation comparée et l'association Henri Capitant des amis de la pensée juridique française qui ont abouti à la rédaction de principes contractuels communs (PCC) publiés en février 2008."

13 Many of the hostile reactions were to the *Communication from the Commission to the Council and the European Parliament on European Contract Law* (OJ 13.9.2001): *see, e.g.*, Y. Lequette, 'Vers un Code Civil Européen?', *Pouvoirs, Revue Française d'Études Constitutionnelles et Politiques*, n°107, 107 – Le Code Civil, 2003, pp. 97-126, p. 97.

14 *See* 2016 President's Report, *supra* note 5, Nos. 3 & 6, p. 1: "3. Affirmer le principe du consensualisme et présenter ses exceptions, en indiquant les principales règles applicables à la forme du contrat ; [...] 6° Préciser les règles relatives aux effets du contrat entre les parties et à l'égard des tiers, en consacrant la possibilité pour celles-ci d'adapter leur contrat en cas de changement imprévisible de circonstances".

15 2016 President's Report, *supra* note 5, p. 3: "Le deuxième objectif poursuivi par l'ordonnance est de renforcer l'attractivité du droit français, au plan politique, culturel, et économique. La sécurité juridique conférée à

In fact, as this chapter will make clear, introducing the concept of unforeseen circumstances not only meets the need for legal certainty,[16] but can be regarded as a logical complement of the ('formal', as rather ambiguously specified in the 2016 President's Report) abolition of the concept of *cause*.[17]

6.3 CANAL DE CRAPONNE:[18] THE COURT'S REJECTION OF IMPRÉVISION

Before the enactment of the *Ordonnance*, the French Law of Obligations lacked any remedies for the case of unforeseen circumstances arising after the conclusion of the contract, which render the performance of the duty much harder than scheduled, although not impossible.

This hypothesis differs both from inherent inequalities affecting the balance of the contract from the moment of its conclusion (*lésion*, new Article 1168 *Code Civil*)[19] and from the hypotheses of objective and insurmountable supervening impossibility to perform the contract not depending on a creditor's behavior (*impossibilité survenant d'exécuter*, new Article 1351 *Code Civil*).[20] From a different perspective, this phenomenon does not affect aleatory contracts (in which the possibility of unforeseen circumstances to unbalance the contract is implicit) or contracts in which parties insert specific clauses to manage future incidents.

---

notre droit des obligations, qui constitue le socle des échanges économiques, devrait ainsi faciliter son application dans des contrats de droit international. A cet égard, l'abandon *formel* de la notion de cause, qui a suscité de nombreux débats, permettra à la France de se rapprocher de la législation de nombreux droits étrangers, tout en consacrant dans la loi les différentes fonctions, dont celle de rééquilibrage du contrat, que la jurisprudence lui avait assignées."

16 2016 President's Report, *supra* note 5, p. 15: "La France est l'un des derniers pays d'Europe à ne pas reconnaître la théorie de l'imprévision comme cause modératrice de la force obligatoire du contrat. Cette consécration, inspirée du droit comparé comme des projets d'harmonisation européens, permet de lutter contre les déséquilibres contractuels majeurs qui surviennent en cours d'exécution, conformément à l'objectif de justice contractuelle poursuivi par l'ordonnance".

17 2016 President's Report, *supra* note 5, p. 2: "Par ailleurs, l'ordonnance abandonne certaines notions présentes dans le code actuel et historiquement très ancrées dans le droit français, mais qui ne sont pas définies, dont le régime n'est pas déterminé par la loi, et dont le maintien ne paraît pas nécessaire, telles que les obligations de faire, de ne pas faire, et de donner. A l'inverse, il est apparu nécessaire de consacrer certains mécanismes juridiques essentiels pour les praticiens".

18 *De Galliffet c/ Commune de Pélissann* (*Canal de Craponne*), Civ. 6 March 1876 (D.76.1.193, note Giboulot) in *Les Grand Arrêts de la Jurisprudence Civile*, 12th edn, Dalloz, Paris, 2008, p. 183 [hereinafter '*Canal de Craponne*'].

19 As for the old version (new Article 1118 *Code Civil*), this article states the exceptional nature of hypotheses (especially in case of sales of immoveables), whereby a party can rescind or ask for the adaptation "when a substantial difference of value of the performances can be assessed in the agreement".

20 Such supervening impossibility to perform extinguishes the obligation when not due to fault of the debtor: *see also*, in the version of *Code Civil* before the Reform, the equivalent rule in old Article 1302.

Therefore, monetary devaluation, war, and economic crises are among the most significant examples of the unforeseen circumstances taken into account in the case of *imprévision*.[21]

France was, for a long time, the only European country lacking a formal *ad hoc* regulation of these hypotheses, as repeatedly pointed out by comparative lawyers after David did so in 1974;[22] furthermore, most (academic or official) projects for the harmonization of European contract law established some kind of legal mechanism for managing unforeseen circumstances affecting contractual equality.[23]

Indeed, the *Code civil* (1804), derived from natural law doctrines[24] and the 'sacrality' of the principle of consent in contract law (set out in Article 1134, clause 1), rejected both the *rebus-sic-stantibus*-clause doctrine elaborated by medieval legal culture and the different remedies tracing back to Roman law and acknowledged in *Corpus iuris civilis*.[25]

In fact, during the nineteenth century, neither scholars nor courts interpreted this principle strictly:[26] treatises by, first, Larombière[27] and, then, M. Planiol and G. Ripert,[28] attempted to ground the theory of *imprévision* on the *rebus-sic-stantibus clause* and on the notion of *abus du droit*', respectively; in the same period, different *tribunaux du fond*

---

21 *See, generally*, L. Thibierge, *Le Contrat Face à l'Imprévu*, Economica, Paris, 2011, p. 309 *et seq.*

22 R. David, 'L'imprévision dans les droits européens', *in Mélanges Jauffret*, D'Aix-Marseille, Publications de la Faculté de Droit et Science Politique, 1974, pp. 211-230. More recently, *see* D. Tallon, 'La Révision du Contrat Pour Imprévision au Regard des Enseignements Récents du Droit Comparé', *in* J. Carbonnier (Ed.), *Droit et Vie des affaires. Études à la Mémoire d'Alain Sayag*, Paris, Litec, 1997, pp. 403-417.

23 *See* E. Savaux, 'L'introduction de la Révision ou de la Résiliation pour Imprévision – Rapport Français', *Revue des contrats*, 2010, pp. 1057-1067, p. 1058; *see also* Tallon, *supra* note 22, p. 405; A. Veneziano, 'Le "Changement de Circonstances" dans le Cadre Commun de Référence sur le Droit Européen des Contrats', 200 (2) *Revue de contrats* 2009, pp. 873-882.

24 *See, in particular*, D. Deroussin, *Histoire du droit Privé (XVIe-XXIe siècle)*, LGDJ, Paris, 2010, p. 478.

25 On these antecedents, *see* P. Pichonnaz, 'De la clausola rebus sic stantibus au hardship: Aspects d'une Evolution du Rôle du Jege, *in* A. Ruelle & M. Berlingin (Eds.), *Le droit romain d'hier à aujourd'hui: collationes et oblationes: liber amicorum en l'honneur du professeur Gilbert Hanard*, Bruxelles, Facultés Universitaires Saint-Louis, 2009, p. 149 *et seq.*; R. Feenstra, '*Impossibilitas* and *Clausola rebus sic stantibus*: Some aspects of Frustration of Contract in Continental Legal History up to Grotius", *in* A. Watson (Ed.), *Daube Noster: Essays in Legal History for David Daube*, Scottish Academic Press, London-Edinburgh, 1974, pp. 77; R. Cardilli, 'Sopravvenienza e pericoli contrattuali', *in* R. Fiori (Ed.), *Modelli teorici* e *metodologici nella storia del diritto privato*, Naples, Jovene, 2004, pp. 1-37; M. Rummel, *Die clausula rebus sic stantibus: eine dogmengeschichtliche Untersuchung unter Berucksichtigung der Zeit von der Rezeption im 14. Jahrhundert bis zum jungeren Usus Modernus in der ersten Halfte des 18. Jahrhunderts*, Nomos, Baden Baden, 1991.

26 D. Philippe, *Changement de Circonstances et Bouleversement de l'Économie Contractuelle*, Émile Bruylant, Bruxelles, 1986, p. 109; and Thibierge, *supra* note 21, p. 178 (calling this period 'une révolution silencieuse').

27 "Les obligations s'éteignent encore par la survenance de circonstances telles que les parties n'auraient pas contractées, si elles les avaient prévues", M.L. Larombière, *Théorie et Pratique des Obligations, ou Commentaire aux Titres III et IV, Livre III, du Code Napoléon, Article 1101 à 1386*, Vol. III, Paris, A. Durand, 1857-1858, Article 1234, n°4, p. 33.

28 M. Planiol & G. Ripert, *Traité de droit civil français*, Vol. VI, 2nd edn, LGDJ, Paris, 1952-1962, no 396; and G. Ripert, *La règle morale dans les obligations civiles*, LGDJ, Paris, 1949, n°83, 86, & 87.

applied the notion of *force majeur* to unforeseen circumstances[29] or, again, the *rebus-sic-stantibus* clause.[30]

These attempts were disclaimed after the draconian assertion in the *Canal de Craponne* decision in 1876, in which the *Cour de Cassation* explicitly stated that:

> dans aucun cas, il n'appartient aux tribunaux, quelque équitable que puisse apparaître leur décision, de prendre en considération le temps et les circonstances pour modifier les conventions des parties et substituer des clauses nouvelles à celles qui ont été librement acceptées par les contractants.[31]

This *arrêt* has been interpreted as a radical rejection of the concept of *imprévision* in French contract law, both for long-term contracts and for so-called spot contracts,[32] and the courts had since held fast to the apparently uncompromising assertion of the 'consent principle', even when monetary 'stagflation' made performance of monetary obligations objectively harder for debtors, especially during World War I.[33]

6.4 The 'Flood Tide'

Although the *Cour de Cassation* held tight to this definitive assertion of the consent principle up until the *Ordonnance*,[34] some exceptions were quietly introduced into French contract law. We have been able to distinguish three situations in which unforeseen circumstances could lead to a revision of the contract.[35]

Firstly, a few exceptions were explicitly introduced by the legislature with respect to particular private law contracts,[36] namely: agricultural and commercial leases (*bail à*

29 *See* Cour d'Appel Douai, 3 May 1851, DP18 54.2.130; Cour d'Appel Grenoble, 18 August 1854, DP 1855.2.78; Tribunal Commercial Toulouse, 1 June 1915, DP 1916.2.112, S. 1916.2.29; and Tribunal Commercial Rouen, 18 December 1919, DP 1920.2.33.

30 *See, e.g.*, Cour d'Appel Rouen, 9 February 1844, DP 1845.2.4; and Cour d'Appel Bordeaux, 18 May 1852, DP 1853.2.105.

31 *See Canal de Craponne, supra* note 18.

32 The *Cour de Cassation* explicitly stated that "la règle qu'il consacre est générale, absolue et régit les contrats dont l'exécution s'étend à des époques successives de même qu'à ceux de toute autre nature". Id.

33 *E.g.*, Cass. Civ. 15 November 1933. *See, generally*, J. Ghestin, M. Biliau, & C. Jamin, *Traité de droit civil: Les obligations: Les Effets du Contrat*, 3rd edn, LGDJ, Paris, 1993, p. 368; P. Stoffel-Munk, *Regards sur l'Imprévision: Vers une Souplesse Contractuelle en Droit Prive Français Contemporain*, Presses Universitaires d'Aix-Marseille, Aix-en-Provence, 1994, p. 15; Philippe, *supra* note 26, p. 54.

34 *Canal de Craponne, supra* note 18. On this point, *see* C. Witz, 'Force Obligatoire et Durée du Contrat', *in* Rémy-Corlay & Fenouillet 2003, *supra* note 2, p. 178.

35 Ghestin *et al.*, *supra* note 33, p. 361.

36 Already noticed by J. Savatier, 'La théorie de l'imprévision dans les contrats', *in Études de Droit Contemporain: Contributions Françaises aux 3. et 4. Congrès Internationaux de Droit Comparé*, Vol. II, Paris, Sirey, 1959, p. 1; *see also* Philippe, *supra* note 26, p. 105 and Thibierge, *supra* note 21, p. 190.

ferme[37] and *bail commercial*[38]); assignments of copyrights (*cession de droit d'auteur*[39]); changes to gift contracts (*révision des charges des donations*[40]); and lifetime annuity (*rente viagère*[41]). It is not redundant to highlight that they are all hypotheses of long-term contracts.

Secondly, an explicit, exceptional application of *imprévision* was admitted early by the *Cour de Cassation* within contractual relations with public administrations, starting in the leading case commonly known as *Gaz de Bordeaux*[42] in 1916.[43] Facing an increase in the price of coal due to World War I, a gas provider, Gaz de Bordeaux, requested an additional sum from the City of Bordeaux: the *Conseil d'État* acknowledged the fundamental, public interest in the provision of gas and, thus, ordered the City of Bordeaux to pay the extra charge to Gaz de Bordeaux. It is important to note how this jurisprudential application of *imprévision* to contracts with public administration was grounded on the *Cour de Cassation*'s belief that the interests at the basis of some contracts are particularly essential for society.

Thirdly, also with reference to contractual relationships in private law, French courts prudently took charge of the equitable need to adjust the content and extent of contractual obligations when confronted with unpredictable circumstances not ascribable to any of the contracting parties' fault. An equitable revision of the contract has, in recent years,[44] been accepted by the court, which grounded its decisions on two different arguments.[45]

On the one hand, by imposing, on the contracting parties, a specific obligation to renegotiate contractual terms on the basis of the general duty to perform their obligations in good faith (old Article 1134, clause 3 *Code Civil*).[46] The leading cases decided by the *Cour de Cassation* on this legal basis concern the execution of the contract of supply

37 Article 812 Code Rural et de la Pêche Maritime.

38 Arts. 26-28 Décret n°53-960 of 30 September 1953 réglant les rapports entre bailleurs et locataires en ce qui concerne le renouvellement des baux à loyer d'immeubles ou de locaux à usage commercial, industriel ou artisanal.

39 Article 37 loi 11 mars 1957 (codified as Article 131-5 *Code de la Propriété Intellectuelle*); Philippe, *supra* note 26, p. 107 and Witz, *supra* note 33, p. 178.

40 Article 900-2 (modified by Loi 84-562, 6 July 1984).

41 *See* Article 2(e) 2bis loi du 25 March 1921: *cf.* Philippe, *supra* note 26, p. 106.

42 *Conseil d'État*, 30 March 1916, 59928, published in *Recueil Lebon* (commonly known as *Gaz de Bordeaux*).

43 Philippe, *supra* note 26, p. 69; Witz, *supra* note 33, p. 179.

44 In older jurisprudence, as we pointed out *supra*, courts in particular applied notions as *abus de droit* and *force majeur*.

45 *See, generally*, Witz, *supra* note 33, p. 175; Ghestin *et al.*, *supra* note 33, p. 368; Fauvarque-Cosson, *supra* note 9, p. 78; and Thibierge, *supra* note 21, p. 211.

46 *See* C. Jamin, 'Révision et Intangibilité du Contrat ou la Double Philosophie de l'Article 1134 du Code Civil', 58 *Droit et Patrimoine* 1998, pp. 46-57. This approach can be traced back to Ripert, *supra* note 28, n° 83. More generally, one could notice that good faith (Trau und Glauben, § 242 BGB) is the legal basis through which Oertmann's theory of *Geschäftsgrundlage* (now codified in § 313 BGB) has been firstly introduced in German legal system: *see* H. Rösler, 'Hardship in German Codified Private Law – In Comparative Perspective to English, French and International Contract Law', 3 *Eur. Rev. Private Law* 2007, pp. 483-513.

(*contrat de distribution*) and date back to the 1990s:[47] in the *Huard* (3 November 1992)[48] and *Danone* (24 November 1998),[49] the *Cour de Cassation* established that, in the field of commercial supply, a change of economic circumstances imposes a duty on the parties to renegotiate the contract.[50] According to this jurisprudence, the judge (*le juge du fond)* is never allowed to redefine the content of the contract, but a breach of the duty to renegotiate in good faith is a contractual breach for which a claim for damages (including interest) can be made.

This jurisprudence was later confirmed and moved forward by the *Cour de Cassation*. Whereas the previous decisions established a duty to renegotiate in good faith based on the nature of the particular contract (e.g., supply contracts and long-term contracts), in a rather ambiguous decision dated 16 March 2004,[51] the first *Chambre Civile* of the *Cour de Cassation* recognized a general duty to renegotiate, in good faith, the content of the contract in light of supervening unforeseen circumstances[52] and, apparently, the right to terminate a contract in the event the other contracting party breaches that obligation. Nevertheless, the right to seek termination of the contract due to such a breach of *bonne foi*, via a refusal to renegotiate the contract, is still disputed.[53]

On the other hand, the *Cour de Cassation* recently started to accept the disappearance of the *cause contractuelle* when unforeseen circumstances critically undermine the contractual balance (*synallagma*). Unfortunately, any definition of the extent or function of *cause* is disputed[54] and, in many respects, impossible for foreign lawyers to understand. Among the different roles the notion of *cause* plays in French contract law, it has been frequently used by courts as a means to ensure equality in the contractual relationship. With particular reference to supervening circumstances affecting the balance of the con-

47 *See also Arrêt de la Court d'appel de Paris*, 28 Sep. 1976, EDF v. Shell, JCP 1978.II.18810, note J. Robert.

48 Cass. com, 3 November 1992, Bull. 1992 IV n° 338 p. 241.

49 Cass. com, 24 November 1998, 96-18.357, published in the official bulletin.

50 *Cf.* Ghestin *et al., supra* note 33, p. 377.

51 Cass. 1st Chambre civile, 16 March 2004, 01-15.804, published in the official bulletin, with a note by D. Mazeaud, 'Du Nouveau sur l'Obligation de Renégocier', *Recueil Dalloz* 2004 p. 1754.

52 According to Mazeaud, *supra* note 51, p. 1757 ("avec cet arrêt, et pour la première fois de façon claire et nette, la Cour de cassation appréhende l'obligation de renégocier comme un tempérament, indirect mais général, à l'intangibilité des contrats devenus déséquilibrés lors de leur exécution, autrement dit au refus de la révision pour imprévision qu'elle a exprimé en 1876").

53 In a subsequent decision on the power of judge to sanction a breach of good faith obligation, the *Cour de Cassation* stated that "qu'en statuant ainsi, alors que si la règle selon laquelle les conventions doivent être exécutées de bonne foi permet au juge de sanctionner l'usage déloyal d'une prérogative contractuelle, elle ne l'autorise pas à porter atteinte à la substance même des droits et obligations légalement convenus entre les parties, la cour a violé, par fausse application, le second des textes susvisés et, par refus d'application, le premier de ces textes" (arrêt rendu le 10 juillet 2007 (n°06-14.768). *Cf.* P. Jacques, *Regards sur l'Article 1135 du Code Civil*, Dalloz, Paris, 2005; and P. Ancel, 'Les Sanctions du Manquement à la Bonne Foi dans l'Exécution du Contrat (Retour sur l'Arrêt de la Chambre Commerciale du 10 juillet 2007)', in *Mélanges en Hommage à Daniel Tricot*, Paris, Dalloz-Sirey/Litec, 2011, p. 61.

54 *See* J. Ghestin, *Droit Civil. Les obligations: Le Contrat: Formation*, 2nd edn, LGDJ, Paris, 1988, p. 747; H. Mazeaud & F. Chabas, *Leçons de Droit Civil: Obligations*, 9th edn, Montchrestien, Paris, 1998, p. 265; F. Terré, P. Simler & Y. Lequette, *Droit civil. Les obligations*, 7th edn, Dalloz, Paris, 1999, p. 314.

tract, the decision given by *Cour de Cassation* on 29 June 2010,[55] before the adoption of the *Ordonnance* and thus, before the introduction of an *ad hoc* regulation for cases of *imprévision*, seems to have opened up a new method to address unforeseen circumstances in the French legal system. As different scholars have pointed out,[56] the *Cour de Cassation* implicitly acknowledged the termination of a contract (for the maintenance, for a period of twelve years, of industrial devices) due to unforeseen circumstances (*imprévision*) on the basis of old Article 1131 *Code Civil* ("L'obligation sans cause, ou sur une fausse cause, ou sur une cause illicite, ne peut avoir aucun effet").

6.5 The Ordonnance and New Article 1195 *Code Civil*

The foregoing review of the development of the French legal system in relation to the concept of unforeseen circumstances that substantially affect the balance of contractual obligations between the parties demonstrates a clear tendency toward allowing stronger intervention by a judge in reforming the content of a contract. After the harsh decision in *Canal de Craponne*, lots of exceptions to the so-called *Canal de Craponne* doctrine have been introduced, both by legislature and by the courts; the role of the judge has also developed, as the threat of termination (*résiliation*) in case of an inability to renegotiate the relevant contract gives courts more power to intervene in the relationship between the contracting parties.

On the one hand, one might think that the introduction, via the *Ordonnance*, of a specific concept of *imprévision* in the *Code civil* is a further (and congruent) step on the path suggested by the jurisprudential exceptions to the consent principle. New Article 1195 *Code civil* states:

> Si un changement de circonstances imprévisible lors de la conclusion du contrat rend l'exécution excessivement onéreuse pour une partie qui n'avait pas accepté d'en assumer le risque, celle-ci peut demander une renégociation du contrat à son cocontractant. Elle continue à exécuter ses obligations durant la renégociation.
>
> En cas de refus ou d'échec de la renégociation, les parties peuvent convenir de la résolution du contrat, à la date et aux conditions qu'elles déterminent, ou demander d'un commun accord au juge de procéder à son adaptation. À défaut

55 Cass. com, 29 June 2010, 09-11.841, published in the official bulletin. *See* D. Mazeaud, 'L'arrêt Canal "moins"?', *in Recueil Dalloz* 2010, p. 2481; and T. Genicon, 'Théorie de l'Imprévision… ou de l'Imprévoyance ?', *in Recueil Dalloz* 2010, p. 2485.

56 *See* Genicon, *supra* note 55, p. 2485; Mazeaud, *supra* note 51, p. 2481; and M. J.-D. Bretzner, 'Brèves Réflexions sur un Outil Alternatif en Temps de Crise: La Caducité (ou Comment Faire du Neuf avec du Vieux!)', *Revue des contrats* 2010, p. 487.

> d'accord dans un délai raisonnable, le juge peut, à la demande d'une partie, réviser le contrat ou y mettre fin, à la date et aux conditions qu'il fixe.

Several critical remarks can be made about the actual formulation of this new article. Among the many interpretative problems, one notices that it is difficult to figure out how a party can, *ex ante*, assume the risk of the realization of an 'unforeseeable' change of circumstances.[57] The legislature probably meant to refer to aleatory contracts, where the assignment of risk to one of the parties is a fundamental element of the contract.

The mechanism established by new Article 1195 *Code civil* mixes the tendencies that first started to emerge from French jurisprudence in the 1990s. It primarily imposes, on the contracting parties, a duty to cooperate in a renegotiation of a contract suffering from a major imbalance due to unforeseen circumstances; if the parties are unable to renegotiate the contract, they can either agree to terminate the contract or jointly seek the assistance of a judge to help them to modify it; if no agreement can be found within a reasonable amount of time, either party can ask the court to terminate or modify the contract. Thus, the power of the judge to modify or terminate the contract (clause 2) depends on either the common will of the parties or a lack of agreement within a "reasonable period of time".

This new power certainly represents a 'revolutionary' innovation compared with the Catala *Avant-Projet*: its proposed Article 1135-1[58] could only be applied to long-term contractual relationships and, moreover, it did not give the judge power to adapt or terminate the contract and thus, the whole responsibility for adaptation was placed on renegotiation by the parties.[59] Furthermore, in the Catala *Avant-Projet*, the notion of *cause contractuelle* was maintained, but its proposed Article 1125 explicitly restricted its relevance to the moment of contract formation: consequently, there would have been no possibility to use the Catala *Avant-Projet*'s notion of *cause contractuelle* to modify a supervening imbalance within the contractual relationship. Finally, in the Catala *Avant-Projet*, the role of the court was subsidiary, as it could only act as an auxiliary of the parties which are the only subjects entitled by the Catala *Avant- Projet* to claim for termination in case of failure of the renegotiation.

---

57 R. Cabrillac, 'L'Article 1196: La Porte Entrouverte à l'Admission de l'Imprévision,' 3 *Revue des contrats* 2015, p. 771.

58 The *Catala Avant-Projet*'s proposed Article 1135-1 read as follows: "Dans les contrats à exécution successive ou échelonnée, les parties peuvent s'engager à négocier une modification de leur convention pour le cas où il adviendrait que, par l'effet des circonstances, l'équilibre initial des prestations réciproques fût perturbé au point que le contrat perde tout intérêt pour l'une d'entre elles."

59 *Cf. Catala Avant-Projet*, Article 1135-1 *et seq.* The commentary attached to the Catala *Avant-Projet* explicitly stated that "la prévention contractuelle des difficultés d'exécution à venir, ou, à défaut, l'organisation d'une renégociation sous l'impulsion du Juge" (A. Gohzi, Effet des conventions, Interprétation, Qualification (Article 1134 à 1143), *in* the Catala *Avant-Projet, supra* note 2, p. 34 *et seq.*, p. 35). *See also* Thibierge, *supra* note 21, p. 235; R. Cabrillac, 'Crises Financières et Contrats: Le Droit Positif Français Refuse la Révision d'un Contrat Devenu Déséquilibré mais le Projet de Réforme Entr'ouvre la Porte à l'Imprévision', *in* Basak Basoglu (Ed.), *The Effects of Financial Crises on the Binding Force of Contracts: Renegotiation, Rescission or Revision*, Switzerland, Springer International Publishing Switzerland, p. 140.

On the other hand, however, new Article 1195 *Code civil* apparently takes a step backward when compared with the jurisprudence analyzed above. The ability of a judge to intervene on behalf of a contracting party, through adaptation or termination, is carefully (although ambiguously!) confined.

The main responsibility for restoring balance to the contractual relationship is put on the parties, which are given a duty to renegotiate the contract in good faith. The court may only intervene, at the request of a party, when the parties cannot find any agreement (neither on the contract's termination nor on its adaptation). Because the nature and limits of the court's ability to modify the contract are unclear, one must find that the entire mechanism set out in the new Article 1195 *Code Civil* is unclear.

Referring to the duty of parties to renegotiate in good faith, new Article 1195 does not explicitly address the court's ability to award damages if it finds a lack of good faith on the part of one or more of the contracting parties. Before the *Ordonnance* came into effect, the *Cour de Cassation* prudently acknowledged the court's prerogative to do so, based on its ability to rectify a failure to the general duty to perform obligations in good faith (old Article 1134, clause 3 *Code civil*), but it is disputable if this will be possible after the enactment of a specific regulation for *imprévision* that did not envisage this option.

As for the ability of the court to directly intervene, the meaning of the term *mettre fin* is unclear and, this, so is the nature and effect of the judicial termination of the contract.[60]

Furthermore, the extent of the court's power to act in case of failure of the parties' renegotiations remains uncertain. Firstly, it is not specified whether the court must hold to the request put forward by the party seeking the court's assistance or if it is free to choose between termination and adaptation of the contract, regardless of that party's request. Secondly, new Article 1195 does not provide any criterion for the court's choice between termination and adaptation:[61] the provision's actual formulation suggests that either result is equally feasible. Thirdly, when there is a case for the court to revise the contract, the extent of the power of the judge to rewrite the contract remains unspecified: while the contracting parties are obviously free to substantially modify the original contract during their renegotiations, the court's intervention should probably not go so far. Furthermore, in the case of judicial adaptation, new Article 1195 does not specify the goal the court should pursue when modifying the contract: one might consider the rule set by Article 441-8 *Code de commerce* regarding price renegotiations in long-term contracts, according to which "la renégociation [...] tend à une répartition équitable entre les parties de l'accroissement ou de la réduction des coûts de production."

---

60 Savaux, *supra* note 23, p. 1062.

61 Id.

The actual phrasing of new Article 1195 is shaped by the analogous rules provided in both the UNIDROIT Principles (Article 6.2.3)[62] and the Principles of European Contract Law (PECL) (i.e., proposed by the Lando Commission, Article 6:11).[63] Both provisions design a mechanism whereby renegotiations among the contracting parties have priority over any judicial intervention that can eventually oblige the termination or adaptation of the contract. This correspondence can be explained by the political goals pursued through the Reform Project, which was intended to make French contract law attractive to international business: a reference to a standard used in international contract practice (UNIDROIT Principles) and in European *lex mercatoria* (e.g., PECL) clearly supported that goal.

Despite the criticism of the French legislature's decision to base its new Article 1195 on those international standards, one should note that the phrasing of the international rules is less ambiguous than the French language. For example:

- the phrase "the risk of the change of circumstances is not one which, according to the contract, the party affected should be required to bear" is far clearer than "pour une partie qui n'avait pas accepté d'en assumer le risqué";
- the ability to award damages "for the loss suffered through a party refusing to negotiate or breaking off negotiations contrary to good faith" is explicit; and
- the international provisions specifically state that adaptation of the contract should aim "to distribute between the parties in a just and equitable manner the losses and gains resulting from the change of circumstances".

6.6 CONCLUSIONS

In conclusion, I would like to make some critical remarks about the introduction, in French contract law, of the concept of *imprévision*, in light of the research on Life Time Contracts.[64] My first criticism concerns the general attitude of the French government toward the Europeanization of contract law, the remainder deal with the legislative technique used to draft new Article 1195 *Code civil*.

Firstly, the attitude of the French government toward the Europeanization of contract law seems paradoxical: on the one hand, it intended to give the French national *Code civil* a central role in the current, globalized scenario of international business and "forum

62 S. Vogenauer & J. Kleinheisterkamp (Eds.), *Commentary on the UNIDROIT Principles of International Commercial Law*, Oxford, Oxford University Press, 2009, p. 709 (with further bibliography); and M. J. Bonell, *An International Restatement of Contract Law: The UNIDROIT Principles of International Commercial Contracts*, 3rd edn, Brill, Ardsley, 2005, p. 117.

63 *See, generally*, O. Lando & H. Beale (Eds.), *Principles of European Contract Law. 1 Performance, Non-Performance, Remedies*, Dordrecht, Kluwer, 1995, p. 112; and B. Fauvaurque-Cosson & D. Mazeaud, *European Contract Law*, De Gruyter, Munich, 2008, p. 457.

64 *Cf.* L. Nogler & U. Reifner (Eds.), *Life Time Contracts. Social Long Term Contracts in Labour, Tenancy and Consumer Credit Law*, The Hague, Eleven International Publishing, 2014.

shopping" and, therefore, appears to take a step back from the project of harmonization (or unification) of European contract law; on the other hand, in doing so, the French legislature apparently repudiated French legal tradition (such as the French law notion of *cause*) and pointed to international standards more fitting to the common law tradition.

Secondly, all of the specific situations in which either the legislature or the *Cour de Cassation* has recognized the judge's ability to intervene in a contractual relationship after an unforeseen circumstance affects the contractual balance can be traced back to the notion of long-term contracts. Both the legislative exceptions for private law contracts and the jurisprudential exceptions for contracts with public administrations affect contractual relationships that endure over time and through which fundamental interests are pursued. The jurisprudential developments in this regard, starting in 1990, also primarily affect long-term contractual relationships that establish a sort of institutional cooperation between economic agents, even though the *Cour de Cassation* has always grounded its decisions on general rules of contract law (i.e., good faith and *cause contractuelle*).

In light of this observation, one could ask whether regulating *imprévision* should be a part of the general law of contracts or should be explicitly prescribed only with reference to long-term contracts. I think this latter solution (one followed, for instance, by Italian Civil Code, in which its Article 1467 explicitly restricts the applicability *eccessiva onerosità sopravventuta*" to "contracts for continuous or periodic performance")[65] could make it easier to fashion a more precise mechanism for relief in the context of *imprévision*, based on the needs and goals typical of long-term relations.

The connection between France's *imprévision* doctrine and long-term contractual relationships has been acknowledged by French civil lawyers since 1926, when Hariou first published his article entitled "*L'imprévision et les contrats dominés par des institutions sociales*",[66] and more recently by supporters of Ian McNeil's theory of 'relational contracts'.[67] These researches highlighted the connection between long-term contracts and the pursuit of commodities essential for survival and development of human existence: when this is the case, the problem of unforeseen circumstances arising after the conclusion of the contract clearly assume a particular significance and should be regulated accordingly. From this point of view, the traditional view of *Cour de Cassation*, according to which contracts with public administrations are exceptionally subject to *imprévision*

65 *See* A. Veneziano & L. Antoniolli (Eds.), *Principles of European Contract Law and Italian Law*, The Hague, Kluwer, 2005, p. 311.

66 M. Hauriou, 'L'Imprévision et les Contrats Dominés par des Institutions Sociales', republished *in Aux Sources du Droit: Le Pouvoir, l'Ordre et la Liberté*, Caen, Publication du Centre de Philosophie Politique et Juridique, 1986 (originally published in 1926), pp. 129-146, p. 131.

67 *See, in particular*, I. McNeil, 'Contracts: Adjustment of Long-Term Economic Relations under Classical, Neoclassical, and Relational Contract Law', 72 *Nw. Univ. L. Rev.* 1978, pp. 854-901; among French scholars, *see* C. Boisman, *Les contrats relationnels*, Press Universitaire, Aix-Marseille, 2005, p. 327 *et seq.*; and H. Bounthinon-Dumas, 'Les Contrats Relationnelles et la Théorie de l'Imprévision', 15 (3) *Revue Internationale de Droit Économique* 2001, pp. 339-373.

because they ensure the enjoyment of essential services for the public, seems at least biased. As elegantly pointed out by Hariou, "ce qui justifie la théorie de l'imprévision dans les relations du droit administratif doit la justifier aussi dans celles du droit Privé":[68] no difference should be made on the account of the character (public or private) of the provider because also contracts of private law are means to achieve essential goods and services.[69]

Furthermore, when regarded from the point of view of economic efficiency,[70] the connection between long-time contracts and supervening circumstances affecting the balance of the contract suggests that the main goal of a regulation of unforeseen circumstances in these contracts is to ensure stability and endurance through adaptation of the content of the contract. Termination should be an *extrema ratio*, a means to put pressure on the parties rather than a feasible result. Paradoxically, the power to adapt the contract is the best way to preserve its stability and thus, its binding force (*force obligatoire*). By adopting a specific regulation for *imprévision* in long-time contracts, the legislature could have had pursued the goal of adapting the contract more clearly, whereas actual Article 1195 still enables the judge to terminate the contract regardless of what the party claimed.

Finally, the vague formulation of Article 1195 (modeled on international contractual practice and its set of rules) seems to be more fitting for international business-to-business contractual relations and (related) arbitral jurisdictions, where parties' equal power can lead to a satisfactory renegotiation of the contractual terms even when the relevant regulation is vague. On the contrary, when unbalanced contractual relations are concerned this semi-arbitral mechanism might be less effective and the power of the Court should have been more defined.[71]

BIBLIOGRAPHY

Ancel, P., 'Les Sanctions du Manquement à la Bonne Foi dans l'Exécution du Contrat (Retour sur l'Arrêt de la Chambre Commerciale du 10 juillet 2007)', *in Mélanges en Hommage à Daniel Tricot*, Paris: Dalloz-Sirey/Litec, 2011.

Association Henri Capitant, *Les Droits de Tradition Civiliste en Question. À Propos des Rapports* Doing Business *de la Banque Mondiale, Contributions des Groupes Autres que le Groupe Français de l'Association Henri Capitant des Amis de la Culture Juridique Française*, Paris: Société de Législation Comparée, 2006.

68 Hauriou, *supra* note 66, p. 138.

69 *See also* J. Carbonnier, *Droit civil. Obligations*, 12th edn, Press Universitaire de France, Paris, 1994, n°149; and Tallon, *supra* note 22, p. 404.

70 C. Ménard, 'Imprévision et Contrats de Longue Durée: Un Économiste à l'Écoute du Juriste', *in Le Contrat au Début du XXIème Siècle (Études Offertes à Jacques Ghestin)*, Paris, LGDJ, 2001, p. 667.

71 Savaux, *supra* note 23, p. 1065.

Boisman, C., *Les Contrats Relationnels*, Aix-Marseille: Press Universitaire, 2005.

Bonell, M.J., *An International Restatement of Contract Law: The UNIDROIT Principles of International Commercial Contracts* (3rd ed.), Ardsley: Brill, 2005.

Bounthinon-Dumas, H., 'Les Contrats Relationnelles et la Théorie de l'Imprévision', 15 (3) *Rev. Int. Droit Écon.* 2001, pp. 339-373.

Bretzner, M.J.-D., 'Brèves Réflexions sur un Outil Alternatif en Temps de Crise: La Caducité (ou Comment Faire du Neuf avec du Vieux?)', *Revue des Contrats* 2010, p. 487.

Cabrillac, R., 'Crises Financières et Contrats: Le Droit Positif Français Refuse la Révision d'un Contrat Devenu Déséquilibré mais le Projet de Réforme Entr'ouvre la Porte à l'Imprévision', *in* B. Basoglu (Ed.), *The Effects of Financial Crises on the Binding Force of Contracts: Renegotiation, Rescission or Revision*, Springer International Publishing: Switzerland, 2016, p. 140.

Cabrillac, R., 'L'Article 1196 : La Porte Entrouverte à l'Admission de l'Imprévision', 3 *Revue des Contrats* 2015, p. 771.

Carbonnier, J., *Droit Civil. Obligations* (12th ed.), Paris: Press Universitaire de France, 1994.

Cardilli, R., 'Sopravvenienza e Pericoli Contrattuali', *in* R. Fiori (Ed.), *Modelli Teorici e Metodologici nella Storia del Diritto Privato*, Naples: Jovene, 2004, pp. 1-37.

Cartwright, J., Vogenauer, S. &Whittaker, S. (Eds.), *Reforming the French Law of Obligations*, Oxford/Portland: Hart, 2009.

Catala, P., Viney, G., Ancel, P., *et al.*, "La Réforme du Droit des Contrats : Projet et Perspectives'», 1 *Revue des Contrats* 2006.

David, R., 'L'imprévision dans les Droits Européens', *in Mélanges Jauffret*, D'Aix-Marseille : Publications de la Faculté de Droit et Science Politique, 1974, pp. 211-230.

Deroussin, D., *Histoire du Droit Privé (XVIe-XXIe siècle)*, Paris: LGDJ, 2010.

Deshayes, O., *et al.* (Eds.), *Réforme du Droit des Contrats, du Régime Général et de la Preuve des Obligations: Commentaire Article par Article*, Paris: Lexis-Nexis, 2016.

Fauvaurque-Cosson, B. & Mazeaud, D., *European Contract Law*, Munich: De Gruyter, 2008.

Fauvarque-Cosson, B., & Patris-Godechot, S. (Eds.), *Le Code Civil Face à Son Destin, la Documentation Française*, Paris: La Documentation Française, 2006.

Feenstra, R., '*Impossibilitas* and *Clausola Rebus Sic Stantibus*: Some Aspects of Frustration of Contract in Continental Legal History up to Grotius', *in* A. Watson (Ed.), *Daube Noster: Essays in Legal History for David Daube*, London/Edinburgh: Scottish Academic Press, 1974, p. 77.

Genicon, T., 'Théorie de l'Imprévision… ou de l'Imprévoyance ?', 2010 *Recueil Dalloz*, p. 2485.

Ghestin, J., *Droit Civil. Les obligations: Le Contrat: Formation* (2nd ed.), Paris: LGDJ, 1988.

Ghestin, J., Biliau, M. & Jamin, C., *Traité de droit civil: Les obligations: Les Effets du Contrat* (3rd ed.), Paris: LGDJ, 1993.

Gohzi, A., 'Effet des conventions, Interprétation, Qualification (Article 1134 à 1143)', *in Avant-Projet de Reforme du Droit des Obligations (Articles 1101 A 1386 Du Code Civil) et du Droit de la Prescription (Articles 2234 à 2281 du Code civil)*, 2005, p. 34.

Hauriou, M., 'L'Imprévision et les Contrats Dominés par des Institutions Sociales', Republished *in Aux Sources du Droit: Le Pouvoir, l'Ordre et la Liberté*, Caen: Publication du Centre de Philosophie Politique et Juridique, 1986.

Jacques, P., *Regards sur l'Article 1135 du Code Civil*, Paris: Dalloz, 2005.

Jamin, C., 'Révision et Intangibilité du Contrat ou la Double Philosophie de l'Article 1134 du Code Civil', 58 *Droit et Patrimoine* 1998, pp. 46-57.

Lando, O. & Beale, H. (Eds.), *Principles of European Contract Law. 1 Performance, Non-Performance, Remedies*, Dordrecht: Kluwer, 1995.

Larombière, M.L., *Théorie et Pratique des Obligations, ou Commentaire aux Titres III et IV, Livre III, du Code Napoléon, Article 1101 à 1386*, Vol. III, Paris: A. Durand.

Lequette, Y., 'Vers un Code Civil Européen?', 107 *Pouvoirs, Revue Française d'Études Constitutionnelles et Politiques* 2003, pp. 97-126.

Mazeaud, D., 'Du Nouveau sur l'Obligation de Renégocier', *Recueil Dalloz* 2004, p. 1754.

Mazeaud, D., 'L'arrêt Canal «Moins»?', *Recueil Dalloz* 2010, p. 2481.

Mazeaud, H. & Chabas, F., *Leçons de Droit Civil : Obligations* (9th ed.), Paris: Montchrestien, 1998.

McNeil, I., 'Contracts: Adjustment of Long-Term Economic Relations under Classical, Neoclassical, and Relational Contract Law', 72 *Nw. Univ. L. Rev.* 1978, pp. 854-901.

Ménard, C., 'Imprévision et Contrats de Longue Durée: Un Économiste à l'Écoute du Juriste', *in Le Contrat au Début du XXIème Siècle (Études Offertes à Jacques Ghestin)*, Paris: LGDJ, 2001, p. 667.

Nogler, L. & Reifner, U. (Eds.), *Life Time Contracts. Social Long Term Contracts in Labour, Tenancy and Consumer Credit Law*, The Hague: Eleven International Publishing, 2014.

Philippe, D., *Changement de Circonstances et Bouleversement de l'Économie Contractuelle*, Bruxelles: Émile Bruylant, 1986, p. 109.

Pichonnaz, P., 'De la Clausola Rebus Sic Stantibus au Hardship: Aspects d'une Evolution du Rôle du Jege', *in* A. Ruelle & M. Berlingin (Eds.), *Le Droit Romain d'hier à Aujourd'hui: Collationes et Oblationes: Liber Amicorum en l'Honneur du Professeur Gilbert Hanard*, Bruxelles: Facultés Universitaires Saint-Louis, 2009, p. 149 *et seq.*

Planiol, M., & Ripert, G., *Traité de Droit Civil Français* (2nd ed.), Vol. VI, Paris: LGDJ, 1952-1962.

Rémy-Corlay, P. & Fenouillet, D. (Eds.), *Les Concepts Contractuels Français à l'Heure des Principes du Droit Européen des Contrats*, Paris: Dalloz, 2003.

Ripert, G., *La Règle Morale dans les Obligations Civiles*, Paris: LGDJ, 1949.

Rösler, H., 'Hardship in German Codified Private Law – In Comparative Perspective to English, French and International Contract Law', 3 *Eur. Rev. Private Law* 2007, pp. 483-513.

Rummel, M., *Die Clausula Rebus Sic Stantibus : eine Dogmengeschichtliche Untersuchung unter Berucksichtigung der Zeit von der Rezeption im 14. Jahrhundert bis zum Jungeren Usus Modernus in der ersten Halfte des 18. Jahrhunderts*, Baden-Baden: Nomos, 1991.

Savatier, J., 'La Théorie de l'Imprévision dans les Contrats', *in Études de Droit Contemporain: Contributions Françaises aux 3. et 4. Congrès Internationaux de Droit Comparé*, Vol. II, Paris: Sirey, 1959, p. 1.

Savaux, E., 'L'introduction de la Révision ou de la Résiliation pour Imprévision – Rapport Français', *Revue des Contrats* 2010, pp. 1057-1067.

Stoffel-Munk, P., *Regards sur l'Imprévision: Vers une Souplesse Contractuelle en Droit Prive Français Contemporain*, Aix-en-Provence: Presses Universitaires d'Aix-Marseille, 1994.

Stoffel-Munk, P., *Réforme du Droit des Obligations : la Force Obligatoire du Contrat en Danger*, Retrieved on 7 June 2017 from <www.dalloz-actualite.fr/interview/reforme-du-droit-des-obligations-force-obligatoire-du-contrat-en-danger#.VoF_waTZg-8>.

Tallon, D., 'La Révision du Contrat Pour Imprévision au Regard des Enseignements Récents du Droit Comparé', *in* J. Carbonnier (Ed.), *Droit et Vie des Affaires. Études à la Mémoire d'Alain Sayag*, Paris: Litec, 1997, pp. 403-417.

Terré, F., Simler, P. & Lequette, Y., *Droit civil. Les obligations* (7th ed.), Paris: Dalloz, 1999.

Thibierge, L., *Le Contrat Face à l'Imprévu*, Paris: Economica, 2011.

Veneziano, A., 'Le "Changement de Circonstances» dans le Cadre Commun de Référence sur le Droit Européen des Contrats', 200 (2) *Revue de Contrats* 2009, pp. 873-882.

Veneziano, A. & Antoniolli, L. (Eds.), *Principles of European Contract Law and Italian Law*, The Hague: Kluwer, 2005.

Vogenauer, S. & Kleinheisterkamp, J. (Eds.), *Commentary on the UNIDROIT Principles of International Commercial Law*, Oxford: Oxford University Press, 2009.

Witz, C., 'Force Obligatoire et Durée du Contrat', *in* P. Rémy-Corlay & D. Fenouillet (Eds.), *Les Concepts Contractuels Français à l'Heure des Principes du Droit Européen des Contrats*, Paris: Dalloz, 2003.

World Bank, *Doing Business in 2004: Understanding Regulations*, Washington, DC: World Bank/Oxford University Press, 2004.

7 Le Rôle de la Formation dans le Cadre des Contrats à Temps Essentiels à l'Existence de la Personne

Giulia Merlo[*]

7.1 Introduction. Le Principe de Formation dans les Contrats à Temps Pour l'Existence de la Personne et sa Dimension Collective.

Le renforcement des principes sur la catégorie juridique des contrats à temps pour l'existence de la personne[1] et la réalisation de son spécifique cadre juridique sont essentiels pour assurer un "model contractuel européen" véritablement social dans lequel l'être humain et ses besoins sont considérés importants autant que l'efficacité économique contractuelle. Et ce besoin est encore plus manifeste dans l'actuel crise de légitimité du projet politique européen.

En ce qui concerne les "contrats d'existence" (c'est-à-dire les contrats à temps qui sont essentiels pour la conservation des biens et services, l'accès à un travail et à une source de revenus pour le développement de la personne dans toute forme), le modèle européen mis en œuvre jusqu'à présent a montré peu d'attention envers la protection substantielle des intérêts économiques et existentiels de la partie contraignante "faible". En effet, le modèle contractuel proposée[2] a transformé le rapport du temps d'existence en des "*relations synallagmatiques ponctues*"[3] fondés sur la fiction d'un parfait équilibre entre les deux parties contraignantes, en utilisant l'archétype du contrat de vente.

Afin d'améliorer le cadre juridique dans la matière, il est donc nécessaire d'étudier les formes contractuelles élémentaires et rechercher des principes communs à ces contrats. De cette manière, nous trouverons des remèdes plus appropriés pour assurer une protection substantielle à la partie faible du contrat.

---

* École de Doctorat d'Études Juridiques Européennes et Comparés, Faculté de Droit-Université de Trente.

1 Pour un approfondissement et une définition précise de cette "macro" catégorie contractuel, *voy.* L. Nogler & U. Reifner (Eds.), *Life Time Contracts Social Long-term Contracts in Labour, Tenancy and Consumer Credit Law*, The Hague, Eleven International Publishing, 2014, p. XVII *et seq.*, pp. 1-4. "*Les contrats d'existence sont des relations sociales à long terme par lesquelles les individus se fournissent des biens ou des services, accèdent à un travail ou à une source de revenus. Ces contrats sont essentiels à la réalisation et à l'insertion de l'individu dans la vie sociale, à différents stades de celle-ci*", p. XXII.

2 *Voy.* Les directives en matière de protection du consommateur (Directive n. 2011/83/UE du Parlement européen et du Conseil du 25 octobre 2011) où en matière du crédit à consommation (Directive n. 2008/48/CE du Parlement européen et du conseil du 26 avril 2008).

3 Nogler & Reifner (Eds.), *supra* note 1, p. XXXVI.

Dans le but de protéger la faiblesse sociale des contraignants, il est particulièrement important de regarder à la dimension sociale et collective des contrats d'existence, exprimée par les conventions collectives, mais aussi, en général, par les principes généraux. L'organisation collective des contrats d'existence sera une façon pour assurer une majeure protection à la partie faible, dans les situations de déplacement du pouvoir contractuel.

Afin de rechercher des solutions collectives de protection des intérêts économiques et sociales des consommateurs, des travailleurs et des locataires, dans toutes les étapes du rapport et, notamment, pendant la durée du rapport, nous essayerons de comprendre quel est le rôle de la formation et de l'éducation de la partie faible dans les contrats à temps qui sont essentiels à l'existence de la personne. Plus précisément, le but sera de comprendre si un principe d'éducation, au sein de la dimension collective des contrats d'existence, puisse être opérationnel pour assurer une relation véritablement équilibrée et durable[4] afin d'éviter que le risque d'un déplacement de pouvoir contractuel puisse se traduire par l'exclusion sociale.

Nous essayerons donc de comprendre si l'affirmation d'un principe d'éducation peut être utile pour renforcer le cadre juridique en matière des contrats d'existence.

Dans ce but, la recherche essayera d'analyser quel est le rôle de la formation du contraignant faible dans deux types de contrats d'existence, entre lesquels il y a un fort lien fonctionnel: le contrat de travail subordonné et les contrats qui rentrent dans le domaine du crédit à la consommation.[5] Les deux domaines contractuels sont destinés à la satisfaction des besoins humains, parfois essentiels, car ils fournissent les moyens nécessaires pour les atteindre.[6]

Aujourd'hui, au sein d'une société capitaliste de consommation, la capacité de générer des revenus présentes grâce au travail n'est plus suffisante pour garantir la satisfaction des nécessites primaires des individus. Ainsi, toujours plus fréquemment, les besoins essentiels sont satisfaits par l'accès au crédit à la consommation, qui va affecter directement la capacité du travail future des individus[7] et, donc, leur capacité de percevoir des revenus. C'est pour cette raison qu'il y a une forte relation parmi ces contrats; la stabilité de l'emploi devient ainsi fondamentale afin de garantir soit la capacité de générer des revenus présents, soit la capacité de générer des revenus futurs face aux dettes éventuelles.[8] En

4 Principe n. 2 sur les contrats d'existence, *in* Nogler & Reifner (Eds.), *supra* note 1, p. XXII.

5 Pour une définition du contrat de "crédit à la consommation", G.A. Bennacchio, *Diritto Privato dell'Unione europea (fonti, modelli, regole)*, Padova, CEDAM-Wolters Kluwer Italia, 2013, p. 431 *et seq*: "*concession dans le domaine d'une activité non-commercial, d'un crédit, en faveur d'une personne physique agissant à des fins non commerciales*".

6 "*A feature of consumer credit is that its purpose is not to make investments but just to finance the current spent of the family*", L. Nogler & U. Reifner, 'The New Dimension: Life Time in the Law of Contracts and Obligations', *in* Nogler & Reifner (Eds.), *supra* note 1, p. 16.

7 L. Nogler, 'The Historical Contribution of Employment Law to General Civil Law: A Lost Dimension?', *in* Nogler & Reifner (Eds.), *supra* note 1, pp. 305-307.

8 La stabilité de l'emploi sera donc indispensable pour éviter le risque d'insolvabilité et surendettement, qui actuellement est d'ailleurs une de majeure cause de pauvreté. "*In relation to consumer credit, the work*

particulier, dans les cadre de contrats à l'existence, nous essayerons de comprendre comment la formation peut influencer la coopération durable entre les deux parties contraignantes où la rupture anticipé doit être considérée seulement que l'*extrema ratio* (de sorte que la confiance mutuelle sur la durée du contrat soit protégé). D'une part, en envisagent comment la formation va influencer la stabilité de la relation de travail; d'autre part, comment elle influence la durée du contrat de crédit, de sorte que le possibles situations d'insolvabilité soient évitées.

Une discipline générale, individuelle et collective, des contractas à l'existence sera opérationnel afin d'améliorer la qualité de vie des individus dans la moderne société de la consommation.

À cette fin, donc, nous envisagerons la possibilité d'introduire un principe général de formation dans les contrats d'existence.

Dans les différentes langues romanes, la signification étymologique de ce terme (*formation* en français, *formazione* en italien, *formación* en espagnol, *formação* en portugués qui dérive du mot latin, *formatio, -onis*), rappelle quelque chose qui prend une forme, qui est modelée sur la base d'un projet extérieur.[9] Dans un sens figuré cette expression renvoie à l'acquisition progressive, par l'étude ou l'expérience, d'un particulière "physionomie culturelle ou morale" aussi bien que de l'expertise technique dans un domaine particulier.[10] Ainsi conçue, le concept de "formation" est directement lié à la notion d'"éducation", où un individu donne une "forme" a ses connaissances et compétences grâce à un processus d'apprentissage.[11] La notion de formation que nous choisissons d'utiliser est donc très générique, étant donné que ce principe sera décliné différemment selon chaque types de contrats et se réfère à la croissance des connaissances des chaque individus dans le domaine de chaque relation contractuelle.

Dans l'optique de créer une réglementation unitaire des contrats d'existence, malgré les approches différentes utilisées, nous rechercherons dans quelle manière la formation de la partie la plus faible au contrat peut assurer une relation contractuelle équilibrée, afin de préserver la capacité de pouvoir pourvoir à ses besoins vitaux et prévenir le risque d'exclusion social.

---

required to repay the loan takes on legal relevance once again, so that the subdivision so of people's lives into 'two parts which are estranged from one another' is dissolved [...] But above all in the credit society work is shifted over from production to consumption, as it can be appreciated in the new term 'prosumer'". Nogler & Reifner (Eds.), *supra* note 1, pp. 2, 17.

9 Entrée *"formazione"*, *in Enciclopedia Treccani on-line*, Retrieved on June 19 2017 from <www.treccani.it/enciclopedia/formazione/>.

10 Entrée *"formazione", in Dizionario Sabatini-Coletti on-line*', Retrieved on 19 June 2017 from <http://dizionari.corriere.it/dizionario_italiano/F/formazione.shtml>,

11 Entrée *"formation", in Dictionnaire de la langue française 'Le Petit Robert'*, Le Robert-VUEF, 2003.

7.2 LA FORMATION DANS LA RELATION DE TRAVAIL

7.2.1 *La Formation au Sein du Contrat de Travail. L'Objet du Contrat de Travail*

La transition entre le mode de production fordiste-tayloriste, caractérisée par une structuration de l'organisation du travail répétitive et standardisé, vers une production plus légère et flexible, où la réorganisation continue, l'information et surtout la connaissance, ont un rôle primaire[12] (on parle de post-fordisme), a mis en évidence que la qualité de la prestation du travail est la clé fondamentale pour améliorer la productivité des entreprises.

Les processus d'automatisation typiques du post-fordisme exigent des profils d'emploi intelligent, avec un professionnalisme très adaptable aux rapides changements technologiques et organisationnels.[13] Nous pouvons observer que le contenu du contrat de travail devient plus cognitif et coopératif; dans l'exécution de ses propres taches le travailleur doit posséder une forte attitude polyvalente.[14]

Dans ce contexte, un rôle très important est joué par la formation tout au long de la vie.[15] Les entreprises, en effet, cherchent toujours plus de développer leurs produits grâce à l'augmentation des investissements dans le capital humane, afin de permettre l'apprentissage des capacités nouvelles (et plus élevées).[16] L'importance de la formation continue a été soulignée par de nombreuses sources européennes, notamment depuis le début des années '90 avec "le livre Blanc" de la Commission Européenne sur l'éducation e la formation,[17] et le processus de Luxembourg du 1997. Dans le domaine de la politique européenne sur l'emploi, les Traités de Maastricht et Amsterdam ont mis en relief l'importance des politiques de

---

12 C. Dell'Arringa, 'Professionalità e approccio economico', in M. Napoli (Ed.), *La professionalità*, Milano, Vita e Pensiero, 2004, p. 95.

13 R. Nacamulli, 'Professionalità e organizzazione', in Napoli (Ed.), *supra* note 12, p. 65 *et seq*. Pour approfondir, U. Carabelli, Organizzazione del lavoro e professionalità: una riflessione su contratto di lavoro e post-taylorismo, *DLRI*, n. 101, 2004, p. 1 *et seq*.; M. Corti, 'L'edificazione del sistema italiano di formazione continua dei lavoratori', n. 1, *RGL*, 2007, p. 173.

14 M. Magnani, 'Organizzazione del lavoro e professionalità tra rapporti e mercato del lavoro", *DLRI*, 2004, n. 101, p. 168.

15 La définition de formation professionnelle et, notamment, de formation tout au long de la vie n'est pas toujours claire et certaine. Dans le contexte du droit européen (art. 166 TFUE et art. 166 (ex art. 150 TCE) et dans la jurisprudence de la CJUE (Arrêt du 11 juin 1991, Royaume-Uni e.a. / Conseil (Affaires jointes C-51/89, C-90/89 et C-94/89, Rec. 1991 p. I-2757) on utilise l'expression "formation tout au long de la vie" ou "formation professionnelle continue" soit pour reconnaître le droit d'entreprendre des cours de formation tout au long de la vie, soit, d'autres fois, dans le cadre de l'exécution du contrat du travail. M. Roccella, 'Formazione, occupabilità, occupazione nell'Europa comunitaria', *DLRI*, n. 1, 2007, pp. 187-236.

16 Travailleurs: W. Streek, 'L'impresa come luogo di formazione e conoscenza, *in* P. Ceri (Ed.), *Impresa e lavoro in trasformazione*, p. 84, Bologna, Il Mulino, 1988, *in* Magnani, *supra* note 14, p. 167. On parle, à ce propos, de "travailleurs de la connaissance". Cette expression indique que les performances personnelles sont adressées vers l'obtention d'un résultat final. Magnani, *supra* note 14, p. 168.

17 "*Livre Blanc sur l'éducation et la formation, enseigner et apprendre, vers la société cognitive*" Com (95) 590 final du 29 novembre 1995, où pour la première fois, la formation professionnelle continue est considérée essentiale pour l'intégration sociale et le développement de la personne.

formation professionnelle en donnant une spécifique compétence à l'Union[18] en matière de formation professionnelle. Même la Charte européenne de Nice a reconnu le droit fondamental à l'accès à la formation professionnelle et continue (art. 14).[19]

La formation professionnelle continue devient donc un "*élément structurel*" des politiques européennes,[20] attendu que les stratégies de *lifelong learning* sont opérationnelles à une meilleure compétitivité et innovation de la production des entreprises. L'objectif est de promouvoir la formation des ressources humaines expertes et qualifiés, selon les innovations organisationnelles et technologiques.

Mais, on reconnait aussi que l'apprentissage continu des compétences des travailleurs est l'élément qui garantit pleinement leur employabilité durable. Dans un marché du travail très complexe et compétitif, où la quatrième révolution industrielle et l'informatisation profonde du travail exige un professionnalisme toujours plus avancé, où les processus organisationnels sont en constante évolution, la formation continue des compétences semble un moyen très sûr pour assurer la stabilité de l'emploi.

La formation professionnelle est définie comme le "droit du futur", et "la plus grande garantie de stabilité de l'emploi face aux grands changements en cours".[21]

Il faut donc s'interroger sur les conséquences, par rapport au contenu du contrat de travail, de la valorisation de la formation professionnelle dans le cadre d'une réalité productive et organisationnelle qui a changé profondément.[22]

En particulier, il faut comprendre si, comment et dans quelles situations, la reconnaissance formelle du droit subjectif à la formation au sein de la relation contractuelle sera utile afin de donner une plus grande stabilité à l'emploi, en veillant à ce que la rupture anticipée ne soit que l'*extrema ratio*, et garantissant ainsi les revenues présentes et futures du sujet pour éviter le risque d'exclusion sociale et de chômage. Il faut comprendre si la formation doit être un outil effectif de protection substantielle du travailleur (principes n. 1, 11 e 15 sur les contrats d'existence).

Dans le système juridique italien la formation professionnelle est un droit fondamental reconnu par l'art. 35.2 de la Constitution, selon lequel "*la Repubblica cura la formazione e l'elevazione professionale dei lavoratori*". Il peut être ainsi considéré comme un "droit social à prestation",[23] c'est-à-dire un droit fondamental qui engage la République et ses institutions, y compris les partenaires sociaux, à sa mise en œuvre par des différentes mesures politiques.[24]

---

18 Art 166 TFUE.

19 Roccella, *supra* note 15, p. 187 *et seq.*

20 Corti, *supra* note 13, pp. 163-164.

21 Déclaration de M. Bentivogli, secrétaire général de FIM-CISL, "La formazione aumenta i posti" extrait de "*Il Sole 24 Ore*", 18 mars 2016, p. 20

22 En particulier, par rapport au system italien.

23 G. Loy, *La professionalità*, *RGL*, n. 4, 2003, pp. 763-798.

24 B. Caruso, 'Occupabilità, formazione e "capability" nei modelli di regolazione dei mercati del lavoro', *DLRI*, n. 1, 2007, pp. 1-31. Par exemple: le financement de la formation, la certification des compétences etc.

Dans le système italien, le droit à la formation n'a jamais été positivement reconnu dans le cadre du contrat de travail. La jurisprudence n'a jamais reconnu une obligation de formation de l'employeur (à l'exception, bien sûr, des contrats de travail dont la cause même est la formation, tels que le soi-disant contrat d' "*apprendistato*").[25]

Cependant, la doctrine a souvent essayé de faire valoir l'existence de ce droit à travers les données normatives. Mais, surtout, en se fondant sur la reconnaissance du professionnalisme comme l'objet principal du contrat de travail.

La thèse, selon laquelle le professionnalisme constitue l'objet du contrat de travail, a été avancée à plusieurs reprises par Mario Napoli.[26] Selon cet auteur, en opposition à la thèse (traditionnelle) qui voit la raison du contrat de travail dans l'échange entre énergies psycho physique et rétribution,[27] le professionnalisme est le vrai objet de l'échange, la vraie raison du contrat de travail. l'évolution des processus productifs a changé la notion du travail même et, notamment, du travail subordonné. Aujourd'hui, les entreprises demandent une collaboration intelligente, active, *multitasking*.

Dans cet optique, la synthèse des connaissances, les compétences, les capacités interpersonnelles, c'est-à-dire le professionnalisme dans le sens subjectif,[28] doit être placé au centre du contrat.

Mario Napoli affirme que, en conséquence, la formation professionnelle sera une "effet légal naturel du contrat de travail subordonné". Le travailleur jouira donc du droit d'être formé, en raison de la conclusion du contrat et dans certaines circonstances, telles que les innovations organisationnelles ou technologiques (voy paragraphes suivantes). Cette obligation de l'employeur vise essentiellement à préserver les compétences professionnelles du travailleur.[29] Cette approche a été partagée par de nombreux autres auteurs,[30] mais avec quelques différences. Selon une partie de la doctrine, l'obligation

---

25 Corti, *supra* note 13, p. 180.

26 M. Napoli, 'Disciplina del mercato del lavoro ed esigenze formative', *RGL*, n. 3-4, 1997, p. 269 *et seq.*; M. Napoli, *Le dimensioni della professionalità*, relation au XIV Congrès AIDLASS, Teramo -Silvi Marini, 30-31 mai 2003; partage cette conceptualisation, L. Nogler, 'La subordinazione nel d.lgs. n. 81 del 2015: alla ricerca dell' "autorità del punto di vista giuridico"', *WP C.S.D.L.E. 'Massimo D'Antona'.IT*, n. 267, 2015, p. 27 Retrieved on 22 March 2016, from<http://csdle.lex.unict.it/Archive/WP/WP%20CSDLE%20M%20DAN TONA/WP%20CSDLE%20M%20DAN TONA-IT/20150923-014624_nogler_n267-2015itpdf.pdf>.

27 A. Supiot, *Critique du droit du travail*, Press Universitaires de France, Paris, 1996, p. 86. G. Giugni indique les tâches convenues comme l'objet du contrat: Giugni G., *Mansioni e qualifica nel rapporto di lavoro*, Jovene, Napoli, 1963, p. 3.

28 S. Ciucciovino, *Apprendimento e tutela del lavoro*, Giappichelli, Torino, 2013, p. 156.

29 Selon M. Napoli cet obligation doit être fondé sur l'art. 35. 2 de la Constitution italienne et sur la combinaison des art. 2094 du code civil italien, norme qui définit la subordination, et sur l'art. 2103, norme qui régule le *jus variandi* de l'employeur qui, selon nombreuses auteurs, protège le professionnalisme subjective des travailleurs.

30 U. Romagnoli, 'Il Diritto del secolo e poi?', *in Il Diritto del Mercato del lavoro*, 1999, 2, p. 238; C. Alessi, *Professionalità e diritto del lavoro*, Giuffrè, Milano, 2004, p. 81 *et seq.*; A. Loffredo, *Diritto alla formazione. Realtà e retorica*, Cacucci, Bari, 2012, p. 131 *et seq.*; Corti, *supra* note 13, pp. 243-244.

d'adaptation professionnelle est dérivée d'une interprétation évolutive de l'article. art. 2087[31] du Code civil, conjointement avec l'article. 2103 du Code civil. D'autres auteurs identifient le fondement de cette obligation dans l'obligation générale de bonne foi,[32] d'autres dans l'accomplissement de l'obligation du créancier de coopérer, conformément à l'art. 1206 du Code civil.[33]

Une autre partie de la doctrine, au contraire, rejette l'idée que dans la relation de travail il existe un droit individuel juridiquement exécutoire de formation et de perfectionnement des compétences.[34] Selon cette interprétation, le professionnalisme est quand même une conditionne préalable fondamentale pour l'exécution des tâches assignées qui, cependant, restent le seul objet du contrat[35] et, par conséquent, elle ne détecte pas par rapport aux contraintes contractuelles. Sa pertinence se déroule seulement sur le marché du travail. Selon cette approche, donc, en l'absence de données normatives, l'intérêt mentionné ci-dessus ne peut pas se traduire par des obligations de comportement réelles pour les parties de la relation de travail, au point de mettre en place un droit individuel juridiquement exécutoire.[36]

Dans les paragraphes suivants, nous essayerons de spécifier dans quelles situations concrètes l'introduction d'un spécifique devoir d'adaptation et de formation est réellement opérationnelle pour assurer une majeure stabilité à l'emploi, dans l'optique de préserver une relation durable véritablement synallagmatique dans les contrats à temps d'existence.

7.2.2 *Les Effets Systématiques de l'Obligation de Formation au Sein du Contrat de Travail*

Dans le cadre de la relation de travail l'inadaptation des connaissances des travailleurs dans certaines situations peut sérieusement mettre en péril la stabilité de l'emploi.

Cet situation peut se produire en premier lieu si l'entreprise met en place les changements organisationnels conduisant l'employeur à exercer le pouvoir du dit "*jus variandi*", conformément à l'art. 2013 Cod. civ. italien, c'est-à-dire la variation unilatérale des tâches

31 Romagnoli, *supra* note 30, p. 3. L'art. 2087 du Code Civil est visé à la protection, par l'employeur, de l'intégrité physique et morale du travailleur. Aussi Corti, *supra* note 13, pp. 243-244. Selon Matteo Corti cet article doit être interprété, conjointement avec l'art. 35 cost., comme la disposition visant à la protection du professionnalisme.

32 Art. 1175 Cod. civ.

33 L. Galantino, 'I profili giuslavoristici della qualità', L. Galantino (Ed.), *Qualità e Rapporto di Lavora, Milano: Giuffrè*, 1995, pp. 138-139.

34 Ciucciovino, *supra* note 28, p. 180; Roccella, *supra* note 15; Loy, *supra* note 23, pp. 763-798; R. Del Punta, 'Diritti della persona e contratto di lavoro, *DRLI*, n. 2, 2006, p. 195 *et seq.*; Carabelli 2004, *supra* note 13, p. 1 *et seq.*

35 Loy, *supra* note 23; Ciucciovino, *supra* note 28, p. 180.

36 Des auteurs ont également rejeté la thèse de l'obligations de formation, en raison de la crainte que cela pourrait conduire à l'extension de la dette de l'employé. Carabelli, *supra* note 13, pp .71-73.

auxquels l'employé est affecté selon le contrat de travail[37] qui, normalement, se réfère aux classes de classification contenues dans la négociation collective.[38]

La légitimité des modifications de la position professionnelle du travailleur, selon la formulation précédente de l'article 2013[39] du Code Civil italien, était limitée par le critère d' "équivalence professionnelle".

L'employeur pouvait demander exclusivement l'exécution des tâches pour lesquelles le travailleur avait été embauché ou celles qui équivalaient aux dernières réellement effectuées (sans aucun changement de salaire). La jurisprudence a longtemps interprété ce principe d'une façon rigide, car elle légitimait la modification unilatérale uniquement si les nouvelles taches tombaient dans le même niveau contractuel et, surtout, si le bagage d'expertise et de l'expérience professionnelle déjà acquis précédemment, pouvait être entièrement utilisé[40] ("professionnalisme statique"). Plus récemment, la jurisprudence avait montré des petites ouvertures vers une conception du professionnalisme plus dynamique, dans lequel les tâches pouvaient également être considérées comme équivalentes si elles permettaient d'utiliser des connaissances professionnelles potentielles.[41]

La plus moderne conception d'un professionnalisme "dynamique" semble plus cohérente avec les besoins actuels des entreprises, qui demandent des ressources humaines flexibles et adaptables.

Selon une partie de la doctrine,[42] la modification du contenu de la prestation du travail, qui suit un changement organisationnel et où le travailleur ne possède pas les connaissances techniques pour l'exacte exécution, dans l'optique d'un développement dynamique du professionnalisme, exige par l'employeur un devoir d'adaptation (à travers des parcours de formation). Cette reconstruction est basée sur la reconnaissance du professionnalisme comme l'objet du contrat.[43]

---

37 Son contenu est réglé par l'art. 2103 du Code civil tel que modifié par l'art. 13 du Statut des travailleurs et successivement par le décret législatif n. 81 du 2015.

38 Les méthodes de la classification professionnel (en italien "*inquadramento*") ont peu à peu changé au fil des années, sous la pression des mouvements syndicaux des années 70, jusqu'à la consolidation dans le système de la "gestion unique" (en italien "*inquadramento unico*"). Ce système, qui d'ailleurs est très commun dans des nombreuses conventions collectives, prévoit le la prédisposition d'une série de niveaux, à l'intérieur desquels il y a des multiples profils professionnels énucléés et le contenu des tâches liées à ces derniers. Pour en savoir plus, O. Mazzotta *Manuale di diritto del lavoro*, CEDAM, Padova, 2015, pp. 369-371; *aussi* M. Borzaga, 'Contrattazione collettiva di prossimità e disciplina delle mansioni: una via per aumentare la flessibilità interna del rapporto di lavoro e la produttività delle imprese?', *DRI*, n. 4, 2013, p. 983.

39 En vigueur jusqu'à 2015, quand l'art. 2013 cod. civ. a été visiblement modifié par le décret législatif n. 81-2015

40 Borzaga, *supra* note 38, pp. 984-985; Cass., n. 14815/2005.

41 Cass. n. 25.033/2006, *Poste Italiane.*

42 *Ex multis*, Alessi, *supra* note 30, p. 143; Roccella, *supra* note 15, p. 187 *et seq,; contra* Ciucciovino, *supra* note 28, p. 175.

43 Et, aussi, par le devoir de coopération du créancier à la diligente exécution du débiteur et au devoir de loyauté et bonne foi *dans l'exécution.*

De toute évidence, cela aura des conséquences directes sur l'imputabilité de l'inexécution,[44] et donc pourra être considérable pour la légitimité des licenciements pour raisons subjectives.[45]

Par rapport à l'objet principal de notre recherche, la reconnaissance d'un devoir d'adaptation face aux modifications de l'organisation et dans la domaine d'un professionnalisme dynamique a aussi des importantes conséquences pour la légitimité des licenciements économiques. Au sein du précédent cadre législatif, selon une jurisprudence constante, l'employeur qui voulait mettre en place des licenciements économiques, devait démontrer d'avoir respecté le dit devoir de "repêchage", c'est-à-dire, il devait prouver qu'il n'existait pas des autres positions dans lesquelles le travailleur pouvait être attaché, *au sein de tâches équivalentes (art. 2013 Cod. civ)*[46] ("*physiologiquement absorbables par l'organisation productive*"[47]). Selon cette interprétation, l'affirmation d'une obligation de formation pouvait se révéler ainsi opérationnelle afin d'étendre le "devoir de repêchage" également aux taches "équivalentes" qui exigent des initiatives d'éducation préventive. Cela implique une plus grande difficulté à mettre en place un licenciement pour des raisonnes économiques et devient ainsi une mesure de protection de la sécurité de l'emploi en cas de changements organisationnels.

Néanmoins, la jurisprudence italienne concernant les allégations de preuve du licenciement pour des raisons objectives (*giustificato motivo oggettivo* art. 5 l. 604/1966), étant donné l'absence d'une disposition législative spécifique, a montré une position restrictive visant à rejeter l'extension du devoir "qualifié" de "repêchage[48]", exigeant en fait la seule preuve de l'impossibilité d'utiliser le travailleur dans des tâches équivalentes en relation avec le professionnalisme possédé.[49] Dans le précédent cadre législatif, l'obligation de repêchage semble être déconnectée des initiatives de formation possibles.

Maintenant, il est nécessaire de se demander si la situation proposée peut changer à la suite de récentes modifications législatives qui ont profondément modifié le texte de l'art. 2103 Cod. civ.[50]

---

44 Alessi, *supra* note 30, p. 144.

45 Il s'agit du licenciement pour l'inexacte exécution pour violation du devoir de diligence (parfois défini comme licenciement pour "*scarso rendimento*"), Ciucciovino, *supra* note 28, p. 168.

46 *"L'obligation de repêchage est un élément indissociable des raisons économiques et organisationnelles à la base de la résolution de l'emploi, dont la preuve doit être considérée comme entièrement payée par l'employeur, conformément aux dispositions de l'article 5 de la loi 604/1966"*. Cass., n. 5592/2016.

47 Magnani, *supra* note 14, p. 182.

48 Conformément à cette interprétation, Carabelli, *supra* note 13, p. 88, qui parle d' "*inconsistente dato normativo per fondare l'onere di repechâge dinamico*". *Contra* C. Cester, 'La diligenza del lavoratore', *in* C. Cester & M.G. Mattarolo (Eds.), *Diligenza e obbedienza del prestatore del lavoro. Art. 2104, in Commentario al codice civile diretto da P. Schlesinger*, Giuffrè, Milano, 2007, p. 159.

49 Cass. n. 14815/2005.

50 U. Gargiulo, 'Lo jus variandi nel "nuovo" art. 2013 cod.civ.', WP C.S.D.L.E 'Massimo D'Antona'.IT, n. 268, 2015, pp. 1-23, Retreived on 15 june 2017 from <http://csdle.lex.unict.it/Archive/WP/WP%20CSDLE%20M%20DANTONA/WP%20CSDLE%20M%20DANTONA.IT/20150930-084343_gargiulo_n268-2015itpdf.pdf>.

Dans l'optique d'un professionnalisme plus moderne et dynamique, la nouvelle législation[51] a élargi les limites du pouvoir de modifier les tâches du travailleur, en l'étendant à celles liées au même niveau de classification (et, à certaines conditions, au niveau inférieur). Le troisième paragraphe du même article prévoit que la modification des tâches doit être suivie, s'il est nécessaire, par l'obligation de formation.

Cependant cette obligation est expressément dépourvue d'une pénalité.[52]

La doctrine s'est interrogée sur le possible caractère contraignant de cette exigence et sur la capacité de cette nouvelle à introduire un devoir d'adaptation et de formation imposé à l'employeur. Cette obligation est le corollaire naturel du choix d'élargir l'éventail des tâches de chaque travailleur, développer le professionnalisme potentiel, ainsi que de donner une majeure stabilité à l'emploi.

Néanmoins, en raison de l'absence d'une spécifique sanction, une partie de la doctrine a nié cet effet,[53] même si elle reconnait que cela peut avoir de conséquences sur la non imputabilité de l'inexacte exécution.[54] Selon cette interprétation, le devoir de formation est complètement en dehors de l'objet du contrat, qui est reconnu dans les taches déduites dans le contrat. Nous devons attendre les évolutions jurisprudentielles pour comprendre le champ d'application de cette nouvelle disposition de loi et la possible extension du devoir du "repêchage".

Pour l'instant, nous pouvons constater que la première interprétation jurisprudentielle sur cette disposition (Trib. Milano, n. 3370 du 16 décembre 2016) a reconnu que le devoir de "repêchage", conformément au nouveau cadre législatif, est devenue plus rigide. En effet, la Cour affirme que maintenant, dans le cas d'un licenciement économique, le contrôle préalable sur la possibilité d'affecter le travailleur aux différentes tâches dans le domaine de l'organisation de l'entreprise, ne trouve plus la limite de "*l'équivalence*" mais doit être étendue aux tâches liées au même niveau (et catégorie) de classification. La majeure flexibilité dans l'organisation implique donc le parallèle alourdissement de la charge de la preuve en relation au repêchage (et donc une majeure difficulté à mettre en place un licenciement économique). Cette interprétation n'était pas évidente, et probablement pas conforme aux intentions originaires du législateur, même si la doctrine

51 Décret législatif n. 81/2015. Ceci est un des nombreux décrets qui font partie du projet de réforme du marché du travail nommé *Jobs Act*.

52 "*Il mancato assolvimento dell'obbligo formativo non determina comunque la nullità dell'atto di assegnazione delle nuove mansioni*".

53 Gargiulo, *supra* note 50, p. 10; une autre partie de la doctrine affirme que cette obligation est à la charge du travailleur, F. Liso, 'Brevi osservazioni sulla revisione della disciplina della mansioni contenuta nel decreto legislativo n. 81/2015 e su alcune recenti tendenze di politica legislativa in materia di rapporto di lavoro', *WP C.S.D.L.E 'Massimo D'Antona'.IT*, n. 257, 2015, p. 1 *et seq.* Retreived on 15 june 2017 from <http://csdle.-lex.unict.it/Archive/WP/WP%20CSDLE%20M%20DANTONA/WP%20CSDLE%20M%20DANTONA-IT/20150723-100120_lliso_n257-2015itpdf.pdf>.

54 "*Ne discende che nell'assolvimento di quell'attività non potrà essere richiesta la diligenza connessa alla natura della prestazione (art. 2104 cod. civ.) e dunque eventuale inadempimento non potrà essere sanzionato disciplinarmente*", Gargiulo, *supra* note 50, p. 10.

avait déjà envisagé ce scénario[55] car il a toujours été reconnu qu' "il y a une connexion entre la latitude du pouvoir de l'employeur de changer les taches assignés (*jus variandi*) et latitude du pouvoir du licenciement pour des raisons objectives".[56]

En tous cas, il faudra attendre les futures interprétations pour que cette jurisprudence puisse être confirmée. Pour l'instant il est important de souligner que cette jurisprudence ne clarifie pas la portée de l'obligation de formation de l'employeur dans le cas de l'attribution aux nouvelles tâches et donc tous les problèmes d'interprétation associés, notamment en ce qui concerne les contours du repêchage, restent profondément incertains.

Selon nous, dans le contexte de l'élargissement des tâches exigibles, la reconnaissance du devoir de formation lié aux nouvelles tâches serait plus cohérente avec une vision de l'emploi plus dynamique; elle serait également opérationnelle pour assurer, avec plus de certitude, la résistance de la relation contractuelle aux changements organisationnels. Il serait donc nécessaire le législateur intervenait pour mieux définir le contenu de l'obligation de formation mentionnée par le nouveau art. 2103 Cod. civ. italien.

De toute façon, la connexion entre la mise en valeur de la flexibilité "fonctionnelle" qui, cependant, doit valoriser les compétences professionnelles du travailleur et la parallèle mis en relief de la formation professionnelle dans l'organisation, demandent un renouvèlement des systèmes de classification du personnelle, qu'exaltent le rôle du travailleur, ses compétences, ses capacités.[57]

Or, le devoir d'adaptation et de formation au sein du contrat, peut être utile aussi par rapport aux obsolescences des connaissances professionnelles des travailleurs dans l'exécution de ses performances, face aux innovations techniques, changements organisationnels et productif et à l'évolution de l'emploi. L'obsolescence peut, à la fois, aboutir dans un licenciement pour raisons subjectives,[58] à la fois peut conduire à un licenciement pour des raisonnes économiques, si les capacités professionnelles possédées ne sont plus utiles dans la cadre organisationnel, notamment, pour ce qui concerne les innovations techno-

55 A. Tursi, *Nuova disciplina delle mansioni con effetti preterintenzionali*, Retrieved on 9 July 2016, from <www.ipsoa.it/documents/lavoro-e-previdenza/rapporto-di-lavoro/quotidiano/2016/07/09/nuova-disciplina-delle-mansioni-con-effetti-preterintenzionali>.

56 R. Del Punta, *Disciplina del licenziamento e modelli organizzativi delle imprese, in GDL*, 1998, p. 717

57 Beaucoup d'auteurs (soit juristes que économistes de l'organisation) ont détecté l'obsolescence de la plupart des systèmes de classification de la négociation collective (en Italie) parce qu'ils contaient des tâches et des qualifications statiques, qui ne correspondent pas à l'actuel réalité professionnelle. F. Carinci, 'Rivoluzione tecnologica e diritto del lavoro: Il rapporto individuale', *in* Aidlass (Ed.), *Rivoluzione tecnologica e rapporto di lavoro, Atti del VIII Congresso nazionale di diritto del lavoro, Napoli 12-14 aprile 1985*, Giuffrè, Milano, 1985, p. 32; F. Butera, *L'orologio e l'organismo, il cambiamento organizzativo nella grande impresa italiana*, Franco Angeli, Milano, 1992, p. 87 *et seq;* F. Guarriello, *Trasformazioni organizzative e contratto di lavoro*, Jovene, Napoli, 2000, p. 167 *et seq.*; Magnani, *supra* note 14, p. 175. Très souvent tels systèmes sont "indifférentes" aux politiques de formation dans l'entreprise.

58 Le manque survenant d'expertise technique au cours de la relation peut conduire à la non-exécution pour violation de la diligence (art. 2104 Cod. civ.).

logiques.[59] Dans ce dernier cas, l'ajustement professionnel conséquent au spécifique devoir d'adaptation et formation, mise en place tout au long de la durée du contrat (et non seulement à l'occasion du licenciement économique) va maintenir un état d'employabilité du salarié pendant la durée de la relation, réduisant ainsi à l'origine les situations qui peuvent mener à la rupture anticipé (du contrat).

Jusqu'ici, nous avons essayé de démontrer que l'introduction d'un devoir général de formation tout au long du contrat de travail peut être essentiel pour la protection de l'emploi et pour la persécution d'une relation contractuelle équilibrée, car il maintient inchangés les raisons de la relation synallagmatique;[60] c'est-à-dire, il est opérationnel à l'adaptation de la relation contractuelle à des possibles modifies qui peuvent survenir au cours de sa durée.

L'introduction d'un devoir général d'adaptation, sur la base d'autres importantes expériences étrangères (paragraphe successif), serait souhaitable dans notre contexte, car il devient un outil indispensable pour le maintien des compétences professionnelles par rapport à la dynamique d'organisation liés aux nouveaux modes de production. Mais aussi la formation est le véritable moteur de la croissance et compétitivité, ainsi que moyen de développement de la personnalité du travailleur.

Cependant, en l'absence d'une disposition expresse de la loi, une telle obligation devrait être appliquée par l'interprétation jurisprudentielle, qui, peut-être inadéquate pour résoudre les nombreuses incertitudes pratiques (Quel niveau de formation ? Dans quels moments précis ?) et d'équilibrer les différents intérêts en jeu. Comme Massimo Roccella indiquait en 2007, "*dans une économie de marché, l'équilibre entre la liberté d'initiative économique et de l'intérêt à l'emploi peut être tracée que par le législateur*".[61]

7.2.3 *Le Droit de Formation au Sein du Contrat de Travail dans une Perspective Comparée. L'Expérience Française.*

Ce qui se ressort d'une analyse comparée est le fait que les différents systèmes ont introduit un devoir d'adaptation, dans l'optique d'installer un lien entre le professionnalisme et la stabilité à l'emploi.

Le system français est exemplaire en la matière.[62]

En observant des nombreuses dispositions de loi, nous pouvons constater que ce système met le professionnalisme, considéré comme la synthèse de capacités et compétences

---

59 Cela se produit dans le cas des transformations technologiques qui excluent le professionnalisme lié aux techniques de production dépassées.

60 Selon des auteurs le devoir de formation est opérationnel pour la manutention de l'objet du contrat: la professionnalité, Guarriello, *supra* note 57, p. 222.

61 Roccella, *supra* note 15, p. 236. De la même opinion, Magnani, *supra* note 14, p. 183, tout en partageant l'idée du professionnalisme comme l'objet de l'échange.

62 M. Biagi, 'Recessione e mercato del lavoro: la formazione alla flessibilità', DRL, n. 1, 1993, p. 267.

professionnelles, au centre du contrat de travail.[63] Cela a impliqué que le législateur français et les partenaires sociaux ont développé, pendent les années, un très articulé système des règles relatives à la promotion de la formation continue dans la relation de travail, visant notamment à la manutention de la capacité du travailleur d'effectuer correctement sa performance et de sauvegarder l'employabilité du salarié face aux risques d'obsolescence des connaissances professionnelles issues des progrès scientifiques et technologiques appliquées dans la production.

Dans ce but, le système français contient une disposition législative, qui reconnait un vrai droit réel subjective d'adaptation professionnelle aux besoins organisationnels et productifs, prévisibles à moyenne et à long terme. De cette manière le salarié peut continuer à offrir utilement sa performance, même face à des changements profonds dans l'organisation.[64] L'actuelle formulation de l'obligation d'adaptation contenue à l'art. L.6321-1 du Code du travail, prévoit que "*L'employeur assure l'adaptation des salariés à leur poste de travail. Il veille au maintien de leur capacité à occuper un emploi, au regard notamment de l'évolution des emplois, des technologies et des organisations*". L'obligation d'adaptation est une obligation contractuelle, à la charge de l'employeur, strictement liée au pouvoir de direction de ce dernier.[65] C'est en effet l'employeur le maitre de ses choisies économiques et, par conséquent, c'est à lui de choisir comment faire évoluer l'emploi dans l'entreprise et être vigilant aux effets de ses décisions sur l'emploi de ses salariés.

Dès le début, l'adaptation, résultant de l'exécution de bonne foi du contrat de travail, s'impose lorsque "*il est porté atteinte à l'équilibre initial du contrat quand des nouvelle compétence sont requises par des technologies ou encore des modification de l'organisation du travail, impliquant la mise en œuvre d'un nouveau savoir-faire*".[66] Selon les premières interprétations jurisprudentielles, qui ont été transposée dans la première formulation de l'obligation dans le Code du travail, l'adaptation est visée au maintien du lien contractuel,

63 S. Brun, 'Capacità, valutazione e insufficienza professionale nell'ordinamento francese', *DRLI*, n. 1, 2016, pp. 51-52. La doctrine française a néanmoins évité de spécifier si cette conception peut être envisagée dans la structure du contrat de travail. Id.

64 Biagi, *supra* note 62, p. 262. C'est dans l'arrêt Expovit, (Cass. Soc., 25 février 1992, n. 89-41.634) que la Chambre Sociale de la Cour de Cassation a posé le principe selon lequel: "*l'employeur, tenu d'exécuter de bonne foi le contrat de travail, a le devoir d'assurer l'adaptation des salariés à l'évolution de leurs emplois*". L'obligation d'adaptation trouve sa source dans le contrat de travail. Dans l'espèce la Cour avait nié la légitimité du licenciement "technologique" d'une travailleuse qui aurait de l'être affectée à un outre emploi si adéquatement formée. Alessi, *supra* note 30, p. 184. M. Correia & N. Maggi-Germain, 'l'évolution de la formation professionnelle continue', *Dr. Soc.*, n. 9-10, 2001, pp. 830-840.
Par la suite, la loi n. 2000-37 du 19 janvier 2000, modifiée par la loi n. 2004-391 du 4 mai 2004 a mis en place une obligation générale d'adaptation, consolidée par l'article L.6321-1 du Code du travail.

65 N. Maggi-Germain, 'La capacité du salarié à occuper un emploi', Dr. Soc., n. 12, 2009, p. 1235.

66 N. Maggi-Germain, 'Inconstance et contingence de la définition juridique de la formation professionnelle', en '*Les évolutions de la formation professionnelle: regards croisés, Actes du séminaire de la DARES sur le droit de la formation professionnelle*' sous la direction de N. Maggi-Germain et A. Pélage, La documentation française, Paris, 2003, p. 159.

grâce à la mise au jour des connaissances professionnelles liées au *poste* du travail du salarié.

Ensuite, le devoir d'adoption a été étendu jusqu'à comprendre aussi le devoir de l'employeur de veiller au maintien de la capacité à occuper un emploi (deuxième alinéa art. L.6321-1). l'évolution jurisprudentielle française a joué un rôle fondamental dans la définition du contenu et des contours de l'obligation d'adaptation.[67] En particulière, la jurisprudence a reconnu l'existence de deux obligations séparées, qui impliquent un niveau de responsabilité de l'employeur différente. Selon le plus récentes interprétations,[68] le concept de 'capacité d'occuper un emploi', mentionné au deuxième alinéa du même article, ne se réfère pas à la mise au jour des compétences professionnelles en relation à l'évolution du poste du travail, quant plutôt aux compétences qui s'expliquent sur le marché du travail.[69] Précisément, l'employeur doit veiller à que les compétences de ses salariés soient toujours adaptées (et donc pas obsolètes) à l'évolution prévisible des métiers et des qualifications dans un certain secteur d'activité.[70] L'obligation d'adaptation est opérationnelle au maintien de la capacité à occuper un emploi et donc nécessaire pour rendre les travailleurs employables *dans le marché du travail*, dans l'optique de construire un système de formation professionnelle qui accompagne les salariés dans toute leur vie *active* et pas seulement dans le spécifique rapport du travail.[71] Autrement dit, l'obligation d'adaptation, dont l'obligation de formation est le naturel corollaire et le moyen principal pour la mettre en œuvre, était envisagée uniquement dans des situations qui pouvaient porter atteinte à la stabilité de la relation contractuelle. Pour ces raisons des auteurs avaient défini le devoir d'adaptation comme "le signal de la tendance perpétuelle de la relation contractuelle".[72] Ensuite, le législateur et l'interprétation jurisprudentielle ont élargi la portée de l'adaptation, en la lient à la personne et au développement de ses capacités dans un contexte plus large que celui de la seule relation contractuelle.

---

67 Pour approfondir *voy* E. Barthélémy, 'Le rôle de la jurisprudence dans le droit de la formation', *Dr. Soc.*, n. 12, 2014, pp. 1007-1112.

68 *Ex multis* Cass. soc., 23 oct. 2007, n. 06-40950.

69 N. Maggi-Germain, *supra* note 65 , p. 1234 *et seq.*

70 Les observatoires sur les métiers ou qualifications, crées par la négociation collective de branche et les CPNE (Commissionnes Nationales pour l'emploi) peuvent aider les entreprises dans l'évaluation des priorités de formation professionnelle. Id.

71 Sur la base de cette interprétation dans un arrêt du 5 juin 2013 (Cass. Soc., 5 juin 2013, n. 11-21.255) a précisé que même dans le cas où le salarié n'aurait pas vu son poste évoluer depuis son embauche, l'employeur ne pouvait s'exonérer de son obligation en soutenant que l'expérience acquise était suffisante. Dans des autres arrêtes (Cass. Soc., 18 juin 2014, n.13-14.916, Cass. Soc. 24 juin 2015 n. 13- 28784), la Cour de Cassation a précisé que l'obligation de veiller à la capacité à occuper un emploi est tout à fait à la charge de l'employeur et le fait que les salariés ne demandent pas à bénéficier de formation ne dispense pas l'employeur de son obligation de veiller à leur employabilité. Encore, une formation *adaptive* de courte durée, bien qu'elle soit suffisante pour satisfaire l'obligation au premier alinéa, ne sera pas adéquate pour satisfaire celle contenue au deuxième alinéa. Cass. soc., 23 oct. 2007, n. 06-40950.

72 G. Coutrier, *Plan sociaux et exigences de reclassement*, Dr. Soc., 1994, p. 435 *et seq.*

Il est nécessaire préciser quelles sont les limites de l'obligation en question. L'adaptation du salarié doit se mesurer par rapport aux capacités professionnelles et personnelles du travailleur.[73] Quant aux capacités professionnelles, celle-ci se réfèrent aux compétences entraînées dedans et dehors l'entreprise, régulièrement et périodiquement certifiées[74] et à ses qualifications possédées.[75] La limite "extérieure" du devoir d'adaptation est donc constituée par la qualification contenue dans le contrat[76] et le domaine du devoir n'inclue pas le développement des nouvelles compétences.

Le système français a envisagé une série de mesures spécifiques et procédures qui rendent effectif l'accès à la formation et favorisent la mise en œuvre de l'obligation d'adaptation. Le non-respect de ces procédures de gestion des compétences des salariés (même dans le cas où leur exécution n'est pas obligatoire), pourrait constituer un élément de preuve, à charge de l'employeur, dans le cas où il se verrait reprocher l'inexécution de son obligation d'adaptation.[77]

En premier lieu, tous les deux ans, un entretien professionnel (art. L. 6315-1), destiné à envisager les perspectives d'évolution professionnelle du salarié et les formations qui peuvent y contribuer, doit être organisé entre le salarié et l'employeur, quel que soit la nature de leur contrat de travail. De plus, tous les 6 ans, l'entretien professionnel doit faire un sommaire du parcours professionnel du salarié, permettant ainsi de vérifier que le travailleur a effectivement bénéficié des entretiens professionnels prévus au cours des 6 dernières années.[78] Malgré la discrétion à disposition de l'entreprise quant au choix des activités de formation, sa non-exécution, en plus d'affecter le contrôle global sur l'accom-

73 Brun, *supra* note 63, p. 56.

74 En France la loi de Modernisation sociale du 17 janvier 2002 a eu un fort impact sur le système formel de validation des compétences (VAE, validation des acquis de l'expérience). Grace à cette réforme il est accordée à toutes les personnes embouchées d'obtenir une certification professionnelle, avec la même valeur d'une certification obtenue grâce à l'apprentissage ou la formation initiale ou continue. En particulier, les travailleurs ayant au moins trois années d'expérience peuvent demander la reconnaissance des acquis afin d'obtenir une validation formelle, à condition que ces soient partie du Répertoire national Certification Professionnelle (RNCP). "Dans le cadre de l'amélioration de l'employabilité des individus le VAE accorde alors la possibilité à ceux qui ne disposent pas d'une qualification professionnelle, mais juste de l'expérience professionnelle, qui est synonyme de compétence, d'enrichir le curriculum personnel en conformité un system fortement orienté à la formation professionnelle continue". G.R. Simoncini, 'La certificazione delle competenze: definizione e inquadramento giuridico: una rassegna sulla letteratura di riferimento', *Adapt Working Paper*, n. 4, 2016, pp. 21-23.

75 Brun, *supra* note 63, p. 56.

76 Id., Cass. Soc., 17 mai 2006 n. 04-43022.

77 M. Gomez-Mustel, 'Les enjeux de l'obligation d'adaptation', Dr. Soc., n. 5, 2004, p. 509.

78 1. *"A l'occasion de son embauche, le salarié est informé qu'il bénéficie tous les deux ans d'un entretien professionnel avec son employeur consacré à ses perspectives d'évolution professionnelle, notamment en termes de qualifications et d'emploi. Cet entretien ne porte pas sur l'évaluation du travail du salarié. Cet entretien comporte également des informations relatives à la validation des acquis de l'expérience (...)".*

2. *"Tous les six ans, l'entretien professionnel mentionné au I du présent article fait un état des lieux récapitulatif du parcours professionnel du salarié. Cette durée s'apprécie par référence à l'ancienneté du salarié dans l'entreprise"* Retrieved on 9 July 2017 from <https://www.service-public.fr/professionnels-entreprises/vosdroits/F23466>.

plissement du devoir lié à l'art. L. 6321-1, aura des répercussions sur le montant de l'indemnité fixée pour cette violation.[79]

Ensuite, les actions de formation envisagées dans le cadre de l'adaptation sont prévues, le cas échéant, par le plan de formation mentionné par l'article L. 6312-1 du code du travail.[80] Bien que cet article prévoie que la rédaction d'un tel document soit une simple possibilité, la pratique courante montre que la plupart des entreprises[81] choisissent de le mettre en œuvre.[82]

La planification et l'exécution est gérée en consultation avec le comité d'entreprise.[83] Dans ce plan, en particulier, il sera prévu de mettre à jour les différentes obsolescences des compétences afin de combler l'écart entre l'expertise professionnelle présente et celle nécessaire à l'avenir.

De plus, l'art. L. 2242-13 prévoit, dans les entreprises et les groupes d'entreprises d'au moins trois cents salariés, ainsi que dans les entreprises et groupes d'entreprises de dimension communautaire, une obligation de négocier, tous les trois ans, la gestion des emplois et des parcours professionnels en mettant en place un dispositif de "gestion prévisionnelle des emplois et des compétences", lié aux mesures d'accompagnement susceptibles de lui être associées, en particulier en matière de formation, d'abondement du compte personnel de formation, de validation des acquis de l'expérience. Cette négociation représente la forme "embryonnaire" de l'accomplissement des devoirs de formation continue conformément au devoir d'adaptation.[84]

La participation aux activités prévues dans le cadre de l'adaptation représente l'exécution du contrat en vigueur. Le temps consacré à ces activités éducatives est considéré comme temps du travail régulièrement rémunéré. Le refus par le travailleur constitue un motif valide de licenciement.[85] Cette circonstance ne peut que confirmer le fait que la formation liée à l'adaptation, dans le système français, est un corollaire naturel du contrat de travail.

Maintenant, nous allons analyser quelles sont les conséquences de la non-exécution de l'obligation contractuelle d'adaptation et son incidence sur la légitimité du licenciement.

---

79 Brun, *supra* note 63, p. 58.

80 *[...] L'accès des salariés à des actions de formation professionnelle continue est assuré: 1° A l'initiative de l'employeur, le cas échéant, dans le cadre d'un plan de formation [...].*

81 N. Maggi Germain, *Le plan de formation de l'entreprise*. Dr. Soc. 2013, p. 949.

82 l'élaboration du plan est conçue pour aider le juge qui décide de l'exécution des obligations de formation. En outre, seulement les actions envisagées dans le plan sont couvertes, conformément à l'art. L. 6331-1, par le financement du système de formation continue. Brun, *supra* note 63, p. 58.

83 Biagi, *supra* note 62, p. 268.
En application de l'art. L. 2323-34, le Comité d'Entreprise au cours de l'année exprime dans deux réunions séparées, respectivement, un avis sur le niveau de la formation de l'année précédente et un avis sur le projet de plan pour l'année suivante.

84 Brun 2016, *supra* note 63, p. 58.

85 M. Gomez-Mustel, 2004, *supra* note 77, p. 505.

Encore un fois, nous pouvons constater que la jurisprudence a joué un rôle fondamental à cet égard.

Lorsque l'employeur veut mettre en œuvre des licenciements pour des raisonnes économiques, en application de l'art. L. 1233-4 du Code du travail, afin de garantir la légitimité du licenciement, il doit démontrer d'avoir essayé de mettre en place tous les efforts de formation et d'adaptation possibles, y compris par rapport à différentes tâches. De plus, l'employeur doit démontrer "*que le reclassement de l'intéressé ne peut être opéré dans l'entreprise ou dans les entreprises du groupe auquel l'entreprise appartient*" (art. L. 1233-3).[86]

Dans ce cas, la prévision d'un devoir de formation est opérationnelle premièrement afin de garantir la stabilité de l'emploi en garantissant au salarié la possibilité d'occuper un emploi différent de celui aboli en raison des décisions techniques et organisationnelles.

Dans le cadre de l'art. L. 1233-3, l'obligation de formation permet au salarié soit de s'adapter à l'évolution de son emploi, soit de s'adapter aux possibles différentes tâches car le reclassement inclut tous les postes pertinents de la même catégorie de classification ou même du niveau inférieur. Dans ce contexte, l'adaptation en fonction du licenciement, représente l'accomplissement du devoir d'adaptation de l'emploi dans le moment précise du licenciement, qui peut être opérationnel au reclassement, et qui n'a pas été inclus dans la programmation de la formation continue conformément aux dispositions du code du travail.[87]

Selon une jurisprudence constante le devoir d'adaptation et, par conséquent, le devoir de reclassement rencontre des limitations supplémentaires par rapport à ce qui est génériquement indiqué par l'article L. 1233. Le travailleur pourrait en fait continuer à être utilisé dans l'entreprise âpres une période de formation aux nouvelles taches lorsque les mêmes sont complémentaires et à court terme.[88]

En ce qui concerne la violation du devoir d'adaptation au sens de l'art. L. 6321-1 et suivant, au départ la jurisprudence ne reconnaissait pas l'existence d'une cause réelle et sérieuse de licenciement sans la preuve d'avoir accompli l'obligation d'adaptation préalable (au licenciement).[89] La formation dans l'adaptation était en effet conçue comme le moyen essentiel pour satisfaire l'obligation de reclassement.[90]

86 "*le licenciement pour motif économique d'un salarié ne peut intervenir que lorsque tous les efforts de formation et d'adaptation ont été réalisés et que le reclassement de l'intéressé ne peut être opéré dans l'entreprise ou dans les entreprises du groupe auquel l'entreprise appartient* [...] *Un licenciement économique ne repose pas sur une cause réelle et sérieuse dès lors que l'employeur ne justifie pas de l'impossibilité d'affecter la salariée au poste disponible moyennant une formation permettant son adaptation à ce nouvel emploi conformément à l'article L. 1233- 4 du Code du travail*" (Cass. Soc. 28 mai 2008).

87 Brun 2016, *supra* note 63, 2016, p. 58.

88 Cass. Soc. 3 avril 2001 n. 99-42188, Nancy 15 mai 1995 *in* Brun 2016, *supra* note 63, p. 60.

89 Cass. Soc. 6 juillet 1999 n. 96-45665, Cass. Soc. 7 juin 2000, 98-42267.

90 L'adaptation était donc un fort outil de protection et de gestion des licenciements économiques: "La gestion prévisionnelle de l'emploi devient non seulement un élément permanent de la gestion des ressources hu-

Néanmoins, la plus récente jurisprudence,[91] après une période de contrastes,[92] la doctrine et même les partenariaux sociaux ont nié un lien direct entre les devoirs de formation continue e la légitimité du licenciement. Il y a donc une dissociation entre le préjudice qui dépend de l'inexécution du contrat à cause de l'absence ou insuffisance de formation liée à l'adaptation et celui qui dérive de l'illégitimité du licenciement économique.[93]

Même dans le cadre du licenciement pour insuffisance professionnelle la jurisprudence est évolué d'une façon similaire. Dans un premier moment elle avait étendu au licenciement pour insuffisance professionnelle la portée de l'obligation d'adaptation.[94] En effet, elle reconnaissait la nullité du licenciement d'un salarié qui aurait pu être évité si l'employeur avait fourni les moyens d'adaptation, notamment en formation, suite à un changement imposé, lui permettant de maintenir les compétences professionnelles pour la correcte exécution.[95] Ensuite, afin de sanctionner l'inexécution de l'obligation d'adaptation, la jurisprudence s'est positionné sur le terrain de la réparation du dommage subi par le salarié, envisageant ainsi un préjudice distinct de celui résultant de la rupture du contrat.[96]

Cependant, la prévision d'un devoir général d'adaptation, qui est rendu effectif dans le contexte de l'entreprise par nombreux outils et dont l'inexécution conduit à la condamne de l'employeur à la réparation des dommages soufferts par le salarié, se révèle fondamental pour garantir la stabilité de la relation contractuelle car il vise au maintien de l'état d'employabilité du travailleur, en garantissant que ses connaissances professionnelles ne deviennent pas obsolètes. L'accomplissement constante de ce devoir, dans toutes ses articulations, dans une optique de prévision organisationnelle à long terme, réduit à l'origine les situations où l'obsolescence peut être une possible cause de la perte de l'emploi et se révèle complémentaire à la correcte exécution de l'obligation de reclassement prévue par l'art. 1233-3 Cod. Trav. En outre, il est fondamental pour garantir la constante mise au jour des connaissances des travailleurs, utilisables sur le marché de l'emploi, dans le but de construire un système d'apprentissage professionnel permanente.

maines, mais un instrument de protection des licenciements". P.H. Antonmattei, 'L'obligation de reclassement préalable pour motifs économiques: nouvelles dispositions', *Dr. Soc.*, n. 3, 2002, p. 275.

91 Cass. Soc. 5 mars 2014 n. 11-1442.

92 C. Neua-Leduc, 'Les sanctions de la GPEC', *Dr. Soc.*, 2007, p. 1081 *et seq.*, *in* Brun (Ed.), *supra* note 63, p. 61.

93 Cass. Soc. 5 mars 2014 n. 11-14426; Cass. Soc., 5 mars 2014 n. 12-27701

94 M. Gomez-Mustel, 2004, supra note 77, p. 503; Cass. soc. 12 mars 1999, n. 90-46.029

95 "*Ainsi, les erreurs commises sur une courte période après la mise en place d'un nouveau logiciel ne peuvent justifier un licenciement pour insuffisance professionnelle, l'employeur n'ayant pas satisfait à son obligation d'adaptation*". Id.

96 Cass. Soc., 23 oct. 2007, n. 06-40.950, Barthelemy, 2014, *supra* note 67, p. 1113.

7.2.4 *Le Droit à la Formation dans la Dimension Collective*

L'expérience comparative, et notamment l'expérience française, a mis en relief l'importance de l'affirmation d'une obligation de formation liée à l'évolution des processus de l'organisation, compte tenu des considérables répercussions sur la stabilité de l'emploi. Il est également apparu, cependant, qu'il est très important compléter cette obligation avec une série de mesures opérationnelles qui peuvent en garantir l'efficacité.

Néanmoins, en l'absence d'un complet système légal, un rôle stratégique peut être joué par l'autonomie collective. Les partenaires sociaux peuvent en effet avoir une place fondamentale dans la planification de tout politique en matière d'emploi et, d'abord, dans l'orientation des relations industrielles vers la modernisation stratégique du système de formation professionnelle.[97]

Dans cette optique, la négociation collective, même au niveau d'entreprise, peut traiter l'amélioration et la croissance des connaissances, en vue d'un professionnalisme dynamique dans le contrat de travail. La négociation collective est en fait un acteur capable de mieux interpréter les besoins de formation d'un secteur spécifique et d'évaluer rationnellement la compatibilité du développement des connaissances avec les besoins de l'organisation.[98]

Quant à la valorisation de la formation dans le contrat de travail l'autonomie collective peut agir de deux manières.[99] En premier lieu, le lien entre la formation et le contrat peut être récupéré grâce à un système dynamique collectif de classification des emplois,[100] qui valorise le professionnalisme en évolution à travers la formation continue.[101] Les dernières conventions collectives ont connu des formes de classification qui renforcent le "rôle" individuel des travailleurs au sein de l'organisation productive, en mettant l'accent sur les éléments de professionnalisme subjectif tels que le degré d'autonomie ou le degré de responsabilité.[102]

Un exemple très intéressant par rapport à une conception d'un professionnalisme plus dynamique, par ailleurs conformément à la logique des dernières modifications législatives (par. 2), est représenté par l'accord collectif signé le 26 novembre 2016 par FIM-CISL,

---

97 D. Garofalo, *Formazione e lavoro fra diritto e contratto. L'occupabilità*, Cacucci, Bari, 2004, p. 325.

98 De nombreuses conventions collectives rappellent le rôle important des organismes paritaires bilatéraux dans l'analyse des besoins de formation et dans la promotion et la gestion des initiatives de formation. Id., p. 333 *et seq*.

99 Ciucciovino 2013, *supra* note 28, p. 182 *et seq*.

100 Napoli 1997, *supra* note 26, p. 269.

101 Beaucoup d'auteurs ont souligné l' "insuffisance" des communs systèmes de classification par rapport aux modernes processus d'organisations, Guarriello 2000, *supra* note 57, p. 167; Magnani 2004, *supra* note 14, p. 175. Il faut mettre en œuvre des modèles "competenced oriented". F. Butera, 'Come cambia nel mondo l'organizzazione del lavoro ad alta qualificazione', *Rapporti Rassegna Monitor*, n. 1, 1997, p. 83 *et seq*.

102 Convention collective nationale (CCNL) "Poste italiane" 14 avril 2011, *CCNL du secteur du crédit*, 8 décembre 2007; Ciucciovino 2013, *supra* note 28, p. 182 *et seq*. Pour approfondir Magnani, 2004, *supra* note 14, pp. 165 -200.

FIOM-CGIL, UIM-UIL et Federmaccanica- Assistal pour le renouvellement de la convention collective des métallurgistes pour la période 2016-2019 (et approuvé par la majorité des travailleurs). L'accorde contiens la prévision de créer un comité bilatéral visant à réviser l'actuel système de classification des ressources humaines.[103] Le but est de favoriser, dans l'évaluation professionnelle des travailleurs, la polyvalence et la multifonctionnalité, ainsi que les compétences personnelles transversales (un système de classification ainsi conçu, peut sans aucun doute favoriser les chemins de mobilité d'entreprise grâce à des activités de formation).

Ensuite, la négociation collective peut agir en renforçant la formation continue au sein du contrat par l'introduction du droit individuel à la charge de l'employeur. Souvent, le droit est lié aux tâches à accomplir[104] ou par des "pactes de formation" qui engageant les deux parties contraignantes.[105]

Une expérience intéressante est contenue, encore une fois, dans le renouvellement de la convention collective des métallurgistes 2016-2019 qui établit un droit individuel de formation avec des spécifique prérogatives, garantissant un standard minimum de formation et un nombre suffisant d'heures au cours des trois années.[106] La consultation et co-planification de la formation est définie avec les représentants syndicaux d'entreprise. L'introduction d'un droit subjectif à la formation, dont chacun est titulaire, essaie de fournir à chaque travailleur une protection plus solide par rapport aux réglementations contractuelles sur les congés de formation en vertu de la loi 53/2000.[107]

L'introduction de ce droit (qui, en tout cas, ne peut pas être comparé au devoir d'adaptation dans le système français, car il manque de tout cette instrumentation juridique qui en garantisse l'application et la force contraignante) est due à la prise de conscience qu'il est nécessaire de faire plus d'investissement dans la formation, grâce à la pratique participative et la construction d'un réseau d'expertise, afin d'obtenir des usines modernes et intelligents.

En conclusion, les exemples ici proposés, montrent comme le droit à la formation peut être effectivement mis en œuvre même dehors du cadre légal. La formation dans la dimension collective du travail peut devenir une ressource stratégique pour assurer une protection de l'emploi, en empêchent les effets négatifs liés aux obsolescences des compétences.

---

103 À cet égard, l'accord appelle les entreprises à donner leur volonté d'expérimenter nouvelles formes de classification; les résultats seront analysés ensuite par le Comité.

104 *CCNL* secteur du crédit 8 décembre 2007.

105 *CCNL* secteur chimique 10 mai 2006.

106 Précisément 24 heures pour tous les travailleurs. En cas de violation, l'employeur doit fournir à l'employé 300 euros à chaque travailleur pour être investis dans activité de formation. Ciucciovino, *supra* note 28, p. 183.

107 Legge, n. 53 du 8 mars 2000 concernant les "Disposizioni per il sostegno della maternità e della paternità, per il diritto alla cura e alla formazione e per il coordinamento dei tempi delle città".

En outre, le contrat collectif (même au niveau d'entreprise) représente un siège particulièrement approprié pour identifier les besoins concrets de formation et ainsi construire des parcours de mobilité professionnelle en ligne avec les exigences de la production.

Selon nous, la formation dans le contrat de travail est fondamentale pour garantir l'équilibre entre les deux parties tout au long de la vie contractuelle. La dimension collective est surement une dimension appropriée pour l'affirmation et la mise en œuvre de ce principe. Dans l'attente de la construction d'un organique système légale de formation continue, il faut donc que les partenaires sociaux collaborent intensivement pour améliorer la relation essentielle entre le travail et la connaissance.

7.3 La Formation dans le Crédit à la Consommation

7.3.1 *Le Crédit à la Consommation et la Protection du Consommateur. Les Informations Précontractuelles et le Crédit Responsable*

Le modèle de capitalisme développé dans le siècle XX a conduit à une expansion très rapide du phénomène du crédit à la consommation. En fait, un nombre croissant de personnes font usage de crédit à la consommation pour l'achat de biens et services ou pour l'achat des biens immobiliers à usage résidentiel.[108] Aujourd'hui ce phénomène est devenu un élément clé du modèle de croissance économique des pays capitalistes avancés ("*credit societies*"), dans lequel la figure de "consommateur-payeur" a été remplacée par celle du "consommateur-débiteur".[109] L'accès au crédit est donc un élément très important dans la moderne société industrialisé car il rende possible l'usage des biens et services essentiels et donc, l'effective participation à la vie sociale,[110] en garantissant l'équilibre entre les variations des revenus et des dépenses (situations qui se vérifient souvent dans les modernes marchés du travail flexibles).[111]

Bien qu'il n'existe pas une définition unitaire dans la législation UE, nous pouvons génériquement définir le crédit à la consommation comme "l'octroi d'un crédit, en faveur d'une personne physique agissant dehors d'une activité commerciale ou profession-

108 Pour une analyse des causes du phénomène, *voy.* Nogler & Reifner, *supra* note 6, p. 14 *et seq.*

109 R. Montinaro, 'Il sovraindebitamento del consumatore: diligenza nell'accesso al credito ed obblighi del finanziatore', *Banca borsa e titoli di credito*, n. 6-1, 2015, p. 781.

110 L'accès au crédit est d'ailleurs vu comme un vrai moyen de participation à la vie sociale. U. Reifner & A. Schelhowe, 'Financial Education', *Journal of Social Science Education*, Vol. 9, n. 2, 2010, p. 32.

111 European Coalition for Responsible Credit (ECRC), *Principes sur le crédit responsable*, Retrieved on 16 June 2017 from <www.credito-responsabile.net/index.php?id=2534>. Les prêts peuvent en effet aider les gens qui ont besoins urgents de liquidité à cause des événements imprévus comme le chômage. Tout comme la situation de surendettement.

nelle"[112] qui est justifié par la dépense à la consommation ou pour différer les paiements.[113] La principale caractéristique du crédit à la consommation est celle d'être adressée au financement des dépenses courantes, sans aucun rapport avec des fins d'investissement et cela peut être réalisée, à niveau européen, par différents types contractuels (qui, généralement, ne sont pas toujours adaptés pour réguler des relations durables qui ont des implications sociales[114]).

L'endettement peut avoir des effets importants sur la vie des individus qui se sont obligés. La situation de constant déséquilibre entre les obligations assumées et le patrimoine, qui mène à la difficulté ou à l'impossibilité de faire face à ses propres dettes, est définie "surendettement".[115]

La doctrine parle de surendettement "actif" pour indiquer les situations de déséquilibre entre la dette et le patrimoine du consommateur, causé par une programmation erronée de la capacité de remboursement.[116] On parle de surendettement "passif" lorsque le déséquilibre ne résulte pas de choix disproportionnés mais, plutôt, il dépend d'événements imprévus et non désirées.[117]

Cette situation se produit souvent lorsque le consommateur ne comprend pas exactement les termes et conditions du contrat, qui peuvent être formulées de manière opaque et trompeuse. Les intermédiaires offrent de plus en plus sur le marché des produits qui sont délibérément inadéquates et opaques.[118] De plus, souvent, ils sont établis des importants coûts pour les situations d'incapacité de remboursement. Le crédit à la consomma-

---

112 Bennacchio, *supra* note 5, p. 431. L'art. 121 du "Testo Unico Bancario" (TUB) d. lgs 385-1993, définit le crédit à la consommation comme "*la forme de subvention, dans l'exercice ou d'une activité professionnelle ou commerciale, de crédit sous forme de paiement différé, financement et autres instituts financières similaires en faveur d'une personne agissant à des fins étrangères à une activité commerciale ou professionnelle* (trad.)".

113 Nogler & Reifner, *supra* note 6, p. 16.

114 Id.

115 Loi (italienne) 27-1-2012, n. 3, concernant les "*Disposizioni in materia di usura e di estorsione, nonché di composizione della crisi da sovra indebitamento*", qui définit le surendettement comme "*la situazione di perdurante squilibrio tra le obbligazioni assunte e il patrimonio prontamente liquidabile per farvi fronte, che determini una "rilevante difficoltà" od una "definitiva incapacità di adempiere."* Néanmoins, la doctrine a mis en évidence la difficulté à rejoindre une complète définition du phénomène: "*While there is converging evidence of the growth of the problem of over-indebtedness in the Member States, there is less agreement on what over-indebtedness actually is*". J. Niemi-Kiesiläinen & A.-S. Hensikson, *Legal Solutions to Debt Problems in Credit Societies. A Report to the Council of Europe*, Juridiska Institutionem (Ed.), Umeå Universitet, Umeå, no. 13/2006, p. 11 "*It might help to narrow the field of analysis and tentatively and roughly describe over-indebtedness as the pathological economic state a non-entrepreneurial individual is in, when permanently unable to regularly fulfil his obligations making use of his own income and properties alone. Let me immediately clarify that even the definition now included in the Italian Law 3/2012, […] does not solve the problem of setting precise borders to the notion of over-indebtedness*". D. Cerini, 'Consumer Over-Indebtedness and Interference with Credit Contracts: An Italian', *in* Ferretti F. (Ed.), *Comparative Perspective of Consumer Over-indebtedness – a View from the UK, Germany, Greece and Italy*, The Hague, Eleven International Publishing, 2016, pp. 347-348.

116 Montinaro, *supra* note 109, p. 781.

117 Comme, par exemple le handicap, la maladie, le licenciement, la séparation conjugale, la responsabilité non assurés, etc.

118 Reifner & Schelhowe, *supra* note 110, p. 34.

tion, comme il est conçu aujourd'hui, vise à promouvoir le profit des intermédiaires, plutôt que faciliter l'utilisation productive du crédit.[119]

C'est pour cette raison qu'il est absolument nécessaire et urgent de parvenir à une législation européenne adéquate dans cette discipline qui est plus protectrice pour les consommateurs. Le problème de surendettement postule la mise en œuvre de mesures spécifiques de protection du consommateur.[120] La nécessité primaire est celle de mettre le débiteur à l'abri du risque d'un endettement disproportionné par rapport aux conditions économiques qui peut le conduire à la pauvreté et à l'exclusion social, grâce à une majeure conscience sur les choix économiques. Le surendettement est d'ailleurs une de majeures causes de pauvreté en Europe.

Le principal instrument de protection et prévention[121] contre le risque de surendettement proposé par le législateur européen, conformément aux dispositions relatives à la protection des consommateurs, est l'obligation de transmettre tout information qui peuvent affecter le choix d'accéder au crédit.

Le devoir d''information a toujours été au centre des mesures de protection du consommateur.[122]

Cette forme de protection est basée sur l'idée de l'asymétrie d'information parmi les deux parties du contrat, où le consommateur est vu comme un sujet inexpert pour prendre sciemment sa décision.

L'information précontractuelle a la fonction de structurer le marché unique comme un lieu de concurrence parfaite, garantissant le libre choix des consommateurs.[123]

Dans ce contexte, l'information à la charge du créancier doit être transparente, claire et complète, afin de faciliter la compréhension des caractéristiques, des risques et des coûts des produits financiers offerts et de comparer facilement les offres.[124]

---

119 ECRC, *supra* note 111.

120 Dir. 2008/48/CE du 23 avril 2008 concernant les contrats de crédit aux consommateurs et la Dir. 2014/17/UE du 4 février 2014 sur les contrats de crédit aux consommateurs relatifs aux biens immobiliers à usage résidentiel.

121 Il faut dire que les États Membres, sous pression dès la législation européenne on introduit des spécifiques procédure pour le traitement de surendettement. En Italie ce discipline est contenue dans la loi n. 3-2012. G. Falcone, 'Il trattamento normativo del sovraindebitamento del consumatore', *Giurisprudenza commerciale*, Vol. 42, 2015, p. 132.
Pour une analyse comparative des modèles proposés et des solutions *ex post* pour recomposer la crise du surendettement, Cerini, *supra* note 115, p. 348 *et seq.*

122 V. Roppo, 'L'informazione precontrattuale: spunti di diritto italiano e prospettive di diritto europeo', *Riv. dir. priv.*, 2004, p. 747 *et seq.*; Art. 169 TFUE; art 4. Code de la consommation italien.

123 A. Jannarelli, 'La disciplina dell'atto e dell'attività: i contratti tra imprese e tra imprese e consumatori', *in* N. Lipari (Ed.), *Trattato di diritto privato europeo: L'attività e il contractto*, Vol. III, Padova, CEDAM, 2003, p. 3 *et seq.*; Montinaro, *supra* note 109, pp. 789-790.

124 Arts. 2 et 5 Code de la consommation italien, D. lgs 206-2005.

Quant au crédit à la consommation, la législation a prévu des obligations d'information précontractuelles concertantes l'évaluation de la conformité du crédit par rapport à la personnelle situation financière du consommateur.[125]

Cependant, malgré la méticuleuse discipline européenne en matière de devoirs d'information, des nombreuses études empiriques, notamment dans la branche de la psychologie cognitive, ont démontré l'inefficacité de ces instruments quant à leur capacité de prévenir le surendettement.[126] Les informations contractuelles, en fait, visent à restaurer le synallagme contractuel dans la conviction que le consommateur possède une parfaite rationalité. Les études sur le comportement des consommateurs, cependant, ont démenti cette prémisse. Très souvent, en effet, le comportement des consommateurs n'est pas inspiré par des critères de rationalité et démontre un manque d'attention sur le calcul du risque.[127]

L'irrationalité de choix est, en outre, exacerbée lorsque le sujet est dans le besoin et doit faire face aux ses nécessités urgentes.[128] De plus, le choix rationnel peut également être affecté par le comportement des intermédiaires financiers qui, grâce à une rédaction fallacieuse et manipulatrice du contact, peut mener le consommateur en erreur sur les conditions de l'accord, seulement en apparence favorables.[129]

Le modèle de protection contractuel choisi pour les contrats en matière de consommation – où le consommateur n'est pas conçu comme un membre d'une catégorie socio-économique caractérisée par l'élément de la faiblesse contractuel[130] et donc exigeant une discipline spécifique, mais comme un contraignante dont il faut combler l'asymétrie d'information – a montré ses limites par rapport au véritable rééquilibre contractuel.

125 Dir. 2008/48/CE. En Italie, en particulier, l'information précontractuelle doit être contenu dans une forme normalisée, dénommé "l'information européenne relative crédit à la consommation "conformément aux instructions l'Autorité de surveillance" conformément au art. 124.2 TUB." La législation italienne prévoit que le prêteur est tenu d'informer le consommateur par écrit sur les principales caractéristiques du produit de crédit; il doit lui transmettre gratuitement, sur demande, une copie du projet de convention de crédit; l'information doit ensuite être mise à la disposition des consommateurs dans le bon moment, avant de signer, ainsi il y aura une séparation temporelle entre la transmission de la même et la conclusion de l'accord. art. 124 TUB.

126 R. Caterina, 'Psicologia della decisione e tutela del consumatore', *Analisi giuridica dell'economia*, n.1, 2012, p. 67 *et seq.;* F.P. Patti, 'L'educazione finanziaria e la direttiva 2014/17/UE (sui contratti di credito ai consumatori relativi a beni immobili residenziali)', in *Contratto Impresa*, n. 6, 2015, p. 1431.

127 F. Ferretti & C. Livada, 'The Over-Indebtedness of European Consumers under EU Policy and Law', *in* Ferretti (Ed.), *supra* note 115, p. 14: "*[...] behavioural economics has demonstrated that borrowers are not rational maximisers of their resources and that they may well take wrong borrowing decisions or have decisional biases even if they are provided with adequate information*".

128 F. Pérez Carrillo & F. Gallardo-Olmedo, 'The EU Consumer Credit Directive 2008 in the light of the EuSoCo Principles', *in* Nogler & Reifner (Eds.), *supra* note 1, pp. 479-480.

129 Patti, *supra* note 126, p. 1430.

130 G. Benedetti, 'Tutela del consumatore e autonomia contrattuale', in G. Vettori (Ed.), *Materiali e commenti sul nuovo diritto dei contratti*, Padova: CEDAM, 1999, p. 803.

Il est nécessaire d'introduire des techniques de protection supplémentaires, destinées à mieux garantir la liberté effective de choix du consommateur et de le protéger contre le risque de surendettement.

À ce but, il a été nécessaire de dépasser les limites du point de vue traditionnel de la réglementation des obligations d'information dans le domaine du droit européen des contrats où trop souvent l'accomplissement des devoirs d'information se traduit par la simple transmission de données.

À cette fin, la Directive 2008/48/CE, concernant le crédit à la consommation, en application du principe du "*responsible lending*", a introduit l'obligation d'évaluer la solvabilité du consommateur, conjointement à celle de lui fournir une assistance personnalisée en ce qui concerne sa situation personnelle et financière. Ce principe est expressément contenu dans l'art. 5 de la même Directive, intitulé "*Informations précontractuelles*". En vertu de cette disposition, le prêteur et, le cas échéant, l'intermédiaire de crédit, "*avant que le consommateur ne soit lié par un contrat ou une offre de crédit,* (doit fournir) *les informations nécessaires à la comparaison des différentes offres pour prendre une décision en connaissance de cause sur la conclusion d'un contrat de crédit*", concertantes les caractéristiques essentielles du crédit, ainsi que les conséquences spécifiques que cela peut avoir sur le consommateur. En particulier, le paragraphe 6 impose aux États Membres de prendre toutes les mesures appropriées pour que le consommateur puisse recevoir toute explication pertinente pour lui permettre de déterminer si le contrat proposé est vraiment conforme à ses besoins et à sa situation financière concrète (illustrant également le contenu des informations précontractuelles fournies en vertu du même article). Notamment, les prêteurs doivent illustrer clairement les conséquences d'un défaut de paiement. Le principe du crédit responsable, établi par cette disposition, implique en outre que "les modalités d'octroi et l'étendue de cette assistance", aussi bien que "l'individuation des sujets que la fournissent", doivent être adaptés par les États Membre selon le contexte particulier dans lequel le contrat est proposé, selon la situation de la personne à qui est proposé et selon le type spécifique du contrat.

Par la suite, la Directive mentionnée, à son art. 8, prévoit que "avant de conclure le contrat de crédit, le prêteur évalue la solvabilité du consommateur, à partir d'un nombre suffisant d'informations, fournies, le cas échéant, par ce dernier et, si nécessaire, en consultant la base de données appropriée".

Le consommateur doit donner des informations adéquates concertantes les éléments qui peuvent influer sur sa capacité à rembourser; informations que le prêteur utilisera pour déterminer si la requête est disproportionnée par rapport au patrimoine.[131] Les intermédiaires ne doivent pas accorder des prêts "irresponsables" c'est-à-dire sans avoir préalablement évalué la solvabilité du débiteur.[132]

131 Art. 124 TUB (*Testo unico bancario*).

132 Considérant n. 26.

Même la Directive 2014/ 17/UE sur les contrats de crédit aux consommateurs relatifs aux biens immobiliers à usage résidentiel, prévoit également l'évaluation de la solvabilité des obligations du débiteur (art. 18).

Un regard plus attentif met en évidence comme le contenu réel du principe du prêt responsable, décrit dans le paragraphe 6 de l'art 5, consiste à rendre le même consommateur protagoniste de ses choix de consommation, grâce à une aide personnalisée et pointée. Avec cela, en fait, le législateur européen veut donner au débiteur la possibilité de prendre l'option la plus appropriée à la lumière de sa situation économique; le principe mentionné, donc ne vise pas à exclure *a priori* la possibilité d'accès au crédit, mais au contraire de l'étendre aux ce qui en ont besoin, d'une façon responsable et consciente. La réflexion sous-jacente est celle de concevoir le crédit comme une ressource qui augmente le bien-être des citoyens est qui essentielle pour la réalisation des besoins fondamentaux des consommateurs et la pleine participation sociale (en leur donnant un plus grand pouvoir d'achat, par rapport à celui à leur disposition grâce à ses revenus).[133]

Grâce à l'accès au crédit, donc, il est possible obtenir l'usage des biens et des services, d'investir dans son propre capital de connaissances, moyennant la formation permanente, et avoir accès à un logement. Sans surprise, des études sociologiques ont démontré que beaucoup de sujets appartenant aux groups plus "vulnérable" de la société (comme les travailleurs précaires, à temps partiels etc.) sont souvent exclus de l'accès au crédit;[134] et cela (comme la situation de surendettement) peut conduire à l'exclusion social de ces sujets-là.

Per ces raisons il est important favoriser l'accès au crédit, sans discrimination aucune, et d'une façon responsable, de sorte qu'il en soit encouragé son "usage productif".[135] Les outils liés à l'information précontractuelle, bien qu'ils soient utiles, ne semblent pas en mesure de compenser vraiment la faible rationalité des consommateurs.

7.3.2 *Le Rôle de l'Éducation Financière dans le Domaine des Contrats à la Consommation. Vers un Soutien Concret à la Participation Active et Critique du Consommateur*

Comme nous avons déjà expliqué, les consommateurs prennent souvent de mauvaises décisions car qu'ils ne sont pas vraiment conscients des coûts et des avantages résultant d'une précise choix.

Le principe du crédit responsable, visant à l'usage productif du même crédit, exige une forme de soutien vers le consommateur plus solide par rapport au simple octroi des

133 ECRC, *supra* note 111.

134 U. Reifner, 'EU General Report', and J. Ford & A. Jones, 'UK Report', tous les deux *in* U. Reifner (Ed.), *Financial Literacy in Europe*, Baden-Baden: Nomos, 2006, p. 19 *et seq.*, et pp. 42-54.

135 ECRC, *supra* note 111.

informations précontractuelles, qui sont standardisé et générales. Le mentionné paragraphe 6 de l'art. 5 adresse le législateur européen justement vers une dimension de l'information plus personnalisé, plus attentive à la situation réelle du contraignante qui se trouve dans la position de faiblesse.

L'espoir est d'aller toujours plus vers à un service d'assistance objective et personnalisé, dans lequel de sujets indépendants fournissent aux consommateurs toutes les instructions nécessaires, en particulier en ce qui concerne l'impact des paiements futurs sur l'avenir de la liquidité familière et sur le futur pouvoir d'achat.[136] Le service de conseil représente donc un outil clé pour la croissance cognitive du consommateur car il réponde à la nécessité de mettre au centre de service l'intérêt du consommateur en relation avec ses besoins spécifiques. Dans cela, le fournisseur du conseil "ajuste" les informations génériques au cas concret, accordant une attention particulière à la situation économique du possible bénéficiaire du prêt mais aussi à sa situation personnelle et psychologique (notamment le possible état de vulnérabilité).

Pour que le crédit soit vraiment responsable, et donc soutenir vraiment le consommateur dans ses choix, il est nécessaire que les services des conseil financiers soient indépendants et impartiaux.[137] Une solution appropriée à ce but peut être envisagée par les conseils offerts par les associations de consommateurs.[138]

Afin de rendre le conseil un "outil" véritablement objectif (notamment dans le cas où il est fourni par le mêmes intermédiaires ou préteurs) il faut que la collectivité soit constamment vigilante quant à son contenu e sa mise en œuvre. Le conseil sur l'endettement doit donc devenir une "tâche publique"[139] (quel que soit le sujet impliqué).

Pour atteindre des résultats appréciables dans le processus éducatif personnalisé du consommateur il est nécessaire que ce sujet soit suffisamment alphabétisé quant aux concepts économiques relevant.

Ce qui est obtenu grâce à la mise en œuvre des programmes d' "éducation financière".

Ce concept est souvent mentionné par les institutions européennes et les différentes organisations internationales qui, de plus en plus, encouragé les États membres à mettre en place des mesures appropriées pour améliorer les connaissances des consommateurs dans l'évaluation des risques et, plus en général, dans la matière financière.[140]

---

136 Id.

137 C. Biasior, Directeur du Centro Ricerca e Tutela dei Consumatori e Degli Utenti (CRTCU), entretien du 13/07/2016, Trento. Il est également important de souligner que le fournisseur du conseil (soit qu'il soit un sujet tiers, soit qu'il soit le même prêteur) doit être sujet à responsabilité dans le cas des informations incomplètes ou fausses.

138 C. Biasior, *Consumer Over-Indebtedness in Italy: The Role of Consumer Organisations to Prevent and Repair Over-Indebtedness, in* Ferretti (Ed.), *supra* note 115, pp. 333-347.

139 ECRC, *supra* note 111.

140 Commission européenne, *Huit principes de base pour la réalisation de programmes d'éducation financière de haute qualité*, COM(2007) 808 final; OCDE, *Improving Financial Literacy: Analysis of Issues and Policies*, The Hague, OECD Publishing, 2005: Règlement n. 254/2014 du Parlement Européen et du Conseil. Opinion 14/7/2011 du Comité économique et Social Européen, *Financial Education and Responsible Consumption*,

Dans ce contexte, l'éducation est conçue comme un outil fondamentale pour l'acquisition, par les consommateurs, de la base de connaissances appropriées pour adresser leurs processus de cognition et d'évaluation.[141] Le terme éducation indique donc un véritable processus de formation du consommateur afin d'apprendre les concepts de base de la matière financière.

La base des dispositions pour la promotion de l'éducation financière est représentée par l'art. 169 du TFUE, selon lequel "1. Afin de promouvoir les intérêts des consommateurs et d'assurer un niveau élevé de protection des consommateurs, l'Union contribue à la protection de la santé, de la sécurité et des intérêts économiques des consommateurs ainsi qu'à la promotion de leur droit à l'information, à l'éducation et à s'organiser afin de préserver leurs intérêts."

Une définition de ce concept est fournie par l'OECD selon laquelle l'éducation financière est: "le processus par lequel les consommateurs / investisseurs améliorent leur compréhension des produits et des concepts financiers et, grâce à un support objectif, développent les compétences et la confiance nécessaires pour devenir plus conscients des risques et des opportunités financières, pour faire des choix éclairés et comprendre la mise en œuvre d'autres mesures efficaces pour améliorer leur bien-être financier".[142]

Même le code de la consommation italien, à l'art. 4, encourage l'adoption des mesures d'éducation financière, en la définissant comme un droit fondamental du consommateur.

l'éducation financière a donc le but d'augmenter le niveau d'efficacité de la législation sur la protection des consommateurs (et bien, rendre effectif le principe du crédit responsable).

l'éducation est d'ailleurs considérée comme un de majeur objectif des politiques publiques car elle fournit les base cognitives, d'aptitude et des compétences pour, après, être plus conscientes dans le successives phases du conseil, et même dans la lecture des information précontractuelles.[143]

l'éducation et l'alphabétisation du consommateur est vue comme un correctif à la faiblesse de la réglementation des devoirs d'information à la charge du créancier et un réel outil de rééquilibrage de l'asymétrie de la relation contractuelle.[144]

ECO-297; Opinion 29/4/2014 du Comité économique et Social Européen, *Consumer Protection and Appropriate Treatment of Over-Indebtedness to Prevent Social Exclusion*, INT/726.

141 Patti, *supra* note 126, p. 1427.

142 OCDE 2005, *supra* note 140, p. 26. La définition donnée par l'OECD a été récemment reprise par le législateur italien qui, à l'Art. 24 *bis* de la loi 15/2017 a, pour la première fois en Italie, prévoit une stratégie pour le développement de l'éducation financière (*voy. infra* note 167).

143 U. Reifner, 'Financial Education', *in* Reifner (Ed.), *supra* note 134, p. 13.

144 "*Directive 2008/48/EC on credit agreements for consumers instructs the Member States to require lenders or intermediaries to provide the consumer with clear information in their advertising, supplying them with bases for comparison, and also sets out the principal financial information that should be included in agreements. This directive, which is based on consumer information, is not sufficient to prevent over-indebtedness. Effective legislation in this area must include measures to educate professionals and consumers*". Opinion 29-4-

Ainsi, dans la perspective européenne, la mise en place des programmes exhaustives d'éducation financière accessible réduit les risques d'exclusion financière et est opérationnelle pour prévenir le surendettement.

L'idée de base est que la protection doit être déplacée de la réglementation des devoirs contractuels à la charge du créancier, vers l' "autoprotection" de la partie fable, à travers des programmes d'éducation et alphabétisation financière pour lui faire prendre conscience de ses choix de consommation. L'individu éduqué est ainsi muni d'une meilleure capacité de sélection.

Néanmoins, ainsi conçue, l'efficacité de l'éducation financière quant à son rôle de protection du contraignait faible contre le risques provenant des services financiers, peut de toute façon rencontrer quelques limites.

Afin d'arriver à une conception de l'éducation financière qui vise à un l'amélioration par rapport à la pratique actuelle et même plus réaliste, comme des Auteurs suggèrent,[145] nous pouvons mettre en œuvre une approche différent, à partir de l'identification du contenu réel de l'éducation financière. Il faut d'abord observer que ce concept diffère du concept de "l'éducation économique". Le deuxième indique l'apprentissage des concepts base de l'économie (soit dans la dimension *macro*, soit dans la dimension *micro*) mais qui sont loin des exigences quotidiennes des consommateurs.[146] l'éducation financière implique un processus d'apprentissage qui concerne aussi la capacité d'utilisation des concepts (délimités dans le domaine de la finance), d'une façon opérationnelle à la satisfaction des besoins essentiels et à l'usage du crédit. Dans ce sens, donc, l'éducation financière se place dans une position complémentarité par rapport à l'éducation économique.[147] Donc, l'éducation financière doit s'occuper soit de donner les connaissances financières objectives (en relation aux besoin essentiaux de consommateurs),[148] soit d'assurer les compétences financières subjectives dans la prise de décision et dans l'évaluation des risques.[149] En particulier les compétences nécessaires pour le consommateur sont:

2014 du Comité Économique et Social Européen, *Consumer Protection and Appropriate Treatment of Over-Indebtedness to Prevent Social Exclusion*, INT/726 (footnote omitted); M.T. Paracampo, 'Educazione finanziaria e protezione dei risparmiatori: miti e realtà', *Analisi Giuridica dell'Economia*, n 2, 2010, p. 535 *et seq.*

145 Reifner & Schelhowe, *supra* note 110, p. 32 *et seq.*

146 Id., p. 33.

147 Beaucoup de programmes d'éducation financière mises en place dans les États Unités ou en Allemagne envisagent comme objectifs primaires ceux de fournir une "capacité financière". Reifner & Schelhowe, *supra* note 110, p. 32.

148 "*Develop numeracy, literacy and information technology skills in the context of personal finance;-Develop an understanding of the nature and use of money in its various form, including credit and debt, savings and investment*". *in* Reifner (Ed.), *supra* note 134, p. 13.

149 "*Learn how to access, interpret, question and evaluate financial information and advice; - learn about the consequences of financial decisions and about consumer rights and responsibilities and – learn how to weigh up risks and benefits in order to choose appropriate solutions to particular financial need.*" Id.
Par exemple, *voy.* la définition de l'éducation financière donné par OCDE (OECD, *Improving Financial Literacy: Analysis of Issues and Policies*, 2005, p. 26). Aussi, la définition fournie par SEDI (Social Enterprise

spécifiquement financières (capacité à utiliser les concepts de base comme l'argent, le temps et le risque); humaines: être en mesure d'évaluer un produit par rapport à sa propre situation personnelle; sociales: capacité d'interagir, de poser des questions et faire des suggestions.[150]

Mais il y a plus. Selon une approche diffèrent, afin d'augmenter la protection du consommateur il est nécessaire[151] utiliser l'éducation pour adapter le marché financier aux besoins du des consommateurs, en construisant des compétences "participés" du consommateur. Nous pouvons concevoir l'éducation financière aussi comme un "processus mutuel", dans lequel les deux parties de la relation contractuel sont engagées. Les consommateurs, grâce à l'éducation financière, peuvent aboutir à "améliorer" le marché des services financiers, et dans ce cas, celui du crédit à la consommation. Cela implique que les consommateurs participent activement à un "processus collectif" pour rendre plus adaptés les services de crédit à leurs besoins. Moyennant la capacité et l'habilité financière, les consommateurs doivent participer, d'une façon critique au processus de création de règles concernent les sévices du crédit, pour ensuite les adapter à leurs besoins et proposer des alternatives. Il n'est pas suffisant la seule entente; il faut donner aux consommateurs la capacité d'exercer des pressions sur les intermédiaires (notamment grâce aux processus de sélection et de plainte).[152]

En parallèle, dans ce processus d'apprentissage dialogique, il devrait être également impliqué le prêteur qui sera amené à comprendre les besoins des consommateurs et moduler l'offre services sur la base des besoins et des considérations de la consommation.[153] Seulement de cette façon, il sera garanti plein effet aux programmes en question. Lorsque que les consommateurs restent dehors du processus de création de l'offre de services au crédit, nous envisageons le risque de réduire l'éducation financière à une connaissance simple et passive des produits et des services qui sont beaucoup plus proche aux exigences du profit du prêteur. Par conséquent, tant que les programmes d'éducation financière ne prennent pas suffisamment en compte les sollicites des consommateurs et

---

Development Innovations*)* 2004, *in* Reifner & Schelhowe, *supra* note 110, p. 33; *Financial Capability and Poverty* <www.mta.ca/library/egovdocs/ca1pv82004f31.pdf>.

150 Reifner & Schelhowe, *supra* note 110, p. 40.

151 Id., p. 33 *et seq.*

152 Reifner, *supra* note 134, p. 17: "*The objective of financial education is the appropriate use of money: consumers need to be capable of managing money flows rationally during the course of their lifetime. … Concepts of financial education should therefore aim at the productive use of financial services, and, at the same time, improve the ability of consumers to exert pressure on providers of financial services. Financial education is thus an essential part of consumer protection*". Pour cette raison une différente et plus critique définition d'éducation financière a été proposée: "*Financial education provides such knowledge, understanding and social competence for a critical evaluation of financial services (…) based on credit opportunities and respond adequately to human needs to allocate own income during lifetime there and then where outside their labour relations sustainable consumption is required*".

153 Reifner & Schelhowe, *supra* note 110, p. 34.

ne font pas participer (activement) toutes les parties du contrat, leur fonction de protection du consommateur ne sera pas efficace.

Concrètement, donc, il faut faire beaucoup d'attention aux programmes d'éducation. Nous souhaitons donc la mise au jour du contenu de ceux-ci afin qu'ils soient véritablement éducatifs[154] même si les résultats obtenus jusqu'ici ne sont pas vraiment satisfaisantes, spécialement dans l'éducation des consommateurs plus vulnérables.[155]

À ce propos, les sources européennes en matière et les avertissements provenant des institutions internationales fournissent des indications très génériques quant aux programmes éducatifs visant à promouvoir et à encourager une amélioration du niveau culturel des consommateurs sur les questions financières.[156] Les États membres disposent donc d'un large pouvoir d'appréciation quant à la mise en œuvre de ces mesures, notamment en ce qui concerne les sujets chargés de sa réalisation concrète.

En Europe, les programmes d'éducation sont, en général, organisés et promus par les associations non lucratives (par exemple associations des consommateurs, les autorités de contrôle, et d'autres institutions de la société civile),[157] par les mêmes préteurs des services financiers, par les écoles et par les media.[158]

En Allemagne le "Sparkassen-Finanzgruppe (SBFIC)" a mis en œuvre un programme d'éducation financière locale et régionale à travers l'élaboration des études et des analyses, la préparation de matériel pédagogique pour l'enseignement de l'éducation financière, l'organisation des forums stratégiques d'organisation pour débattre sur l'avenir de l'éducation financière.[159]

---

154 Les programmes d'éducation réalisés jusqu'à présent, dans de nombreux cas, sont limités à l'explication des produits et services prédéterminées.

155 Pour un aperçu de l'état des différents programmes en Europe, *voy.* Reifner (Ed.), *supra* note 134. Ce report va démontrer qu'en Europe il y a (d'où moins à l'époque de ce report) un manque d'attention vers l'éducation au consommateur des services financiers et en général ils ne sont pas bien éduqués dans ce domaine.

156 Comité Économique et Social Européen "l'éducation financière et de la consommation responsable des produits financiers", 2013. Entre les initiatives institutionnelles Européennes plus importantes il y a la section de formation d'approfondissement et d'analyse financière du projet-DOLCETA (développement d'outils en ligne pour l'éducation des consommateurs adultes) financée par la Commission Européenne et la mise en place en Octobre 2008, par le Commission, le groupe d'experts sur l' analysé les différentes stratégies de développement des programmes d'éducation financière, encourageant la coopération entre les secteurs public et Privé afin de promouvoir une meilleure réalisation. Aujourd'hui, le programme DOLCETA a produit le site web <www.consumerclassroom.eu/it/> qui est d'ailleurs une vaste bibliothèque des ressources de l'éducation de consommateurs de l'UE, il offre des outils interactifs et la collaboration pour aider à préparer et partager les leçons avec les étudiants et les enseignants.

157 Paracampo, *supra* note 144, p. 536 *et seq.*

158 Reifner, *supra* note 134, p. 25.

159 Aussi la Banque d'Italie a été très active dans la promotion de l'éducation financière dans le pays. Les stratégies employées par la Banque de l'Italie consiste à rendre les citoyens plus conscients des services financiers à travers une section de son site web, et, plus important encore, la promotion de programmes d'éducation financière dans les écoles.

G. Comparato, 'The Italian Law Against Over-Indebtedness: Fresh Start, Debt Advice and Financial Education', *in* Ferretti (Ed.), *supra* note 115, p. 389.

En Italie, "PattiChiari Consortium", consortium de banques italiennes, a organisé, dans une cinquantaine de villes, des programmes pour les adultes, en collaboration avec les associations de consommateurs visant à améliorer la compréhension des produits financières et faciliter l'adoption de décisions informés et responsables.

En Italie la "Fondazione per l'Educazione Finanziaria e il Risparmio" créé à l'initiative de l'Association Bancaire Italienne (ABI) qui, à travers le site internet www.feduf.it, développe et diffuse la connaissance financière et économique.[160]

En général, nous observons que les programmes éducatifs mis en place jusqu'à aujourd'hui dans les différentes réalités en Europe impliquent les associations des consommateurs (notamment en Angleterre) et les intermédiaires des services financières.[161] Parfois, des programmes sont expérimentés dans les écoles, soit par des programmes spécifiques,[162] soit par l'enseignement des matières économiques et financières dans les écoles primaires et secondaires. Une rapide analyse montre que ces programmes mettent l'accent sur la transmission de notions et illustrent les produits spécifiques,[163] mais, à part quelques exceptions,[164] ils ne se concentrent pas sur le développement des compétences essentielles et de participation active à la consommation.

En parlant du conseil, nous avons observé qu'il est très important que la mise en œuvre des programmes d'éducation financière soit toujours effectuée par des sujets tiers et impartial, qui ne sont pas en conflit d'intérêts, dans le but d'illustrer objectivement les coûts économiques et les avantages des choix. Pour la même raison, il serait préférable que les programmes éducatifs ne soient pas organisés par les prêteurs qui vendent des produits financiers, mais plutôt par des associations des consommateurs ou de la société

160 Paracampo, *supra* note 144, p. 536 *et seq.*

161 Pour une reconnaissance dans les différents pays, *voy.* Reifner (Ed.), *supra* note 134, pp. 15, 93, 131, 173; 203, 241.

162 Par exemple: "*Schüler Banking Project*" mis en place avec des écoliers de Hambourg 14 à 17 ans depuis 2005 par l'autorité de l'éducation de Hambourg et avec la Banque d'Épargne d'Hambourg e (Haspa); Après son succès à Hambourg, le projet a été étendu à d'autres régions de l'Allemagne, en association avec d'autres Sparkassen (caisses d'épargne) dans les États de Bade-Wurtemberg, Basse-Saxe et de Rhénanie du Nord Westphalie. Dans l'année scolaire 2009/2010, environ 5.700 écoliers participé à ce projet. Reifner & Schelhowe, *supra* note 110, p. 38.

163 Par exemple: l'éducation en Allemagne sur les services des retraites complémentaires *Altersvorsorge macht Schule!* (*Pensions go to school*!) <www.altersvorsorge-macht-schule.de> qui a une impliqué une large coalition formée par: l'éducation allemande, le gouvernement et les institutions du marché; le projet a impliqué plus de 500 institutions d'éducation des adultes à travers l'Allemagne dans le 2010. Reifner & Schelhowe, *supra* note 110, p. 36.

164 Par exemple: en Belgique les programmes collectifs promus pas l'École de Consommateurs (il s'agit d'une communauté di organismes qui s'adressent en particulier aux groups de la société et éviter l'isolation de victimes) plus vulnérables pour prévenir le surendettement et qui concernent les domaines de l'Euro, budget, assurances, surendettement, documents et services bancaires, prêts etc. L'objectif déclaré par ce programme est de former les consommateurs à être autonomes et compétentes pour la prose de décisions et savoir utiliser correctement les services financiers. M. Isidori, 'Belgium Report', *in* Reifner (Ed.), *supra* note 134, p. 138.

civile générale.[165] À ce but, le code de la consommation italien précise (art. 4) que les activités d'éducation des consommateurs, réalisées par des entités publiques ou Privées, ne doivent pas être visées à "des fins promotionnelles".

De plus, l'éducation financière devrait également tenir compte des aspects émotionnels des consommateurs, en les aidant à gérer leurs émotions dans le processus de choix.[166] De plus, il est nécessaire que le consommateur soit véritablement convaincu de sa participation aux programmes d'éducation.

Comme nous avons déjà observé, l'art. 4 du code de la consommation italien et l'art. 169 du TFUE identifient l'éducation financière comme un droit fondamental du consommateur.

Cependant, la recognition de ce droit est simplement programmatique car elle pousse les états membres à mettre en œuvre des mesures de promotion. l'éducation aujourd'hui représente une importante idée de politique du droit mais elle n'est pas à la base d'un droit subjectif du consommateur.

Même les initiatives des États ne sont pas toujours satisfaisantes dans les résultats, dans les objectifs ou dans le nombre de projets promus.[167]

---

165 Biasior, *supra* note 137.

166 Paracampo, *supra* note 144, p. 536 *et seq.*

167 Les initiatives de l'État sont encore très faibles et, contrairement aux autres pays, l'Italie ne possède encore une loi entièrement consacrée à la matière, ni, pour longtemps, il a eu une législation spécifique. Ce n'est seulement que récemment l'Italie a introduit pour la première fois dans un texte législatif des mesures consacrées à la promotion de l'éducation financière. Le récent "*decreto legge*" en matière de protection de l'épargne (D.L. 237/2016 puis converti en loi, n. 15/2017) contient, à l'art. 24*bis*, des "*Disposizioni generali concernenti l'educazione finanziaria, assicurativa e previdenziale*". Plus précisément, il prévoit l'adoption par le Ministère de l'Économie et des Finances d'une "stratégie nationale pour l'éducation financière" (dans le délai des six mois à partir de la conversion en loi du décret) qui a comme but celui d'organiser systématiquement la coordination des acteurs publics et Privés dans le domaine et promouvoir l'échange d'informations et *best practices* entre ces sujets là, aussi bien que créer des synergies entre les initiatives d'enseignement et le système éducatif national. La stratégie prévoit également:
- la définition des politiques nationales en matière de communication et de diffusion d'information pour promouvoir l'éducation financière;
- la possibilité de conclure des accords pour promouvoir la formation dans ce domaine de concert avec les associations représentatives des secteurs productifs, les associations professionnelles, les associations de consommateurs, les associations sans but lucratif et les universités, avec aussi la participation des autorités locales.

Il est prévu que chaque année le Gouvernement transmet aux deux chambre parlementaires une relation sur l'état d'actuation de la stratégie susmentionné. Pour l'actuation de la stratégie le Ministère de l'Économie et des Finances, de concert avec le Ministère pour l'Instruction et le Ministère pour le Développement Économique, constitue le "Comité pour la planification et la coordination des activités d'éducation financière", composé par onze membres ayant une expérience avérée dans le domaine, qui a pour mission celle de promouvoir les initiatives et le programme de sensibilisation sur d'éducation financière. Le Comité a en particulier le but d'identifier des objectifs mesurables, d'améliorer les programmes et les actions à mettre en œuvre, en renforçant les compétences et initiatives accumulées par les acteurs actifs et favorisant la collaboration entre les organismes publics et Privés. La prévision législative d'un programme d'éducation financière est une étape très importante pour l'évolution culturelle et sociale en Italie, qui l'aligne à ce qui est prévu dans des nombreux autres pays. Nous espérons que cette action sera opérationnelle à l'avenir pour mettre en place un système de formation et de l'éducation financière plus organique et capillaire.

Quant au problème de surendettement, compte tenu de son aggravation en Europe et de l'actuelle situation d'instabilité financière, la nécessité d'une éducation financière sérieuse et efficace est maintenant plus pressante, afin d'assurer non seulement la protection des consommateurs mais, également, la stabilité financière. Les institutions européennes et internationales (notamment l'OCDE) continuent à encourager les États à renforcer l'éducation financière en sachant que cela est un outil essentiel pour lutter contre le surendettement et pour sensibiliser les consommateurs.[168] Cependant, il faut souligner que, à l'heure actuelle, les mesures empiriques adéquates pour l'évaluation de l'efficacité de l'éducation financière sont rares.[169] Il semble donc approprié que les États mettent en œuvre également des outils pour la vérification des résultats concrets dans le futur.[170]

En tous cas, à la lumière de ce qui précède, l'éducation financière, mise en pratique selon une conception "active", impliquant la participation du consommateur et de ses compétences multiples, peut avoir un impact positif sur l'utilisation responsable du crédit par toutes les parties impliquées. Et cela ne n'implique pas la stigmatisation de la dette en tant que tel.

Néanmoins, des auteurs soulignent correctement, comme la seule éducation financière n'est pas suffisante sans l'application d'une efficace réglementation de la protection des consommateurs dans le contrat même, surtout, dans le renforcement des profils de la responsabilité des prêteurs.[171] l'éducation des consommateurs ne peut pas être une valide raison pour l'atténuation des profils de responsabilité des intermédiaires.

Un objectif pour l'avenir peut être représentée par le renforcement du cadre de l'éducation financière en fonction de l'amélioration de l'efficacité du conseil à travers la création d'organes crées à ce but, avec une préparation spécifique sur la matière et d'haut niveau,[172] qui serons nécessairement troisièmes et impartiales.

---

168 "*The gradual shrinkage of public welfare resources, the launch of the supplementary private pension system, and the transformation of the few outstanding defined-benefit schemes to the defined-contribution regimes, all contribute to transfer financial responsibility away from the State towards individuals and households, thus requiring strengthened financial capabilities among the public at large*". Bank of Italy, "*Italy: Financial Education Initiatives to Support Financial Stability and Consumer Protection*", in G20 & OECD, *Advancing National Strategies for Financial Education. A Joint Publication by Russia's G20 Presidency and the OECD*, 2013, p. 148.

169 Quelques exemples *in* Reifner (Ed.), *supra* note 134, p. 31.

170 Id.

171 M. Trifilidis, 'L'educazione finanziaria: le iniziative a livello internazionale', *in Consumatori, Diritti e Mercato*, n. 2, 2009, p. 58 *et seq.*; Paracampo, *supra* note 144, p. 536 *et seq.*; Comparato, *supra* note 159, p. 389 *et seq.;* M. Paracampo, 'Il ruolo dell'educazione finanziaria nella recente disciplina del mercato finanziario', *Diritto Bancario.it*, juin 2011, p. 4. Retrieved on 19 June 2017 from <www.dirittobancario.it/rivista/mercati-finanziari-e-regole-di-sistema/ruolo-educazione-finanziaria-nella-recente-disciplina-del-mercato-finanziario>.

172 La formation des prêteurs et des intermédiaires est fondamentale pour que l'octroi de crédit se produise d'une façon responsable. Récemment le législateur français a inséré dans le Code de la consommation de nouvelles règles en matière de formation professionnelle des prêteurs et des intermédiaires en relation aux contrats de crédit relatifs aux biens immobiliers à usage d'habitation (ordonnance n. 2016-351 du 25 mars 2016, décret n. 2016-622 du 19 mai 2016, en application de la Directive /17/UE, *infra*). Le principe introduit

Comme déjà souligné, le control sur les services de conseil et l'exactitude de la formation connexe, ainsi comment le control sur le mise en œuvre des programmes d'éducation financière, représente une tâche publique dont le collectivité (et par conséquence les pouvoirs publiques) doit en assumer la responsabilité.

Nous pouvons affirmer, donc, que soit l'octroi des services de conseil et d'éducation financière, soit leur control doivent respecter la dimension collective.

En conclusion, la formation dans l'en crédit à la consommation apparaît un fort outil de protection de la partie la plus faible au contrat au sein de la durée de la relation contractuelle. Cela donne au consommateur l'habilité d'utiliser les services financiers d'une façon intelligente; notamment, d'être informé sur le plan de crédit plus adapte à ses besoins de liquidité, en prévision de sa situation future et des circonstances qui peuvent se produire à l'avenir (donc choisir le produit financier plus cohérent avec ses flux des revenues); ainsi les situations d'insolvabilité qui mènent à la rupture de la relation contractuelle sont limités. Dans le cadre plus général de la réglementation des contrats à temps essentiels à la personne, la formation est nécessaire à la survie du contrat et donc à la satisfaction des besoins essentiels de la personne.

7.3.3 L'Éducation Financière dans la Directive 2014/17/UE et Son Application

La directive 2014/17/UE[173] sur les contrats de crédit aux consommateurs relatifs aux biens immobiliers à usage résidentiel est le premier acte normatif européenne qui impose une obligation contraignante pour les États à mettre en œuvre des mesures visant à promouvoir l'éducation financière des consommateurs.

L'art. 6 par. 1 de la Directive mentionnée prescrit: "Les États membres promeuvent des mesures encourageant l'éducation des consommateurs en matière d'emprunt responsable et de gestion de l'endettement, en particulier en ce qui concerne les contrats de crédit hypothécaire. Des informations claires et générales sur les procédures d'octroi de

postule que les prêteurs et les intermédiaires de crédit doivent veiller à ce que le personnel placé sous leur autorité possède et maintienne à jour des connaissances et compétences appropriées concernant l'élaboration, la proposition et l'octroi des contrats de crédit, aussi que la fourniture de service de conseil. Les compétences doivent être vérifiées sur la base d'un diplôme spécif, ou la suivie d'une formation professionnelle concernant les opérations de crédit ou, enfin, la preuve d'une précédente expérience professionnelle. La mise au jour des connaissances du personnelle qui s'occupe de l'octroi du crédit à la consommation, qui sans doute se situe dans le cadre juridique concernant la formation professionnelle continue, doit comporter au moins 7 heures de formation par année. On peut observer que le législateur français, en valorisant la formation initiale et continue des travailleurs et leur expérience professionnelle, arrive également à poursuivre l'objectif social de la protection des consommateurs dans le marché du crédit.

173 Patti, *supra* note 126; T. Rumi, 'Profili privatistici della nuova disciplina sul credito relativo agli immobili residenziali', *I Contratti*, n. 23, 2015, p. 1; E. Pellecchia, 'La direttiva 2014/17/UE: sui contratti di credito ai consumatori relativi a beni immobili residenziali', *Banca borsa e titoli di credito* n. 2, 2016, p. 206 *et seq.*

crédit sont nécessaires pour guider les consommateurs, notamment ceux qui souscrivent un crédit hypothécaire pour la première fois. Des informations relatives aux orientations que les organisations de consommateurs et les autorités nationales peuvent fournir aux consommateurs sont également nécessaires".

L'éducation est considérée ainsi particulièrement importante pour le renforcement de la capacité des consommateurs de prendre des décisions informées qui peuvent avoir un impact significatif sur leurs vies et de gérer de façon responsable l'endettement dans le secteur névralgique du crédit hypothécaire.[174]

Dans le contexte de cette directive, donc, l'éducation est complémentaire et antécédente aux devoirs d'informations précontractuels, di conseil et de l'évaluation de la solvabilité di débiteur.

Le par. 2 continue en disposant que: "La Commission publie une évaluation des mesures mises au point par les États membres en matière d'éducation des consommateurs et recense les exemples de bonnes pratiques qui pourraient être approfondies afin de renforcer la sensibilisation des consommateurs aux questions financières". La matière de l'éducation financière est en constante évolution et donc il est important de baser son futur sur les meilleurs pratiques expérimentés à niveau international, en application de ce Directive.

Dans le domaine de la Directive, une correcte éducation peut avoir un rôle fondamental en raison du grand impact économique sur la qualité de la vie de chacun et du haut taux de risque du contrat de crédit relatif aux biens immobiliers.[175] Dans ce marché, plus que dans les autres, en fait, la technicité des contenus et le carence de préparation des consommateurs menacent d'annuler complètement l'utilité de l'information que les prêteurs sont tenus de donner.[176] Le but est donc d'assurer un rapport équilibré de l'endettement et les revenus future, en garantissant aux consommateurs les outils pour évaluer le seuil de risque tolérable.[177]

La Directive impose une obligation générique aux États Membres, que donc peuvent l'appliquer selon les moyens plus appropriés. De tout façon, ils doivent être garanties des mesures éducatives spécifiques par rapport au contexte spécifique du crédit hypothécaire. L'activité d'évaluation, menée par le Commission Européenne, des meilleures pratiques appliquées, contribuera à la diffusion des modèles plus efficaces.

---

174 Considérant 29 "*Afin d'améliorer la capacité des consommateurs à prendre des décisions en connaissance de cause en matière d'emprunt et de gestion responsable de leurs dettes, les États membres devraient promouvoir des mesures visant à renforcer les connaissances des consommateurs en matière d'emprunt responsable et de gestion de l'endettement, en particulier en ce qui concerne les contrats de crédit hypothécaire. Il importe tout particulièrement de fournir des orientations aux consommateurs qui souscrivent un crédit hypothécaire pour la première fois. À cet égard, la Commission devrait recenser des exemples de bonnes pratiques afin de faciliter l'élaboration de nouvelles mesures visant à renforcer la sensibilisation des consommateurs aux questions financières*".

175 Patti, *supra* note 126, p. 1425.

176 En outre, étant donné l'importance de l'affaire économique, cette directive a introduit des dispositions plus strictes quant à l'appréciation préventive de la solvabilité du débiteur.

177 Patti, *supra* note 126, p. 1425.

Pour une majeure protection du consommateur il serait de toute façon préférable assurer que l'éducation soit mise en œuvre par des sujets différents par rapport à ceux qui sont obligés d'"informer" le consommateur et surtout dans une phase antérieure à celle du contrat.[178]

La normative d'application de la Directive vient d'entrer en vigueur dans presque tous les États Membres, compte tenu de l'adoption récente de la Directive. Il est trop tôt pour évaluer concrètement les effets pratiques dans les différents systèmes.

Cependant, nous pouvons faire quelques observations préliminaires sur le cas italien, quant au contenu du décret législatif n. 72 du 26 avril 2016,[179] publié en application de la D. 2014/17 / UE.[180]

Le champ d'application du décret est limité par l'art. 1 "aux contrats de crédit à la consommation qui sont garantis par une hypothèque sur les droits de propriété ou d'autres droits réels ayant pour objet le bien immobilier résidentiel".

En ce qui concerne la matière de l'éducation, le décret simplement spécifique le contenu du service de conseil qui doit être fourni par le prêteur ou l'intermédiaire. En l'espèce, le prêteur doit toujours fournir une assistance au consommateur dans la phase précontractuelle afin de l'aider à comprendre si le contrat de crédit proposé et les services auxiliaires sont adaptés à ses besoins et à sa situation financière.

En plus le décret dispose que le service de conseil peut être effectué par un tiers indépendant qui fournira au consommateur un véritable service rémunéré séparément et consistant en une "*recommandation personnelle sur un ou plusieurs opérations liées aux accords de crédit, nécessaires pour correspondre à ses besoins et à sa situation personnelle et financière*" (art. 120 *terdecies*, par. 3, lettre. c), TUB).

Lae fin du conseil est le contrôle sur la solvabilité du crédit dans le temps, même dans le cas où il y a des événements qui puissent affecter négativement la capacité à rembourser. Le conseil est donc opérationnel pour éviter des phénomènes de surendettement.

Le décret a déclaré que le service de conseil indépendant ne peut être donnée que par des personnes qui exercent exclusivement cette activité et qui sont inscrits dans une section spéciale du "*albo dei mediatori finanziari*" (art. 128 *sexies*, par. 2-bis, TUB). Le service rendu par ces sujets sera payé exclusivement par le consommateur et pas par le prêteur.

Le décret vise à l'amélioration des profils liés à l'indépendance et l'impartialité du service de conseil. Néanmoins, il ne semble pas transposer les indications de la directive UE sur la mise en œuvre des mesures appropriées d'éducation financière.

---

178 Rumi, *supra* note 173.

179 Pour une exégèse, R. Ferretti & A. Santoro, 'Prime osservazioni sul decreto legislativo di recepimento della direttiva mutui', *Diritto Bancario.it*, May 2016, Retrieved 16 June 2017 <www.dirittobancario.it/sites/default/files/allegati/ferretti_r._e_santoro_a._prime_osservazioni_sul_decreto_legislativo_di_recepimento_della_direttiva_mutui_2016.pdf>.

180 Modifiant le décret législatif n.385/1993 (TUB) et le décret- législatif N. 141/2010.

À cet égard, cependant, il convient de noter que l'objectif de parvenir à un service de conseil totalement indépendant n'a pas été atteint. En fait, le conseil peut encore être fournit par le prêteur ou l'intermédiaire.

L'absence de dispositions concernant des programmes spécifiques sur l'éducation financière semble être une occasion perdue pour le législateur national qui aurai pu profiter de la transposition de la directive pour améliorer le cadre dans ce contexte.

Aussi en France l'Ordonnance n° 2016-351 du 25 mars 2016 sur les contrats de crédit aux consommateurs relatifs aux biens immobiliers à usage d'habitation (ensuite appliquée par le Décret n. 2016-607 du 13 mai 2016), qui met en œuvre la directive, ne fait aucune mention des programmes d'éducation spécifiques dans le domaine du crédit hypothécaire. Le législateur français, néanmoins, a souligné la nécessité de renforcer les compétences professionnelles auxquelles sont soumis les prêteurs et les intermédiaires de crédit pour leurs personnels, en matière de crédit immobilier.

L'ordonnance, à l'art. 4, a inséré dans le Code de la consommation de nouvelles règles en matière de formation,[181] imposant aux prêteurs et intermédiaires de crédit de veiller à ce que le personnel placé sous leur autorité possèdent les compétences professionnelles et connaissances adéquates et qu'ils les mettent à jour leurs tout au long de leur activité professionnelle, notamment en ce qui concerne l'élaboration, la proposition et l'octroi des contrats de crédit, la fourniture de service de conseil, ainsi que, l'activité d'intermédiation. De plus, lorsque la conclusion d'un contrat de crédit implique la souscription de services accessoires, il est demandé "*un niveau suffisant de connaissance de ces services et de compétence pour leur fourniture*". En outre, le législateur a établi que les personnes chargées de fournir à l'emprunteur les explications sur les prêts doivent être formées à la distribution du crédit à la consommation et à la prévention du surendettement.[182]

Ces dispositions révèlent comment, encore une fois, la loi française accordent une grande attention au développement des compétences professionnelles des travailleurs, en posant, à cet effet, au chargé de l'employeur des ponctuels obligations de surveillance. En plus, le fait de posséder e de maintenir au jour certaines compétences professionnelles[183] se révèle fondamental pour que l'octroi de crédit soit géré d'une façon véritablement responsable dans l'intérêt des consommateurs.

l'éducation financière est un outil qui peut aider le consommateur à choisir plus rationnellement. La formation du consommateur est donc un moyen de défense, préalable à

181 Art. L 314 -24 du Code de la Consommation. Deux arrêtés du 9 juin 2016 (JO 11 juin 2016) pour l'application de l'article D. 313-10-2 du code de la consommation ont complété les nouveaux principes en particulier en précisant que "*La durée minimale de formation continue mentionnée à l'article D. 313-10-4 du même code est fixée à 7 heures par année civile [...]*".

182 Art. L 314-25 du Code de la Consommation.

183 Le décret n. 2016-622 du 19 mai 2016 précise les modalités de mise en œuvre des obligations de compétences. Elles doivent être attestées soit par la possession d'un diplôme, soit par une formation professionnelle adaptée à la réalisation d'opérations de crédit, soit par l'attestation d'une précédente expérience professionnelle.

la phase contractuelle, contre une partie contractuelle culturellement et économiquement plus forte.

Et l'éducation financière, pour être vraiment efficace, doit être placé dans la dimension collective, si nécessaire, réalisée par des organismes créés à ce but, qui en garantissent toute impartialité.

7.4 Conclusion

Après avoir comparé le rôle joué par la formation dans ces deux domaines contractuels, nous pouvons répondre à la question initiale, c'est-à-dire si la formation peut être incluse dans les contrats pour l'existence en tant que principe général pour équilibrer la relation contractuelle asymétrique.

Nous avons observé que la formation dans le contrat de travail est opérationnelle pour assurer la stabilité de la relation face à des changements qui peuvent en mettre en danger la durée. La formation apparaît un puissant instrument de protection de la partie la plus faible au contrat, car elle empêche la défaillance prématurée de la relation, susceptible de compromettre la capacité de pourvoir à ses besoins essentiels. De plus, compte tenu du lien parmi les contrats que nous avons analysés, la stabilité de l'emploi est également opérationnelle pour éviter le risque de surendettement, de sorte que le flux de revenu reste inchangé et il ne se produit pas le déséquilibre entre le taux de la dette et le taux de revenu.

Nous avons également montré que, en l'absence d'un droit législative expresse, la dimension collective peut ainsi prendre en charge le principe de la formation et le mettre au point par la négociation collective.

Dans le crédit à la consommation nous avons observé que la formation de la partie la plus faible au contrat peut être déclinée de différentes manières et être plus ou moins contraignante, en fonction du son contenu. Nous avons observé que l'obligation d' "informer" le consommateur par le créancier est souvent insuffisante pour corriger l'asymétrie du contrat. Pourtant, une éducation préventive, fournie par des sujets tiers et impartiales, peut augmenter le choix rationnel du consommateur et peut être une défense adéquate contre une partie contractuelle culturellement et économiquement plus forte. Même dans le cas du crédit à la consommation, on peut conclure que la formation de la partie faible, quand elle répond à certaines conditions, aide à équilibrer la relation contractuelle. En effet, comme nous avons observé, elle se révèle utile (même dans ce cas) pour éviter le risque d'une rupture prématurée de la relation contractuelle car elle est dirigée à prévenir les possibles causes d'insolvabilité. Un consommateur formé est un consommateur plus fort puisqu'il sera moins exposé aux risques de surendettement et d'exclusion sociale.

En conclusion, pour ce qui concerne l'idée de création d'une catégorie générale des principes concernant les "contrats d'existence" la formation peut donc devenir un outil collectif de protection de la partie contraignante faible. Bien que dans des termes différents, en fait, nous avons mis en évidence que le principe de formation du sujet faible soit extrêmement important pour assurer un équilibre contractuel.

La partie la plus faible au contrat doit en effet être équipée des moyens nécessaires de formation pour acquérir les connaissances nécessaires pour l'exécution du contrat. Plus précisément, la formation devient un élément fondamental par rapport à la bonne utilisation du capital (bien ou des services) qui appartiennent et sont gérés par l'autre partie contractuel (créancier).

La formation est essentielle pour l'exécution du contrat, qui dans les de contrats d'existence se traduira par l'apprentissage à la correcte utilisation des biens et services. De ce fait la relation contractuelle peut rester durable et équilibrée pour garantir la satisfaction à long terme des exigences essentiels des personnes.

Bibliography

Alessi, C., *Professionalità e Contratto di Lavoro*, Milano: Giuffrè, 2004.

Antonmattei, H., 'L'obligation de Reclassement Préalable pour Motif Economique: Nouvelles Disposition', *Dr. Soc.*, n. 3, 2002, p. 275.

Barthélémy, E., 'Le Rôle de la Jurisprudence dans le Droit de la Formation', *Dr. Soc.*, n. 12, 2014, pp. 1007-1112.

Benedetti, G., 'Tutela del Consumatore e Autonomia Contrattuale', *in* G. Vettori (Ed.), *Materiali e Commenti sul Nuovo Diritto dei Contratti*, Padova: CEDAM, 1999, p. 799 *et seq*.

Bennacchio, G.A., *Diritto Privato dell'Unione Europea (Fonti, Modelli, Regole)*, Padova: CEDAM Wolters Kluwer, 2013.

Biagi, M., 'Recessione e Mercato del Lavoro: la Formazione alla Flessibilità', *DRI*, n. 1, 1993, p. 261 *et seq*.

Biasior, C., 'Consumer Over-Indebtedness in Italy: The Role of Consumer Organisations to Prevent and Repair Over-Indebtedness', *in* Ferretti F. (Ed.), *Comparative Perspective of Consumer Over-Indebtedness – a View from the UK, Germany, Greece and Italy*, The Hague: Eleven International Publishing, 2016, pp. 333-346.

Borzaga, M., 'Contrattazione Collettiva di Prossimità e Disciplina delle Mansioni: una Via per Aumentare la Flessibilità Interna del Rapporto di Lavoro e la Produttività delle Imprese?', *DRI*, n. 4, 2013, pp. 980-1003.

Brun, S., 'Capacità, Valutazione e Insufficienza Professionale nell'Ordinamento Francese', *DRLI*, n. 1, 2016, pp. 51-78.

Butera, F., *L'orologio e l'Organismo, il Cambiamento Organizzativo nella Grande Impresa Italiana*, Milano: Franco Angeli, 1992.

Butera, F., 'Come Cambia nel Mondo l'Organizzazione del Lavoro ad alta Qualificazione', *Rapporti Rassegna Monitor*, n.1, 1997, p. 83 *et seq.*

Carabelli, U., 'Organizzazione del Lavoro e Professionalità: una Riflessione su Contratto di Lavoro e Post Taylorismo', *DLRI*, n. 101, 2004, pp. 1-99.

Carinci, F., 'Rivoluzione Tecnologica e Diritto del Lavoro: Il Rapporto Individuale', *in* Aidlass (Ed.), *Rivoluzione Tecnologica e Rapporto di Lavoro, Atti del VIII Congresso Nazionale di Diritto del Lavoro', Napoli 12-14 aprile 1985*, Milano: Giuffrè, 1985, p. 3 *et seq.*

Caruso, B., 'Occupabilità, Formazione e «capability» nei Modelli di Regolazione dei Mercati del Lavoro', *DLRI*, n. 1, 2007, pp. 1-34.

Caterina, R., 'Psicologia della Decisione e Tutela del Consumatore', *Analisi Giuridica dell'Economia*, n. 1, 2012, pp. 67-84.

Cerini, D., 'Consumer Over-Indebtedness and Interference with Credit Contracts: An Italian' *in* Ferretti F. (Ed.*), Comparative Perspective of Consumer Over-Indebtedness – a View from the UK, Germany, Greece and Italy*, The Hague: Eleven International Publishing, 2016, pp. 347-372.

Cester, C., 'La Diligenza del Lavoratore', *in* C. Cester & M.G. Mattarolo (Eds.), *Diligenza e Obbedienza del Prestatore del Lavoro. Art. 2104*, in *Commentario al Codice Civile Diretto da P. Schlesinger*, Milano: Giuffrè, 2007.

Ciucciovino, S., *Apprendimento e Tutela del Lavoro*, Torino: Giappichelli, 2013.

Comparato, G., 'The Italian Law Against Over-Indebtedness: Fresh Start, Debt Advice and Financial Education', *in* Ferretti F. (Ed.), *Comparative Perspective of Consumer*

Over-indebtedness – a View from the UK, Germany, Greece and Italy, The Hague: Eleven International Publishing, 2016, pp. 373 -392.

Correia, M. &Maggi-Germain, N., 'l'évolution de la Formation Professionnelle Continue', *Dr. Soc.*, n. 9-10, 2001, p. 830 *et seq.*

Corti, M., 'L'edificazione del Sistema Italiano di Formazione Continua dei Lavoratori', *RGL*, n. 1, 2007, pp. 163-244.

Del Punta, R., 'Diritti della Persona e Contratto di Lavoro', *DLRI*, n. 2, 2006, pp. 195-268.

Dell'Arringa, C., 'Professionalità e Approccio Economico', *in* M. Napoli (Ed.), *La Professionalità*, Milano: Vita e Pensiero, 2004.

European Coalition for Responsible Credit (ECRC), *Principes sur le Crédit Responsable*, Retrieved on 16 June 2017 from www.credito-responsabile.net/index.php?id=2534.

Falcone, G., 'Il Trattamento Normativo del Sovraindebitamento del Consumatore', *Giurisprudenza Commerciale*, Vol. 42, 2015, p. 123 *et seq.*

Ferretti, F. & Livada, C., 'The Over-Indebtedness of European Consumers under EU Policy and Law' *in* Ferretti F. (Ed.), *Comparative Perspective of Consumer Over-indebtedness – a View from the UK, Germany, Greece and Italy*, The Hague: Eleven International Publishing, pp. 11- 40.

Ferretti, F. (Ed.), *Comparative Perspective of Consumer Over-indebtedness – A View from the UK, Germany, Greece and Italy*, The Hague: Eleven International Publishing, 2016.

Ferretti, R. & Santoro, A., 'Prime osservazioni sul decreto legislativo di recepimento della direttiva mutui', *Diritto Bancario.it*, May 2016, Retrieved on 16 June 2017 from www.-dirittobancario.it/sites/default/files/allegati/ferretti_r._e_santoro_a._prime_osservazioni_sul_decreto_legislativo_di_recepimento_della_direttiva_mutui_2016.pdf.

Ford, J. & Jones, A., 'UK Report', *in* U. Reifner (Ed), *Financial Literacy in Europe*, Baden-Baden: Nomos, 2006.

Galantino, L., 'I Profili Giuslavoristici Della Qualità', *in* L. Galantino (Ed.), *Qualità e Rapporto di Lavora*, Milano: Giuffrè, 1995.

Gargiulo, U., 'Lo Jus Variandi nel "Nuovo" Art. 2013 Cod.Civ.', *WP C.S.D.L.E 'Massimo D'Antona'.IT*, n. 268, 2015, pp. 1-23.

Garofalo, D., *Formazione e Lavoro tra Diritto e Contratto. L'occupabilità*, Bari: Cacucci, 2004.

Giugni, G., *Mansioni e Qualifica nel Rapporto di Lavoro*, Napoli: Jovene, 1963.

Gomez-Mustel, M., 'Les Enjeux de l'Obligation d'Adaptation', *Dr. Soc.*, n. 5, 2004, pp. 499-515.

Guarriello, F., *Trasformazioni Organizzative e Contratto di Lavoro*, Napoli: Jovene, 2000.

Isidori, M., 'Belgium Report', *in* U. Reifner (Ed.), *Financial Literacy in Europe*, Baden-Baden: Nomos, 2006.

Liso, F., 'Brevi Osservazioni sulla Revisione della Disciplina della Mansioni Contenuta nel Decreto Legislativo n. 81/2015 e su Alcune Recenti Tendenze di Politica Legislativa in Materia di Rapporto di Lavoro', *WP C.S.D.L.E 'Massimo D'Antona'.IT*, n. 257, 2015, pp. 1- 25.

Loffredo, A., *Diritto alla Formazione. Realtà e Retorica*, Bari: Cacucci, 2012.

Loy, G., 'Professionalità e Rapporto di Lavoro', *RGL*, n. 4, 2003.

Maggi-Germain, N., 'Inconstance et Contingence de la Définition Juridique de la Formation Professionnelle', en '*Les Evolutions de la Formation Professionnelle: Regards Croisés, Actes du Séminaire de la DARES sur le Droit de la Formation Professionnelle*', N. Maggi-Germain & A. Pélage (Eds.), Paris: La Documentation Française, 2003, pp. 153-172.

Maggi-Germain, N., 'La Capacité du Salarié à Occuper un Emploi', *Dr. Soc.*, n. 12, 2009, pp. 1234-1252.

Magnani, M., 'Organizzazione del Lavoro e Professionalità tra Rapporti e Mercato del Lavoro', *DLRI*, n. 101, 2004, pp. 165-200.

Mazzotta, O., *Manuale di Diritto del Lavoro*, Padova: CEDAM, 2015.

Montinaro, R., 'Il Sovraindebitamento del Consumatore: Diligenza nell'Accesso al Credito ed Obblighi del Finanziatore', *Banca Borsa e Titoli di Credito*, n. 6-1, 2015, pp. 7801-7820.

Nacamulli, R., 'Professionalità e Organizzazione', *in* M. Napoli (Ed.), *La Professionalità*, Milano: Vita e Pensiero, 2004.

Napoli, M., 'Disciplina del Mercato del Lavoro ed Esigenze Formative', *RGL*, n. 3-4, 1997, pp. 263-271.

Napoli, M. (Ed.), *La professionalità*, Milano: Vita e Pensiero, 2004.

Napoli, M., 'Le Dimensioni della Professionalità, Relazione dell'Intervento al XIV Convegno AIDLASS, Teramo-Silvi Marini, 30 – 31 Maggio 2003', in *'Il Diritto del Lavoro tra Conferme e Sviluppi'* (2001 – 2005), Torino: Giappichelli, 2006, p. 155 *et seq*.

Niemi-Kiesiläinen, J. & Hensikson, A.-S., *Legal Solutions to Debt Problems in Credit Societies. A Report to the Council of Europe*, Skrifter från Juridiska Institutionen vid Umeå Universitet (Ed.), Umeå: Umeå University Publishing, no. 13, 2006.

Nogler, L., 'La Subordinazione nel d.lgs. n. 81 del 2015: alla Ricerca dell «Autorità del Punto di Vista Giuridico»', *WP C.S.D.L.E. 'Massimo D'Antona'.IT* – n. 267, 2015, pp. 1-33.

Nogler, L. & Reifner, U. (Eds.), *Life Time Contracts: Social Long-term Contracts in Labour, Tenancy and Consumer Credit Law*, The Hague: Eleven International Publishing, 2014.

OCDE, *Improving Financial Literacy: Analysis of Issues and Policies*, Paris: OECD Publishing, 2005.

OCDE, *Advancing National Strategies for Financial Education. A Joint Publication by Russia's G20 Presidency and the OECD*, Paris: OECD Publishing, 2013.

Paracampo, M.T., 'Educazione Finanziaria e Protezione dei Risparmiatori: Miti e Realtà', *Analisi Giuridica dell'Economia*, Vol. 2, 2010, pp. 535-560.

Paracampo, M.T., 'Il Ruolo dell'Educazione Finanziaria nella Recente Disciplina del Mercato Finanziario', *Diritto Bancario.it*, Agosto 2011, Available at www.dirittobancario.it/

rivista/mercati-finanziari-e-regole-di-sistema/ruolo-educazione-finanziaria-nella-recente-disciplina-del-mercato-finanziario.

Patti, F.P., 'L'educazione Finanziaria e la Direttiva 2014/17/UE (Sui Contratti di Credito ai Consumatori Relativi a Beni Immobili Residenziali)', *Contratto Impresa*, n. 6, 2015, pp. 1423-1444.

Pellecchia, E., 'La Direttiva 2014/17/UE: sui Contratti di Credito ai Consumatori Relativi a Beni Immobili Residenziali', *Banca Borsa e Titoli di Credito*, n. 2, 2016, pp. 206-226.

Pérez Carrillo, F. & Gallardo Olmedo, F., 'The EU Consumer Credit Directive 2008 in the Light of the EuSoCo Principles', *in* L. Nogler & U. Reifner, *Life Time Contracts Social Long-Term Contracts in Labour, Tenancy and Consumer Credit Law*, The Hague: Eleven International Publishing, 2014, pp. 467-493.

Reifner, U. (Ed.), *Financial Literacy in Europe*, Baden-Baden: Nomos, 2006.

Reifner, U., 'EU General Report', *in* Reifner U. (Ed.), *Financial Literacy in Europe*, Baden-Baden: Nomos, 2006, pp. 15-36.

Reifner, U., 'Financial Education', *in* Reifner U. (Ed.), *Financial Literacy in Europe*, Baden-Baden: Nomos, 2006.

Reifner. U. & Schelhowe A., 'Financial Education', *Journal of Social Science Education*, Vol. 9, n. 2, 2010, pp. 32-42.

Roccella, M., 'Formazione, Occupabilità, Occupazione nell'Europa Comunitaria', *DLRI*, n. 1, 2007, pp. 187-236.

Romagnoli, U., 'Il Diritto del Secolo e Poi?', *Diritti, Lavori, Mercati*, n. 2, 1999, p. 239 *et seq*.

Roppo, V., 'L'Informazione Precontrattuale: Spunti di Diritto Italiano e Prospettive di Diritto Europeo', *Riv. Dir. Priv.*, 2004, pp. 747-764.

Rumi, T., 'Profili Privatistici della Nuova Disciplina sul Credito Relativo agli Immobili Residenziali', *I Contratti*, n. 1, 2015, pp. 70-86.

Rustico, L., 'Nuove Finalità, Strumenti e Mezzi per la Formazione Permanente: l'Apprendimento come Diritto Individuale', *DRI*, n. 4, 2009, pp. 1177-1181.

Simoncini, G.R., 'La Certificazione delle Competenze: Definizione e Inquadramento Giuridico: una Rassegna sulla Letteratura di Riferimento', *Adapt Working Paper*, n. 4, 2016, pp. 1-31.

Social Enterprise Development Innovations (SEDI), prepared for the Canadian Government's Policy Research Initiative Project 'New Approaches for Addressing Poverty and Exclusion', *Financial Capability and Poverty: Discussion Paper*, July 2004, Retrieved on 16 June 2017 from www.mta.ca/library/egovdocs/ca1pv82004f31.pdf.

Streek, W., 'L'Impresa come luogo di Formazione e Conoscenza', *in* P. Ceri (Ed.), *Impresa e Lavoro in Trasformazione*, Bologna: Il Mulino, 1988, p. 84.

Supiot, A., *Critique du droit du travail*, Paris: Press Universitaire de France, 1996.

Entretiens

Dr. Carlo Biasior, Directeur du Centro Ricerca e Tutela dei Consumatori e Degli Utenti (CRTCU), Trento, 13 juillet 2016.

8 Prenuptial and Tenancy Agreements as Relational Contracts

*Alexander Flos**

8.1 Introduction

Contract theory is a much-debated topic. Atiyah, for example, wrote about how contract law has developed over the past three centuries, arguing that we have seen 'the rise and fall of contracts'.[1] Even more radical is Gilmore who, in his ominously titled book, *The Death of Contract*, stressed the artificiality of contract law.[2] There is a general lack of consensus regarding contract theory, partly owing to country-specific differences, as well as to different methods and theories being used to explain contracts. When considering Life Time Contracts, however, one cannot feel other than uneasy about the current state of affairs, where all contracts are forcibly modelled to fit the 'ideal type' of contract, with its emphasis on the principles of consent, freedom of contract, and *pacta sunt servanda*. This applies especially in the case of Life Time Contracts, which tend to be long-term and relate to people's fundamental needs and wants. However, any alternatives to these principles are currently absent in the case of such contracts.

Dutch contract law is based on three general principles derived from classical law theory: consent, freedom of contract, and *pacta sunt servanda*. These general principles were developed to regulate short-term contracts, such as sales contracts. In practice, however, they are applied to all types of contracts. Provisions dealing with long-term contracts – such as employment contracts and tenancy agreements – are considered to be mere exceptions to these general principles, which focus mainly on the relationships between parties at the moment they enter into the contract, rather than on how these relationships may develop over time. Applying these principles to long-term contracts is thus, problematic as it neglects the evolving character of parties' relationships. Given that a long-term contract can last for 30 years or more, it is doubtful that emphasizing on the moment when the parties originally entered into the contract does justice to its long duration. To remedy this deficiency, more attention must be paid to the parties' relationships throughout the duration of a long-term contract. In long-term relational contracts,

---

* Lecturer/researcher at Vrije Universiteit Amsterdam.
I would like to thank Prof. M.V. Antokolskaia and V.S. Parfenchyk for their valuable comments on a draft version of this article. Any errors are mine.

1 P.S. Atiyah, *The Rise and Fall of Freedom of Contract*, Clarendon Press, Oxford, 1979.

2 G. Gilmore, *The Death of Contract*, Ohio State University Press, Columbus, OH, 1974.

the personal relationship between the parties is often more important to them than their contractual relationship. And, in order to fully understand the contractual relationship in a long-term contract, it is necessary to look at behavioural norms.

This chapter first discusses the problems that arise when applying general principles of contract law to the way in which long-term contracts are regulated and then presents an alternative approach – 'Relational Contract Theory' (RCT) – that focuses on the parties' relationship during the term of the contract. The case study chosen for this purpose examines two social long-term contracts:[3] prenuptial agreements and residential tenancy agreements.[4] I will argue that the three general principles of contract law are ill suited to regulate these types of long-term contracts and that more attention should be paid to the parties' evolving relationship. This is a more suitable approach, given the RCT's focus on the parties' relationship, rather than on the 'black and white' letter of the contract itself.

The RCT recognizes that every relationship is guided by behavioural norms. These behavioural norms continue to influence the parties long after the contract has been entered into, guiding how those parties interact, regardless of their formal contractual rights and duties. I will argue that the emphasis on long-term relational contracts should be on the relational dimension and the norms that stem from that relationship during the term of the particular contract. Specifically, I argue in favour of applying the RCT, which conforms to Point 6 of the European Social Contracts Group Declaration ('EuSoCo Declaration'), which states that the law "should be able to cope with long-term relational problems of changes in human lives instead of providing only remedies typical of spot contracts."[5]

The first section discusses the three principles of contracts law and explores the problem of applying them to long-terms contracts, particularly the fact that they give long-term contracts a too-static character. The second section presents the RCT as an alternative way of viewing long-term contracts and as a solution to the problems presented by current contract law. The third section focuses on prenuptial and tenancy agreements, analysing them from an RCT perspective and assessing the extent to which they are in conformity with the RCT.

3 Social long-term contracts are defined as "long-term social relationships providing goods, services and opportunities for work and income-creation, which are essential for the self-realisation of individuals and their participation in society at various stages in their life". *See* Principle 1, 'Principles of Social Long-term Contracts', *in* L. Nogler & U. Reifner (Eds.), *Life Time Contracts: Social Long-term Contracts in Labour, Tenancy and Consumer Credit Law*, Eleven International Publishing, The Hague, 2014, p. 5.

4 This chapter will only focus on residential tenancy agreements, commercial tenancy agreements are excluded.

5 Nogler & Reifner (Eds.), *supra* note 3, p. 22.

8.2 Three General Principles of Contract Law

Three principles of contract law – consent, freedom of contract, and *pacta sunt servanda* – are commonly perceived as general principles of Dutch contract law.[6] These principles cover the various stages of a contract. The principle of consent is most important when the contract is being entered into, while the principle of the freedom of contract mainly relates to the contents of the contract, and *pacta sunt servanda* governs the final stage of the contract. Although these three principles were conceived of with short-term or synallagmatic spot contracts, such as sales contracts, in mind, and they have become general principles applying to all contracts and they form the basis of Dutch contract law. However, these general principles are not as general as they may suggest because they do not apply equally to all contracts. As will be explained below, the application of these principles to long-term contracts can be particularly problematic.

8.2.1 Consent

For a contract to be valid, the only requirement needed to satisfy the principle of consent is the parties' mutual agreement. No other requirements, such as a requirement for the contract to be in writing, have to be met for the contract to be considered valid. The most important element in this mutual agreement is the will of the parties, which can be expressed verbally, either orally or in writing, or non-verbally. Dutch contract law codifies this principle in Article 217, Book 6 Dutch Civil Code (DCC), which states that only 'an offer and its acceptance' are required for the conclusion of a valid contract. Under Article 37, Book 3 DCC, such declarations can be made in any form. The moment at which the parties reach mutual agreement is the moment at which the contract is seen as being concluded. However, there are several exceptions to this general rule.

The most important exception to this principle relates to contracts that are required by law to be in a specific form, such as in writing or in the form of a notarial deed. A contract that fails to comply with the legally required form is void. Article 2, Book 7 DCC states, for example, that a contract for selling a house must be in writing, while Article 115, Book 1 DCC states that prenuptial agreements must be recorded in a notarial deed. Formal requirements for entering into contracts are usually intended to protect the interests of one or both of the parties to the contract and, sometimes, even those of third parties. Most importantly, the requirement of a written contract forces parties to specify their agreements, and so does not allow scope for any unexpressed expectations of the

6 J.H.M. van Erp, *Contract als rechtsbetrekking. Een rechtsvergelijkende studie*, W.E.J. Tjeenk Willink, Zwolle, 1990, p. 10; T. Hartlief, 'Vrijheid en bescherming in het contractenrecht', *Contracteren: tijdschrift voor de contractspraktijk* 2003, p. 5; J.M. Smits, 'Eenheid en verscheidenheid in het contractenrecht. Over het gedetermineerd verleden en de postmoderne toekomst van het privaatrecht', *Rechtsfilosofie & Rechtstheorie* 1998, p. 13.

parties, as opposed to hard and fast agreements, also to become part of the contract. This also means that no implicit agreements or implicit changes in the original agreement can be assumed unless they are recorded in writing. All of these factors add even more weight to the importance of the written contract.

8.2.2 *Freedom of Contract*

The second principle in Dutch contract law is the freedom of contract, which means that parties are free to decide whether to enter into a contract and free to determine its contents. In general, parties are free to shape their contractual relations as they see fit. Under the principle of consent, parties need to agree on all aspects of their contract when they enter into it, because that is when the contract is seen as being concluded. In its classical form, the principle of the freedom of contract reflects that the parties have autonomy when deciding to enter into a contract.

However, this freedom is not unlimited. Certain types of contracts, for example, include provisions to protect the weaker party. In theory, the general principle of the freedom of contract in Dutch law also applies to employment contracts and tenancy agreements. In practice, however, their application is limited by the specific provisions governing these types of contracts, which are specifically designed to protect the employee or tenant. Dutch contract law has also developed over the years and now places more emphasis on solidarity, thereby, forcing parties to take account of the other contractual party's interests.[7] This explains why legal provisions have been introduced to require contracting parties to provide certain information to each other or to protect the interests of the other party. A bank, for example, has to actively warn its customers of the risks of investing in shares. These obligations are based on the general provision of Article 2, Book 6 DCC, which obliges contracting parties to act towards each other in accordance with the requirements of reasonableness and fairness.

The interpretation of contracts also curbs parties' freedom of contract. If parties later disagree on what their contract means, the contract has to be interpreted by a court. The fact that a disagreement has arisen suggests that the parties never reached full, mutual agreement. However, they will be bound by the court's interpretation of their contract. Contract law also provides default rules to fill any minor gaps in the contents of a contract. These default rules are legitimized by the assumption that the parties have implicitly agreed to the missing terms. In reality, however, they represent another exception to the principle of the freedom of contract as the parties never actually reached agreement on those missing terms.

In addition, it is not only the law that curbs the freedom of contract: parties are not always able to foresee all possible eventualities when entering into a contract. This can

7 Hartlief, *supra* note 6, p. 6.

make the freedom of contract illusory, especially in the case of long-term contracts. This is referred to as 'bounded rationality', whereby parties cannot foresee or contemplate, at the time of contracting, all the possibilities that may arise and how their relationship will evolve, especially in the case of long-term contracts.[8] Yet, the law requires parties to cast all the details of their contract in stone at the time they enter into it.

8.2.3 Pacta Sunt Servanda

Under the principle of *pacta sunt servanda*, parties are bound by a contract as soon as they enter into it. According to *pacta sunt servanda*, parties cannot terminate or alter the contract unilaterally, unless they specifically addressed that possibility at the time of concluding the contract. Although the strict rules on the binding nature of contracts do not cause problems in the case of synallagmatic spot relationships, they can cause problems in the case of long-term contracts.

As most sales contracts are short-term contracts, there is usually little need to alter or terminate them at an early stage. As the DCC takes sales contracts to be typical of all contracts, the only opportunity it provides for early termination of a contract is when there is a problem with performance on the part of one or both parties. If one party's performance is inadequate, the other party has a statutory right to terminate the contract (rescission; Article 265, Book 6 DCC). Under the influence of EU law, consumers now also have the right to unilaterally terminate a consumer sales contract within a certain 'cool-off period' in certain circumstances.

In the case of long-term contracts, however, strict application of the principle of *pacta sunt servanda* can be problematic. The only remedies that Dutch law provides for a party wishing to alter or terminate such a contract is the option to invoke the general provisions on reasonableness and fairness (Article 248(2), Book 6 DCC) or to invoke an unforeseen change of circumstances (Article 258, Book 6 DCC). However, both these remedies have a relatively limited scope of application. Contract provisions can be set aside by a court if they go against the requirements of reasonableness and fairness. A contract can also be altered or terminated if the circumstances have changed to such an extent that the petitioner cannot reasonably be expected to remain bound by the contract in its original form. However, this does not give much flexibility to change or terminate a long-term contract unilaterally if parties cannot reach mutual agreement. The Dutch Supreme Court has, therefore, ruled that a long-term contract entered into for an unspecified period can be terminated unilaterally even if the DCC does not make any provision for this.[9]

---

8 A. Sanders, *Statischer Vertrag und dynamische Vertragsbeziehung: Wirksamkeits- und Ausübungskontrolle von Gesellschafts- und Eheverträgen*, Verlag Ernst und Werner Gieseking, Bielefeld, 2008, p. 314.

9 *See* the Dutch Supreme Court ruling: 28 October 2011, ECLI:NL:HR:2011:BQ9854, Nederlandse Jurisprudentie 2012, p. 685 (Ronde Venen/Stedin).

8.2.4 Concluding Remarks

Parties who enter into a contract through which they intend to cooperate for a long period of time are obliged to be flexible. They must be prepared to adjust the contract in light of changes in circumstances or to subsequently tie off issues that were left open or were unforeseen at the time the parties entered into the contract. The decisions that that parties make when they enter into a contract can be limited by bounded rationality (i.e., information, time, and knowledge). When entering into a long-term contract, parties cannot possibly know how their business or other contractual relationships will develop over time. The same is true for future external developments that can affect contractual relationships. All this argues in favour of allowing more flexibility to alter or terminate long-term contracts, including, if necessary, unilaterally. Applying the above-mentioned general principles of contract law to long-term contracts identifies the moment when the contract is concluded as the moment when all of the parties' future rights and obligations are fixed. However, such an emphasis on the moment at which the contract is concluded gives the contract a static character because, from that point onwards, everything becomes cast in stone, potentially for years to come. This is not a problem for short-term contracts, such as the 'spot' sales contract entered into when someone buys a newspaper at a local shop on the spot. In the case of long-term contracts, however, which may last as long as the marriage or until the death of a party, the rigidity of these principles results in potentially detrimental inflexibility.[10]

True, contract law offers little scope for flexibility. However, parties can remedy this shortcoming by incorporating provisions into their contracts that allow them to alter or renegotiate contractual terms in the future. Without such provisions, problems are likely to emerge, particularly when one of the parties is unwilling to cooperate. In addition, the behaviour of parties to a long-term contract differs from the behaviour of parties to a sales contract; the former are more inclined to cooperate, be flexible, and take the interest of the other party into consideration, because they value the ongoing relationship. This behavioural aspect is lacking in current contract law as it treats all contracts as short-term spot contracts. Therefore, it would be better to have a contract theory that takes this difference into account and it is for this the RCT offers an alternative.

8.3 RELATIONAL CONTRACT THEORY

The RCT, as put forward by Macneil, places contracts in their societal context. In this way, a contract is seen firstly as a means to enable rather than to determine cooperation between the contracting parties and so is governed not only by legal rules, but also by behavioural norms. For a clearer view of these norms, it is necessary to study the context

10 M.A. Eisenberg, 'Why There Is No Law of Relational Contracts', 94 *N.W.U. L. Rev.* 2000, p. 807.

of a contract and the relationships between the parties.[11] In other words, contracts should be seen as transactions embedded in complex relationships. To understand the transactions, therefore, we must first understand the underlying relationship.[12] The RCT also makes a distinction between discrete contracts, when the relationship between the parties is of no or less relevance, and relational contracts, when the relationship between the parties is of defining importance. The RCT sees every contract falling somewhere along a continuum of discrete and relational contacts. Although a short-term contract is more likely to be a discrete contract than a relational contract, a short-term contract, too, cannot be fully understood without understanding the relationship in which it is embedded and the norms flowing from that relationship.

Macneil refers to 'common contract norms' that are relevant for any type of contract, regardless of whether it is discrete or relational. However, some of those norms are more applicable to discrete contracts, while others are better suited to relational contracts. By contrast, the general norms of Dutch contract law tend to focus more on discrete contracts, particularly those of a short-term nature.

8.3.1 *The Contract*

According to the RCT, a contract is a means for people to cooperate and to exchange commodities and services. A contract has four primal roots.[13] The first of these primal roots is society.[14] Parties can only understand, conclude, and perform a contract if they have a common frame of reference; in other words, a common means of communication. What is considered to be an offer or acceptance of a contract depends on the specific society and its behavioural codes. In Bulgaria, for example, people nod their head to say 'no' and shake their head to say 'yes', which would lead to misunderstandings if a Bulgarian were to shake his head to indicate his wish to accept an offer and enter into a contract in the Netherlands.

The second primal root is labour specialization, which means that nobody is self-sufficient. As a result, we are all forced to exchange goods and services with other people, and these exchanges are made in the form of contracts.

11 In his later work, Macneil referred to the 'Essential Contract Theory' in order to distinguish this theory from other Relational Contract theories. *See* I.R. Macneil, 'Contracting Worlds and Essential Contract Theory', 9 *Soc. Legal Stud.* 2000, p. 432.

12 I.R. Macneil, 'Relational Contract Theory: Challenges and Queries', 94 *N.W.U. L. Rev.* 2000, p. 881.

13 I.R. Macneil, 'Whither Contracts?', 21 *J. Legal Educ.* 1969, p. 408; I.R. Macneil, 'The Many Futures of Contracts', 47 *S. Cal. L. Rev.* 1974, p. 696 *et seq.*; I.R. Macneil, *The New Social Contract: The Inquiry into Modern Contractual Relations*, Yale University, New Haven, CT, 1980, p. 1 *et seq.*

14 I.R. Macneil, 'Essays on the Nature of Contract', *N.C. Cent. L.J.* 1979, p. 172 *et seq.*

The third root is the freedom of choice. This distinguishes contracts from other types of exchanges, such as forced labour. People enter into a contract of their own free will and are not forced to do so. There is thus, a difference between forced and unforced contracts.

The fourth and final primal root is the awareness of the future. Contracts always involve an exchange in either the near or the distant future. Such an exchange is not possible without an awareness of the future; in other words, if the parties are just living in the 'here and now', they do not contemplate or plan for future needs, wants, or events. Buying a plane ticket to go on a holiday to Greece, for example, requires making plans for the future, even if the contract itself is entered into weeks before this.

A contract, thus, is a means for people to cooperate with each other and can be defined as 'relations among people who have exchanged, are exchanging, or expect to be exchanging in the future'.[15] Contract law's function is to facilitate cooperation between people who want to exchange particular goods or services. The rules set out in contract law are not just directed specifically at the parties in question. They also influence the expectations of other people, who expect the parties in question to behave in such and such a way. In this way, contracts function as a basis for accomplishing exchanges of goods and services and for enabling exchanges between people.

An important aspect of such cooperation is what Macneil refers to as '*presentiation*'.[16] This is the act of bringing future needs into the present and acting accordingly. If people have full *presentiation* at the moment they conclude a contract, they can foresee exactly what they will need in the future. When it comes to long-term contracts, however, full *presentiation* is illusory. The general principles and rules of contract law attempt to contradict this reality by freezing the parties' relationship at the moment they enter into the contract and forcing them to behave accordingly. The principle of *pacta sunt servanda*, for example, requires parties to foresee all of the possible future developments relevant to their long-term contractual relationships at the moment they enter into the contract.[17] However, this is not feasible for long-term contracts.

8.3.2 Discrete versus Relational Contracts

The RCT distinguishes between two types of contracts: discrete contracts and relational contracts. A discrete contract is a contract for which the parties' relationship is frequently of little or no relevance. In general, though not always, these types of contracts tend to be

15 I.R. Macneil, 'Relational Contract Theory as Sociology: A Reply to Professors Lindenberg and de Vos', 143 *J. Inst. Theo. Econ.* 1987, p. 274.

16 I.R. Macneil, 'Restatement (Second) of Contracts and Presentiation', 60 *Va. L. Rev.* 1974, p. 589.

17 Macneil 1974, *supra* note 13, p. 802; P. Linzer, 'Uncontracts: Context, Contorts and the Relational Approach', *Ann. Surv. Am. L.* 1988, p. 155-156.

of short duration, and so cooperation between the parties is relatively limited over time.[18] A relational contract, on the other hand, is typically a long-term contract, for which the relationships between the parties are more important.[19] In both cases, however, the context in which the contract was entered into and the relations between the parties are important.

An example of a discrete contract is one in which a cyclist on a holiday in another country visits a local bicycle repair shop to have his gears fixed. This is a one-off transaction, in which the relationship between the parties is less important. After entering into and performing the contract, the parties will part ways and will most likely never see each other again, let alone enter into a contract again. Even so, the context of the contract is still significant. This context, which is so natural that lawyers tend to overlook it, includes the culture of cycling, the concept of 'money', the legal concept of ownership of the bike, and the social conventions that underlie the parties' interaction.[20] Even in the case of discrete contracts, therefore, it is important not to ignore the context in which contracting takes place.

There are three characteristics that distinguish discrete and relational contracts.[21] Firstly, the duration of the contract is important. Buying a magazine at a newspaper kiosk is limited in time and usually regarded as a discrete contract. This applies unless, for example, the purchase becomes a habit and the buyer chooses to go to the same kiosk on a regular basis. Secondly, the parties' obligations in discrete contracts are more clearly defined. This reflects the often-limited duration of such contracts.[22] Thirdly, the parties involved in discrete contracts are less dependent on each other as their relationship does not normally go beyond a single transaction. These three characteristics indicate whether a contract is of a more discrete or a more relational nature.

Here, we can already see how general contract law (being the general principles and rules of contract law: consent, freedom of contract, and *pacta sunt servanda*) differs from an RCT approach to contracts. The former, which builds upon the general principles and rules of consent, freedom of contract, and *pacta sunt servanda*, tends to treat all contracts as if they were discrete contracts, with the sales contract as a typical example. In this way,

18 Macneil 1987, *supra* note 15, p. 275; N.M. Crystal, 'An Empirical View of Relational Contracts under Article Two of the Uniform Commercial Code', *Ann. Surv. Am. L.* 1988, p. 298; R.C. Bird, 'Employment as a Relational Contract', 8 *U. Pa. J. Lab. & Emp. L.* 2005, p. 152.

19 Bird, *supra* note 18, p. 151.

20 I.R. Macneil, 'Contracts: Adjustment of Long-Term Economic Relations under Classical, Neoclassical, and Relational Contract Law', 72 *N.W.U. L. Rev.* 1978, p. 857, n. 10.

21 R.E. Speidel, 'The Characteristics and Challenges of Relational Contracts', 93 *N.W.U. L. Rev* 2000, p. 823 *et seq*. As well as these three general basic characteristics, Speidel recognizes certain additional features that distinguish discrete contracts from relational contracts: future cooperation is expected and can be facilitated by mechanisms agreed by an authority, while the costs and benefits of the relationship have to be shared instead of divided, transaction-specific investments may be made and, lastly, the personal relation between the contracting parties comprizes an integral part of the relationship.

22 J. Goetz & R.E. Scott, 'Principles of Relational Contracts', 67 *Va. L. Rev.* 1981, p. 1091.

general contract law implicitly gives priority to the norms of discrete contracts, with their focus on the immediate benefits derived by each of the individual contracting parties, instead of focusing on the underlying cooperation and reciprocity between them. This is at odds with relational contracts, where the relevant behavioural norms tend to stress flexibility and reciprocity[23] and even sometimes at odds with discrete contracts themselves, as the relationship is also of importance to these types of contracts, albeit to a lesser extent.

This means that any analysis of relational contracts should start by recognizing such contracts as relational and identifying the relevant behavioural norms that give rise to the specific relationship between the parties. Such an analysis should aim to establish whether contract law contributes positively to these relationships or whether it obstructs them. For this, a more in-depth examination is needed of the various types of behavioural norms that govern contracting parties' behaviour in relational contracts.

8.3.3 Contractual Behavioural Norms

The way parties behave during negotiations, when concluding a contract, during performance, or when terminating a contract is influenced by whether the contract is more discrete or more relational, and the behavioural norms stemming from this.[24] Focussing solely on the 'black and white' contractual arrangements gives an incomplete image of the contract. Classical contract law treats every contract as a discrete contract by emphasizing on discreteness and *presentiation*, thereby, enhancing behaviour linked to discrete contracts.[25] Firstly, the identity of the contracting parties is generally viewed as irrelevant. Secondly, parties themselves determine a contract's duration by including a time limit in the contract. Lastly, few remedies are available to contracting parties wanting to change or terminate their contract and thus, enhance *presentiation*.

The RCT, in contrast, insists that the analysis of contracts should start by analysing the relationships between the contracting parties as governed by behavioural norms,[26] rather than by analysing the terms of the contract as governed by contract law, because this will present a better picture of the contract. Classical contract law, however, still promotes an analysis focussing on the terms of the contract, which it regards as complete and closed. This leaves little, if any, room for analysing the circumstances in which the

23 Macneil 1974, *supra* note 13, p. 761.

24 D. Campbell, 'Ian Macneil and the Relational Theory of Contract', CDAMS Discussion Paper, March 2004, p. 16.

25 Macneil 1978, *supra* note 20, p. 863-864.

26 I.R. Macneil, 'Reflections on Relational Contract Theory after a Neo-classical Seminar', *in* D. Campbell, H. Collins & J. Wightman (Eds.), *Implicit Dimensions of Contract: Discrete, Relational and Network Contracts*, Hart Publishing, Oxford/Portland, OR, 2003, p. 210.

contract is embedded, in other words, for analysing the relationship between the parties and the interplay of behavioural norms.

Macneil described ten common behavioural norms that influence the behaviour of contracting parties.[27] These are: (1) role integrity, or the behaviour expected of a person in a given social position; (2) reciprocity, or the idea that contracting parties will receive benefits from the exchange; (3) implementation of planning, or how things are planned and structured; (4) effectuation of consent: this derives from the primal root of choice, where a party chooses and, if necessary, forces the other party to comply with the exchange; (5) flexibility: this is at odds with the idea of effecting consent and implementing planning; (6) contractual solidarity, or the idea of holding the exchange together; (7) the interests of restitution, reliance, and expectations, which are all based on promises by one party on which the other party has come to rely; (8) creation of the restraint of power: in order to have reciprocity and solidarity, and for the exchange to continue, there should be a balance between the parties; (9) property of means; and (10) harmonization with the particular matrix.

Discrete behaviour gives rise to discrete legal norms, while relational behaviour should give rise to relational legal norms.[28] These two separate groups of norms are intensifications of common contract norms, some of which tend to be more discrete, while others tend to be more relational. The RCT claims that contracting parties' relationship should be at the forefront of the analysis, not their legal contract. This is because the behaviour of contracting parties is guided primarily by behavioural norms, such that it is important that legal norms should reflect those behavioural norms. Otherwise, there will be a discrepancy between the way parties behave, based on behavioural norms, and the legal norms of contract law.

A correlation between behavioural norms and contract law norms is particularly important in the case of relational contracts. Behavioural norms that are relevant for discrete contracts differ from those that are relevant for relational contracts. In long-term relational contracts, reciprocity, restraint of power, and solidarity are all significant as they facilitate the continuation of the contract. In relational contracts, the parties have a greater interest in cooperation and reciprocity because the relationship between the parties is of longer duration and more valuable than the immediate benefits.[29] If a long-term contract is going to last, the parties must be willing to continue to cooperate with each other. This, in turn, requires the contractual obligations to be balanced: "The more an exchange system is perceived as wrongly uneven, the more its beneficiaries must depend

27 Id., p. 213. *See also* M.W. de Hoon, *Conflictbeheersing bij opzegging*, Boom Juridische uitgevers, The Hague, 2005, p. 101 *et seq.*, for a detailed description of the ten behavioural norms, which she describes as behavioural structures.

28 Macneil 1987, *supra* note 15, p. 276.

29 Campbell 2001, *supra* note 24, p. 19.

on external force to maintain it".[30] Flexibility is also important in such contracts, owing to the limited potential for full *presentiation*, especially when a relational contract is of long duration.

In the case of discrete contracts, by contrast, the effectuation of consent is more important, more emphasis is placed on the parties pursuing their own benefits, and there is more competition between the parties. Each party tries to maximize its own benefits from the contract because the contract is of short duration and the relationship between the parties is less important to them than the immediate benefit.

8.4 PRENUPTIAL AND TENANCY AGREEMENTS AS RELATIONAL CONTRACTS

> Parties (to relational contracts) treat their contracts more like marriages than like one night stands. Obligations grow out of the commitment that they have made to one another, and the conventions that the trading community establishes for such commitments; they are not frozen at the initial moment of commitment, but change as circumstances change; the object of contracting is not ... to allocate risks, but to signify commitment to co-operate. In bad times the parties are expected to lend one another mutual support, rather than standing on their rights; each will treat the other's insistence on literal performance as willful obstructionism ... and the sanction for egregiously bad behavior is always ... refusal to deal again.[31]

Prenuptial and tenancy agreements in the Dutch legal system fall within the domain of contract law. Thus, the general rules of contract law, stressing discreteness, apply to both of them. In the case of tenancy agreements, however, there are certain specific provisions that are entirely lacking in the case of prenuptial agreements, even though both types of contracts are highly relational. With this in mind, I now turn to the analysis of such contracts, particularly their underlying relationships, in order to assess whether Dutch contract law takes their relational dimension into consideration. I start by describing the importance of the relationships between the parties to these contracts and then turn to the contracts themselves and the rules of contract law governing them.

---

30 I.R. Macneil, as cited in S. Macaulay, 'Relational Contracts floating on a Sea of Custom? Thoughts about the Ideas of Ian Macneil and Lisa Bernstein', 94 *N.W.U. L. Rev.* 2000, p. 776.

31 R.W. Gordon, 'Macaulay, Macneil, and the Discovery of Solidarity in Contract Law', *Wis. L. Rev.* 1985, p. 569, as cited *in* D. Kimel, 'The Choice of Paradigm for Theory of Contract: Reflections on the Relational Model', 27 *Oxford J. Legal Stud.* 2007, p. 236.

8.4.1 Relationships between Parties and Behavioural Norms

In the Netherlands, the default statutory matrimonial property regime is the universal community of property.[32] All the assets of spouses, acquired before and during marriage, are part of the community of property. To a certain extent, this legal regime reflects the nature of the de facto relationships between spouses. Marriage presupposes affective relations, based on a commitment to share life together until death. This can be the reason why many spouses in the Netherlands choose to follow the default statutory matrimonial property regime and opt for the universal community of property, for it reflects this bond and lifelong commitment.

Instead, in the Netherlands, prenuptial agreements are intended to keep the assets of spouses separated, thereby, avoiding their assets becoming part of a community of property. Typically, spouses will opt for prenuptial agreements that exclude any community of property, with or without a contractual obligation to periodically divide any acquired gains. If one spouse owns his or her own business or is a lot richer than the other spouse, that solution might be advisable. However, spouses conclude prenuptial agreements even if this does not apply to them, for around 20 to 25% of all married couples opt for prenuptial agreements. A prenuptial agreement in the Netherlands consists of a standard model of the notary, and is brief and not very detailed. A future spouse will normally not seek individual legal advice and instead will have legal advice together with their partner by a notary.

A prenuptial agreement is ancillary to marriage and, in the Netherlands, to a registered partnership, both of which are far more important and more far-reaching relationships between the parties than the prenuptial agreement itself. Being connected by marriage makes the relationship of parties who have signed a prenuptial agreement highly relational as their matrimonial relationship can also be described as a 'partnership'. In other words, they are committed to work together for their mutual benefit, which makes the spouses less willing to pursue only their own interests, as the interests of the other spouse are considered to also be the first spouse's own interest. The relationship between parties in a prenuptial agreement is – or at least is intended to be – of long duration. However, their obligations are not clearly defined, as it is not possible to foresee what will happen during the years to come. In addition, the views and opinions of spouses might change over time as well, making it troublesome to rely on the prenuptial agreement that was concluded many years ago. At the moment of entering into a prenuptial agreement, the future spouses do not usually yet know whether, for example, they will have children, or buy a house, or how their careers will develop. The parties to such agreements are interdependent, both emotionally and socio-economically and function as a unity. It is,

32 The law will change in 2018, from which point forwards, the community of property will only consist of assets acquired by spouses during their marriage.

therefore, fair to expect the behaviour of spouses to be determined more by the internal behavioural norms derived from the parties' internal marital relationship than by external contractual or statutory legal norms because, in principle, prenuptial agreements should be relevant throughout the whole marriage, keeping the assets of spouses separated, with the expectation that each spouse looks after his or her own interests, just as with any other contract. This is also due to people not being adequately informed about their own legal arrangements or they might have forgotten such legal arrangements, making it less likely for spouses to have their day-to-day lives influenced by prenuptial agreements.[33] Basically, prenuptial agreements serve to keep the assets of spouses separate, yet spouses will be less influenced by them than by non-legal norms during their marriage when making decisions that could be of relevance to their assets or matrimonial property.

The parties can be expected to behave as contractual partners in a way that reflects their affective relationship and to show a readiness to be attentive to the needs and wishes of the other person, at least as long as the relationship is in a good shape. Translated into terms of behavioural norms, this means that solidarity, role integrity, and harmonization with the social matrix will be particularly important for governing their contractual behaviour, especially within their own internal social matrix.[34] Spouses do not tend to alter prenuptial agreements after they get married as seeking to renegotiate such an agreement would be seen as a 'vote of no confidence'.[35] Role integrity means that even though they are contractual partners, spouses will behave primarily as spouses, rather than strictly in line with their 'black and white' contractual arrangements. Although gradually changing, traditional gender roles still play a significant role, as husbands are still more often the breadwinner, while wives are still more likely to be actively involved in bringing up children and running the household. The evolving nature of a relationship in such circumstances could involve a decision by the wife to sacrifice her career,[36] thus making the spouses even more interdependent and trusting that their relationship will last and not break down. Other important relational aspects include sexual fidelity, open communication and honesty, and interdependence – both economically (gender-specific role division) and emotionally. These behavioural norms, which emphasize on loving cooperation and solidarity, create expectations for spouses that might run counter to the arrangements they made in their prenuptial agreements. Moreover, these expectations, in turn, are not necessarily reflected in the matrimonial property arrangements they make when they conclude a prenuptial agreement.

---

33 A.-R. Poortman & M. Mills, 'Investments in Marriage and Cohabitation: The Role of Legal and Interpersonal Commitment', 72 *J. Marriage Family* 2012, p. 373.

34 Macneil 1987, *supra* note 15, p. 287.

35 E.S. Scott, 'Social Norms and the Legal Regulation of Marriage', 86 *Va. L. Rev.* 2000, p. 1909.

36 S. Thompson, *Prenuptial Agreements and the Presumption of Free Choice: Issues of Power in Theory and Practice*, Hart Publishing, Oxford and Portland, OR, 2015, p. 161.

Relationships between tenants and landlords are admittedly less relational than relationships between spouses or partners, and can vary depending on how close the cooperation is.[37] This is, of course, because parties to a residential tenancy agreement do not have an affective relationship. The relationship itself is also less intense as the tenant only needs to pay rent on a monthly basis, while the landlord just has to allow the tenant to live in the house. In the Netherlands, social housing corporations own 71.5% of all rented housing. This means that the relationship between the parties in a residential tenancy agreement is even less relational because the landlord in such cases is often an anonymous housing corporation. This is different in the case of residential rented properties owned by a private person. In those cases, the relationship between the residential tenant and the landlord is likely to be more relational.

Whatever the situation, tenancy agreements are nevertheless relational because they are long-term contracts. Therefore, not everything that could happen in their relationship can be foreseen at the time the parties enter into the contract. The parties to a residential tenancy agreement are interdependent: the tenant needs housing and the landlord wants to earn money by renting out his house. Such interdependence increases if, for example, the tenant has family members living in the house because these family members will then also depend on the same tenancy agreement for shelter.

Another important aspect of residential tenancy agreements is the existence of a weaker party. Generally, a residential tenant in the Netherlands is the weaker party because there has been a structural shortage of housing since World War II, which makes it more difficult for people to find affordable rental housing than for landlords to find tenants. Contract law assumes all persons are formally equal, so there would be no weaker party. However, the government has tried to balance this material inequality by introducing specific mandatory provisions to curb the contracting parties' freedom of contract and, thereby, protect residential tenants. In itself, this fits well with the nature of relational contracts, especially because it emphasizes solidarity and reciprocity by balancing the parties' obligations and also by the restraint of power.

8.4.2 *Flexibility in Prenuptial and Tenancy Agreements*

Dutch law on tenancy agreements consists largely of mandatory rules that leave little room for contractual freedom. If a home is classified as 'social housing', the rent payable by tenant is set by mandatory rules, and the parties are not allowed to deviate therefrom. It is also not easy to unilaterally change the terms of rental agreement. The landlord can only request the tenant to change the contract if the landlord's offer is reasonable and does not involve the amount of rent to be paid. If they do not reach agreement, the landlord will have to go to court, to get the permission from a judge to change the tenancy

37 Eisenberg, *supra* note 10, p. 814.

agreement if and only if the offer of the landlord is reasonable. Importantly, when a property needs to be renovated (which may occur years after the tenancy agreement is signed), the law allows the landlord to force the tenant to cooperate. This way, the tenant also has a relational obligation to cooperate in order to make sure the property gets the necessary renovation.

Prenuptial agreements are concluded in a different way from tenancy agreements. No specific form is prescribed for tenancy agreements, whereas, under Article 115, Book 1 DCC, future spouses wanting to conclude a prenuptial agreement have to do so in a notarial deed. This enhances the discreteness of the contract as it forces the parties to record all their arrangements in writing at the time they enter into the contract. The reason for this requirement is the desire for legal certainty. The involvement of a notary avoids the risk of antedating and ensures that the parties are properly informed about the relevant law and the consequences of their choices. The downside to this requirement is that it gives prenuptial agreements a static character and makes it impossible for parties to amend them informally, given that every amendment has to be in a notarial deed. By contrast, no form requirements apply to tenancy agreements; even an oral agreement is valid. The absence of form requirements is necessary in order to protect the tenant. Otherwise, it would be easy for landlords to bypass the mandatory rules protecting tenants by refusing to conclude contracts in writing.

As one assumes that their marital relationship is more important to the spouses than their contractual relationship, most couples pay little attention to their prenuptial agreement as long as they remain married. For this reason, few couples decide to change their prenuptial agreement in the course of their marriage. Their relationship will progress and evolve over the years: children may be born, houses may be bought and sold, and careers may be made or given up. However, but most prenuptial agreements are never changed after they have been signed, and so continue to reflect the spouses' original situation. This can lead to problems in the case, for example, of prenuptial agreements that include a total separation of property. If spouses who were economically equal at the time of entering into the prenuptial agreement end up with a traditional role division (in other words, the husband becomes the main breadwinner and the wife gives up her career to look after the children), the wife can be seen as the weaker party, at least from a socio-economic perspective. Unlike in tenancy law, there are no specific provisions aimed at protecting the weaker party in the law governing prenuptial agreements. Although this is not usually a matter of concern during the relationship, the wife could face substantial problems if the relationship breaks down. In the absence of specific provisions under Dutch law allowing an unfair prenuptial agreement to be set aside or terminated, courts are reluctant to apply general principles of contract law, such as reasonableness and fairness, to mitigate unfair consequences for the weaker party in such situations.

8.4.3 *Termination of Prenuptial and Tenancy Agreements*

The grounds on which a Dutch landlord can terminate a residential tenancy agreement that has been entered into for an indefinite period of time are strict and are set down in the law. Firstly, the landlord can terminate the contract if the tenant does not behave as a good tenant should; for example, if the tenant causes nuisances or does not pay the rent. If a landlord needs the house for himself and has made provision for this in the contract, he also has the right to terminate the contract. If no such provision is made in the contract, both parties' interests have to be assessed by the court responsible for ruling whether the contract can be terminated. This provision is used more often by private landlords than by commercial landlords. On the other hand, a housing corporation landlord can terminate the contract if it needs to renovate the building. In this way, Dutch tenancy law takes account of the different types of parties and different types of relationship involved.

In contrast with other contracts, a tenancy agreement does not automatically end when the tenant dies. A spouse or registered partner automatically becomes party to the contract by law and so continues the contract. The contract also automatically continues for a further six months in the case of an unofficial partner who has lived in the house with the tenant. During this six-month extension period, the unofficial partner can request to take over the tenancy. This request will be granted if the partners had a shared household. These rules, which in effect allow a third party to take the contract over, acknowledge the interdependence of parties to the contract and possible third persons.

Prenuptial agreements, on the other hand, are so intertwined with marriage that they end at the moment the marriage ends. Given their affective relationship, it is not desirable to force spouses to continue their marriage and, thereby, their prenuptial agreement against their will by, for example, denying them the right to a divorce. This applies even if it runs counter to other relational contracts that stress the importance of continued cooperation. In this situation, it is the relationship, rather than the prenuptial agreement, that prevails.

8.4.4 *Application of Relational Contract Theory to Prenuptial and Tenancy Agreements*

Classical contract law tends to treat all contracts as sales contracts by emphasizing on the moment when the contract is concluded as the moment when all the parties' future rights and obligations are established. However, long-term contracts require more flexibility. Owing to the relational nature of these contracts, the way in which they are regulated should take account of the parties' behaviour. This differs from the behaviour regulated by short-term contracts as, instead of focusing solely on their own interests, the parties to long-term contracts will normally try to cooperate, to be flexible, and to take account of the other party's wishes, because preserving the ongoing relationship is of more importance than the, possibly out-dated, stipulations of the written contract. Comparing the two long-term contracts – prenuptial agreements and tenancy agreements – shows the pitfalls of applying general contract law to long-term contracts, and the benefits of making specific provisions for such contracts.

One aspect that is important to take into account for the purposes of regulating long-term agreements is – using the terminology of the RCT – *presentiation*: in other words, the possibility for parties to a long-term contract to bring their future needs into the present at the moment of entering into the contract. Here, Dutch law can be seen to differ in its approach to regulating the problems related to *presentiation*. Tenancy law, for example, includes specific provisions to deal with the changes that often arise due to the long duration of tenancy agreements and the impossibility of predicting parties' future circumstances. This makes these contracts more flexible and able to be changed during the term of the agreement.

Prenuptial agreements, by contrast, are treated in Dutch contract law in the same way as sales contracts, with the result that full *presentiation* is not possible. The general principles of consent, freedom of contract, and *pacta sunt servanda* apply to prenuptial agreements, which turns such agreements into static agreements, with little if any scope to redress changed circumstances.[38] This can leave parties destitute and force them to resolve their problems on the basis of an agreement they entered into before their marriage. This applies even if, say, they have been married for thirty or forty years, given that few spouses 'renegotiate' their prenuptial agreement, or, if they do, it will be seen as at least a sign of mistrust.[39] The requirement for a prenuptial agreement to be recorded in a notarial deed makes it even less flexible as the parties cannot then make any adjustments to the agreement without going to a notary, something which rarely occurs in practice. In addition, couples tend to overestimate the chances that they will not divorce. They tend to see their future too rosily and are, therefore, unprepared for the consequences of things turning out differently.[40] This, in turn, can have an adverse impact on one of the parties if the prenuptial agreement provides for a total separation of property and the spouses have a traditional role division, where the wife is then the weaker party to the contract. This is partly due to gender roles in our society, where women tend to work less once they have children and thus become more dependent on their husband.

Another aspect to be considered is the behavioural norms of parties to a long-term contract, and this is emphasized and explained by the RCT. The importance of these

38 The only exception to this is the requirement for prenuptial agreements to be recorded in a notarial deed.

39 Sanders, *supra* note 8, p. 334.

40 L.A. Baker & R.E. Emery, 'When Every Relationship is Above Average: Perceptions and Expectations of Divorce at the Time of Marriage', 17 *Law Hum. Behav.* 1993, p. 446; J.A. Lavner, B.R. Karney & T.N. Bradbury, 'Newlyweds' Optimistic Forecasts of Their Marriage: For Better or for Worse?', 27 *J. Fam. Psychol.* 2013, p. 536.

norms for the way in which agreements are regulated is acknowledged by the Dutch legislature in the case of tenancy agreements, unlike in the case of prenuptial agreements. Specifically, there are already relational elements in the specific provisions of tenancy law that influence parties' behaviour and force them to cooperate in order to protect the weaker party to the contract. Residential tenancy law includes many mandatory provisions aimed at protecting tenants. Landlords are thus forced to take tenants' needs into consideration: rent for social housing, for example, is regulated by the state, while residential tenancy agreements can only be terminated in a limited number of situations, and third parties have a right to take over the tenancy agreement after the death of the original tenant. On the other hand, Dutch tenancy law also leaves some scope for flexibility as a landlord has the right to unilaterally force a tenant to change the tenancy agreement. These special provisions show that contract law can allow more attention to be paid to the relational nature of the contract.

Although Dutch contract law takes no account of behavioural norms in regulating prenuptial agreements, these norms do dictate the way in which parties behave in such agreements. The relationship between spouses in a prenuptial agreement is heavily relational, with a focus on cooperation, flexibility, reciprocity, and solidarity. It is the behaviour of the parties that stems from their relationship that regulates their dealings with each other as spouses are likely to pay little attention to the prenuptial agreement itself, until the marriage starts falling apart and it will become relevant again. This agreement will not, therefore, evolve in the same way as their relationship evolves over the course of their lives. More attention needs to be paid to behaviour than to the 'black and white' letter of the contract that the parties signed before they got married. This behaviour creates expectations, and these expectations should be acknowledged by law, for spouses ignore or deviate from their own prenuptial agreements. In other words, behavioural norms should give rise to legal norms and contract law regulating prenuptial agreements should be amended to take account of and possibly incorporate these insights from RCT.

8.5 Conclusion

Dutch contract law contains three general principles of classical contract law: consent, freedom of contract, and *pacta sunt servanda*. Modelled on synallagmatic spot relationships such as sales contracts, the emphasis in contract law is on the moment that parties enter into the contract. However, the DCC provisions on contract law, which are based on these principles, are problematic when applied to long-term contracts and, more specifically, to Life Time Contracts. This chapter argues that a different model is needed for these types of contracts. The application of RCT, which focuses on the contracting parties' behaviour during the term of the contract rather than on the 'black and white' letter of the contract, is more suited as the general contract theory in the case of long-term contracts.

The conclusion, then, is that, in the case of relational contracts, contract law should focus primarily on the relationship between the parties and only secondarily on the wording of the relevant contract. A discrete contract is more likely to be a contract in which the relationship between the parties is of little or no importance. A relational contract, in contrast, is often a long-term contract in which the relationship between the parties is vitally important. In the case of long-term relational contracts, the contracting parties are primarily influenced by behavioural norms and only secondarily by the provisions of their contract. The expectations that flow from the parties' behaviour should thus be acknowledged in law. After examining the application of the RCT to Life Time Contracts such as tenancy and prenuptial agreements, it can be concluded that Dutch tenancy law is more in line with the RCT, while Dutch law governing prenuptial agreements is much less so, and that this leads to problems when applying classical contract law to this latter type of agreement. The comparison between the way in which these two specific types of contracts are regulated under Dutch law provides an example of a case (tenancy agreements) in which the law has already been amended to take account of the relational nature of the contract and an example of a case (prenuptial agreements) in which this has not yet been done, despite such amendment being sorely needed.

Bibliography

Atiyah, P.S., *The Rise and Fall of Freedom of Contract*, Oxford: Clarendon Press, 1979.

Baker, L.A. & Emery, R.E., 'When Every Relationship is Above Average. Perceptions and Expectations of Divorce at the Time of Marriage', 17 *Law Hum. Behaviour* 1993, pp. 439-450.

Bird, R.C., 'Employment as a Relational Contract', 8 *U. Pa. J. Lab. Emp. L.* 2005, pp. 149-217.

Campbell, D., 'Ian Macneil and the Relational Theory of Contract', CDAMS Discussion Paper, March 2004, Retrieved on 1 March 2017 from <www.lib.kobe-u.ac.jp/repository/80100023.pdf>.

Crystal, N.M., 'An Empirical View of Relational Contracts under Article Two of the Uniform Commercial Code', *Ann. Surv. Am. L.* 1988, pp. 293-306.

Eisenberg, M.A., 'Why There Is No Law of Relational Contracts', 94 *N.W.U. L. Rev.* 2000, pp. 805-821.

Van Erp, J.H.M., *Contract als Rechtsbetrekking. Een Rechtsvergelijkende Studie*, Zwolle: W.E.J. Tjeenk Willink, 1990.

Gilmore, G., *The Death of Contract*, Columbus, OH: Ohio State University Press, 1974.

Goetz, J. & R.E. Scott, R.E., 'Principles of Relational Contracts', 67 *Va. L. Rev.* 1981, pp. 1089-1150.

Hartlief, T., 'Vrijheid en Bescherming in het Contractenrecht', *Contracteren: Tijdschrift voor de Contractspraktijk* 2003, pp. 5-14.

De Hoon, M.W., *Conflictbeheersing bij Opzegging*, The Hague: Boom Juridische Uitgevers, 2005.

Kimel, D., 'The Choice of Paradigm for Theory of Contract: Reflections on the Relational Model', 27 *Oxford J. Legal Stud.* 2007, pp. 233-255.

Lavner, J.A., Karney, B.R. & Bradbury, T.N., 'Newlyweds' Optimistic Forecasts of Their Marriage: For Better or for Worse?', 27 *J. Fam. Psychol.* 2013, pp. 531-540.

Linzer, P., 'Uncontracts: Context, Contorts and the Relational Approach', *Ann. Surv. Am. L.* 1988, pp. 139-211.

Macaulay, S., 'Relational Contracts Floating on a Sea of Custom? Thoughts about the Ideas of Ian Macneil and Lisa Bernstein', 94 *N.W.U. L. Rev.* 2000, pp. 775-804.

Macneil, I.R., 'Whither Contracts?', 21 *J. Legal Educ.* 1969, pp. 403-418.

Macneil, I.R., 'Restatement (Second) of Contracts and Presentiation', 60 *Va. L. Rev.* 1974, pp. 589-610.

Macneil, I.R., 'The Many Futures of Contracts', 47 *S. Cal. L. Rev.* 1974, pp. 691-816.

Macneil, I.R., 'Contracts: Adjustment of Long-Term Economic Relations under Classical, Neoclassical, and Relational Contract Law', 72 *N.W.U. L. Rev.* 1978, pp. 854-905.

Macneil, I.R., 'Essays on the Nature of Contract', *N.C. Centr. L.J.* 1979, pp. 159-200.

Macneil, I.R., *The New Social Contract. The Inquiry into Modern Contractual Relations*, New Haven, CT: Yale University, 1980.

Macneil, I.R., 'Relational Contract Theory as Sociology: A Reply to Professors Lindenberg and de Vos', 143 *J. Institutional & Theoretical Econ.* 1987, pp. 272-290.

Macneil, I.R., 'Contracting Worlds and Essential Contract Theory', 9 *Social Legal Stud.* 2000, pp. 431-438.

Macneil, I.R., 'Relational Contract Theory: Challenges and Queries', 94 *N.W.U. L. Rev.* 2000, pp. 877-907.

Macneil, I.R., 'Reflections on Relational Contract Theory after a Neo-classical Seminar', *in* D. Campbell, H. Collins & J. Wightman (eds.), *Implicit Dimensions of Contract: Discrete, Relational and Network Contracts*, Oxford/Portland, OR: Hart Publishing, 2003, pp. 207-218.

Nogler, L. & Reifner. U. (Eds.), *Life Time Contracts: Social Long-term Contracts in Labour, Tenancy and Consumer Credit Law*, The Hague: Eleven International Publishing, 2014.

Poortman, A.-R. & Mills, M., 'Investments in Marriage and Cohabitation: The Role of Legal and Interpersonal Commitment', 72 *J. Marriage Family* 2012, pp. 357-376.

Sanders, A., *Statischer Vertrag und dynamische Vertragsbeziehung: Wirksamkeits- und Ausübungskontrolle von Gesellschafts- und Eheverträgen*, Bielefeld: Verlag Ernst und Werner Gieseking, 2008.

Scott, E.S., 'Social Norms and the Legal Regulation of Marriage', 86 *Va. L. Rev.* 2000, pp. 1901-1970.

Smits, J.M., 'Eenheid en Verscheidenheid in het Contractenrecht. Over het Gedetermineerd Verleden en de Postmoderne Toekomst van het Privaatrecht', *Rechtsfilosofie & Rechtstheorie* 1998, pp. 10-38.

Speidel, R.E., 'The Characteristics and Challenges of Relational Contracts', 93 *N.W.U. L. Rev.* 2000, pp. 823-846.

Thompson, S., *Prenuptial Agreements and the Presumption of Free Choice: Issues of Power in Theory and Practice*, Oxford/Portland, OR: Hart Publishing, 2015.

Part II
A Spectrum of Problems to Approach the Principles of Life Time Contracts

9 Collective Responses to the New Economy in US Labor Law

*Charles F. Szymanski**

9.1 Introduction

If there is an "American carnage", as stated by US President Trump in his inauguration address, its epicenter is within the American labor movement. Labor unions are not only flat on their backs, they are threatened with virtual extinction or, more optimistically, condemned to indefinite irrelevance. There are many reasons for this. The usual suspects are weak US labor laws, American individualism, technological change/globalization/free trade resulting in the loss of jobs in traditionally unionized industries, and even labor unions themselves (due to outdated thinking and corruption).[1] This list is not anything new; indeed, these factors have been discussed by commentators and academics since the beginning of the steep decline of the labor movement since Ronald Reagan became president in 1981.[2] While ostensibly pro-union Democratic administrations under Presidents Bill Clinton and Barak Obama did produce a more labor-friendly National Labor Relations Board (NLRB) and commensurately more favorable interpretations of the National Labor Relations Act (NLRA),[3] the changes to labor law were not dramatic. In any case, they were not enough to reverse the decline, which kept progressing. Today, labor unions only represent little more than 6% of the private sector workforce.[4] While unions have a stronger base within the public sector,[5] this too, is set to decline with States stripping

* Professor of law, Vytautas Magnus University, Faculty of Law, Kaunas, Lithuania.

1 *See, e.g.*, K. Andrias, 'The New Labor Law', 126 *Yale L.J.* 2016, pp. 13-33, outlining the reasons for demise of American labor unions, ultimately placing most of the blame on the outdated structure of the NLRA.

2 Id., p. 24 (referencing 1984 congressional report entitled *The Failure of Labor Law*); *see also* P. Weiler, 'Promises to Keep: Securing Workers' Rights to Self-Organization under the NLRA', 96 *Harv. L. Rev.* 1983, p. 1769 (seminal, early work stressing that NLRA did not prevent a determined employer from avoiding unionization); I.H. Eliasoph, 'Know your (Lack of) Rights: Examining the Cause and Effect of Phantom Employment Rights', 12 *Emp. Rts. Emp. Pol'y J.* 2008, pp. 197, 225-226 (listing the possibilities for the decline of unions, including perceptions of corruption and increasing individualism).

3 The National Labor Relations Act of 1935 (49 Stat. 449), 29 USC §§ 151-169.

4 *See* U.S. Department of Labor, Bureau of Labor Statistics, *Union Members Summary*, 26 January 2017, Retrieved on 1 March 2017 from <www.bls.gov/news.release/union2.nr0.htm> (private sector union membership at 6.4% in 2016).

5 Id. (public sector union membership at 34.4% in 2016).

away the right of public employees to collectively bargain,[6] and a potential Supreme Court case that would cripple their ability to fund themselves.[7]

While there finally appears to be a push back against globalization, and the outsourcing of industries, and decent jobs, much of the damage has already been done. The US has shifted to a service economy, which has been difficult for unions to organize. Moreover, within the service economy, there has been the emergence of the new, or gig, economy. Individuals who provide various services, including rides, through computer applications (apps) to paying customers, are theoretically their own bosses. They are arguably independent contractors rather than employees.[8] As such, they do not have the right to organize and collectively bargain under the NLRA.[9] To the extent that unions could come up with revolutionary and effective methods to organize the service sector, ever growing percentages of individuals working in this sector would be in any case excluded.[10] Moreover, other gig or sharing economy businesses, such as Airbnb, have had the effective of diminishing the small pockets of unionization that do exist within the service sector. While unions have had modest success in organizing hotel and hospitality workers, Airbnb, by offering more attractive accommodations at lower prices, has seriously hurt that industry. In turn, this has further lowered union membership in this sector. Arguably, then, the new economy may be the final impetus pushing unions into oblivion.

Certainly, technological change that has hurt union jobs has occurred previously in American history.[11] One standard response has been to resist such change, and barring that, negotiate to minimize its impact, or at least to spread out its negative effects (essentially job loss) over time. With the new economy, too, unions have at first taken an aggressive approach, for example using corporate campaign-type methods to hurt Uber

---

6 Most notably Wisconsin in 2011, *see* S. Jones IV, 'Wisconsin's Act 10 Limitations on Collective Bargaining: Balancing a Budget on the Backs of Public Employees', 13 *Geo. J.L. Pub. Pol'y* 2015, p. 543 (summarizing impact of change) and most recently Iowa in early 2017, *see* W. Petroski & B. Pfannenstiel, 'Iowa House, Senate Approve Sweeping Collective Bargaining Changes', *Des Moines Register*, 16 February 2017, Retrieved on 1 March 2017 from <www.desmoinesregister.com/story/news/politics/2017/02/16/amid-marathon-debate-iowa-legislature-barrels-towards-passage-collective-bargaining-bill/97984338/>.

7 *See, e.g.*, C. Szymanski, 'Scalia's Shadow: The Freidrichs Case and the Fate of the American Labor Movement', *Giornale di Diritto Del Lavoro e di Relazioni Industriali* 2016, pp. 759-761.

8 *See, e.g.*, D. Das Acevedo, 'Regulating Employment Relationships in the Sharing Economy', 20 *Emp. Rts. Emp. Pol'y J.* 2016, pp. 1, 3-14 (providing an overview of the sharing economy, which relies upon platform suppliers rather than traditional employees); V. De Stafano, 'The Rise of the "Just-In-Time" Workforce: On-Demand Work, Crowdwork, and Labor Protection in the "Gig Economy"', 37 *Comp. Lab. L. Pol'y J.*, 2016, pp. 1, 3-14 (the "catchphrase 'gig-economy' [...] is often used to indicate a sort of parallel dimension in which labor protection and employment regulation are assumed not to apply by default.").

9 29 U.S.C. § 152(3).

10 *See* G. Brooks & T. Steadman, 'Is the Gig Economy a Fleeting Fad, or an Enduring Legacy?', 33 *J. Compensation Benefits ART 5*, March/April 2017, p. 7 (finding a 66% increase of company use of gig workers in the last 10 years, and projecting that "33% of employers of 100,000 employees or more expect to be using 30% or more contingent workers by 2020.").

11 *See* Andrias, *supra* note 1, pp. 21-22 (reciting the effect of economic restructuring on labor in the U.S. in the 1970s, 1980s, and 1990s).

and Airbnb with an aim of driving them out of business. While this approach has not entirely failed as of yet, to the extent the new economy is here to stay,[12] it looks more like a desperate rear-guard action, only delaying the inevitable.

Unions' ineffectiveness in responding to the new economy is very disconcerting, because, for the sake of employees, a *collective* response is exactly what is required at this moment. Individual lawsuits against new economy businesses are less likely to make a difference – let alone a sea change – in labor law or policy. Even in their weakened state, unions, through collective bargaining and other agreements with new economy companies, have a greater chance to protect workers in this sector. Alternatively, or even in conjunction with these efforts, class action employment law cases are another collective way to effectively alter new economy companies' behavior with respect to labor rights. This essay will analyze both methods and their effectiveness, and provide a legal roadmap for the most-promising collective strategies going forward.

9.2 Collective Bargaining and Other Agreements with New Economy Companies

9.2.1 *Dealing with the Devil: Coming to an Accommodation with the New Economy*

It is one thing to challenge a new economy entity such as Uber and Airbnb at every step – attacking them politically, with a negative media campaign, and administratively – with the goal of destroying them, and quite another to use these tactics as leverage to come to a mutual understanding with them. Again, assuming the sharing economy is not a temporary phenomenon, the latter strategy holds more promise. It was used, in fact, by the Service Employees International Union (SEIU) with Airbnb. While negotiations were ultimately unsuccessful (in part due to resistance from other labor unions locked into a more traditional, confrontational approach), the process of negotiations and the draft agreement itself are worth a closer examination.

In some respects, SEIU and Airbnb were logical partners to try and attempt to come to an innovative, new economy labor agreement. The SEIU is a large labor union oriented toward (as its name suggests) service industries. It has not hesitated to engage in unconventional tactics to gain members and obtain collective bargaining agreements with new employers. The SEIU has applied political, public relations and regulatory pressure on various employers in order to make it easier to represent their employees. Seeing that the formal election process under the NLRB was too time-consuming and more and more ineffectual, it came to card check agreements with employers, whereby the employer

12 *See, e.g.*, Brooks & Steadman, *supra* note 10 (arguing that the gig economy is very much here to stay).

would recognize the SEIU as the exclusive bargaining representative if a majority of employees simply provided signed authorization cards indicating their selection of the SEIU. More recently, the SEIU has been the driving force behind the "Fight for $15", pushing local and state governments to raise the minimum wage to $15 per hour.[13] When it viewed the umbrella organization of American unions, the AFL–CIO, as holding it back, the SEIU pulled out of the organization.[14]

Airbnb, for its part, is different than other gig economy companies in that it does not directly replace employees with independent contractors (as Uber with taxi drivers). Its harm to the labor movement, while real, is more indirect. When owners of a house or apartment use Airbnb to rent out a room or space for an attractive price, it provides consumers with (at times) a cheaper and better alternative than standard hotels. This hurts the business of these hotels, and to the extent they are unionized, this results in job loss for unionized employees. At the same time, Airbnb likes to convey a socially responsible image.[15]

Coalitions of community groups and labor unions have tried to prevent Airbnb from doing business in a number of large US metropolitan markets. Essentially, these coalitions have argued that Airbnb should meet the same regulatory requirements as hotels, and have the same tax and other legal responsibilities. To the extent Airbnb cannot comply, it should be prohibited from doing business in that market. These efforts also hurt Airbnb's socially responsible image, to some extent, as it was portrayed as avoiding taxes and permits and destroying local jobs.[16]

Airbnb made the first move to try to reach an understanding with the SEIU. It hired former SEIU President Andy Stern to negotiate an agreement with the union.[17] As nego-

---

13 *See* D. Lee, 'Bundling "Alt-Labor": How Policy Reform Can Facilitate Political Organization in Emerging Worker Movements', 51 *Harv. C.R.-C.L. L. Rev.* 2016, pp. 509, 517; Andrias, *supra* note 1, pp. 47-48.

14 *See* T.B. Edsall, 'Two Top Unions Split from AFL-CIO', *Washington Post*, 26 July 2005 (quoting SEIU President as stating "Our world has changed, our economy has changed, employers have changed. But the AFL-CIO is not willing to make fundamental change").

15 *See, e.g.*, J. Graham, 'Airbnb Aims #WeAccept Super Bowl Ad at Refugees, Immigrants', *USA Today*, 5 February 2017 (Airbnb also promises to provide 100,000 refugees and others with short-term housing and donate $4 million to support displaced persons); T. Lee, 'Sharing Economy Startups Airbnb and Uber Don't Share Similar CEOs', *San Francisco Chronicle*, 13 February 2015 (contrasting Airbnb and Uber with this analogy – "For if Airbnb is the pleasant waitress who cheerfully offers you an extra cup of coffee, Uber is the Soup Nazi, who behaves as if the customer is lucky to even get a table.").

16 *See* C. Said, 'Airbnb Hurts Hotels, Trade Group and Union Say', *San Francisco Chronicle*, 30 September 2016, Retrieved on 1 March 2017 from <www.sfchronicle.com/business/article/Airbnb-hurts-hotels-says-trade-group-and-union-9517727.php>; J. Dawsey, 'Union Financed Fight to Block Airbnb in New York City', *Wall Street Journal*, 6 May 2016, Retrieved on 1 March 2017 from <www.wsj.com/articles/union-financed-fight-to-block-airbnb-in-new-york-city-1462842763>; K. Bennerjune, 'Airbnb in Disputes with New York and San Francisco', *New York Times*, 28 June 2016, Retrieved on 1 March 2017 from <www.-nytimes.com/2016/06/29/technology/airbnb-sues-san-francisco-over-a-law-it-had-helped-pass.html?_r=0>.

17 *See* S. Levin & J.C. Wong, 'Airbnb Negotiations with Powerful US Labor Union Facing Backlash', *The Guardian*, 18 April 2016, Retrieved on 1 March 2017 from <www.theguardian.com/technology/2016/apr/18/airbnb-seiu-backlash-labor-union-deal-new-york-california>.

tiations progressed, the outline of a deal emerged. Airbnb would take the following steps: (1) support SEIU's "Fight for $15" program, (2) recommend that customers renting properties through Airbnb use cleaning companies that have collective bargaining agreements with SEIU and pay cleaning employees at least $15 per hour, and (3) emphasize that such cleaning companies are "green" certified and thus, environmentally friendly. The SEIU, for its part, would no longer oppose Airbnb's presence in various US cities and markets. This draft agreement was in part based on a local experiment in a segment of the New York City market, whereby Airbnb offered individuals listing rooms through its platform, two (2) free cleanings by the firm Cooperative Cleaners. This firm was employee owned, and paid its workers at least $15 per hour. Approximately 1,300 users of Airbnb took the company up on this offer during the time of the promotion.[18]

A large segment of unionized jobs at hotels consist of cleaning personnel, as well as front desk and reception employees. Through this draft agreement, SEIU was attempting to at least preserve the cleaning jobs. Assuming that Airbnb made appropriate marketing efforts, and unionized cleaning companies provided good, eco-friendly service at a fair price, it was certainly possible that a reasonable portion of people listing property rentals on Airbnb would use these companies. At least, it was better than the alternative option – that over time, most of these jobs would be permanently lost as Airbnb obtained more and more market share from traditional hotels.

However, when information about the draft agreement became publicly available, there was immediate resistance from other labor unions. In particular, HERE/UNITE, the labor union that traditionally represented employees in the hotel and restaurant industry, voiced very strong objections. The HERE/UNITE argued that the agreement did not really commit Airbnb to preserve one union job. Rather, Airbnb simply has to suggest unionized cleaning companies, and its clients were free to reject this suggestion. To the extent due to higher wage, unionized companies were more expensive, it would be more likely that clients would go with cheaper (and lower wage) alternatives. Thus, the deal was allegedly skewed toward Airbnb – while SEIU would withdraw opposition from Airbnb obtaining the right to do business in major US markets, driving unionized hotels out of business, and SIEU was not guaranteed to represent any additional cleaning employees. There was also a suggestion that Airbnb's hiring of the SEIU's former president to negotiate this agreement smacked of an insider deal.[19]

18 *See, e.g.*, id.; E. Dwoskin, 'Airbnb Is Forming an Alliance with One of the Nation's Biggest Labor Unions', *Washington Post*, 18 April 2016, Retrieved on 1 March 2017 from <www.washingtonpost.com/news/the-switch/wp/2016/04/18/airbnb-is-forming-an-alliance-with-one-of-the-nations-biggest-labor-unions/?utm_term=.e357ff05d4ce> (outlining terms of the proposed deal).

19 *See* S. Levin, 'Airbnb's Controversial Deal with Labor Union Falls Apart After Intense Backlash', *The Guardian*, 21 April 2016, Retrieved on 1 March 2017 from <www.theguardian.com/technology/2016/apr/21/airbnb-seiu-labor-union-deal-called-off-after-criticism>; J. Miller, 'Uber, Airbnb, and Other Labor Dilemmas', *The American Prospect*, 26 April 2016, Retrieved on 1 March 2017 from <http://prospect.org/article/uber-airbnb-and-other-labor-dilemmas>.

As a result of this outcry from HERE/UNITE and other unions, SEIU backed out of the agreement.[20] The labor movement went back to its standard model of opposing new economy businesses, to try to protect the hotel jobs its members already had.

This is not the best collective approach. While perhaps there could have been more concrete obligations placed on Airbnb to encourage the use of unionized cleaners (through incentives, for example, as in the pilot program), overall, this was an innovative agreement that certainly had an opportunity to preserve some level of union cleaning jobs, and even the potential for adding such jobs as Airbnb grows. From HERE/UNITE's own perspective, there is some logic in its opposition to the agreement, as that union would have lost members (with hotel job loss) and SEIU would have gained members (through new cleaning companies obtaining work through Airbnb). But, looking at the agreement from the broader perspective of employees and unions in general, it was more beneficial than the alternative. The draft agreement was also innovative, and showed that unions and new economy businesses can coexist and work for mutual gain. While confrontation has a place in labor's struggle with the new economy, it is only a means to a realistic end. The SEIU used its leverage in this regard to good effect, and came up with a good offer from Airbnb to resolve the matter. This agreement should be revisited by SEIU and Airbnb and should provoke other unions to think of other kinds of outside-the-box understandings with new economy businesses.

9.2.2 Do Not Mourn, Organize!

In order to continue to exist, in both the old and new economies, unions must organize new members. This is not easy under any circumstances in the United States, but, nonetheless, it has to happen. Thus, instead of trying to destroy new economy businesses, an alternative strategy is for unions to organize new economy workers. In all fairness to unions, the organizing in the new economy presents special challenges, to say the least. The business model of gig economy firms such as Uber presumes that they are technology companies, which provide an application that self-employed individuals may use (for a fee) to earn extra money by offering a service to customers (providing a ride, shopping, giving home care, etc.). Thus, according to Uber, all its drivers are simply independent contractors and not employees. This saves Uber tremendous amounts of money, as it does not have to comply with wage and hour, antidiscrimination and other labor laws, nor does it have to pay extra employment taxes, insurance, or other fringe benefits (especially mileage reimbursement). Critically, for unions, it also means that the drivers – as independent contractors rather than employees – do not have the right to organize and collectively bargain.

20 Id.

While the NLRA generally provides private sector employees the right to organize, join, and form labor organizations and collectively bargain, it also specifically excludes independent contractors from its coverage. As nonemployees, they do not enjoy any of the protections of the Act, and cannot be represented (or protected) by unions.[21] The key legal question, then, is whether new economy workers such as Uber drivers are really independent contractors, or whether they are actually employees within the meaning of the NLRA. In this regard, the employer's own designation is not determinative. Rather, the individual's actual duties and relationship with the company are examined to see if an actual employment relationship exists.

The NLRB has not directly ruled on this issue in the context of new economy companies. Outside the context of the NLRA, there have been scattered decisions on this question involving other labor law claims (such as wage/overtime, fringe benefit and unemployment matters). These are not directly determinative of the collective bargaining issue, as the NLRB uses a different test to determine whether an individual is an employee than other federal and State labor laws. Moreover, in the few reported decisions on this issue, a consensus opinion has not yet emerged among the courts and administrative bodies that have dealt with it. The California Labor Commissioner found that an Uber driver was an employee in a claim for wages, benefits, and other damages, while a Florida tribunal came to an opposite conclusion in a claim for unemployment benefits under Florida law, ruling that the drivers were independent contractors.[22] In *O'Connor v. Uber*,[23] a massive class action case involving a claim for fringe benefits such as tips and mileage and penalties under the California labor code, a federal district court ruled that the question of employee/independent contractor status could go to a jury for a determination. In doing so, the court found that it was arguable that the Uber drivers were employees, in that Uber was a transportation company, its drivers provided a service to it, and Uber exercised substantial control over the drivers' working conditions.[24]

As the *O'Connor* court explained, part of the difficulty the courts are facing in determining this issue is in using legal tests from the old economy to determine whether someone is an employee in the new economy:

> The application of the traditional test of employment – a test which evolved under an economic model very different from the new "sharing economy" – to Uber's business model creates significant challenges. Arguably, many of the

21 29 U.S.C. § 152.

22 *See* C.A. Olson, T.F. Haley & A.L. Stoklas, 'The Contingent and On-Demand Workforce and the "Gig Economy"', SY002 Am. L. Inst. Continuing Legal Education, 28-30 June 2016, citing *Berwick v. Uber Technologies*, No. 11-46739 EK (Cal. Labor Comm'r 3 June 2015) and *Florida Department of Economic Opportunity v. Raiser, LLC*, No. 00262825 90-02, *Ewers*, No. 0026 282 468-02, *McGillis*, No. 0026 2850 33-02 Hutton (PP) (Dep't. of Econ. Opportunity 13 May 2015).

23 *O'Connor v. Uber*, 82 F.Supp.3d 1133 (N.D. Ca. 2015).

24 Id., pp. 1148-1153.

> factors in that test appear outmoded in this context. Other factors, which might arguably be reflective of the current economic realities (such as the proportion of revenues generated and shared by the respective parties, their relative bargaining power, and the range of alternatives available to each), are not expressly encompassed by the *Borello* test. It may be that the legislature or appellate courts may eventually refine or revise that test in the context of the new economy. It is conceivable that the legislature would enact rules particular to the new so-called "sharing economy." Until then, this Court is tasked with applying the traditional multifactor test.[25]

Still, until a new legal standard emerges (by a statutory amendment or by a decision of a higher court), courts and administrative bodies must make do applying the older, traditional tests. While not a new economy decision, in *Sisters' Camelot*,[26] the NLRB did apply its traditional test for employee status in a case that has some strong parallels with sharing or gig work, and found that the individuals in question were employees covered by the Act.[27]

In *Sisters' Camelot*, a nonprofit cooperative provided food for low-income people and funded itself by soliciting contributions from the public. It solicited money by using canvassers, with people who went door-to-door to various homes asking for donations. These canvassers were free to work as often or as little as they liked. If they chose to work on a given day, they were assigned a specific geographic area in which to solicit, and were prohibited from soliciting outside of this area. They were required to keep detailed notes and records of their home visits, which would be reviewed by the cooperative. While the canvassers could work for other companies and even charities, once they appeared for work on a given day, they could only solicit for Sisters' Camelot during that day. The canvassers received a nonnegotiable commission based on the amount of donations they were able to solicit.[28]

One of the canvassers was interested in forming a union, but was told by management that this was impossible, as they were not employees. The cooperative then terminated the canvasser. The union filed an unfair labor practice charge, alleging that the company violated the employees' right to join a labor union guaranteed under Section 7 of the Act. The key legal question in the case was whether or not canvassers were employees covered by the NLRA, or excluded as independent contractors.[29]

---

25 Id., p. 1153 (internal citations omitted).

26 *Sisters' Camelot*, 363 N.L.R.B. No. 13 (2015) (slip. op).

27 *See* 'Employment Law – National Labor Relations Act – NLRB Classifies Canvassers as Employees, Not Independent Contractors – *Sisters' Camelot*', 363 N.L.R.B. NO. 13 (SEPT. 25, 2015)', 129 *Harv. L. Rev.* 2016, p. 2039 (arguing the relevance of the case to the gig economy) [hereinafter "Employment Law"].

28 *Sisters' Camelot, supra* note 26, pp. 1-4.

29 Id., p. 1.

The NLRB's test for determining employee status consists of 11 factors. These are: "(1) the extent of control by the employer; (2) whether the individual is engaged in a distinct occupation or business; (3) the extent of supervision by the employer; (4) the skill required in the occupation; (5) whether the employer supplies the instrumentalities, tools, and place of work; (6) the length of time the individual is employed; (7) the method of payment; (8) whether the work is part of the regular business of the employer; (9) the understanding between the parties…; (10) whether the employer is in the business, and […] (11) whether the individual in question is rendering services as an independent business."[30]

Applying this test, the NLRB concluded that 9 of the 11 factors favored a finding of employee status (only length of employment and the parties' understanding of the nature of their relationship weighed in favor of independent contractor status). Critically, the NLRB found that, while a canvasser could choose when to work and how hard she would work, once she made the decision to work a particular day she was substantially under the control of the company. The canvassers' pay was nonnegotiable, specific recordkeeping requirements were enforced, they had a specific start and end time once they decided to work a particular day, they could only solicit in a specific geographic area, they could not work for other companies the days when they were working for Sisters' Camelot, and they could be disciplined for violating these rules.

Analogizing this case to new economy relationships, many similarities are present.[31] Like gig workers, the canvassers decided when and how much to work. They did not have direct, in-person supervision when soliciting funds, but had detailed recordkeeping requirements which enabled the company to determine how the solicitations could be conducted. The key for the NLRB was that while the canvassers worked, the cooperative had extensive control over what they did. While there are differences, to be sure, with new economy cases (for example, unlike Uber, where drivers use their own cars, the canvassers did not use their own equipment), *Sisters' Camelot* suggests that there is a reasonable chance that the NLRB could find Uber drivers and other gig workers to be employees once this case is put before it, even using its traditional old economy test.[32] Therefore, if gig workers such as Uber drivers are truly disgruntled with their work, this should present an opportunity for a labor union to try to organize them.

Even with the *Sisters' Camelot* decision, however, formidable obstacles remain for labor unions. First, as mentioned, there may be significant differences between the canvassers in that case and gig workers in a given case, and the applicable factors may tilt in favor of independent contractor status.[33] Second, the NLRB has become more and more

30 *See* Employment Law, *supra* note 27, pp. 2041, nn. 24 & 28 (listing factors applied by the NLRB).

31 *See* M.W. Finkin, 'Beclouded Work, Beclouded Workers in Historical Perspective', 37 *Comp. Lab. L. Pol'y J.* 2016, p. 603 (pointing out that task and home work has existed for thousands of years, and despite the new technology facilitating this type of work, the concept itself is not new in labor relations).

32 *See* Employment Law, *supra* note 27, pp. 2044-2046.

33 Id., pp. 2045-2046 & n. 60.

political over the last 30 years.[34] While the Trump administration is difficult to classify in many respects, the Republican Party is still quite pro-business and he will likely nominate pro-management members to the NLRB. It is, therefore, quite possible that a newly constituted NLRB with a majority of Republican members will not be so eager to expand or interpret the *Sisters' Camelot* ruling to encompass gig workers. Third, for some new economy companies, such as Uber, their business model – and even existence – depends upon using independent contractors rather than employees. If Uber had to reimburse drivers for mileage (for example), and pay all applicable employment taxes and insurance, it is not clear if it could remain in business as it is currently designed. A win at the NLRB might be a pyrrhic victory for labor, if the employer goes out of business and the drivers lose their jobs. However, one should not presume the bankruptcy of a company like Uber in this situation too quickly, as it is possible negotiations and changes to the business model may provide some solutions.[35]

Whether or not a union could persuade the NLRB to find that gig workers are employees, and thus eligible for collective bargaining, there still is another alternative route for union representation of individuals working for new economy companies. Unions could lobby local and State governments to provide bargaining rights for certain gig workers, who are independent contractors. These efforts have already borne fruit in one major US city, Seattle.

Seattle recently passed an ordinance that provides drivers who are independent contractors for companies like Uber the right to union representation and collective bargaining.[36] The ordinance contains elements of typical state and federal labor law regarding the selection of bargaining representatives and the collective bargaining process. Unions who wish to represent such drivers must be pre-approved as a potential Qualified Drivers Representative (QDR) by Seattle. This should not be an obstacle for most established labor unions, as eligibility requirements include whether or not the prospective QDR has prior experience representing employees and has a democratic structure.[37] Once approved, a prospective QDR seeking to represent drivers has the right to receive the drivers' names, addresses, e-mails, and contact information from the company.[38] Only drivers who have provided at least 52 rides for the company in Seattle in any three-month

34 *See* A. Semet, 'Political Decision-Making at the National Labor Relations Board: An Empirical Examination of the Board's Unfair Labor Practice Decisions through the Clinton and Bush II Years', 37 *Berkeley J. Emp. Lab. L.* 2016, p. 223.

35 *See* Olson *et al., supra* note 22, p. 5 (Westlaw pagination) (giving examples of the range of possibilities: one gig company went out of business in the face of 4 employee misclassification lawsuits, another converted all its workers from independent contractors to employees, while a third gave its workers the option of reclassifying themselves as employees pending ongoing litigation).

36 *See* City of Seattle Ordinance No. 124968 (23 December 2015), amending § 125132 6.310.110 of the Seattle Municipal Code (SMC) and adding § 6.310.735 to that Code; *amended* by Seattle Ordinance No. 125132 (12 September 2016).

37 SMC § 6.310.735(B).

38 SMC § 6.310.735(D).

period within the preceding 12 months are eligible to vote.[39] Within 120 days of receiving the drivers' contact information, the QDR should submit evidence that a majority of the drivers has selected it as the Exclusive Drivers' Representative (EDR). If it presents this evidence, the QDR will be certified as the EDR. If more than one QDR is seeking to represent the drivers, the QDR with the highest number of authorizations will be certified as the EDR.[40]

The EDR and the company then have 90 days to reach an agreement "over terms and conditions or work, such as best practices regarding vehicle equipment standards, safe driving practices, the nature and amount of payments to be made by, or withheld from, the driver coordinator to or by the drivers, minimum hours of work, and conditions of work and applicable rules."[41] The parties may also agree on a clause providing that drivers become members of the QDR as a condition of employment.[42]

Any agreement reached must be sent to Seattle's Director for Financial and Administrative Services (Director) for approval. The Director will either approve the agreement or reject it. If the Director rejects it, she will send it back to the parties with an explanation about the deficiencies of the agreement and instructions to the parties to correct it.[43]

If no agreement is reached, an interest arbitrator will make a decision on the terms of the agreement. The interest arbitrator may be directly selected by the parties or selected by them from a list of seven (7) arbitrators supplied by the American Arbitration Association.[44] In making a decision on the terms of the new contract, the arbitrator should consider: "a. stipulations of the parties; b. the cost of expenses incurred by drivers (e.g., fuel, wear and tear on vehicles, and insurance) c. comparison of the amount and/or proportion of revenue received from customers by the driver coordinators and the income provided to or retained by the drivers; d. the wages, hours, and conditions of employment of other persons, whether employees or independent contractors, employed as for-hire or taxicab drivers in Seattle and its environs, as well as other comparably sized urban areas; and e. any other factors that are normally or traditionally taken into consideration in the determination of wages, hours, and conditions of employment."[45]

The Seattle ordinance is therefore quite comprehensive, and, through the use of interest arbitration, avoids the possibility of a strike and related disruption to transportation in the city. While it has the great advantage of bypassing the whole employee/independent contractor issue, by directly giving bargaining rights to independent contractor drivers, it

39 *See* City of Seattle Dept. of Financial and Administrative Services (FAS) Director's Rule FHDR-1; SMC 6.310.110.

40 SMC § 6.310.735 (F).

41 SMC § 6.310.735 (H)(1); *see also* Director's Rule FHDR-4 (providing detailed list of mandatory subjects of bargaining).

42 SMC § 6.310.735 (H)(4).

43 SMC § 6.310.735(H)(2).

44 SMC § 6.310.735(I)(1).

45 SMC § 6.310.735(I)(2)(a)-(g).

nevertheless has its share of potential legal difficulties. The US Chamber of Commerce filed a lawsuit arguing that the ordinance was illegal,[46] and Uber subsequently challenged the ordinance in a separate lawsuit.[47] The Chamber of Commerce lawsuit was dismissed by the court on the grounds that the Chamber lacked standing – the ordinance was not yet in effect and there was no evidence that it had suffered any actual harm as of the date the case was filed.[48] Uber's lawsuit is pending. While there has not yet been a decision on the merits of either the Chamber's or Uber's claims, both parties have raised strong arguments about the ordinance's validity.

The Chamber contended that Seattle's ordinance was pre-empted by the NLRA and was illegal under the Sherman Anti-Trust Act.[49, 50] Under the pre-emption doctrine, federal law prevails over any inconsistent state or local law.[51] NLRA pre-emption is quite broad.[52] There are two specific forms of NLRA pre-emption – *Garmon*[53] pre-emption and *Machinists*[54] pre-emption. Under *Garmon* pre-emption, any state or local law that deals with a subject that is arguably protected or prohibited by the NLRA is pre-empted and thus invalid.[55] With respect to *Machinists* pre-emption, state or local law that regulates an area purposely left unregulated by the NLRA is also invalid, to the extent that Congress intended to let the "free play of economic forces" resolve the issue.[56]

The Chamber's *Garmon* pre-emption argument is that it is arguable whether Uber's drivers are employees protected by the NLRA, and therefore the ordinance is pre-empted.[57] Under *Machinists*, the Chamber contends that independent contractors were intentionally excluded from the coverage of the act, so that the "free play of economic forces" would govern their relationship with other companies.[58] While superficially appealing, both arguments are not likely to succeed. Uber contends that its drivers are independent contractors, and to the extent a union seeking to represent them under the

---

46 Complaint, *Chamber of Commerce v. City of Seattle*, case no. 2:16-cv-00322 (W.D. Wash., 3 March 2016), Retrieved on 1 March 2017 from <www.documentcloud.org/documents/2746828-U-S-Chamber-Lawsuit-Against-Seattle.html> (hereinafter "*Chamber* Complaint").

47 Complaint, *Raiser, LLC v. City of Seattle*, Superior Ct. of Wash., King County (17 January 2017), Retrieved on 1 March 2017 from <www.geekwire.com/2017/uber-sues-city-seattle-block-new-rules-landmark-unionzation-ordinance/> (hereinafter "*Uber* Complaint").

48 *Chamber of Commerce v. City of Seattle*, C16-0322RSL (W.D. Wash., 9 August 2016) (Order granting motion to dismiss), Retrieved on 1 March 2017 from <www.documentcloud.org/documents/3009511-19717037450.html>.

49 15 U.S.C. § 1.

50 *Chamber* Complaint, *supra* note 46, at Counts One through Four.

51 U.S. Constitution, Article VI (2).

52 *See* B. Sachs, 'Despite Preemption: Making Labor Law in Cities and States', 124 *Harv. L. Rev.* 2011, pp. 1153, 1154 ("It would be difficult to find a regime of federal preemption broader than the one grounded in the National Labor Relations Act").

53 *San Diego Bldg. Trades Council v. Garmon*, 359 U.S. 236 (1959).

54 *Int'l Ass'n of Machinists v. Wisconsin Emp't Relations Comm'n*, 427 U.S. 132 (1976).

55 *See Garmon, supra* note 53.

56 *See Machinists, supra* note 54.

57 *See Chamber* Complaint, *supra* note 46, at Count Three.

58 Id., at Count Four.

Seattle ordinance agreed, it would not even be arguable that they are protected by the NLRA. Even if the issue was disputed, ultimately there would be a finding one way or another on their status under the NLRA. If the drivers were excluded as independent contractors, they would be indisputably covered by the ordinance. Independent contractors' exclusion from the coverage of the NLRA likewise does not mean that Congress intentionally kept their relationship with other businesses unregulated. Agricultural workers are likewise excluded from the NLRA,[59] as are public employees,[60] but California has a law permitting collective bargaining for agricultural employees,[61] and many States permit public employee bargaining.[62] In both cases, these State bargaining laws are not pre-empted, and likewise a law permitting independent contractors to collectively bargain would also not be pre-empted.[63]

The antitrust argument is potentially stronger. On their face, labor agreements are anticompetitive, as they set wages and benefits for numerous employees without the possibility of individual negotiations.[64] However, as labor is not regarded as a commodity, there is a specific exemption for labor activity (including collective bargaining agreements) in US antitrust law.[65] For the most part, however, this exemption would not apply to the independent contractor drivers covered by the Seattle ordinance, as they are not employees. There is extensive case law on this issue. For example, when a group of criminal defense lawyers organized a strike against Washington, D.C., to pressure the city to pay higher hourly rates to lawyers defending indigent clients, the Supreme Court ruled that the strike violated antitrust law and was unlawful anticompetitive behavior. The labor exemption did not apply since the lawyers were not employees, but small businesses.[66] Likewise, the concerted activity (strike or boycott) of other individuals, making much less than lawyers, in protest of their income has also been effectively challenged as

59 29 U.S.C. § 152(3).

60 Id. (individuals employed by an entity that is not an employer covered under the Act are likewise not considered employees within the meaning of the NLRA, and 29 U.S.C. § 152(2) specifically excludes states and their subdivisions as employers).

61 California Agricultural Labor Relations Act, codified at California Labor Code §§ 1140 through 1166.3.

62 *See* R.T. Clark, Jr., 'Public Sector Collective Bargaining at the Crossroads', 44 *Urb. Law.* 2012, pp. 186-187 (listing states with collective bargaining laws for public employees, but focusing on trend to strip away these rights, starting with Wisconsin).

63 *See* E. Kennedy, 'Freedom from Independence: Collective Bargaining Rights for "Dependent Contractors"', 26 *Berkeley J. Emp. Lab. L.* 2005, p. 143 (persuasively arguing that neither *Garmon* nor *Machinists* preemption should apply to a state or local law giving collective bargaining rights to independent contractors, citing *Willmar Poultry Co. v. Jones* 430 F. Supp. 573, 576 (D. Minn. 1977) (holding state regulation of agricultural workers is not covered by *Machinists* preemption)).

64 *See* P.M. Sanjukta, 'The Enduring Ambiguities of Antitrust Liability for Worker Collective Action', 47 *Loy. U. Chi. L.J.* 2016, pp. 969, 997-1020 (noting the original application of the Sherman Act to labor activity).

65 Id., p. 1021, citing both the Clayton Act, 15 U.S.C. § 12, and the Norris-LaGuardia Act, 29 U.S.C. Secs. 101-115.

66 Id., pp. 978-979, summarizing *Fed. Trade Comm'n v. Superior Court Trial Lawyers Ass'n*, 493 U.S. 411, 423 (1990).

an unlawful restraint on trade and outside of the scope of the labor exemption.[67] So long as the drivers are not employees, the labor exemption would not apply and any concerted activity to influence their pay would likely violate antitrust law.[68]

Some commentators have suggested an exceptional scenario, one in which independent contractors could be covered by the labor exemption, however. Where independent contractors work alongside of employees, and take action supporting the employees in the employees' own concerted activity, such conduct may be protected.[69] The key is whether the independent contractors are directly affecting the wages and working conditions of actual employees. If they are, union activity to eliminate this threat to employee working conditions – for example, by regulating wages/income – is covered by the labor exemption, even though independent contractors are involved.[70]

This scenario does not appear to be directly applicable to the drivers covered by the Seattle ordinance. Uber does not use a mix of employee and independent contractor drivers, and therefore this is not a situation where the independent contractor drivers are supporting the concerted activity of employee drivers for overall better working conditions. Nor is this a situation where unions of competing taxi drivers are pressuring Uber to raise incomes for independent contractor drivers to protect taxi employee wages. Rather, the Seattle ordinance is a separate collective bargaining law for independent contractors.[71]

Even though the labor exemption to antitrust liability would likely not apply, another exemption might. The State action exemption permits States to make laws with anticompetitive effects, so long as the law that permits anticompetitive behavior is clearly expressed as State policy. The idea behind this exception is that State legislative policy was not something intended to be regulated by federal antitrust law. Instead, federal antitrust law was designed to regulate the anticompetitive behavior of private actors.[72] This exception is not limited to action taken by the State itself; instead, it may also be extended to subdivisions of the State, such as municipalities, if certain conditions are met.

67 Id., pp. 980-982.

68 *See* Kennedy, *supra* note 63, p. 169 ("Workers who are viewed as independent contractors, rather than employees, lack the legal status to bargain collectively under labor law. Strikes and other concerted action in support of increased compensation could also constitute unlawful horizontal restraints of trade. In addition, collectively bargaining pay rates would constitute illegal price fixing and a per se violation of antitrust law.")

69 Id.; *see also* Lee, *supra* note 13, p. 530.

70 Id.; *see also* Sanjukta, *supra* note 64, pp. 1032-1033.

71 *See* Sanjukta, *supra* note 64, pp. 1032-1033. (concluding that these exceptional situations where independent contractors are covered by the labor exemption to antitrust laws do not really apply to the classic gig worker/independent contractor situation); *see also* Lee, *supra* note 13, p. 531 (acknowledging the obstacles antitrust law places upon independent contractors taking collective action, and suggesting that the Federal Trade Commission use its rule-making authority to clarify the labor exemption to encompass such contractors that are in a dependent work relationship).

72 *See Parker v. Brown*, 317 U.S. 341 (1943); Kennedy, *supra* note 63, pp. 175-178; Andrias, *supra* note 1, p. 92, n. 485.

Specifically, the municipal action must be clearly authorized by the State. To establish this factor, the municipality "need not 'point to a specific, detailed legislative authorization.' Rather, the anticompetitive effects of the challenged municipal restraint must constitute the kind of action contemplated by the State legislature and must be a foreseeable consequence of engaging in the authorized activity. The State action doctrine immunizes from antitrust liability a municipal restraint that meets these criteria."[73]

The Seattle ordinance arguably meets these criteria. The State of Washington has specifically given its political subdivisions, such as Seattle, the power to "regulate for hire transportation services without liability under federal antitrust laws."[74] A foreseeable consequence of this regulation is the ability of Seattle to make regulations that would set fares and otherwise stabilize working conditions for drivers, among other reasons in order to better ensure public health and safety.

Uber, in its more recent complaint filed against Seattle, focuses on the ordinance's rules for the eligibility of drivers to vote to be represented by a union. Uber complains that setting a minimum number of rides in Seattle (52) in a three-month period for a driver to be eligible contradicts standards for voter eligibility found in federal and State labor law (which generally have a more liberal threshold).[75] Clearly, Uber would like to broaden the pool of voters to include drivers who have a much smaller number of rides, and would be less concerned with forming a union than drivers who depend on Uber for their livelihoods. Uber also raised a number of procedural arguments, for example, that Seattle did not comply with applicable administrative law by allegedly failing to give the public a proper notice and comment period before the ordinance went into effect.[76]

Whatever the merits of these objections, they are less existential than the antitrust and pre-emption challenges. Even if Uber is correct, these eligibility and procedural objections could be addressed by Seattle making amendments to the ordinance or by a delay in the effective date of the ordinance, and they would not take away the right of Seattle to introduce a collective bargaining law for the drivers. Regarding Uber's eligibility arguments, even State and federal labor law do have their own voter eligibility cut-off requirements, and it would seem as if Seattle would have the right to extend voting rights to those drivers who are most dependent upon Uber in this specific circumstance. Precisely, because the drivers are considered to be independent contractors, in any case there is no

---

73 *See* A.M. Perry, 'Municipal State Action Antitrust Immunity: A Federalism Argument Against the Bad Faith Exception', 56 *Fordham L. Rev.* 1987, p. 475. An additional requirement for state action immunity, that the state actively supervise the regulation at issue, is not applicable to municipalities. Id., p. 475 n.26, *citing Town of Hallie v. City of Eau Claire*, 471 U.S. 34, 46 (1985), *accord North Carolina Bd. of Dental Examiners v. F.T.C.*, 135 S.Ct. 1101, 1112-1113 (2015).

74 *See* Seattle Ordinance No. 124968, *supra* note 36, at Preamble and § 1.C, *quoting* Revised Code of Washington (RCW) 46.72.001.

75 *See Uber* Complaint, *supra* note 47, as discussed in Section 9.3, *supra*.

76 Id.

obligation that the ordinance exactly mirrors State or federal labor law in this or any other respect.

While a complex issue, it appears as if collective bargaining laws covering independent contractor drivers (such as Uber drivers) set by municipalities are lawful.[77] Consequently, if they can spread beyond Seattle to other major US urban markets, they represent a degree of hope for both unions and drivers trying to navigate the new economy. Such local bargaining laws have several major advantages over more traditional approaches: they avoid costly and drawn out litigation over the this issue of whether gig workers are independent contractors or employees; if the Seattle ordinance is used as a template, they avoid the weakness of federal labor law by having a streamlined representation process (unlike an NLRB election and more similar to a card check) and avoids strikes by utilizing an interest arbitration process that has been successful with public safety unions; and from the company's standpoint, they do not destroy or undermine a business model, which avoids certain taxes and payments that would otherwise be required if the drivers (for example) are considered employees.

Whether unions will exploit this opportunity is another matter. But, it is one of the best opportunities for them to extend their relevance in the new economy.

9.3 Employment Law Class Actions in the New Economy

Collective bargaining, if possible, is a favorable solution for new economy workers to protect their rights. Labor unions, while in a weakened state in the United States, still possess resources to bargain from a position of greater equality with large new economy companies, than would gig workers attempting to do so on an individual basis. Still, the severe decline of labor unions and various legal obstacles to organizing gig workers may prevent collective bargaining from becoming a realistic solution in many circumstances. New economy workers, therefore, may be in a position that they have to fend for themselves to protect their rights.

77 This question, however, has yet to be definitively settled by a court. In *Chamber of Commerce v. City of Seattle*, 2:17-cv.00370-RBL (W.D. Wash. April 4, 2017), the federal district court did issue a preliminary injunction on the implementation of Seattle's collective bargaining ordinance for drivers. *See* Order Granting Preliminary Injunction, at p. 18, Retrieved on 10 June 2017 from <www.documentcloud.org/documents/3535403-Lasnik-Order.html>. In that (and a related) case, the Chamber of Commerce and a group of Uber and Lyft drivers sued to enjoin the law, mainly on the grounds that it was preempted by the NLRA and federal antitrust law. While the court found that the plaintiffs did not have a strong likelihood of success on the NLRA preemption claim, their antitrust argument was potentially stronger, as there were "serious questions" as to whether the state governmental immunity exception was applicable. Id., p. 6. The court concluded that because of the importance and novelty of the legal issues involved, it would be best to suspend the collective bargaining law until these questions could be fully briefed and litigated by the parties. It emphasized that this preliminary decision "should not be read as a harbinger of what the ultimate decision in this case will be…." Id., p. 18.

They may do so by filing individual employment law claims against new economy companies, primarily arguing that they have been misclassified as independent contractors. There are some basic problems with this approach. Unlike European labor law, being classified as an employee does not entitle workers to have job protection in the United States. Under the American employment at will doctrine, employees may be terminated for any or no reason (with a major exception that they may not be fired for unlawful discriminatory reasons).[78] So, by seeking reclassification as an employee, an individual lawsuit must seek other relief besides job security.

What may be at issue in a misclassification case are certain wages and benefits that are due only to employees. This may include minimum wage, overtime, workers compensation, insurance, and other employee benefits such as pensions or participation in profit-sharing plans. As the US minimum wage is set at a relatively low level, many misclassification claims involve the loss of certain types of fringe benefits. However, many of these kinds of claims do not involve large amounts of money on an individual level. It may, in fact, be uneconomical for a gig worker to retain a lawyer and pursue a court case to pursue only $1000 in lost benefits.

Fortunately, outside of collective bargaining, there is another method for new economy workers to protect their rights in a collective manner. The US federal and state procedural law allows plaintiffs to bring a combined claim as a class action if certain standards are met. The essential requirements are numerosity, typicality, commonality, and adequacy of representation.[79] If there are a relatively large number of workers who share the same basic claim that arose under the same kinds of circumstances, their claims may be combined into one case. While a $1000 claim for lost wages may not be worth bringing, 200,000 workers each alleging a similar loss because they were misclassified would be, and certainly would be better able to get to the attention of the company.

Federal wage and overtime claims brought under the Fair Labor Standards Act (FLSA)[80] have the procedural disadvantage of being akin to an "opt-in" class action.[81] That is, every worker with an FLSA claim stemming from being misclassified as an independent contractor would have to affirmatively agree (or opt-in) to the class action. Typical civil class actions, in contrast, have an "opt-out" model. All affected individuals are automatically included in the class action unless they notify the court that they do not wish to be part of the class.[82] In employment cases, with potentially hundreds of thousands of workers in various locations, it would clearly be beneficial to use the opt-out

78 *See* B. Means & J.A. Seiner, 'Navigating the Uber Economy', 49 *U.C. Davis L. Rev.* 2016, p. 1519 ("Employment-at-will is the governing principle of the United States labor markets [...] Because employment is a wholly voluntary status, either party can terminate the employment relationship at any time, for any reason.").

79 *See* Fed.R.Civ.P. 23.

80 29 U.S.C. § 201.

81 29 U.S.C. § 216(b), formally known as a collective action rather than a class action.

82 *See* Fed.R.Civ.P. 23(b)(3).

model. In practice, it is difficult to track down and persuade individuals to specifically agree to opt-in to a case, and much easier if all affected individuals were included at the outset. In wage and overtime cases, employment lawyers have overcome this problem by filing class actions under state law, rather than the FLSA. State law is generally more favorable, in that it often allows state wage and hour claims to proceed as a typical opt-out class action.[83] One disadvantage is that the class is limited to workers located in that particular state, although there are procedural mechanisms in multidistrict litigation to combine different state law class actions before one federal court.[84]

Once an employee misclassification case is filed as a class action, the next important step is the court's decision to *certify* the case as a class action. In so doing, the court certifies that the requirements for numerosity, typicality, commonality, and adequacy of representation have been satisfied and the case can proceed as a class action.[85] Certification is significant in that it exposes the company/defendant to substantial financial risk going forward: the case could be about 100,000 individuals claiming $1,000 each, rather than a single claim for $1,000. As a form of risk management, the company faces considerable pressure to think about settling the case, rather than try its chances at a jury trial. The pressure to settle is raised even higher if the company loses a summary judgement motion to dismiss the case. A summary judgement motion is a procedural mechanism that enables the judge to dismiss a case before it goes to a jury for a decision.[86] It usually occurs after discovery is concluded (i.e., after the parties have gathered all relevant information, from documents and witnesses, about the case). To win a summary judgment motion, a party would have to show that there are no disputed material facts, and based on these undisputed facts, that party should prevail as a matter of law.[87] Putting this in perspective, if there is certified employment law class action potentially worth 2 billion dollars, the company has a strong motivation to settle for even 10% of that amount to avoid the risk of a jury ruling against it.

The *O'Connor v. Uber* case is an excellent example of how an employment law class action case can put substantial pressure on a new economy company, and even force it to change its behavior. It also illustrates some particular legal hurdles gig workers face in making out a successful claim. *O'Connor* is a class action case involving – potentially – hundreds of thousands of California and Massachusetts drivers working for Uber. The primary claims of the drivers were that they were misclassified as independent contrac-

---

83 *See, e.g.*, A. Beilmana, '"A Fair Day's Pay for a Fair Day's Work": A Defense of Kentucky Wage and Hour Class Actions', 55 *U. Louisville L. Rev.* 2017, pp. 65-69 (summarizing the advantages of state law wage and hour class actions).

84 *See* B. Bartlett, 'Rising Tide of Multidistrict FLSA Cases is Met by Better-Equipped Employers', 13 *FLSA Emp. Exemption Handbook News* 2007, p. 3) (commenting on multidistrict FLSA collective actions, but also noting similar phenomenon with combined state law wage and hour class actions).

85 *See* Fed.R.Civ.P. 23(c).

86 *See* Fed.R.Civ.P. 56.

87 *See Celotex Corp. v. Catrett*, 477 U.S. 317 (1986).

tors, and as a result suffered the following injuries: they did not receive tips allegedly withheld by Uber (Uber's promotional materials indicated that the tip for the ride is included in the price, but never remitted any tips to the drivers; employees would be entitled to such tips under state law); they were not reimbursed for mileage (state law requires employers to compensate employees for the use of their vehicles for work purposes); and they were not paid "on-call time", i.e., time driving around waiting to pick up the next ride.[88] Also, for the California drivers, the Private Attorney General Act (PAGA) permitted private parties to sue to collect statutory penalties levied under the California Labor Code. These penalties might be relatively small per violation (failing to remit tips, pay mileage, etc.), but aggregated in a class action, they would be substantial. Private parties would keep 25% of the penalties recovered, with the state recovering 75%.[89]

In total, the claims of the 240,000 drivers[90] in the *O'Connor* case were worth almost 1.9 billion dollars. The mileage claim was worth 700 million dollars, lost tips 122 million dollars, phone reimbursement 30 million dollars, overtime/on call time 2.4 million dollars,[91] and the PAGA claims approximately 1 billion dollars.[92] Even if Uber could afford to pay out 1.9 billion dollars, the class action posed an existential threat to the company in another manner: as Uber premised its business model on using independent contractors rather than employees (and thus avoiding substantial tax, insurance, and benefit obligations), a ruling that its drivers were employees might even drive it out of business.[93]

These risks increased exponentially after the *O'Connor* case was certified as a class action. The court found that the standards for a class action were satisfied, particularly since one common issue dominated the case – whether or not the drivers were employees or independent contractors. If they were employees, then all the drivers would be entitled to mileage and tips and possibly on-call time.[94]

The court also ruled that the drivers were not required to present their claims on an individual (or other) basis to an arbitrator. The PAGA claims were not arbitrable under California law, and moreover could not be separated from the general arbitration agreement. In this way, the entire arbitration agreement was rendered invalid.[95]

They also were raised when Uber lost its summary judgment motion, in an attempt to dismiss the case. In its motion, Uber argued that the drivers were – as a matter of law – independent contractors and not employees, and in any event, the drivers signed arbitration agreements with Uber requiring them to submit their claims individually before an

88 *See O'Connor v. Uber*, 2016 WL 4398271, at *1, 11 (N.D.Ca. 2016).
89 Id., at *17.
90 Id., at *3.
91 Id., at *13.
92 Id., at *17.
93 Perhaps this is why, as another form of risk management, Uber has been focusing on developing driverless cars.
94 *O'Connor v. Uber*, 2015 WL 5138097 (N.D. Ca. 2015), certifying class, modified by *O'Connor v. Uber*, 311 F.R.D. 547 (9 December 2015) (expanding class).
95 *O'Connor, supra* note 94, 311 F.R.D. pp. 554-565.

arbitrator (rather than a court). As mentioned earlier, applying the California common law test for employee status, the court found that it was a question for the jury to decide. Since the drivers were providing a service to a transportation company, a presumption existed that they were employees. Moreover, Uber had a strong indicium of control over its drivers, ranging from how they behaved in the car to the manner in which they picked up rides. Uber would have an opportunity to prove otherwise to the jury, but at this point, the court could not say as a matter of law that the drivers were not employees, and in fact the indications from the record were otherwise.[96]

After these losses, and with the case headed for a jury trial, Uber reached a settlement with the drivers. Again, there was a risk of enormous damages and the obliteration of Uber's business model if it lost before a presumably unsympathetic jury, making a settlement the most reasonable option. Under the terms of the settlement, Uber would pay 84 million dollars, plus an additional 16 million dollars if Uber's expected initial public offering was valued more than 1.5 times what was anticipated. The attorneys for the class were entitled to a 25-million-dollar contingency fee, but later agreed to take "only" 15 million so that more money could be distributed to the drivers in the class. In individual terms, this meant that each driver would receive between $12 and $1950, depending upon how much miles they had driven and whether or not they signed an arbitration agreement with Uber. On average, a typical driver would receive approximately $100 as a result of the settlement.[97]

The settlement also included various noneconomic terms. Uber would no longer "deactivate" (fire) drivers at will. Instead, drivers will receive two warnings, except where safety, discrimination, fraud, or illegal conduct was alleged. Uber would provide drivers with more information on star ratings, which are critical in determining whether they will be selected by customers for rides. The parties agreed that Uber's most recent arbitration agreement is valid, except that Uber will now pay the costs of any arbitration. A mechanism would also be put in place for drivers to complain about fares set by Uber. Finally, Uber agreed to fund and help create a drivers' association, which will not be considered a union.[98]

As is typical with class action cases, the court was required to review and approve the settlement before it would become effective.[99] In so doing, the court found that the $84 (or possibly $100) million-dollar settlement for the mileage, tip, and wage claims was reasonable. While it was a 90% discount on the value of these claims, the court determined that there was a risk that the arbitration agreements would be found to be valid, and this risk justified the substantial mark-down.[100] However, this settlement amount

96 *O'Connor, supra* note 23, pp. 1148-1153.
97 *O'Connor, supra* note 88, 2016 WL 4398271, at *4-6.
98 Id., at *5.
99 Id., at *7, *citing* Fed.R.Civ.P. 23(e).
100 Id., at *14.

was not sufficient taking into account the one billion dollar PAGA claims, which according to the court were definitely not subject to arbitration under California law.[101] The noneconomic terms of the settlement were not regarded of being of significant value.[102] Consequently, the court rejected the proposed settlement.[103]

This decision was particularly unfortunate for the drivers. One month later, the US Court of Appeals for the 9th Circuit (whose rulings were binding on the trial court in *O'Connor*) ruled in a related case that the Uber arbitration agreements *were* valid, and thus deprived the Uber drivers the right to bring a class action in court.[104] The Court of Appeals held that the arbitration agreements signed in 2014 required the parties to submit the question of whether or not the claims (including PAGA claims) were arbitrable to an arbitrator in the first instance.[105] While the 2013 arbitration agreements reserved the arbitrability question to the court, and the PAGA claims were not arbitrable under California public policy, this part of the arbitration agreement was severable from the rest of the agreement. Thus, the drivers' non-PAGA claims against Uber must proceed to arbitration.[106]

The arbitration agreements also did not run afoul of the NLRB's ruling that arbitration agreements that take away employees' rights to bring a case about working conditions as a class action violated Section 7 of the NLRA. Section 7 guarantees the right of employees to engage in concerted action for mutual aid or protection, and this included the right to bring a class action in court (which itself was a collective act for mutual aid or protection). However, the Court of Appeals reasoned that the Uber arbitration agreements did not violate Section 7 because they were voluntary – the Uber drivers were not required to sign them and suffered no retaliation if they refused to do so. To the extent that Section 7 applied, the Uber drivers voluntarily waived whatever protections they might have had by signing the agreements.[107] If the Court of Appeals ruling on this point applied to the *O'Connor* class, the number of California drivers would potentially be reduced to only 8,000 (those drivers who chose not to sign the arbitration agreements), and this would drastically reduce the value of the case.[108]

---

101 Id., at *17-18.

102 Id., at *14-15.

103 Id., at *19.

104 *See Mohamed v. Uber*, 836 F.3d 1102 (9th Cir. 2016).

105 Id., pp. 1112-1113.

106 Id., pp. 1113-1114; *see also Cobarruviaz v. Maplebear, Inc.*, 143 F.Supp.3d 930 (N.D. Ca. 2015) (also severing PAGA claims from arbitration agreement in a new economy (Instacart) misclassification case).

107 *Mohamed, supra* note 104, p. 1112, n. 6 (also indicating that plaintiffs waived this argument by raising it too late on appeal). The NLRB's position that employee waivers of the right to bring a class action in an arbitration agreement may violate the NLRA has been accepted by the U.S. Courts of Appeal for the 9th Circuit and the 7th Circuit (*see Lewis v. Epic Sys. Corp.*, 823 F.3d 1147, 1155 (7th Cir. 2016)), but three other Circuits have disagreed. *See Cellular Sales of Missouri, LLC v. NLRB*, 824 F.3d 772, 775 (8th Cir. 2016); *D.R. Horton*, 737 F.3d 344, 362 (5th Cir. 2013); *Sutherland v. Ernst & Young LLP*, 726 F.3d 290, 297 n.8 (2d Cir. 2013). The U.S. Supreme Court will decide this question and resolve this split between the Circuits in *NLRB v. Murphy Oil USA, Inc.*, 137 S.Ct. 809 (13 January 2017) (granting petition for writ of certiorari).

108 *See O'Connor, supra* note 88, 2016 WL 4398271, at *9.

In November, 2016, the trial court delayed the trial pending Uber's appeal of various rulings in the case, including the court's decision on the validity of the arbitration agreements.[109]

There are a number of lessons for gig economy workers to be gleaned from the *O'Connor* case. First, by the sheer size of the class, gig workers can gain considerable leverage in forcing a settlement. This leverage is increased by the fact that the legal question of whether or not they are employees or independent contractors is both appropriate to be brought as a class action and at least debatable so that a jury should make the final determination on that issue.[110]

Second, this leverage may be employed not only to get a substantial financial recovery, but also to extract useful noneconomic terms. While the trial court in *O'Connor* did not place much value on the noneconomic terms in the proposed settlement in that case, it did contain some valuable concessions to the drivers. With some exceptions for serious offences, the settlement removed the drivers from "at will" status and gave them a right to warnings before they would be deactivated by Uber.[111] It also provided for the establishment of a drivers' organization financially supported by Uber. While such an organization would likely run afoul of Section 8(a)(2) of the NLRA,[112] which broadly prohibits any sort of company union,[113] it is an indication that – perhaps – both the drivers and Uber recognize that their relationship might be better handled in a collective manner, rather than by a case-by-case, individual way. It may be a bridge to an actual collective bargaining relationship.[114]

Third, arbitration agreements signed by gig workers may be a strong defense for new economy companies against such class actions. While the NLRB has argued with some success that arbitration agreements that preclude an employee from participating in a class action case violates their Section 7 right to engage in mutual aid or protection, truly voluntary arbitration agreements – such as those arguably used by Uber – could amount to a voluntary waiver of that right. One question that may remain is under what circumstances a "voluntary" arbitration agreement handed to a worker for signature is truly

---

109 *See* <http://uberlawsuit.com/>.

110 There are different views about the ultimate prospects of success on the merits for this type of litigation. For an optimistic view, *see* B. Roger, 'Employment Rights in the Platform Economy: Getting Back to Basics', 10 *Harv. L. Pol'y Rev.* 2016, p. 479 (gig workers should be classified as employees). Other commentators have adopted a more neutral, wait-and-see attitude, *see* S.A. Duaban, *Workers for On-Demand Businesses – Employees or Independent Contractors?*, 63-*MAY Fed. Law.* 2016, p. 8.

111 A 27-million-dollar class action settlement was also approved by the court in *Cotter v. Lyft Inc.*, 193 F.-Supp.3d 1030 (N.D.Ca. 2016); Lyft provides services similar to Uber, and Lyft's drivers likewise claimed they had been misclassified as independent contractors. In addition to the financial terms, as in the proposed *O'Connor* settlement, the agreement also restricted Lyft from terminating drivers at will. Id., p. 1033.

112 29 U.S.C. § 158(a)(2).

113 *See Electromation, Inc.*, 309 NLRB 990 (1992).

114 *See* B. Roger, 'The Social Costs of Uber', 82 *U. Chi. L. Rev. Dialogue* 2015, pp. 99-100 (2015) (suggesting some hope for collective action as a solution for Uber drivers' problems, but also acknowledging some difficulties, including the drivers' lack of "communal ties.").

voluntary, and whether there are any implied or other pressures placed upon the individual to sign. The Court of Appeal may well clarify this point in the *O'Connor* case.

Finally, while *O'Connor* is instructive for drivers at new economy companies like Uber, the availability of effective class actions for other types of gig workers is not as clear. As noted earlier, given the employment at will rule, a case holding that independent contractors are employees does not entitle them to job security. The drivers in *O'Connor* were able to craft an effective class action by making some fairly specific claims about mileage reimbursement and the failure to remit tips. Other gig workers who are not drivers would likely not have these same type of claims, and might have to be even more creative in coming up with meaningful damages to make the class action worthwhile.

9.4 CONCLUSIONS

Collective approaches to resolving the labor law dilemmas presented by the new economy have a number of advantages. Revitalized labor unions, though collective bargaining and other agreements, may effectively protect the interests of gig workers. They may do so through by organizing them as traditional employees under the NLRA, or by representing them as independent contractors through local labor laws such as the Seattle ordinance that gives drivers the right to bargain. Once in a collective bargaining relationship, the union and new economy employer have an interest in making the company successful, and having the workers share in that success. The gig economy appears to be here to stay, and a war waged by weakened labor unions to drive new economy companies out of business is not like to succeed in the longer term.

The Seattle ordinance and the scuttled SEIU–Airbnb agreement are perhaps the best roadmaps for the success of collective bargaining in the new economy. Unions could use their remaining political influence to have cities and municipalities, and even states, introduce collective bargaining laws for independent contractors performing gig work. This has multiple advantages, including avoiding the difficult legal question of the status of the gig workers as contractors or employees, providing a new labor law with improvements over the NLRA process, and for the new economy companies preserving a business model that relies on independent contractors. These local laws should be carefully drafted to ensure they do not run afoul of NLRA pre-emption arguments or federal antitrust laws, as outline herein.

While the SEIU–Airbnb draft agreement is rather specific to the room/house sharing business, its very originality should push unions and new economy businesses to come up with equally innovative "win–win" agreements that preserve some measure of union jobs, increase the socially responsible image of these companies, and ease the regulatory environment in which they operate. On a broader level, the concept of getting new economy companies to pledge their support for union policy goals (the fight for $15) will be beneficial for the labor movement in general. Likewise, the idea of employee owned or unionized businesses working within (or a part of) the new economy (for example, unionized cleaning companies being promoted by Airbnb) may have a wider application. One could envision a union hiring hall model, for example, being utilized in the new economy. As authorized by the NLRA,[115] and is the practice in the US construction industry, labor unions have hiring halls with workers skilled in their respective fields (electricians, plumbers, pipefitters, carpenters, etc.). When a construction project arises, the various contractors and subcontractors with collective bargaining agreements with construction trade unions are obligated to obtain workers for the project from the hiring hall. These workers are paid the wages and benefits outlined in the collective bargaining agreement, and the employer reaps the advantage of having an immediately available, highly trained, and skilled workforce at its disposal for the duration of the project.[116] Perhaps a different kind of union hiring hall could place gig workers at the disposal of new economy employers in various fields, such as drivers for Uber. These workers, like construction workers on a building site, would be used as necessary to complete a particular task.

To the extent that collective bargaining is not an option, for legal or other reasons, gig workers may turn to class action litigation as an alternative collective method to protect their interests. The potential sheer size of the class action (and commensurate exposure of the new economy company to damages) can be used as leverage for financial and, importantly, noneconomic concessions that could lead to greater job security and a path to some form of greater collective voice in the workplace. However, at the same time, arbitration agreements prohibiting such class actions at the moment appear to be a formidable obstacle to the use of this type of collective action, so long as they are truly voluntary. This issue will have to be more fully litigated, and in the meantime employees/independent contractors should be encouraged to refuse to sign these arbitration agreements where possible, so as to preserve their class action rights.

Regardless of the era, workers – however they are particularly classified – generally have an unbalanced power relationship with their employers. Collective action is the best correction to this imbalance.

115 *See* 29 U.S.C. § 158(f).

116 *See* E. Naduris-Weissman, 'The Worker Center Movement and Traditional Labor Law: A Contextual Analysis', 30 *Berkeley J. Emp. Lab. L.* 2009, p. 268.

BIBLIOGRAPHY

Andrias, K., 'The New Labor Law', 126 *Yale L.J.* 2016, p. 13.

Bartlett, B., 'Rising Tide of Multidistrict FLSA Cases is Met by Better-Equipped Employers', 13 *FLSA Emp. Exemption Handbook News* 2007, pp. 3-6.

Beilman, A., '"A Fair Day's Pay for a Fair Day's Work": A Defense of Kentucky Wage and Hour Class Actions', 55 *U. Louisville L. Rev.* 2017, pp. 57-80.

Bennerjune, K., 'Airbnb in Disputes with New York and San Francisco', *New York Times*, 28 June 2016, Retrieved on 1 March 2017 from <www.nytimes.com/2016/06/29/technology/airbnb-sues-san-francisco-over-a-law-it-had-helped-pass.html?_r=0>.

Brooks, G. & Steadman, T., 'Is the Gig Economy a Fleeting Fad, or an Enduring Legacy?', 33 *J. Compensation Benefits ART* 5, March/April 2017, p. 7.

Clark, Jr., R.T., 'Public Sector Collective Bargaining at the Crossroads', 44 *Urb. Law.* 2012, p. 186.

Das Acevedo, D., 'Regulating Employment Relationships in the Sharing Economy', 20 *Emp. Rts. Emp. Pol'y J.* 2016, p. 1.

Dawsey, J., 'Union Financed Fight to Block Airbnb in New York City', *Wall Street Journal*, 6 May 2016, Retrieved on 1 March 2017 from <www.wsj.com/articles/union-financed-fight-to-block-airbnb-in-new-york-city-1462842763>.

De Stefano, V., 'The Rise of the "Just-In-Time" Workforce: On-Demand Work, Crowdwork, and Labor Protection in the "Gig Economy"', 37 *Comp. Lab. L. Pol'y J.* 2016, p. 1.

Duaban, S.A., 'Workers for On-Demand Businesses – Employees or Independent Contractors?', 63 *MAY Fed. Law.* 2016, p. 8.

Dwoskin, E., 'Airbnb Is Forming an Alliance with One of the Nation's Biggest Labor Unions', *Washington Post*, 18 April 2016, Retrieved on 1 March 2017 from <www.washingtonpost.com/news/the-switch/wp/2016/04/18/airbnb-is-forming-an-alliance-with-one-of-the-nations-biggest-labor-unions/?utm_term=.e357ff05d4ce>.

Edsall, T.B., 'Two Top Unions Split from AFL-CIO', *Washington Post*, 26 July 2005.

Eliasoph, I.H., 'Know your (Lack of) Rights: Examining the Cause and Effect of Phantom Employment Rights', 12 *Emp. Rts. Emp. Pol'y J.* 2008, p. 197.

Finkin, M.W., 'Beclouded Work, Beclouded Workers in Historical Perspective', 37 *Comp. Lab. L. Pol'y J.* 2016, p. 603.

Graham, J., 'Airbnb Aims #WeAccept Super Bowl Ad at Refugees, Immigrants', *USA Today*, 5 February 2017.

Jones IV, S., 'Wisconsin's Act 10 Limitations on Collective Bargaining: Balancing a Budget on the Backs of Public Employees', 13 *Geo. J.L. Pub. Pol'y* 2015, p. 543.

Kennedy, E., 'Freedom from Independence: Collective Bargaining Rights for "Dependent Contractors"', 26 *Berkeley J. Emp. Lab. L.*, 2005, pp. 143-178.

Lee, D., 'Bundling "Alt-Labor": How Policy Reform Can Facilitate Political Organization in Emerging Worker Movements', 51 *Harv. C.R.-C.L. L. Rev.* 2016, pp. 509-535.

Lee, T., 'Sharing Economy Startups Airbnb and Uber Don't Share Similar CEOs', *San Francisco Chronicle*, 13 February 2015.

Levin, S., 'Airbnb's Controversial Deal with Labor Union Falls Apart after Intense Backlash', *The Guardian*, 21 April 2016, Retrieved on 1 March 2017 from <www.theguardian.com/technology/2016/apr/21/airbnb-seiu-labor-union-deal-called-off-after-criticism>.

Levin, S. & Wong, J.C., 'Airbnb Negotiations with Powerful US Labor Union Facing Backlash', *The Guardian*, 18 April 2016, Retrieved on 1 March 2017 from <www.theguardian.com/technology/2016/apr/18/airbnb-seiu-backlash-labor-union-deal-new-york-california>.

Means, B. & Seiner, J.A., 'Navigating the Uber Economy', 49 *U.C. Davis L. Rev.* 2016, pp. 1511-1546.

Miller, J., 'Uber, Airbnb, and Other Labor Dilemmas', *The American Prospect*, 26 April 2016, Retrieved on 1 March 2017 from <http://prospect.org/article/uber-airbnb-and-other-labor-dilemmas>.

Naduris-Weissman, E., 'The Worker Center Movement and Traditional Labor Law: A Contextual Analysis', 30 *Berkeley J. Emp. Lab. L.* 2009, p. 268.

Olson, C.A., Haley, T.F. & Stoklas, A.L., 'The Contingent and On-Demand Workforce and the "Gig Economy"', SY002 *Am. L. Inst. Continuing Legal Education* 28-30 June 2016.

Perry, A.M., 'Municipal State Action Antitrust Immunity: A Federalism Argument against the Bad Faith Exception', 56 *Fordham L. Rev.* 1987, pp. 471-486.

Petroski, W. & Pfannenstiel, B., 'Iowa House, Senate Approve Sweeping Collective Bargaining Changes', *Des Moines Register*, 16 February 2017, Retrieved on 1 March 2017 from <www.desmoinesregister.com/story/news/politics/2017/02/16/amid-marathon-debate-iowa-legislature-barrels-towards-passage-collective-bargaining-bill/97984338/>.

Roger, B., 'The Social Costs of Uber', 82 *U. Chi. L. Rev. Dialogue* 2015, pp. 85-102.

Roger, B., 'Employment Rights in the Platform Economy: Getting Back to Basics', 10 *Harv. L. Pol'y Rev.* 2016, pp. 479-519.

Sachs, B., 'Despite Preemption: Making Labor Law in Cities and States', 124 *Harv. L. Rev.* 2011, pp. 1153-1223.

Said, C., 'Airbnb Hurts Hotels, Trade Group and Union Say', *San Francisco Chronicle*, 30 September 2016, Retrieved on 1 March 2017 from <www.sfchronicle.com/business/article/Airbnb-hurts-hotels-says-trade-group-and-union-9517727.php>.

Sanjukta, P.M., 'The Enduring Ambiguities of Antitrust Liability for Worker Collective Action', 47 *Loy. U. Chi. L.J.* 2016, pp. 969-1048.

Semet, A., 'Political Decision-Making at the National Labor Relations Board: An Empirical Examination of the Board's Unfair Labor Practice Decisions through the Clinton and Bush II Years', 37 *Berkeley J. Emp. Lab. L.* 2016, p. 223.

Szymanski, C., 'Scalia's Shadow: The Freidrichs Case and the Fate of the American Labor Movement', *Giornale di Diritto Del Lavoro e di Relazioni Industriali* 2016, pp. 761-772.

Weiler, P., 'Promises to Keep: Securing Workers' Rights to Self-Organization under the NLRA', 96 *Harv. L. Rev.* 1983, p. 1769.

10 Back to the Roots: Re-embedding Labour Law into Civil Law to Prevent Evasion of Labour Law

*Elisabeth Brameshuber**

10.1 Introduction

Labour law is based on the idea that the employee owes his employer no success, but only to work diligently. According to the principle of subordination, the employer decides where and when the employee has to work, what devices to use, etc. Furthermore, the employer has the power of control. Thus, only to a certain extent can the employee influence whether the outcome of his work will be an economic success; the responsibility for guaranteeing a specific success must not be shifted from the employer to the employee.

However, the so-called new forms of labour (of which Uber is the most prominent example) challenge this basic idea. On the one hand, it is argued that Uber drivers are not 'real' employees; as a result, the creation of new legal regimes is promoted.[1] As reported by the media, such new forms of labour are carried out by 'independent purchasers', or 'independent' persons, such as those working for TaskRabbit, carrying out various tasks for another, including queuing for concert tickets or walking the dog.[2] On the other hand, though, classic labour law actions, such as surveillance of said independent person, are still implemented.[3] Not only do such measures raise privacy concerns, but also the question of what happens if a Uber driver goes too fast or brakes too harshly and is, therefore,

---

* Assistant Professor, WU Vienna University of Economics and Business, Institute for Austrian and European Labour Law and Social Security Law.

1 *Cf.* the development in Spain, where a specific type of contract was introduced only recently, the *Trabajador Autónomo Económicamente Dependiente. See also* E. Kocher, 'Schutz und kollektive Privatautonomie – das Arbeitsverhältnis in seiner Besonderheit', *in* L. Nogler & U. Reifner (Eds.), *Life Time Contracts: Social Long-Term Contracts in Labour, Tenancy and Consumer Credit Law*, The Hague, Eleven International Publishing, 2014, p. 366, and O. Razzolini, 'Self-Employment and Economic Dependency in the Light of the Social Contract Law', *in* Nogler & Reifner (Eds.), *supra* note 1, p. 388. However, only recently, a London tribunal held that Uber drivers have to be classed as 'workers' and thus are entitled to minimum wage and holiday pay. Retrieved on 4 January 2017 from <www.ft.com/content/a0bb02b2-9d0a-11e6-a6e4-8b8e77dd083a>.

2 *See, e.g.*, T. Klebe, 'Wenn Arbeitnehmer selbständige Crowdworker werden', *Börsen-Zeitung*, 18 December 2015, p. 8.

3 *Cf.* D. MacMillan, 'Uber's App Will Soon Begin Tracking Driving Behavior: The Software Is Aimed at Improving Driver Safety, but Could Raise Privacy Concerns,' *Wall Street Journal (Online)*, 29 June 2016.

classified as a low performer. Negative consequences, up to and including termination of the contract, are only moderated if labour law applies.

Yet, some scholars argue that by focusing on the basic principles of labour law, we will soon realize that no new legal regime is necessary, but that these new phenomena already fit into the well-accepted labour law categories.[4] They argue that a more-holistic approach is necessary (e.g., by looking at personal work contracts as a whole).[5] Nevertheless, we have to be aware of the fact that, not only in the digital work business or 'gig economy', but also in general, employers are going to continue to avoid the application of traditional labour law.[6] It is our task, as legal scholars, to ask why this evasion takes place and what remedies exist. Such new forms of work, therefore, serve as starting point for addressing the more-general question of how such evasion could be prevented.

As the economic crisis of the past years has proven, the more protection for workers a legal system provides for, the stronger the employers' tendency is to try to avoid the application of labour law.[7] However, it is not this chapter's aim to advocate for less protection in labour law in general. On the contrary, as the examples of Uber,[8] City Sprint,[9] and foodora show, a certain minimum protection standard is not only highly necessary, but must also be enforceable in front of labour courts. Nevertheless, this chapter wants to explore ways to adjust the employment relationship, not only in times of economic crisis, but also in cases of employee's low performance (e.g., by cutting wages as sanction for his poor performance). In a nutshell, as *advocatus diaboli*: could an acknowledged ability to cut wages – under certain circumstances – be an alternative path, helping to prevent the above-mentioned evasion of labour law, by giving employers another tool not only to better react to employees' low performance, but also, for example, to its own economic difficulties? In other words, this chapter widens the sometimes-narrow focus regarding the possible reasons for the evasion, bearing in mind that, in many States, strict

4 *Cf.* M. Freedland & N. Kountouris, 'The Legal Characterization of Personal Work Relations and the Idea of Labour Law', *in* G. Davidov & B. Langille (Eds.), *The Idea of Labour Law*, Oxford University Press, Oxford, 2011, p. 195.

5 *See also* M. Freedland & N. Kountouris, *The Legal Construction of Personal Work Relations*, Oxford University Press, Oxford, 2011, p. 120.

6 *Cf.* regarding work in the 'gig economy' W. Däubler & T. Klebe, 'Crowdwork: Die neue Form der Arbeit – Arbeitgeber auf der Flucht?', *Neue Zeitschrift für Arbeitsrecht*, 2015, p. 1032.

7 Apparently, even labour reforms in various Member States could not prevent that development. *Cf.* C. Barnard, *EU Employment Law*, 4th edn, Oxford University Press, Oxford, 2012, p. 133 *et seq.*, on the crisis-related labour law reforms in various Member States.

8 *See* the case in front of a London tribunal of two Uber drivers who, according to the tribunal, should be classified as 'workers'. This status entitles the drivers to the minimum wage and holiday pay. However, they are not protected from unfair dismissal, which would only be the case if they had been classed as 'employees', Available from <www.ft.com/content/a0bb02b2-9d0a-11e6-a6e4-8b8e77dd083a>. According to the media, Uber is going to appeal against the ruling, Retrieved on 4 January 2017 from <www.theguardian.com/technology/2016/oct/28/uber-uk-tribunal-self-employed-status>.

9 *See* the case of a bicycle courier who has just recently been granted worker-status instead of self-employed-status by a London Employment Tribunal, Retrieved on 10 January 2017 from <www.bbc.com/news/business-38534524>.

provisions regarding protection against termination are perceived as one of its main drivers.

From the perspective of Life Time Contracts[10] and their Principles,[11] it is obvious that Principle 10 (Adaptation) is the underlying dogmatic provision of this chapter. After a short overview of the main characteristics of the employment relationship (Section 10.2), which is followed by Section 10.3 that, in turn, highlights some major changes from a legal, as well as from a factual, perspective, regarding employment relationships in Europe over the past few years, and Section 10.4 focusses on the legal bases for adjusting wages. One of the questions to be dealt with is whether Principle 10 follows any specific rules when applied in an employment relationship, compared with civil law, in general. Another crucial point is to explore is if there is a bottom line regarding the adjustment of wages, which is particularly contentious in those legal systems where there is no mandatory statutory or collectively agreed minimum wage or where the minimum wage is extremely low. At this stage, Principle 14 (Securing Livelihood) comes to the fore, according to which a minimum level of income must be guaranteed. It is argued that, within this principle, more focus should be put on the employment relationship.

10.2 THE MAIN CHARACTERISTICS OF THE EMPLOYMENT RELATIONSHIP

Although the concept of the employment relationship has recently been challenged and, despite various peculiarities regarding the definition and the status of the employee in the different EU Member States,[12] there is a common consensus about the main characteristics of the employment relationship, which is also displayed in the CJEU's definition of the employee. Since there is no general legal definition of the terms 'worker', as referred to in Article 45 TFEU or 'employee', as referred to in various Directives, and since the Court only has had few opportunities to develop on the term 'employee', the focus is on its – broad – interpretation of the term 'worker'.[13] According to the Court, "the essential feature of an employment relationship [...] is that for a certain period of time a person performs services for and under the direction of another person in return for which he receives remuneration."[14]

10 L. Nogler & U. Reifner, 'Introduction: The New Dimension of Life Time in the Law of Contracts and Obligations', *in* Nogler & Reifner (Eds.), *supra* note 1, Ch. 1, pp. 1-60 [hereafter, Nogler & Reifner 'Introduction'].

11 'Principles of Life Time Contracts', *in* Nogler & Reifner (Eds.), *supra* note 1, pp. 5-10 [hereinafter the 'Principles'].

12 *See, e.g.*, Barnard, *supra* note 7, p. 154, on the difference between employee and worker status in the UK, or F. Marhold & M. Friedrich, *Österreichisches Arbeitsrecht*, 3rd edn, Verlag Österreich, Wien, 2016, pp. 40-42, on the difference between 'Dienstnehmer' (fully protected employee) and 'freier Dienstnehmer' (dependent self-employed who enjoys only some basic labour protection rights), in Austria.

13 Barnard, *supra* note 7, p. 148.

14 Judgment of 1 October 2015, *Bio Phillipe Auguste*, C-432/14, EU:C:2015:643, para. 22, and cases cited therein (regarding, inter alia, the concept of 'worker' and 'employment relationship' in the EU Treaties and EU

In opposition to someone who fulfills tasks independently, an employee[15] is – in contrast to a self-employed person – in a position of subordination that allows the employer to give instructions about when, where, and how to work and to control the employee. Consequently, the employer bears the risk of the success or 'failure' of the employee's work: since the employee is, generally speaking, not in a position to strongly influence the employer's success, he or she does not have to bear the risk of failure. By paying the employee a monthly salary in exchange for the employee's effort or labour for a certain amount of time, the risk of failure lies entirely with the employer. Because of the subordinate position and the general distribution of risk, the employee does not owe any success, but only to work diligently.[16] The employment relationship is thus, characterized mainly by the employee's subordinate position to and his or her dependency on an employer.[17] A 'self-employed' person, on the contrary, performs his or her economic activity outside of a relationship of subordination,[18] bears the risk of the success or failure of his or her activity,[19] and is paid directly and in most cases in full.[20] Several years later, in 2006, the Commission stated:

> [t]he concept of '*economically dependent work*' covers situations which fall between the two established concepts of subordinate employment and independent self-employment. These workers do not have a contract of employment. They may not be covered by labour law since they occupy a "grey area" between labour law and commercial law. Although formally 'self-employed', they remain economically dependent on a single principal or client/employer for their source of income.[21]

Especially with regard to the new forms of work outlined in Section 10.1, *supra*, it is noteworthy that the Commission expressed its awareness that such economically dependent work was to be "clearly distinguished from the deliberate mis-classification [*sic*] of

---

Directives) and Judgment of 14 October 2010, *Union syndicale Solidaires Isère*, C-428/09, EU:C:2010:612, para. 28 (regarding the concept of an employment relationship for purposes of Directive 2003/88/EC of the European Parliament and of the Council of 4 November 2003 Concerning Certain Aspects of the Organisation of Working Time, OJ 2003 L 299/9).

15 In the following, the term 'employee' is used in its wider sense, thus not paying attention to the distinction between 'employee' and 'worker' as applied in the UK.

16 For Austria, *cf.* Marhold & Friedrich, *supra* note 12, p. 39; for Germany *cf.* U. Preis, *Arbeitsrecht*, 4th edn, Verlag Dr. Otto Schmidt, Köln, 2012, pp. 344-345; for France *cf.* J.M. Verdier, A. Coeuret & M.-A. Souriac, *Droit du travail Volume 2 Rapport individuels*, 16th edn, Dalloz, 2011, pp. 88-89 ('*accomplissement consciencieux*').

17 Barnard, *supra* note 7, p. 145; Marhold & Friedrich, *supra* note 12, p. 34 *et seq.*

18 Judgment of 20 November 2001, *Jany*, C-268/99, EU:C:2001:616, paras. 34, 70.

19 Id., para. 70.

20 Id.; *also* Barnard, *supra* note 7, p. 151.

21 Commission Green Paper of 22 November 2006,'Modernising Labour Law to Meet the Challenges of the 21st Century' COM(2006) 708 final, p. 11

self-employment."[22] That awareness highlights one of the main problems behind working in the gig economy: the use of a workforce made up of purportedly self-employed persons when, in fact, looking at the essential criteria of subordination and dependency, said persons would have to be classed as employees or 'workers'[23] and would, therefore, fall under the scope of labour legislation, or at least part of it.[24]

10.3 Evasion of Labour Law Obligations

Over the past few years, the number of self-employed persons has continually risen. Taking into account the period between the first quarter of 2008 and the second quarter of 2014, of the 1.1 million rise in employment in the UK, 732,000 were self-employed. Of the microbusinesses (i.e., up to nine employees) set up in the UK over past decade, 95 per cent are one-person outfits.[25] In Germany, in 2013, the Federal Council approved a Draft Act of a Bill to fight the misuse of contracts for services and prevent evasion of labour law obligations,[26] but it never entered into force. Subsequently, in 2016, a revised version of that Draft Act was approved, and on 1 April 2017, the Act entered into force.[27] Among others, it intends to provide more legal certainty regarding the classification of persons who provide services, either as employees or as self-employed.[28] One pillar of that Act is a new legal definition of the term 'employee' in § 611a BGB (*Bürgerliches Gesetzbuch*).

Although labour law evasion can be perceived as constant problem, it appears that during the past several years, we have experienced an increase in problems associated with labour law's coverage and its obsolescence.[29] As developments in some countries

22 Id.

23 Only to name a particular specificity of one Member State, the UK.

24 For an alternative path to defining the employment relationship, *see* J. Prassl, *The Concept of the Employer*, Oxford University Press, Oxford, 2015.

25 J. Gapper, 'The Sharing Economy Must Share the Risks', *Financial Times*, 18 December 2014, Retrieved on 4 January 2017 from<www.ft.com/content/d3bd6750-848d-11e4-bae9-00144feabdc0>.

26 Gesetzesentwurf des Bundesrates. Entwurf eines Gesetzes zur Bekämpfung des Missbrauchs von Werkverträgen und zur Verhinderung der Umgehung von arbeitsrechtlichen Verpflichtungen, Federal Council Printing Matter 18/14, 28.10.2013, Retrieved on 4 January 2017 from <http://dipbt.bundestag.de/dip21/btd/18/000/1800014.pdf>. *See also* European Labour Law Network, 'Bill to Fight the Misuse of Contracts for Work and to Prevent Evasion of Labour Law Obligations', Retrieved on 10 January 2017 from <www.labourlawnetwork.eu/national_labour_law/national_legislation/legislative_developments/prm/109/v__detail/id__3501/category__13/index.html>.

27 Gesetz zur Änderung des Arbeitnehmerüberlassungsgesetzes und anderer Gesetze, BGBl Nr 8/2017, 258.

28 Gesetzesentwurf der Bundesregierung. Entwurf eines Gesetzes zur Änderung des Arbeitnehmerüberlassungsgesetzes und anderer Gesetze, Federal Council Printing Matter 18/9232, 20.07.2016, Retrieved on 10 January 2017 from <http://dipbt.bundestag.de/doc/btd/18/092/1809232.pdf>.

29 G. Davidov, *A Purposive Approach to Labour Law*, Oxford University Press, Oxford, 2012, pp. 3-4; *also* Prassl, *supra* note 24, pp. 4-5.

show, legislatures try to prevent a reduction of employee protections by introducing new categories or statuses for persons who provide services. However, such protections are often rather minimal,[30] while the legislation opens up new possibilities for misclassification.[31]

10.4 Applying Civil-Law Instruments to Prevent Evasion of Labour Law?

Since an employment contract is a contract following the general rules of civil law, prima facie civil-law constructs, such as contract avoidance on account of mistake or error (*Irrtumsanfechtung* in German) or contract adaptation because of a change in circumstances, can apply. However, unlike specific labour-law rules, which typically enhance employee protections,[32] general civil law constructs do not necessarily take into account the weaker position of one of the contracting parties. Generally speaking, private law assumes that the freedom of contract guarantees the parties' 'right' to establish the terms and conditions of their contract.[33] But, because of the weaker position of the employee (in most cases), the 'reign of free market private law rules' and, thus, the application of general civil law is regarded as means of granting 'unfettered control' to employers.[34]

Yet, according to Davidov, it appears that in many countries that the resort to standards or principles, rather than to rules, in labour law has increased over the past years (e.g., good faith, proportionality,[35] and managerial prerogative).[36] Good faith and managerial prerogative are two particularly classic standards of general civil law, as depicted, for example, by § 242 BGB.[37] As G. Davidov has shown, the application of these general standards, in addition to labour law rules, could prove useful in preventing evasion of labour law, on the one hand, and in adapting the law, on the other hand,[38] although it is obvious that their application only helps in those cases in which the threshold necessary

30 *See, e.g.*, the so-called 'freier Dienstnehmer' status in Austria, which guarantees only basic labour rights (*e.g.*, regarding equal treatment in case of maternity and some basic rights regarding periods of notice in case of termination) and further, guarantees mandatory social security coverage. However, persons with that status do not fall within the scope of collective bargaining agreements, which is particularly important as there is no statutory minimum wage in Austria.

31 Davidov, *supra* note 29, pp. 136-137.

32 This is at least true for most of the European Civil-law-based systems. The English common-law-based system, on the contrary, is deemed to be rather employer-protective. *See* Freedland & Kountouris, *supra* note 5, p. 184.

33 *Cf.* F. Bydlinski, *System und Prinzipien des Privatrechts*, Springer, Wien/New York, 1996, p. 147 *et seq.*

34 Davidov, *supra* note 29, p. 157.

35 *See* P. Loi, *Il principio di ragionevolezza e proporzionalità nel diritto del lavoro*, G. Giapichelli Editore, Torino, 2016, passim.

36 *See also* Davidov, *supra* note 29, p. 158.

37 "Der Schuldner ist verpflichtet, die Leistung so zu bewirken, wie Treu und Glauben mit Rücksicht auf die Verkehrssitte es erfordern." For other examples of the notion of good faith in the legal systems of the Member States, *see* Freedland & Kountouris, *supra* note 5, p. 195.

38 Davidov, *supra* note 29, pp. 158-159.

to gain access to the courts can be overcome.[39] In addition, recourse to such general standards always entails the risk of legal uncertainty. Thus, it is indispensable to establish specific preconditions, criteria, and limits regarding the application of these general civil-law standards or principles.[40]

The wording of the Principles points in the same direction. The rules concerning good faith (bona fide) are, for example, regarded as principles of Life Time Contracts.[41] From a life-time perspective, the differentiation between subordinated work (generally speaking, work carried out by employees) and work carried out by the self-employed pursuant to a contract for services is obsolete.[42] Under either type of contract, the person providing the services is – in one way or the other – interested in the stability of the contract itself, as well as in the stability of its conditions, because usually, the person providing the services, above all, wants to satisfy his or her basic social needs with the generated income.[43] Applying unified general standards or principles to such contracts could help overcome evasion tendencies. By referring to the 'fundamental obligation of a human being' as one of the relevant circumstances to be considered in case of an adaptation of an Life Time Contract, especially Principle 10, it shows that not only the economic, but also the social dimension has to be taken into account.

Yet, it is questionable whether the focus should indeed be on the question of how to 'bring more labour law into civil law' in order to foster the effectiveness of labour law.[44] One could also rephrase it by asking which principles of general contract law, on the one hand, and of labour law, on the other hand, must be consolidated in order to guarantee the maximum amount of contractual freedom while, at the same time, providing for the necessary social protections.

10.4.1 Adaptation of Life Time Contracts in General

The ability to adapt a contract is one of the issues identified as an underlying reason or justification for developing the Life Time Contract concept. One of the common features of Life Time Contracts is that the parties to the Life Time Contract (should) have the ability to adapt the contract. This basic idea is closely linked to the possibility of alteration

---

39 For the current developments in the UK on the contested UK tribunal fees that obviously deny workers access to justice, *cf.* A. Adams & J. Prassl, 'Oxford Study Shows UK Employment Tribunal Fees Deny Workers Access to Justice', *University of Oxford News & Events*, 20 March 2017, Retrieved on 23 March 2017 from <www.ox.ac.uk/news/2017-03-20-oxford-study-shows-uk-employment-tribunal-fees-deny-workers-access-justice>.

40 *See also* I. Ehrlich & R. Posner, 'An Economic Analysis of Legal Rulemaking', 3 *J. L. Stud.* 1974, p. 265.

41 Nogler & Reifner, 'Introduction', *supra* note 10, p. 46.

42 Freedland & Kountouris, *supra* note 5, p. 198 *et seq. See also*, Nogler & Reifner, 'Introduction', *supra* note 10, pp. 25.

43 Nogler & Reifner, 'Introduction', *supra* note 10, pp. 22-23, 26.

44 Kocher 2014, *supra* note 1, p. 352.

in case of an underlying economic imbalance (also known as *clausula rebus sic stantibus*).[45] Under German[46] and Austrian[47] law, for example, this might also lead to adaptation of the contract, although it is highly contentious whether said adaptation should be the outcome of a supplementary interpretation of the contract or, rather, of a right to be exercised by the party excessively burdened by living up to the Life Time Contract.[48] Yet, recourse to *clausula rebus sic stantibus* in order to terminate an employment relationship is prohibited because it would lead to evasion of labour legislation.[49]

10.4.2 *Adaptation of the Employment Contract*

By definition, generally speaking, the employee does not owe his or her employer any economic success, but only his or her services which are to be carried out diligently. It is the employer's risk whether the services provided by the employee lead to economic success or not. Because of the employer's managerial prerogative, it is the employer's task to specify the services to be carried out by the employee.[50] As a result, the employee cannot be held liable for not completing a certain task.[51] However, opinions differ whether (and, if so, how) an employee can be held liable for not adhering to the employer's instructions or for not working diligently. In case of damages, liability for a tort is an option, and as a disciplinary tool, termination of the contract might be possible. Cutting of wages, however, is broadly regarded as illicit.[52] On the contrary, according to Nogler and Reifner, it is widely acknowledged that illness, for example, is a reason for adapting a labour contract to new circumstances,[53] although, apparently, without adjusting wages as well. It is this chapter's aim to critically discuss this approach, especially taking into

45 Nogler & Reifner, 'Introduction', *supra* note 10, pp. 4-5.

46 *See* § 313 BGB. For applying § 313 BGB subsequent to the interpretation of the employment contract, *see* R. Wank, '§ 93 Änderung von Arbeitsbedingungen', *in* R. Richardi *et al.* (Eds.), *Münchener Handbuch zum Arbeitsrecht*, 3rd edn, C.H.Beck, München, 2009, para 14.

47 *See, e.g.*, C. Bezemek, *Die Geschäftsgrundlage im österreichischen Zivilrecht*, Springer, Wien New York, 2010.

48 *See, e.g.*, P. Rummel, '§ 901 BGB', *in* P. Rummel & M. Lukas (Eds.), *Kommentar zum Allgemeinen Bürgerlichen Gesetzbuch*, Manz, Wien, 2016, para 15.

49 For Germany, *see, e.g.*, U. Preis, '1. Teil. Grundlagen zur Beendigung von Arbeitsverhältnissen', *in* R. Ascheid *et al.*, *Kündigungsrecht*, 5th edn, C.H.Beck, München, 2017, K.IV. para. 72.

50 Kocher, *supra* note 1, p. 357.

51 Marhold & Friedrich, *supra* note 12, p. 39. *See also* Razzolini, *supra* note 1, p. 390.

52 For the applicable French law before the 2016 amendments to its Code du Travail, *see* Article L. 1331-2 Code du Travail, according to which "fines or other pecuniary sanctions are prohibited" (translation by Freedland & Kountouris, *supra* note 5, p. 203). As M. Freedland & N. Kountouris have shown, French courts have interpreted that former provision broadly by prohibiting "any deduction from the salary applied by reason of bad performance of the work", id., pp. 202-203 (reference is also made to a similar legal situation in Italy). As they further point out, in the UK, though, more leeway is given to contractual arrangements that might allow for deductions from remuneration with respect to incomplete or defective performance of work. Id.

53 Nogler & Reifner, 'Introduction', *supra* note 10, p. 45.

account that under certain circumstances, adaptation of wages could be an alternative solution to terminating the employment contract.[54]

This also brings us to the second scenario in which an adaptation of the employment contract might be a sensible solution. As the economic crisis has shown, under specific circumstances, adaptation of an employment contract by cutting wages might be the only way for the employer to keep the personnel in employment. In other words, can the employer unilaterally adapt wages if the only other solution to live through unforeseen economic difficulties would be termination of the employment contract?[55] And if so, is there a limit and at what level is it set?

10.4.3 Prerequisites

Principle 10, on the adaptation of Life Time Contracts, establishes specific prerequisites regarding the adaptation of social long-term contracts, which also apply to the adaptation of wages because of the employee's non-diligent work or a lack of quality in the employee's work.[56] First, a 'significant' change in the 'social and economic circumstances' on which the employment contract is based must have occurred. It is, therefore, necessary to decide whether not adhering to the level of diligence is a (social) change in the circumstances and of significance.

As termination of an employment relationship for disciplinary reasons in a broad sense (i.e., the quality of the employee's work does not correspond to his or her contractual obligations), is, in most of countries, limited to certain circumstances and as adjusting wages is also a disciplinary measure, the same preconditions regarding termination could be applied. On the other hand, adjusting wages is the more lenient consequence. However, since application of the *clausula rebus sic stantibus* must not diminish the protection provided by rules regarding termination of the employment relationship, the application of the same prerequisites is likely to be necessary. From a synallagmatic point of view, it might also be helpful to take a look at the wage levels of other employees in comparable positions. If employees providing the same services at the same level of diligence earn much less, the element 'significant' might be fulfilled. This is also demonstrated by Principle 9 (Remuneration), according to which "[t]he mutual obligations of life time contracts shall not be grossly disproportionate."[57]

54 Yet, it is clear that in practice it is most difficult to decide whether the employee indeed has not been working diligently. The concrete parameter is going to be the single employment contract, and in case of absence the average diligence of comparable employees. For Austria, *see* R. Rebhahn & C. Kietaibl, *in* M. Neumayr & G. P. Reissner (Eds.), *Zeller Kommentar zum Arbeitsrecht*, 2nd edn, Manz, Wien, 2011, § 1153, paras 13, 15, 32.

55 As Freedland & Kountouris further demonstrate, this possibility exists, for example, under Italian law (*supra* note 5, pp. 210-211).

56 Principles, *supra* note 11, p. 7.

57 Id.

Another reason for adaptation according to Principle 10 arises out of "material circumstances from which the parties derived [*sic*] ... are ... at variance with its original situation to such an extent that the social nature of the contract is jeopardised".[58] Again, it is not clear when circumstances are 'material'. However, it is quite obvious that not working diligently, alone, is not going to change the social nature of the contract. Thus, it should be clear that not working diligently can only be subsumed under the first alternative of Principle 10.

The second prerequisite to be fulfilled is that the change in circumstances must be 'unforeseen'. By stating that "all the circumstances of the specific case"[59] have to be taken into account, and especially by referring to the "contractual or statutory allocation of risk and the fundamental obligation of a human being", Principle 10 can be interpreted in a way that the specificities of the employment contract have to be respected. Due to the social long-term dimension of the employment contract, the employer cannot argue that circumstances related to aging or illness were unforeseen, as long as the amount of reduction of the employee's diligence lies within the norm of comparable employees. Any other argument would be contrary to the employer's duty of care.[60] Aspects of this line of argumentation can also be found in Principle 5, according to which "physical, social and psychological considerations [have to] be taken into account in order to ensure the protection of the weaker party to the contract."[61]

Finally, adaptation is only legitimate if the "one of the parties cannot reasonably be expected to continue to comply with the contract without variation of its terms".[62] This suggests that the change in circumstances has to reach a certain gravity; it further objectifies the possible adjustment to a certain degree, by introducing a reasonability criterion, which cannot be assessed without taking into consideration what other employers in comparable circumstances would do.

Thus, adjustment of wages because of a lack of quality in the employee's work under the Principle 10 (Adaptation) is rather unlikely. Due to the social long-term dimension of employment contracts, adjustment because of illness- or age-related lack of diligence/quality has to be ruled out. Consequently, only severe decreases in the employee's performance, unrelated to physical or psychological circumstances, not foreseen by the parties when concluding the contract can allow for an adaptation. Although such cases might be rare, such an approach could also lead to an enhancement of employee capacities: in parallel to adjustment measures due to lack of quality, employers might be inclined to

58 Id.

59 Id.

60 On the employer's duty of care, *see, e.g.*, E.A. Kramer, *Arbeitsvertragliche Verbindlichkeiten neben Lohnzahlung und Dienstleistung*, Manz, Wien, 1975, pp. 21, 28-29.

61 Principles, *supra* note 11, p. 6.

62 Id., p. 7.

establish high-performance work systems in order to promote, for example, capacity-building by their employees.[63]

In the second scenario, in which the employer faces severe economic difficulties, adaptation of the employment relationship is more likely, which is due to the fact that the circumstances under which compliance with the terms of the contract cannot be reasonably expected by the employer could, indeed, be 'unforeseen'. As legislation regarding company pension systems shows, adaptation in case of severe economic difficulties is accepted in social long-term relationships.[64] Yet, adaptation must not lead to a shift in the allocation of risk to the employee. Furthermore, as comparative analyses show, unilateral adaptation must be the *ultima ratio* for the employer,[65] not only in the second, but also in the first, scenario.

Thus, although not very likely, adaptation of wages is imaginable in both scenarios. However, as taken into account in, especially, Principles 5 (Basic Needs) and 14 (Securing Livelihood),[66] even if an adaptation takes place, it is limited due to the social long-term relationship.

10.4.4 Limits

By offering his or her services to another person, an employee or a self-employed person usually strives to provide for, at least, him- or herself and, often, for others, such as family members, with essential goods in order to guarantee a decent livelihood.[67] If there is a statutory, or collectively agreed, minimum wage that only allows for deviations to the employee's advantage, that minimum is the bottom line regarding the adaptation of wages. Yet, especially in the scenario where the employer faces severe economic difficulties, application of Principle 10 (Adaptation), interpreted in the light of Principle 15 (Exclusion) might lead to a more diversified outcome. If the only alternative to adapting the contract and, thus, reducing wages to the employee's detriment, in comparison to mandatory minimum standards, were the termination of the contract and consequently unemployment, adaptation that undercuts such minimum standards could be imaginable. However, as recent legislative initiatives regarding the fight against wage-dumping show,[68] such an outcome is extremely unlikely.

---

63 For the capacity-building approach, *see* H. Arthurs, 'Labour Law after Labour', *in* Davidov & Langille (Eds.), *supra* note 4, pp. 24-26.

64 *See, e.g.*, § 6 of the Austrian Act on Company Pensions (Betriebspensionsgesetz, BGBl 1990/282).

65 *See* the English and Italian examples mentioned in Freedland & Kountouris, *supra* note 5, pp 210-211.

66 Principles, *supra* note 11, pp. 6 (Principle 5) & 9 (Principle 14).

67 *Cf.* B. Langille, 'Labour Law's Theory of Justice', *in* Davidov & Langille (Eds.), *supra* note 4, p. 116 (the idea behind labour law and its true end is a notion of human freedom that enables 'human beings leading lives [they] have a reason to value', referring to A. Sen).

68 *Cf.* the recent initiative in Germany against wage-dumping: Gesetzesentwurf der Bundesregierung. Entwurf eines Gesetzes zur Änderung des Arbeitnehmerüberlassungsgesetzes und anderer Gesetze, Federal Council

10.5 CONCLUDING REMARKS

The EuSoCo Group and the drafting of the Principles show that although labour law is widely regarded as *Sonderprivatrecht*, it is strongly rooted in the private-law system. Yet, due to the social long-term aspect of employment relationships, not all private-law prerogatives apply in a relationship focussed on providing services for a certain amount of time in a position of – sometimes more, sometimes less – subordination. As illustrated by, especially, Principles 5 (Basic Needs), 7 (Collective and Ethical Dimensions), 14 (Securing livelihood), and 15 (Exclusion), the social and human dimensions have to be taken into account.

The drafting of the Principles also shows that the contentious differentiation between employee, worker, and self-employed statuses, only to name a few of the various categories under which services can be provided, could be overcome, as long as the focus is on the social long-term aspect of the relationship. Under these circumstances, this chapter took a look at one specific private-law construct, the ability to adapt the contract and argued that, despite the general tendency in academia to object to the possibility of unilateral adaptation by the employer, this private-law construct should be considered a potential option in two specific cases. First, the employer should be able to adjust wages in case of significantly reduced quality of the employee's services. Second, adaptation should be possible in case of severe economic difficulties. However, as Principle 10 (Adaptation) shows, the specificities of the labour relationship prevent the employer from recourse to that adjustment option in the majority of cases. It limits that possibility by simultaneously recognizing the employee's need for protection.

By applying Principle 10 to labour relationships and thereby re-thinking labour law in light of its private-law roots, a new pathway for preventing evasion of labour law could be established. By applying private-law constructs in light of modern labour-law principles, such as the protection of employees' health and safety and the prevention of risk shifts from the employer to the employee, to only name two important cornerstones, the existing system could be exploited. Employers could be given, on the one hand, more leverage in case of significant changes in circumstances under which they cannot reasonably be expected to comply with the contract and employees could be offered, on the other hand, an alternative to contract termination. In this way, the tendency to create parallel struc-

Printing Matter 18/9232, 20.07.2016, Retrieved on 12 January 2017 from <http://dipbt.bundestag.de/doc/btd/18/092/1809232.pdf>. *See also* the press release by the German Federal Ministry of Labour and Social Affairs: 'Einigung bei Leiharbeit und Werkverträgen, Der von Arbeitsministerin Nahles vorgelegte Gesetzentwurf geht zur Beratung ins Kabinett', Retrieved on 12 January 2017 from <www.bmas.de/DE/Presse/Meldungen/2016/einigung-bei-leiharbeit-und-werkvertraegen.html;jsessionid=F52B7195E0F11B2863-DE80D1A6A6E7FF>.

tures and statuses, such as the *Trabajador Autónomo Económicamente Dependiente*, and, therefore, the misclassification of persons providing their services might be contained.

Bibliography

Adams, A. & Prassl, J., 'Oxford Study Shows UK Employment Tribunal Fees Deny Workers Access to Justice', *University of Oxford News & Events*, 20 March 2017, Retrieved on 23 March 2017 from <www.ox.ac.uk/news/2017-03-20-oxford-study-shows-uk-employment-tribunal-fees-deny-workers-access-justice>.

Arthurs, H., 'Labour Law after Labour', *in* G. Davidov & B. Langille (Eds.), *The Idea of Labour Law*, Oxford: Oxford University Press, 2011.

Barnard, C., *EU Employment Law* (4th ed.), Oxford: Oxford University Press, 2012.

Bezemek, C., *Die Geschäftsgrundlage im österreichischen Zivilrecht*, Wien New York: Springer, 2010.

Bydlinski, F., *System und Prinzipien des Privatrechts*, Wien/New York: Springer, 1996.

Commission Green Paper of 22 November 2006, 'Modernising Labour Law to Meet the Challenges of the 21st Century', COM(2006) 708 final.

Däubler, W. & Klebe, T., 'Crowdwork: Die neue Form der Arbeit – Arbeitgeber auf der Flucht?', *Neue Zeitschrift für Arbeitsrecht* 2015, p. 1032.

Davidov, G., *A Purposive Approach to Labour Law*, Oxford: Oxford University Press, 2012.

Ehrlich, I. & Posner, R., 'An Economic Analysis of Legal Rulemaking', 3 *J. L. Studies* 1974, p. 265.

European Labour Law Network, 'Bill to Fight the Misuse of Contracts for Work and to Prevent Evasion of Labour Law Obligations', Retrieved on 10 January 2017 from <www.labourlawnetwork.eu/national_labour_law/national_legislation/legislative_developments/prm/109/v__detail/id__3501/category__13/index.html>.

Freedland, M. & Kountouris, N., 'The Legal Characterization of Personal Work Relations and the Idea of Labour Law', *in* G. Davidov & B. Langille (Eds.), *The Idea of Labour Law*, Oxford: Oxford University Press, 2011, p. 195.

Freedland, M. & Kountouris, N., *The Legal Construction of Personal Work Relations*, Oxford: Oxford University Press, 2011.

Gapper, J., 'The Sharing Economy Must Share the Risks', *Financial Times*, 18 December 2014, Retrieved on 4 January 2017 from <www.ft.com/content/d3bd6750-848d-11e4-bae9-00144feabdc0>.

German Federal Ministry of Labour and Social Affairs, 'Einigung bei Leiharbeit und Werkverträgen, Der von Arbeitsministerin Nahles vorgelegte Gesetzentwurf geht zur Beratung ins Kabinett', Retrieved on 12 January 2017 from <www.bmas.de/DE/Presse/Meldungen/2016/einigung-bei-leiharbeit-und-werkvertraegen.html;jsessionid=F52-B7195E0F11B2863DE80D1A6A6E7FF>.

Klebe, T., 'Wenn Arbeitnehmer selbständige Crowdworker werden', *Börsen-Zeitung*, 18 December 2015, p. 8.

Kocher, E., 'Schutz und Kollektive Privatautonomie – das Arbeitsverhältnis in seiner Besonderheit', *in* L. Nogler & U. Reifner (Eds.), *Life Time Contracts: Social Long-Term Contracts in Labour, Tenancy and Consumer Credit Law*, The Hague: Eleven International Publishing, 2014, p. 366.

Kramer, E.A., *Arbeitsvertragliche Verbindlichkeiten neben Lohnzahlung und Dienstleistung*, Wien: Manz, 1975.

Langille, B., 'Labour Law's Theory of Justice', *in* G. Davidov & B. Langille (Eds.), *The Idea of Labour Law*, Oxford: Oxford University Press, 2011.

Loi, P., *Il Principio di Ragionevolezza e Proporzionalità nel Diritto del Lavoro*, Torino: G. Giapichelli Editore, 2016.

MacMillan, D., 'Uber's App Will Soon Begin Tracking Driving Behavior: The Software Is Aimed at Improving Driver Safety, but Could Raise Privacy Concerns,' *Wall Street Journal (Online)*, 29 June 2016.

Marhold, F. & Friedrich, M., *Österreichisches Arbeitsrecht* (3rd ed.), Wien: Verlag Österreich, 2016.

Nogler, L. & Reifner, U., 'Introduction: The New Dimension of Life Time in the Law of Contracts and Obligations', *in* L. Nogler & U. Reifner (Eds.), *Life Time Contracts: Social Long-Term Contracts in Labour, Tenancy and Consumer Credit Law*, The Hague: Eleven International Publishing, 2014, pp. 1-60.

Prassl, J., *The Concept of the Employer*, Oxford: Oxford University Press, 2015.

Preis, U., *Arbeitsrecht* (4th ed.), Köln: Verlag Dr. Otto Schmidt, 2012.

Preis, U., '1. Teil. Grundlagen zur Beendigung von Arbeitsverhältnissen', *in* R. Ascheid *et al., Kündigungsrecht* (5th ed.), München: C.H. Beck, 2017.

Razzolini, O., 'Self-Employment and Economic Dependency in the Light of the Social Contract Law', *in* L. Nogler & U. Reifner (Eds.), *Life Time Contracts: Social Long-Term Contracts in Labour, Tenancy and Consumer Credit Law*, The Hague: Eleven International Publishing, 2014, p. 388.

Rebhahn, R. & Kietaibl, C., *in* M. Neumayr & G. P. Reissner (Eds.), *Zeller Kommentar zum Arbeitsrecht* (2nd ed.), Wien: Manz, 2011.

Rummel, P., '§ 901 BGB', *in* P. Rummel & M. Lukas (Eds.), *Kommentar zum Allgemeinen Bürgerlichen Gesetzbuch*, Wien: Manz, 2016.

Verdier, J.M., Coeuret, A. & Souriac, M.-A., *Droit du Travail Vol. 2: Rapport Individuels* (16th ed.), Paris: Dalloz, 2011.

Wank, R., '§ 93 Änderung von Arbeitsbedingungen', *in* R. Richardi *et al.* (Eds.), *Münchener Handbuch zum Arbeitsrecht* (3rd ed.), München: C.H. Beck, 2009.

11 Plateformes, Crowdsourcing, et Principes des Life Time Contracts

Julien-Alexis Defromont[*]

À l'époque de l'*Uberisation*, la frontière séparant traditionnellement l'entreprenariat ou, plus modestement, le travail indépendant d'une part, et les relations de travail classiquement caractérisées par un lien de subordination et un contrôle de l'employeur sur l'employé d'autre part, devient de plus en plus floue. En termes économiques, ce néologisme peut être analysé comme une "désintermédiation", c'est-à-dire un processus facilitant une rencontre directe entre l'offre et la demande. Pour autant, il peut sembler paradoxal de parler de désintermédiation puisque ce phénomène est caractérisé et se généralise au moyen d'un nouveau type d'intermédiaire, numérique cette fois, les plateformes dont l'entreprise Uber est devenue un exemple emblématique.

En fonction de la manière dont opèrent les plateformes, elles peuvent servir de "ponts" permettant à leurs utilisateurs de se rencontrer et de redécouvrir les vertus de la collaboration et du partage à la faveur de la révolution numérique. Nous verrons qu'elles peuvent surtout jouer le rôle de donneurs d'ordres masqués, en contrôlant, par divers moyens, non seulement la rencontre des utilisateurs qui perdent toute liberté réelle de choix de leur cocontractant, mais également l'exécution des tâches, leurs conditions financières, leurs évaluations, ainsi que les conséquences de ces dernières sur la possibilité de recourir à nouveau à la plateforme. Pourtant, au gré de levées de fonds considérables et d'un certain laissez-faire des pouvoirs publics qui voient probablement dans ce phénomène des opportunités de croissance, ce sont ces plateformes qui, réinventant le taylorisme,[1] imposent leur modèle en attirant de plus en plus d'utilisateurs.

Cette contribution cherchera d'abord à identifier les marqueurs du contrôle que peuvent exercer les plateformes à l'encontre d'utilisateurs prestataires de services (Section 11.1). Nous montrerons que ces derniers se retrouvent enserrés dans un état de dépendance alors que la plateforme devient, dans une large mesure, un moyen prépondérant de leur épanouissement social et personnel en leur procurant des moyens de subsistance. Nos constatations appelleront à une redéfinition et à un encadrement, via le droit Privé, des rapports contractuels que les plateformes entretiennent avec leurs utilisateurs (Sec-

* Junior Researcher - Universités du Luxembourg et Paris 1 Panthéon-Sorbonne - jalexis.defromont@gmail.com

1 A. Aloisi, 'Commoditized Workers: Case Study Research on Labor Law Issues Arising From a set of "On Demand/Gig Economy" Platforms', 37 *Comp. Labor L. Pol'y J.* 2016, p. 653.

tion 11.2). La proposition d'appréhension par la catégorie des *Life Time Contracts*[2] devrait favoriser un indispensable rééquilibrage de la relation, en limitant les considérables pouvoirs des plateformes à l'encontre des prestataires de services. Ceci nous permettra, enfin, de nous décentrer quelque peu pour montrer que, plus généralement, c'est bien l'approche des pouvoirs publics à l'égard des plateformes qui pose question. En effet, la posture consistant à vanter les mérites de l'autorégulation et à assurer l'absence de responsabilité des plateformes montrent également ses limites en droit européen des contrats.

11.1 L'identification du Contrôle Que les Plateformes Peuvent Exercer sur les Crowdworkers

Il s'agit ici, par l'étude des modèles d'affaire et des contrats proposés, de prendre la mesure de l'intensité du contrôle que les plateformes exercent sur leurs utilisateurs.

Nous avons globalement pu identifier un modèle économique et contractuel dominant au sein d'une relation associant la plateforme, un prestataire de service (Crowdworkers) et un utilisateur final (crowdsourcer). Il nous est apparu qu'un certain nombre de curseurs marquent le degré de dépendance du Crowdworkers envers la plateforme et conduisent à sérieusement douter de la réalité de son prétendu statut au regard des conditions extrêmement pesantes dans lesquelles il accomplit ses missions. Ainsi, après une brève présentation du modèle économique des plateformes (Section 11.1.1), nous verrons comment la simple activité de mise en relation revendiquée par ces dernières se trouve dévoyée par le large contrôle qu'elles exercent (Section 11.1.2).

11.1.1 Brève Présentation du Modèle Economique des Plateformes Pourvoyeuses d'Activité et Identification des Acteurs

La désintermédiation qu'illustre l'*Uberisation* est consubstantielle aux technologies de réseaux et liée au récent développement des plateformes. Pourtant, derrière chaque désintermédiation se cache une réintermédiation qui voit l'arrivée sur un marché d'un nouvel intermédiaire. Amazon a remplacé les librairies, eBay les salles de ventes, Apple les disquaires, Google est devenu le courtier dominant du marché de l'information gratuite, Facebook celui des liens sociaux, LinkedIn des contacts professionnels. Uber ne cherche, pour sa part, pas à prendre la place des chauffeurs de taxis puisqu'il lui suffit de les inféoder et de prendre celle des centrales de réservation.[3] Sauf à devenir un service public, dont la perspective est probablement à creuser, ou à ce que le secteur associatif et non

---

2 L. Nogler. & U. Reifner (Eds.), *Life Time Contracts: Social Long-Term Contracts in Labour, Tenancy and Consumer Credit Law*, Eleven International Publishing, The Hague, 2014.

3 C. Deshayes, 'Uberisation: Le Temps de la Contre-Attaque', *ParisTech Rev.*, 21 January 2016, Accessible à <www.paristechreview.com/2016/01/21/uberisation-contre-attaque/>.

marchand soit capable de s'organiser pour survivre dans la jungle du libéralisme, l'intermédiation électronique sert (presque) toujours les intérêts d'un ou de plusieurs acteurs, en l'occurrence des entreprises désireuses de croitre et les rapports de domination n'ont pas disparu avec l'avènement de l'économie 2.0.

Telle qu'elles se développent sous la houlette d'une industrie au modèle capitalistique, l'économie collaborative et les plateformes qui l'accompagnent ont tout intérêt à recourir à une forme de travail précaire. Si l'on considère que l'économie du travail à la demande permet d'exploiter des ressources inutilisées ou sous-exploitées pour dégager un profit, augmenter la concurrence sur les marchés, et proposer davantage de choix aux utilisateurs, il faut inclure le capital humain parmi ses ressources.[4] *Amazon Mechanical Turk* (AMT) semble être un pionnier[5] en matière d'apparition de travailleurs 2.0 et de désintermédiation de tâches puisqu'il a démocratisé le *crowdsourcing* que Jeff Howe a en substance défini comme le fait de prendre un travail traditionnellement accompli par un employé en l'externalisant au profit d'un grand groupe de personne via un appel à candidature.[6]

Notre étude repose notamment sur quatre plateformes de livraison de repas (Deliveroo, Foodora, UberEat, TakeEatEasy), trois plateformes permettant la location de matériel ou la réalisation de prestations de services diverses comme le ménage, le jardinage, les travaux et la garde d'enfants (Care, AlloVoisins), deux plateformes de transport (Felix, Uber), et une plateforme d'acheminement de colis (Cocolis). Elle a consisté en l'étude des communications commerciales et conditions générales d'utilisation françaises[7]. On retrouve néanmoins des dispositions comparables dans les éventuelles autres versions linguistiques ou lorsque, présentes sur plusieurs marchés nationaux, les plateformes disposent de différentes conditions générales d'utilisation. Plus généralement, le but de l'analyse consiste à décrire certaines tendances dont le curseur peut être plus ou moins marqué en fonction des plateformes. Identifions dès maintenant les acteurs des relations qui se nouent sous l'égide de la plateforme quel que soit leur secteur d'activité. On découvre d'un côté le crowdsourcer, utilisateur de la plateforme, à la fois pourvoyeur d'un travail ou d'une tâche, et bénéficiaire final du service. Il s'agit de vous-même lorsque vous "prenez un Uber" ou que vous faîtes appel à AlloVoisins, du restaurant lorsque vous passez par un service de livraison de repas de type Deliveroo. À l'autre bout, on trouve le *Crowdworkers* qui sera votre prestataire de service (votre chauffeur chez Uber, votre employé de maison chez Care), ou celui du restaurant (le livreur chez Deliveroo). Entre ces deux extrémités, la plateforme, qui aime laisser à penser qu'elle ne fait que faciliter la création d'un lien, mais qui, en réalité, exerce un large contrôle, notamment sur l'exécutant.

---

4 Aloisi, *supra* note 1, p. 664.

5 L. Ratti, 'Online Platforms and Crowdwork in Europe: A Two-Step Approach to Expanding Agency Work Provisions?', 38 *Comp. Labor L. & Pol'y J.* 2017, pp. 477-511.

6 J. Howe, 'The Rise of Crowdsourcing', *WIRED*, 1 June 2006, Accessible à <www.wired.com/2006/06/crowds/>.

7 Sur la base des documents disponibles en ligne en date du 21 septembre 2016.

11.1.2 Une Prétendue Simple Activité de Mise en Relation Dévoyée par un Large Contrôle des Plateformes

Passée l'euphorie des débuts et dès lors que l'activité disruptive des plateformes met aujourd'hui sensiblement à mal les modèles traditionnels, une question centrale a commencé a émergé tant dans le débat public que parmi certains Crowdworkers désabusés et dont les médias se font progressivement les relais. Les Crowdworkers sont-ils des travailleurs indépendants opérant pour leur compte propre ou pour celui de leur micro-entreprise ou devraient-ils au contraire être considérés comme des employés? Quel est le rôle exact des plateformes dans la nébuleuse des algorithmes qu'elles mettent en place?

La réponse des plateformes est pour sa part sans ambiguïté et emprunte d'une étonnante unanimité puisque toutes se présentent comme des intermédiaires se contentant de connecter des crowdsourcers demandeurs d'une prestation de service à des Crowdworkers entrepreneurs indépendants. Aussi, si les conditions générales d'utilisation sont sensiblement différentes en fonction de l'activité des plateformes et des pays dans lesquelles elles opèrent puisqu'elles tentent de tenir compte des circonstances locales, elles poursuivent bien un but identique consistant à rejeter en bloc le statut d'employeur.[8]

Comme l'illustre une étude notamment axée sur AMT, l'argument central des plateformes pour défendre l'appellation de simple activité de mise en relation et justifier la classification parmi les travailleurs indépendants des Crowdworkers, repose notamment sur une prétendue absence totale d'obligation envers elles.[9] Nous avons passé en revue les conditions générales d'utilisation de quelques plateformes déjà bien installées ou semblant être en phase de développement sur le marché français ainsi que les arguments publicitaires qu'elles développent pour présenter leur activité et attirer de nouveau Crowdworkers. Notre analyse confirme bien la tentative de mise en avant d'une liberté totale offerte au Crowdworkers. Il arrive toutefois fréquemment que ces mêmes documents laissent planer un sérieux doute sur la véracité de l'allégation. Par ailleurs, à l'analyse des différents documents, on ne peut qu'approuver le constat tendant à dire que le nombre important de précautions prises par les plateformes pour éviter d'être considérées comme employeurs laisse fortement présager leur parfaite connaissance de l'ambiguïté de leurs relations avec les Crowdworkers.[10]

8 J. Prassl & M. Risak, 'Uber, Taskrabbit, & co: Platforms as Employers? Rethinking the Legal Analysis of Crowdwork', *Oxford Legal Stud. Res. Paper* No. 8/2016, p. 2.

9 Ratti, *supra* note 5.

10 Id.

11.1.2.1 Des Dispositions Contractuelles ou Publicitaires Vantant l'Indépendance et la Liberté

Toutes les plateformes étudiées se présentent comme des hébergeurs d'annonces ou des plateformes de mise en relation entre deux utilisateurs: un demandeur de service (le crowdsourcer) et un fournisseur de service d'autre part (le Crowdworkers). Elles veillent scrupuleusement à préciser et à répéter qu'elles ne sont nullement partie à l'accord ou au contrat qui se nouera entre les parties.[11]

Le pendant de la totale indépendance du fournisseur de service se retrouve dans l'exclusion de toute forme de responsabilité de la plateforme à l'égard du demandeur de service,[12] et ce parfois même, au titre de la seule mission revendiquée, à savoir la mise

---

11 ALLOVOISINS: "AlloVoisins héberge seulement le contenu des annonces mises en ligne par les Utilisateurs (textes, images, etc.) et n'est qu'une plate-forme électronique mise à disposition de ses utilisateurs, en vue de mettre en contact ces derniers."
CARE: "Relativement aux prestations demandées et offertes, le contrat est établi exclusivement entre les utilisateurs concernés."
COCOLIS: "Le Site constitue une plateforme en ligne de mise en relation d'Expéditeurs souhaitant envoyer un (ou des) Bien(s) à des Destinataires et de Porteurs disposés à les acheminer. Vous comprenez et acceptez que Cocolis n'est partie à aucun accord entre l'Expéditeur, le Porteur et le Destinataire, et qu'elle n'a pas la qualité de transporteur professionnel ou d'opérateur postal. Le Site <www.cocolis.fr> constitue une simple plateforme de mise en relation, et à aucun moment la société Cocolis n'interfère dans les déplacements effectués, les destinations, ainsi que les horaires."
DELIVEROO: "Notre Service a pour but la fourniture d'un service simple et pratique en vous mettant en relation avec le Restaurant partenaire et le menu de son choix et en vous permettant de lui passer commande de Repas. Deliveroo commercialise des Repas pour le compte de ses Restaurants partenaires, prend les commandes pour leur compte et vous livre les Repas."
FELIX:"L'Application est destinée à la mise en relation de Conducteurs et de Passagers [...] Félix ne propose aucun service de transport de personnes, de taxi ou de véhicule de tourisme avec chauffeur. [...]Félix intervient uniquement en qualité d'intermédiaire en ce qu'elle met à la disposition des Passagers et des Conducteurs des outils et moyens techniques leur permettant d'entrer en relation aux fins de partager des trajets entre particulier. Sa responsabilité se limite à la fourniture de ces moyens, tels que décrits aux présentes et à la mise en relation des Passagers et des Conducteurs. [...] Félix agit en son nom personnel et ne passe aucun acte juridique au nom et pour le compte des Passagers ou des Conducteurs, qui conviennent d'effectuer les Trajets et les exécutent directement entre eux."
UBER: "Les Services constituent une plate-forme technologique permettant aux utilisateurs des applications mobiles ou des sites Web d'Uber, qui sont fournis dans le cadre des Services (chacun desquels étant désigné "Application"), d'organiser et de planifier des déplacements et/ou des services logistiques avec des prestataires tiers indépendants desdits services incluant en cela des prestataires tiers indépendants de services de transport et des prestataires tiers indépendants de services logistiques sous contrat avec Uber ou certains affiliés d'Uber."
TAKEEATEASY: "[...] s'agissant des prestations de restauration, les services de Take Eat Easy sont uniquement des services de mise en relation entre l'Utilisateur et le Restaurateur. En effet, Take Eat Easy ne vend pas de plats et de boissons, ni ne fournit des services de restauration. Il appartient au Restaurateur, tiers indépendant de Take Eat Easy, de réaliser les prestations de restauration des Offres qu'il propose et qui sont susceptibles d'être commandées par le biais de Plateforme."

12 ALLOVOISINS: "AlloVoisins n'intervenant pas dans les transactions entre Utilisateurs, les membres dégagent AlloVoisins de toute responsabilité (ainsi que sa maison mère, ses filiales éventuelles et sociétés du groupe, mandataires sociaux, directeurs, agents et employés) en cas de litige, de réclamation, ou tout dommage présent ou futur, présumé ou non, constaté ou non, résultant de manière directe ou indirecte de l'utilisation des services de AlloVoisins."

en relation, puisque certaines prévoient expressément ne pas garantir la continuité de leur service.[13]

A cette simple activité de mise en relation exempte de toute responsabilité s'ajoute souvent la communication autour de la collaboration dans laquelle les fournisseurs de services potentiels s'apprêtent à entrer avec la plateforme. Ce sont ici les promesses d'"autonomie", de "flexibilité", de "revenus rapides et significatifs" tout en vantant les mérites d'une collaboration avec une entreprise "jeune", "ambitieuse" ou "révolutionnaire" qui sont mises à l'honneur. De plus, quand la législation française a compliqué la vie des chauffeurs avec la nécessité de devenir VTC, l'activité de coursier exercée chez Deliveroo, Uber dans le cadre de UberEat, Foodora, Cocolis ou TakeEatEasy ne demande ni licence, ni documents spécifiques (si ce n'est bien sûr la nécessité d'adopter le statut d'autoentrepreneur).

Par ailleurs, et toujours pour justifier le statut de travailleurs indépendants des Crowdworkers, les plateformes mettent en avant, à des degrés divers, l'absence d'obligation pesant sur eux, qu'il s'agisse d'accepter une tâche, de l'accomplir dans un délai ou même de satisfaire le demandeur.[14] L'argument massue consiste à prétendre que le Crowdworkers pourrait, à tout moment, choisir d'allumer ou d'éteindre l'application

---

CARE: "Ainsi, Care.com ne se porte pas garante des prestations des utilisateurs impliqués. Par conséquent, toute affaire ayant trait exclusivement au lien entre le demandeur et le fournisseur des services, et sans exception, aux services fournis à un demandeur ou aux paiements exigibles par le fournisseur, doit être adressée directement à la partie concernée, à savoir le demandeur ou le fournisseur."

COCOLIS: "le bon déroulement du Service rendu par le Porteur en accord avec l'Expéditeur ne saurait entraîner de responsabilité imputable à Cocolis, pour quelque raison que ce soit, le Service proposé par Cocolis étant un simple Service de mise en relation."

FELIX: "Félix ne saurait en aucun cas voir sa responsabilité engagée au titre des difficultés pouvant intervenir lors de la conclusion ou de l'exécution des Trajets, ni être partie à quelques litiges éventuels que ce soit entre un Passager et un Conducteur concernant notamment les garanties, déclarations et autres obligations quelconques auxquelles le Passager ou le Conducteur seraient tenus."

UBER et UBEREAT: "Les services sont fournis "tels quels" et "selon disponibilité". uber décline toute attestation et garantie, expresse, tacite ou prévue par la loi, non expressément énoncée aux présentes conditions, y compris les garanties tacites de qualité marchande, d'adéquation à une finalité particulière et d'absence de contrefaçon. de plus, uber ne livre aucune attestation, garantie ou assurance concernant la fiabilité, la ponctualité, la qualité, le caractère adéquat ou la disponibilité des services ou de tout bien ou service sollicité en utilisant les services, ou que le fonctionnement des services se fera sans interruptions ou erreurs. uber ne garantit pas la qualité, le caractère adéquat, la sécurité ou la capacité des prestataires tiers. vous acceptez que les risques découlant de l'utilisation que vous faites des services et de tout bien ou service sollicité en lien avec ces derniers, vous appartiennent intégralement et n'appartiennent qu'à vous seul(e), dans la mesure la plus large consentie par la loi applicable. (Majuscules supprimées)"

13 ALLOVOISINS: "AlloVoisins n'apporte aucune garantie de bon fonctionnement, de pérennité, de bonne disponibilité, de continuité, de sauvegarde et de mise à disposition des contenus transférés vers le Service."

DELIVEROO: "L'accès à notre Site et à notre Service est autorisé de manière temporaire et nous nous réservons le droit de supprimer ou de modifier sans préavis l'accès à notre Site ou à notre Service (voir ci-dessous). Nous ne sommes pas responsables si, pour quelque motif que ce soit, notre Site ou notre Service n'est pas disponible à un moment donné ou pendant une période donnée."

14 Ratti, *supra* note 5.

sur son téléphone mobile et qu'il resterait ainsi totalement maître de son emploi du temps. C'est évidemment oublier que la demande pour la livraison de repas ou le transport de personnes connaît d'inéluctables périodes dites d'"heures creuses". Aussi, s'il veut travailler, le Crowdworkers a tout intérêt à être connecté au bon moment.

11.1.2.2 D'évidents Marqueurs du Contrôle

Malgré les efforts déployés par les plateformes pour tenter de s'affranchir de toute responsabilité et ne pas risquer d'être considérées comme des employeurs, le débat s'est notamment cristallisé autour de cette question et de celle de la requalification éventuelle des contrats les liant aux Crowdworkers.

Une analyse plus poussée du fonctionnement des plateformes et des contraintes qu'elles font *in fine* peser sur les Crowdworkers plaident indéniablement en faveur d'une relation de dépendance de ces derniers. D'aucuns diront qu'il s'agit d'une relation de travail et donc de salariat déguisé masquant une relation employeur-employé, d'autres se contenteront d'assimiler les plateformes à des agences d'intérim des temps modernes. Nous ne chercherons pas ici à répondre à cette question puisque l'analyse ne peut se faire qu'au cas par cas et que nous pensons que les modèles juridiques traditionnels ne sont, en tout état de cause, pas adaptés à cette forme de travail. Néanmoins, si nous ne savons pas de quel type de rapports il s'agit exactement, nous sommes convaincus que ce n'est pas de celui qu'entendent nous vendre les plateformes. Aussi, nous nous contenterons de faire état des arguments permettant d'étayer cette assertion. On peut, à ce titre, penser aux dispositions contractuelles imposées unilatéralement par la plateforme au Crowdworkers qui ne peut que les accepter s'il veut travailler par son biais. Il doit ainsi par exemple fournir un certain nombre de garanties. De plus, la plateforme peut à tout moment décider de mettre fin au contrat.[15]

Mais l'on doit ici mentionner le montant de la rémunération et sa fixation qui, dans les modèles de type UBER n'est absolument pas maîtrisée par le Crowdworkers. Certaines plateformes ont adopté un modèle encore plus pernicieux et cynique. On le retrouve originellement chez AMT[16] et, plus récemment, chez FELIX.[17] C'est la possibilité, pour l'utilisateur final, de refuser de payer le prix de la prestation, tout en conservant les bénéfices du service accompli. Lié à la problématique du classement développée *infra*, ce mécanisme peut avoir un effet désastreux sur le Crowdworkers qui en plus de ne pas être payé, perdra des chances d'être à nouveau sollicité. En tout état de cause, dès qu'il y a

---

15 Aloisi, *supra* note 1, p. 667.

16 AMT: "If a Requester is not reasonably satisfied with the Services, the Requester may reject the Services." "Amazon mechanical turk Participation Agreement" consultable à l'adresse: <https://www.mturk.com/mturk/conditionsofuse>.

17 FELIX: "Le Passager peut accepter ou refuser ce montant, à sa libre discrétion. S'il choisit de payer une Participation Aux Frais, il doit la régler à travers l'Application. Ainsi, le Passager décide librement et sous sa seule responsabilité de verser ou non la Participation Aux Frais."

rémunération, la plateforme retient une partie du prix, et elle a le plus souvent l'entière maîtrise du moyen de paiement[18] puisqu'elle centralise celui-ci et reversera au Crowdworkers la part qui, selon elle, lui revient.

L'autre aspect à nos yeux fondamental pour tenter de mieux cerner le rôle réel des plateformes dans le contrôle qu'elles exercent sur l'activité du Crowdworkers repose sur le système de notation que la plupart d'entre elles mettent en place.[19] Si l'idée d'être évalué dans le cadre d'une prestation de service payant n'a, en soi, rien de choquant dans la mesure où elle participe à la bonne information du client, ce sont davantage les critères de l'évaluation et les conséquences que celle-ci peuvent emporter sur l'activité du Crowdworkers qui posent question. En effet, si le système d'évaluation n'est pas mauvais par nature, c'est l'éventuelle utilisation qu'en fait la plateforme -via des algorithmes dont elle seule a le secret- qui vient asseoir davantage le contrôle qu'exerce celle-ci sur le Crowdworkers, éloignant définitivement ce-dernier du statut d'indépendant. En réalité, l'utilisateur n'a bien souvent aucune possibilité de choisir celui que la plateforme présente pourtant comme son cocontractant. De son côté, s'il n'a en théorie, aucune obligation d'accepter une tâche, le système de notation basé sur le nombre de retours positifs va indubitablement pousser le Crowdworkers à travailler le plus possible pour maintenir

18 Prassl & Risak, *supra* note 8, p. 11.

19 Notons au passage que les extraits ci-dessous proviennent soit des Conditions générales d'utilisation des plateformes, soit des rubriques "aides" ou "questions fréquentes" de leur site internet. Par ailleurs, si la notation est présentée comme une possibilité offerte à l'utilisateur, dans les faits, la plupart des plateformes invitent ces derniers à évaluer le Crowdworkers par le biais d'une fenêtre de type "pop-up" immédiatement à l'issue de la prestation.
ALLOVOISINS: "La notation réciproque est obligatoire à l'issue d'une transaction. Une note est attribuée à l'utilisateur (de 1 à 5 étoile, 5 étoiles étant la note maximale) sur chacun des 4 critères suivants:
Réactivité / Flexibilité;
Ponctualité / Respect des délais;
Rapport Qualité / Prix de la transaction: conformité;
Courtoisie / Sympathie;
C'est la moyenne pondérée des évaluations globales obtenues que l'on retrouve associée au profil de chaque Utilisateur."
COCOLIS: "Sur Cocolis, chaque membre est évalué: notations et appréciations laissées par les autres membres vous permettent de compter sur des personnes de confiance pour votre envoi de colis."
FELIX: "A l'issue du Trajet, le Passager peut formuler des commentaires sur le Conducteur et l'évaluer. Ces commentaires et évaluations sont exclusivement destinés à Félix et ne sont pas publiés dans l'Application, qui ne fait apparaître que la moyenne des évaluations du Conducteur."
TAKEEATEASY: "Dans le cas où les Utilisateurs ne seraient pas satisfait de la réalisation des commandes par les Restaurateurs, de la qualité des Offres ou des services de quelque nature que ce soit fournis par le Restaurateur, ils ont en tout état de cause la possibilité d'apporter leurs observations en notant les Restaurateur".
UBER: "Après chaque course, le passager peut évaluer son expérience par une note allant de 1 à 5 étoiles. Sélectionnez l'onglet Notes dans votre application pour accéder à votre note globale actuelle et aux commentaires laissés par les passagers sur les courses effectuées dans votre véhicule. Les commentaires des passagers sont toujours anonymes. Nous encourageons les passagers à fournir une note qui reflète l'ensemble de leur expérience. Les passagers peuvent faire des commentaires libres sur le sujet de leur choix, de votre conduite, en passant par la propreté de votre voiture ou la facilité à communiquer avec vous. La note la plus élevée que peuvent accorder les passagers comme les chauffeurs est de 5 étoiles."

un bon classement et se voir proposer de nouvelles tâches. Ceci est d'autant plus vrai que l'algorithme peut tout à fait valoriser les Crowdworkers présentant les plus courtes périodes d'inactivé (les plateformes ayant intérêt à bénéficier du plus grand nombre de Crowdworkers disponibles pour les mettre en concurrence et assurer leur activité).[20]

La grande force de ces systèmes de notation est de permettre de transférer une prérogative relevant traditionnellement du management interne à une entreprise vers les utilisateurs.[21] Si elles sont parvenues à faire sous-traiter l'évaluation par leurs utilisateurs, les plateformes maintiennent toutefois le contrôle suprême avec une arme redoutable: la possibilité de déréférencer purement et simplement et de manière totalement arbitraire le Crowdworkers et de supprimer[22] son profil utilisateur si celui-ci n'est, par exemple, pas actif pendant un certain temps,[23] s'il ne satisfait pas à un critère de notation déterminée par la plateforme, ou s'il ne respecte pas les conditions générales d'utilisations et leurs nombreuses clauses abusives.

Dans le cas d'Uber, si la note d'un chauffeur passe en-dessous de 4,6 sur 5, il peut perdre accès à l'application,[24] ce qui démontre bien qu'en l'espèce, la plateforme exerce avec beaucoup de rigueur les prérogatives d'un employeur s'agissant de la cessation de la relation contractuelle. De toutes manières, nous avons vu qu'étant donné l'opacité des algorithmes utilisés pour répartir les missions entre les Crowdworkers, les plateformes peuvent tout à fait cesser d'alimenter en tâches ceux qu'elle aura décidé de mettre sur la touche sans même devoir recourir à cette extrémité.

Après avoir tenté de décrypter l'ampleur du pouvoir dont bénéficient les plateformes à la faveur de conditions contractuelles particulièrement défavorables au Crowdworkers,

---

20 Prassl & Risak, *supra* note 8, p. 12.

21 Aloisi, *supra* note 1, p. 662.

22 Ratti, *supra* note 5.

23 ALLOVOSINS: "AlloVoisins sera libre de supprimer tout compte resté inutilisé pendant 1 année.
CARE: "Care.com peut résilier le contrat, à sa seule discrétion, avec ou sans préavis, sans motif, à tout moment. En outre, Care.com se réserve le droit d'effacer les profils et/ou de retirer tout contenu du site Internet publié par l'utilisateur. Si Care.com met un terme à l'inscription d'un utilisateur, efface son profil et/ou retire des contenus qu'il a publiés, Care.com n'est pas dans l'obligation d'en informer l'utilisateur en question, ni même de lui en indiquer les raisons".
FELIX, dont les CGU prévoient entre autres exemples grotesques que "Le Conducteur ne doit en aucun cas utiliser les services afin d'exercer une activité de transport rémunérée ou réaliser un quelconque bénéfice ou profit" précise par ailleurs qu' "En cas de manquement de l'Utilisateur à une obligation essentielle visée ou découlant des présentes conditions générales, Félix se réserve le droit de résilier son accès à tout ou partie des services par l'envoi d'une lettre, d'un fax ou d'un courriel. La résiliation prend effet de plein droit à la date d'envoi, par Félix, de l'écrit à l'Utilisateur. Sans préjudice des autres conséquences possibles, elle entraîne automatiquement et sans mise en demeure préalable la suppression du Compte de l'Utilisateur"
UBER: "Uber peut résilier immédiatement les présentes Conditions ou tout Service à votre égard ou, d'une manière générale, cesser d'offrir les Services ou toute partie de ces derniers ou en interdire l'accès, et ce à tout moment et pour quelque motif que ce soit". "Uber se réserve le droit, à tout moment et à la seule discrétion d'Uber, de désactiver, supprimer et/ou revoir les Frais de tout bien ou service ou de l'ensemble d'entre eux obtenus en utilisant les Services".

24 Aloisi, *supra* note 1, p. 674.

nous allons plaider en faveur d'un rééquilibrage de ces relations par l'intervention de la règle de droit Privé.

11.2 Encadrer les Relations Contractuelles des Plateformes via le Droit Privé

La dureté des modèles économique et contractuel des plateformes évoluant jusqu'ici dans un environnement juridique inadapté d'une part et l'état de dépendance dans lequel se trouve les Crowdworkers d'autre part, appellent conjointement à une adaptation du droit Privé. Nous plaiderons pour que les relations entre plateformes et Crowdworkers soient appréhendées via le régime des *Life Time Contracts* (Section 11.2.1) et, plus prospectivement, pour une réorientation de l'approche envisagée par le droit européen des contrats (Section 11.2.2).

11.2.1 Appréhender les Relations des Plateformes et des Crowdworkers via le Régime des Life Time Contracts

Nous l'avons évoqué, les caractéristiques des modèles économiques et contractuels des plateformes rendent délicate leur appréhension par le droit du travail, notamment parce que les différentes législations utilisent des critères non adaptés. Pour autant, il nous semble bien que l'activité des plateformes, en généralisant une nouvelle forme de travail, réinvente le taylorisme, à savoir l'exploitation efficace du travail au détriment de la sécurité, de l'éducation et du développement des capacités des travailleurs.[25] Par ailleurs, le statut de travailleur indépendant n'assure pas une protection sociale satisfaisante au Crowdworkers qui peut pourtant se voir priver de son activité par la plateforme du jour au lendemain. Enfin, en se prétendant en dehors de la relation contractuelle, les plateformes évitent toute responsabilité à l'égard des utilisateurs pour les risques qu'ils peuvent encourir. On pense par exemple au risque d'accident dans le cadre d'un transport ou d'intoxication dans le cadre d'une livraison de repas. Ici encore, les plateformes s'assurent de ne pas couvrir de tels coûts et s'en remettent aux Crowdworkers et à leurs éventuelles assurances. Si l'exemple de la création de la catégorie des voitures de tourisme avec chauffeur a en France tenté d'apporter des garanties en régulant l'accès à la profession, celle-ci n'a pas pour autant réglé le problème de la précarité des chauffeurs opérant via les plateformes. Au contraire, elle n'a fait que développer l'activité d'intermédiaires supplémentaires: les "capacitaires". Il s'agit de sociétés disposant de la capacité de transport ainsi que d'une flotte de véhicules qu'elles proposent moyennant location à de futurs chauffeurs UBER. Pour autant, ces deniers restent enfermés dans leur statut de travailleurs indépen-

25 Id., p. 658.

dants alors qu'ils perdent paradoxalement un peu plus encore en indépendance puisque leur rémunération transite cette-fois par le capacitaire avant de leur parvenir.

Ce n'est pas parce que la tentative de régulation par la mise en place de procédures administratives a montré ses limites qu'elle doit être abandonnée. Néanmoins, le droit Privé doit également déployer des ressources originales et se réinventer pour appréhender ce nouveau paradigme et ainsi garantir une protection adéquate aux Crowdworkers. La première partie de notre exposé a notamment identifié certains éléments propices à caractériser la dépendance du Crowdworkers vis-à-vis de la plateforme: l'impossibilité de choisir le bénéficiaire du service, la fixation unilatérale du prix, la mise à disposition exclusive des moyens de paiement, l'utilisation d'algorithmes exploitant les évaluations des Crowdworkers pour leur attribuer ou non de nouvelles tâches. Cette liste non-exhaustive peut constituer une très forte présomption de la dépendance du Crowdworkers vis-à-vis de la plateforme via laquelle il opère. La caractérisation de cette dépendance doit permettre de tracer une ligne entre les rares plateformes se contentant de permettre à deux futurs cocontractants de se rencontrer pour nouer un contrat tombant naturellement sous le coup du droit commun (à la manière d'une petite annonce dans un journal), et celles qui vont au-delà en exerçant un contrôle sur le prestataire de service et pour lesquelles le Crowdworkers doit pouvoir bénéficier d'une protection renforcée.

Puisqu'il permet au Crowdworkers de bénéficier d'une source de revenus et qu'il devient essentiel à la réalisation de celui-ci dans la vie sociale, le contrat qui lie le Crowdworkers à la plateforme répond pleinement aux contrats d'existence que souhaite appréhender la catégorie des *Life Time Contracts*.[26] Il devrait en conséquence être soumis aux différents principes énoncés dans sa déclaration par le groupe EuSoCo qui milite pour la prise en compte de la dimension social du contrat alors que la fragilité d'un cocontractant est évidente.

Comme nous l'avons notamment présenté, le système de notation peut avoir d'importantes conséquences sur l'attribution de nouvelles missions au Crowdworkers en ce sens que l'évaluation *ex post* affecte très largement l'attribution *ex ante* et place le Crowdworkers dans une sorte de période d'essai infinie. Ceci ne fait qu'ajouter à sa précarité et à sa vulnérabilité. De plus, l'intervention de l'algorithme valorisant les travailleurs assidus, contribue à le lier encore davantage à une plateforme en particulier.[27] Il est pourtant évident que l'activité que lui assure la plateforme représente une part importante du revenu du travailleur. Une étude britannique montre que, parmi les personnes ayant accepté de divulguer cette information, plus d'un tiers déclarent que les revenus qu'ils tirent de leur activité de Crowdworkers constituent leur seule ou principale source de revenus.[28]

26 Nogler. & Reifner, *supra* note 2.

27 Aloisi, *supra* note 1, p. 671.

28 Etude réalisée en collaboration avec l'University of Hertfordshire, *Size of the UK's "Gig Economy" revealed for the first time*, février 2016, consultable à l'adresse <www.feps-europe.eu/assets/a82bcd12-fb97-43a6-9346-24242695a183/crowd-working-surveypdf.pdf>.

Appliquer le régime juridique proposé pour les *Life Time Contracts* à la relation plateforme/Crowdworkers permettrait de répondre aux préoccupations de ces deniers et de prendre en compte la dimension humaine et à long terme de leurs rapports en encadrant notamment l'éventuelle fin de leur contrat (principes 2, 3 et 11), en prenant en considération la dimension collective de leurs intérêts aujourd'hui atomisés (principe 7), en les protégeant d'évidentes discriminations dans l'accès aux tâches (principe 8) et dans la fixation du prix (principe 9), en assurant leur information et la transparence du fonctionnement de la plateforme (principe 13) et en leur garantissant des moyens de subsistance et de couverture contre les risques sociaux (principes 14 et 15). En effet, par opposition à celle qu'il entretient avec l'utilisateur final, la relation entre la plateforme et le travailleur s'étale largement dans le temps et, comme nous l'avons vu, la plateforme maîtrise pleinement le contrôle de l'existence de la relation.[29] A la lumière des relations contractuels que la catégorie des *Life-Time-Contracts* entend appréhender, il nous semble naturel que celles des Crowdworkers avec leur plateforme aient vocation à être y incluses. Puisque nous avons démontré que, loin d'être un travailleur indépendant, le Crowdworkers se situe au mieux dans une relation de type "contrat de travail", au pire dans un contrat encore innomé, quelque part entre la relation de travail classique et le très petit entrepreneur. Nous savons aussi que les tribunaux éprouvent parfois des difficultés à trouver les bases juridiques pour requalifier les contrats des Crowdworkers en contrats de travail alors que les divers tests utilisés dans les différentes traditions juridiques ne sont pas adaptés. Nous avons également compris que les législateurs, soucieux de trouver de la croissance à tout prix, semblent favoriser les intérêts économiques au détriment des droits des travailleurs et tardent à légiférer pour qualifier ces contrats et apporter un peu de sécurité aux Crowdworkers. Enfin et en tout état de cause, nous partageons l'idée selon laquelle les très petits entrepreneurs sont déjà des candidats tout à fait légitimes à entrer dans le régime juridique des *Life Time Contracts*.[30] Aussi, étudier les contrats liant les plateformes aux Crowdworkers à la lumière des *Principles of Life Time Contracts* permettrait de rééquilibrer leurs relations contractuelles, en apportant un minimum de protection aux Crowdworkers.

11.2.2 Réorienter le Droit Européen des Contrats

Plus généralement mais toujours dans le prolongement des travaux du groupe EuSoCo qui tendent à offrir un nouveau regard sur le droit européen des contrats, notre analyse nous pousse à un élargissement du sujet pour questionner l'approche qu'en font les instances européennes dans leur agenda politique.

29 Prassl & Risak, *supra* note 8, p. 19.

30 D. Hiez, 'À Propos des Life Time Contracts', 4 *RTD CIV.* 2014, p. 817.

Notons que, dans le cadre de sa stratégie pour un marché unique numérique en Europe où elle s'est notamment engagée à entreprendre une analyse du rôle des plateformes, la Commission a récemment souligné que, s'agissant des plateformes, il conviendrait de privilégier l'autorégulation dans la mesure où ce serait le meilleur moyen d'assurer le développement d'un secteur présumé assurer à l'économie européenne une croissance soutenue dans les prochaines années.[31] Pourtant, les conséquences de cette approche ne font que conforter l'angle adopté par la Commission ces dernières années en limitant le développement du droit européen des contrats à l'expansion du marché. Cette crainte se confirme lorsque l'on se penche sur le champ d'application des deux dernières propositions de directives concernant le droit européen des contrats.[32] Elles sont d'abord strictement limitées aux transactions B2C, au détriment des plateformes réellement collaboratives qui permettent aux individus de redécouvrir les valeurs simples du partage et de l'échange. Par ailleurs, dans sa proposition de directive relative à la fourniture de contenu numérique, la Commission semble avoir habilement esquivé la question des plateformes en les excluant de la définition de fournisseur et en leur évitant ainsi toute responsabilité en cas défaut de fourniture ou de conformité, dans des cas où le consommateur pourrait légitimement croire qu'elle est son cocontractant. Ainsi, si comme nous avons tenté de le démontrer plus haut, l'activité des plateformes se fait au détriment des Crowdworkers, elles échappent également, en l'absence de réglementation et par le biais de leurs conditions générales d'utilisation, à toute source possible de responsabilité vis-à-vis des utilisateurs-consommateurs. À ce sujet et en conclusion, on ne peut que se faire le relai d'une intéressante proposition doctrinale visant, sur la base d'un faisceau d'indices, à créer une coresponsabilité des plateformes et des fournisseurs lorsqu'elles ont une influence prédominante sur ces deniers.[33]

Bibliography

Aloisi, A., 'Commoditized Workers: Case Study Research on Labor Law Issues Arising From a set of "On Demand/Gig Economy" Platforms', 37 *Comp. Labor L. Pol'y J.* 2016, p. 653-690.

31 COM(2016) 288 final, '*Communication de la Commission au Parlement Européen, au Conseil, au Comité Economique et Social Européen et au Comité des Régions – Les Plateformes en Ligne et le Marché Unique Numérique – Perspectives et Défis pour l'Europe*', 25 mai 2016.

32 COM(2015) 634 final, '*Proposition de Directive du Parlement Européen et du Conseil Concernant Certains Aspects des Contrats de Fourniture de Contenu Numérique*' et COM(2015) 635 final 2015/0288 (COD) '*Proposition de Directive du Parlement Européen et du Conseil Concernant Certains Aspects des Contrats de Ventes en Ligne et de Toute Autre Vente à Distance de Biens*', 9 décembre 2015.

33 Research Group on the Law of Digital Services, 'Discussion Draft of a Directive on Online Intermediary Platforms', 5 *J. Eur. Consumer & Mkt L.* 2016, p. 164.

Deshayes, C., 'Uberisation: Le Temps de la Contre-Attaque', *ParisTech Rev.*, Retrieved on 21 January 2016, from <www.paristechreview.com/2016/01/21/uberisation-contre-attaque/>.

European Commission, '*Proposition de Directive du Parlement Européen et du Conseil Concernant Certains Aspects des Contrats de Fourniture de Contenu Numérique*' et COM(2015) 635 final 2015/0288 (COD) '*Proposition de Directive du Parlement Européen et du Conseil Concernant Certains Aspects des Contrats de Ventes en Ligne et de Toute Autre Vente à Distance de Biens*', COM(2015) 634 final.

European Commission, '*Communication de la Commission au Parlement Européen, au Conseil, au Comité Economique et Social Européen et au Comité des Régions – Les Plateformes en Ligne et le Marché Unique Numérique – Perspectives et Défis pour l'Europe*', COM(2016) 288 final.

Hiez, D., 'À Propos des Life Time Contracts', 4 *RTD CIV.* 2014, p. 817.

Howe, J., 'The Rise of Crowdsourcing', *WIRED*, Retrieved on 1 June 2006, from <www.wired.com/2006/06/crowds/>.

Huws, U. & Joyce, S., *Size of the UK's "Gig Economy" revealed for the first time*, Retrieved on 13 October 2017, from <www.feps-europe.eu/assets/a82bcd12-fb97-43a6-9346-24242695a183/crowd-working-surveypdf.pdf>.

Nogler, L. & Reifner, U. (Eds.), *Life Time Contracts: Social Long-Term Contracts in Labour, Tenancy and Consumer Credit Law*, The Hague: Eleven International Publishing, 2014.

Prassl, J. & Risak, M., 'Uber, Taskrabbit, & Co: Platforms as Employers? Rethinking the Legal Analysis of Crowdwork', *Oxford Legal Stud. Res. Paper No. 8/2016.*

Ratti, L., 'Online Platforms and Crowdwork in Europe: A Two-Step Approach to Expanding Agency Work Provisions?', 38 *Comp. Labor L. & Pol'y J.* 2017, pp. 477-511.

Research Group on the Law of Digital Services, 'Discussion Draft of a Directive on Online Intermediary Platforms', 5 *J. Eur. Consumer & Mkt L.* 2016, p. 164.

12 The Protection of the Primary Residence of Mortgage Debtors: Embedding the 'Basic Needs' Principle in Mortgage Repossession Proceedings

*Anthi Beka**

12.1 Introduction: Rethinking Repossessions in a Postcrisis World

The 2008 global credit-crunch exposed the "failures of capitalism",[1] triggering the Great Recession. By all means, the least prepared to face its consequences were its "silent victims",[2] namely the citizens. At the level of the European Union (EU), the recession and the politics of austerity, which prevailed as a means of the sovereign-debt crisis management,[3] had a heavy impact on citizens, particularly in the member states subject to fiscal

* Legal administrator at the Court of Justice of the European Union. All opinions expressed in this study are personal.
The author would wish to thank Professor Luca Ratti, as well as Suzanne M. Larsen, Research Assistant at the University of Luxembourg, for their comments on an earlier draft. The usual disclaimer applies. The author can be contacted at anthi.beka@curia.europa.eu.

1 R. Posner, *A Failure of Capitalism, The Crisis of '08 and the Descent into Depression*, Harvard University Press, Cambridge, MA & London, 2009.

2 A. Touraine, *Après la crise*, Éditions du Seuil, Paris, 2010, p. 37. *See also* J. Habermas, *The Crisis of the European Union, A Response*, C. Cronin (Tr.), Polity Press, Cambridge, 2013, p. 102, on the "scandalous social injustice that the most vulnerable social groups will have to bear the brunt of the socialized costs for the market failure".

3 The literature refers, with negative connotation, to the measures adopted in the framework of the euro-crisis management as 'Euro-Crisis law': *see* Law Department at the European University Institute, *Constitutional Change Through Euro-Crisis Law: A Multi-Level Legal Analysis of Economic and Monetary Union*, Retrieved on 2 October 2017 from <http://eurocrisislaw.eui.eu/>; M. Everson & C. Joerges, 'Between Constitutional Command and Technocratic Rule: Post-Crisis Governance and the Treaty on Stability, Coordination and Governance ("The Fiscal Compact")', *in* C. Harlow et al. (Eds.), *Research Handbook on EU Administrative Law*, Edward Elgar, Cheltenham, UK & Northampton, MA, USA, 2017.
The European Court of Justice, in its Judgment of 13 June 2017, *Florescu and Others*, C-258/14, EU:C:2017:448, the European Court of Justice examined the compatibility of national measures of austerity, which were adopted in Romania in implementation of a Union law mechanism of financial assistance pursuant to Article 143 TFEU, with the Charter of Fundamental Rights. It its Judgment of 20 September 2016, *Ledra Advertising and Others v Commission and ECB*, C-8/15 P, EU:C:2016:701, it had already found that the Charter applies to the Union institutions when they act outside the EU legal framework and that, therefore, even if the Memorandum of Understanding concluded within the framework of the European Stability Mechanism (ESM) falls outside Union law, the participation of the Commission in its conclusion obliges the latter to ensure its consistency with the fundamental rights guaranteed by the Charter.

surveillance.[4] A reduction of wages in the public and private sectors, a reduction in welfare state expenditures, a sharp rise in unemployment rates (reaching dramatic levels in Greece and Spain[5]), collective redundancies, and a rise in part-time and precarious employment are just some manifestations of this impact. Under such circumstances, households became, as Ian Ramsay puts it, the "shock absorbers"[6] of the crisis. The financial turmoil seriously aggravated the situation of over-indebted households,[7] generating causes of difficulty or inability for the proper execution of obligations assumed in the framework of consumer credit contracts.

This study concentrates on residential mortgage credit agreements, coined by Luca Nogler and Udo Reifner as the "prototype consumer credit contract[s]"[8] and, more particularly, on mortgage repossession proceedings initiated against the primary residence of mortgage debtors. In this framework, it examines ways of '*embedding*' the Principles of Life Time Contracts within the procedural framework for residential mortgage repossession. Of particular relevance in that regard is the 'Basic Needs' principle (EuSoCo Principles, Principle 5) on the essential need that the security subject represents, as well as the 'Exclusion' principle (EuSoCo Principles, Principle 15), on the social risks of exclusion and homelessness that must be taken into account in order "to ensure the protection of the weaker party" to the residential mortgage contract, but also within the framework of repossession proceedings.

Mortgage repossession proceedings are generally fashioned in such a way as to allow for the quick realization of the security. This is perfectly in line with the very reason for the existence of secured credit. It is necessary, however, to examine, at all times, whether the design of those proceedings, in terms of procedural safeguards afforded to the mort-

4 For an account of the measures of austerity in the countries subject to a fiscal surveillance program and the impact on social rights and welfare, *see* C. Kilpatrick & B. de Witte, *Social Rights in Times of Crisis in the Eurozone: The Role of Fundamental Rights' Challenges*, EUI Working Papers, Law 2014/05. *See also* A. Nolan (Ed.), *Economic and Social Rights After the Global Financial Crisis*, Cambridge University Press, Cambridge, 2014; N. Countouris & M. Freedland (Eds.), *Resocialising Europe in a Time of Crisis*, Cambridge University Press, Cambridge, 2013.

5 At the height of the eurozone crisis, the highest unemployment rates for the general population were observed in Greece (27.5%) and Spain (26.1%) (data for 2013 published by Eurostat). The rates reached alarming levels at the same period with regard to youth unemployment, exceeding the threshold of 50%. According to latest statistics (May 2017), despite the downward trend, the same two counties still recorded the highest unemployment rates within the euro-area (Greece: 21.7% and Spain 17.1%).

6 I. Ramsay, 'Two Cheers for Europe: Austerity, Mortgage Foreclosures and Personal Insolvency Policy in the EU', *in* H.-W. Micklitz & I. Domurath (Eds.), *Consumer Debt and Social Exclusion in Europe*, Abingdon Oxon, Routledge, 2015, pp. 189-227, 191.

7 J. Spooner, 'Fresh Start or Stalemate? European Consumer Insolvency Law Reform and the Politics of Household Debt', *ERPL* 2013, pp. 747-794, 748, uses the expression "wreaked-upon" in order to underscore the gravity of the impact upon "debt-laden European households".

8 L. Nogler & U. Reifner, 'Introduction: The New Dimension of Life Time in the Law of Contracts and Obligations', *in* L. Nogler & U. Reifner (Eds.), *Life Time Contracts, Social Long Term Contracts in Labour, Tenancy and Consumer Credit Law*, Eleven International Publishing, The Hague, Netherlands, 2014, pp. 29-75, p. 44.

gage debtors, is sufficiently in line with the evolution of the use of mortgage credit as a major vehicle of access to homeownership.[9] The lowering of standards of procedural protection is a direct consequence of the progressive 'commodification' of housing, a common theme in the housing literature understood as the "conceptual transformation of adequate housing from a social good into a commodity".[10] The marketing of mortgage-backed securities demonstrated the extent of this transformation at the expense of the social aspect of housing. But, the subprime 'meltdown' stripped things of their market 'clothing' and revealed their real nature: the asset on sale was nothing less than the home of a person with family life and the consumer debtor was a citizen[11] in need of protection.

This chapter first traces the procedural safeguards drawn from the EU's 'mortgage-crisis' case-law and then discusses the requirement of "reasonable forbearance" that figures in Directive 2014/17/EU on credit agreements for consumers relating to residential immovable property (the 'Mortgage Credit Directive').[12] We concentrate, in particular, on the ways that requirement can evolve from soft-law encouragement into a mandatory pre-action obligation. Enhanced involvement, by the courts, in the assessment of compliance with such requirement can, we argue, ensure that repossession is a means of last resort, which takes us to the conditions under which proportionality can or should enter into judicial review of repossession. Finally, illustrations are given of measures of absolute protection against residential repossession adopted at the height of the crisis as a temporary solution to ease social pressure.

The ultimate objective of this chapter is to demonstrate some tools through which ingrained attitudes on repossession can be tested and rooted power-imbalances unveiled and addressed. The significance of the developments in this area is not limited to the 2008 financial turmoil and its aftermath. Failures in the supervision of the residential mortgage markets and the absence of a solid protective framework for debtors facing repossession can render housing crises, as well as their social consequences, a recurring feature of the global economy.

---

9 The studies of Lisa Whitehouse offer a thorough insight into problematic aspects of English repossession procedure and the path to reform in order to offer home-owners "the highest degree of procedural stringency within the repossession process": L. Whitehouse, 'The Home-Owner: Citizen or Consumer?', *in* S. Bright & J. Dewar, *Land Law Themes and Perspectives*, Oxford University Press, Oxford, 1998, pp. 183-205; L. Whitehouse, 'A Longitudinal Analysis of the Mortgage Repossession Process 1995-2010: Stability, Regulation and Reform', *in* S. Bright (Ed.), *Modern Studies in Property Law*, Hart Publishing, Oxford, 2011, pp. 151-174.

10 P. Kenna, 'Introduction', *in* P. Kenna (Ed.), *Contemporary Housing Issues in a Globalised World*, Ashgate Publishing, Farnham, 2014, p. 12. *See also* R. Rolnik & L. Rabinovich, 'Late-Neoliberalism: The Financialisation of Homeownership and the Housing Rights of the Poor', *in* Nolan (Ed.), *supra* note 4, pp. 57-89.

11 On the impact of the "rhetoric of consumerism" upon the rights of home-owners, *see* Whitehouse 1998, *supra* note 9.

12 Directive 2014/17/EU of the European Parliament and of the Council of 4 February 2014 on credit agreements for consumers relating to residential immovable property and amending Directives 2008/48/EC and 2013/36/EU and Regulation (EU) No 1093/2010 (OJ 2014, L 60, p. 34) [hereinafter the 'Mortgage Credit Directive'].

12.2 PROCEDURAL PROTECTION OF RESIDENTIAL MORTGAGE DEBTORS IN THE COURT OF JUSTICE'S CASE LAW

Residential mortgage contracts have been, for long time, a matter excluded from regulation at the EU level. The Consumer Credit Directive[13] explicitly excluded from its scope credit for mortgage contracts.[14] Those contracts entered the scope of EU law by virtue of the Mortgage Credit Directive, although the latter is not applicable to credit agreements concluded before 21 March 2016.[15] The provisions of the Mortgage Credit Directive on arrears and foreclosure are discussed in the following section. This section, however, examines another way through which EU law influenced the content of the terms of residential mortgage credit agreements as well as their enforcement: on the basis of the Unfair Contract Terms Directive (the 'Unfair Terms Directive').[16] The procedural protection of mortgage debtors developed within a broader jurisprudential strengthening of the effective protection of consumers from the use of unfair terms by means of the recognition of the powers of national courts to raise such terms on their own motion. The adoption of the Mortgage Credit Directive removes nothing from the relevance of the Unfair Terms Directive as an instrument of protection of consumer-mortgage debtors.[17]

To cut a very long story short,[18] according to the Court of Justice's (Court) now-settled case law, national courts are obliged to raise, on their own motion, mandatory rules of Union consumer contract law, provided that they have available the factual and legal elements necessary for that task and that the right of the parties to be heard is observed. The most prominent field of application of this case law is the legislation on

13 Directive 2008/48 of the European Parliament and of the Council of 23 April 2008 on credit agreements for consumers and repealing Council Directive 87/102/EEC (OJ 2008, L 133, p. 66) [hereinafter the 'Consumer Credit Directive'].

14 Art. 2, Consumer Credit Directive; *see* Judgment of 12 July 2012, *SC Volksbank România*, C-602/10, EU:C:2012:443.

15 Art. 43, Mortgage Credit Directive.

16 Council Directive 93/13/EEC of 5 April 1993 on unfair terms in consumer contracts (OJ 1993, L 95, p. 29) [hereinafter the 'Unfair Terms Directive'].

17 I. Ramsay, 'Changing Policy Paradigms of EU Consumer Credit and Debt Regulation', *in* D. Leczykiewicz & S. Weatherill (Eds.), *The Images of the Consumer in EU Law, Legislation, Free Movement and Competition Law*, Hart Publishing, Oxford and Portland, OR, 2016, pp. 159-182, 172, pointing out the importance of due process in repossession proceedings of the family home, as expressed in the relevant case-law of the Court, concludes that "[t]his 'embedding' of credit markets through minimum standards at the European level complements the provisions of the Mortgage Directive". *See also* O.O. Cherednychenko, 'The EU Charter of Fundamental Rights and Consumer Credit', *in* H. Collins (Ed.), *European Contract Law and the Charter of Fundamental Rights*, Intersentia, Cambridge, Antwerp & Portland, 2017, pp. 139-166.

18 I extensively develop this case-law in: A. Beka, *The Doctrine of the 'Active Consumer Court'*, Intersentia, Cambridge (forthcoming, 2018); *see also* B. Fekete & A. M. Mancaleoni, 'Application of Primary and Secondary EU Law on the National Courts' Own Motion', *in* A. Hartkamp, C. Sieburg & W. Devroe (Eds.), *Cases, Materials and Text on European Law and Private Law*, Hart Publishing, Oxford and Portland, OR, 2017, pp. 421-461; V. Trstenjak & E. Beysen, 'European Consumer Protection Law: Curia Semper Dabit Remedium?', 48 *Common Mkt L. Rev.* 2011, pp. 95-124; F. Ferretti, 'The Over-Indebted European Consumers: *Quo Vadis* Personal Insolvency Law?', 41 *E.L. Rev.* 2016, pp. 843-864, 857 *et seq.*

unfair terms.[19] The origin of this obligation lies with the mandatory nature of Article 6 of the Unfair Terms Directive (according to which unfair terms are not binding on consumers) and with the acknowledgment of the public interest that consumer protection represents.[20] In view of the weaker position of the consumer in terms of bargaining power and level of knowledge, the Court has inferred the existence of an obligation for the courts to take positive action that redresses the contractual imbalance in the procedural plane.

In many instances, the Court has been invited, more specifically, to decide on the interplay of this doctrine with the powers of the courts at the stage of enforcement. In the absence of a harmonized framework for national mechanisms of enforcement, the point of departure to decide such cases has been the long-established principle of national procedural autonomy, limited by the principles of equivalence and effectiveness.[21] The "specific characteristics" of the national procedural system should not be a factor that affects the effective protection of the rights from which the consumer (mortgage) debtor benefits under the Unfair Terms Directive.[22]

Following this line of thinking, national mortgage enforcement proceedings should not undermine the powers of the courts to assess unfair terms of their own motion or afford interim relief so as to ensure the full effectiveness of a final decision declaring the unfairness of a certain term of the mortgage instrument.

On the basis of this case law, the *ex officio* doctrine has progressively evolved into a mechanism affecting different procedural constellations, such as mortgage enforcement proceedings, payment order proceedings, or consumer insolvency proceedings.

The landmark judgment – as far as due process in mortgage enforcement proceedings against the primary residence is concerned – is *Aziz*,[23] a case involving a reference for preliminary ruling from Spain.[24] Three features can be pointed out that make this case stand out. The first one is what Hans-Wolfgang Micklitz and Norbert Reich have called

---

19 The authority of principle is acknowledged in Judgment of 27 June 2000, *Océano Grupo Editorial and Salvat Editores*, C-240/98 to C-244/98, EU:C:2000:346. For recent restatement, *see* Judgment of 21 December 2016, *Gutiérrez Naranjo and Others*, C-154/15, C-307/15 and C-308/15, EU:C:2016:980; Judgment of 18 February 2016, *Finanmadrid EFC*, C-49/14, EU:C:2016:98; Judgment of 21 April 2016, *Radlinger and Radlingerová*, C-377/14, EU:C:2016:283; and judgment of 1 October 2015, *ERSTE Bank Hungary*, C-32/14, EU:C:2015:637.

20 For the most recent restatement, *see* Judgment of 21 December 2016, *Gutiérrez Naranjo and Others*, C-154/15, C-307/15 and C-308/15, EU:C:2016:980, paras. 53-56, and Judgment of 21 December 2016, *Biuro podróży 'Partner'*, C-119/15, EU:C:2016:987, paras. 28-30 and the case-law cited therein.

21 On the most recent statement, outside the field of consumer law, on the principle of national procedural autonomy as limited by Article 47 of the Charter, *see* Judgment of 8 November 2016, *Lesoochranárske zoskupenie VLK*, C-243/15, EU:C:2016:838, para. 65 and the case-law cited.

22 Judgment of 14 March 2013, *Aziz*, C-415/11, EU:C:2013:164, para. 62.

23 Id.

24 For a detailed account of this case and the Spanish procedural context connected to it, *see* J.M. Fernández Seijo, *La Tutela de los Consumidores en los Procedimientos Judiciales, Especial Referencia a las Ejecuciones Hipotecarias*, Bosch, Barcelona, 2017.

the "hidden constitutionalization"[25] of the residential mortgage relationship, in the sense that constitutional values permeate the reasoning of the Court in the assessment of compatibility of national rules on enforcement with Union law.[26] The second feature is the accelerating effect that it has had on legislative change in Spain, which is intended to advance the protection of consumer debtors.[27] It also paved the way for a series of preliminary references to the Court, having as their main theme the challenge to transitional or other[28] provisions of the law that overhauled the Spanish mortgage repossession law. The final element is the backdrop against which the facts of this case unraveled, namely serious social upheaval against evictions.[29]

The main issue in *Aziz* was that the Spanish legislation at that time,[30] while excluding in mortgage enforcement proceedings grounds of objection based on the unfairness of a clause contained in the mortgage credit contract (forming the basis for the nonjudicial enforcement title), it provided that the merits of such claim could only be referred to a different court for the declaratory proceedings, which was deprived of the power to order suspension of enforcement. The Court noted that, although the mechanisms of enforcement, as well as the determination of the grounds of objection in enforcement proceedings were a matter for the national legal orders, national procedural autonomy should not

25 H.-W. Micklitz & N. Reich, 'The Court and Sleeping Beauty: The Revival of the Unfair Contract Terms Directive', 51 *Common Mkt L. Rev.* 2014, pp. 771-808, 800; H.-W. Micklitz, 'Unfair Contract Terms: Public Interest Litigation Before European Courts', *in* E. Terryn, G. Straetmans & V. Colaert (Eds.), *Landmark Cases of EU Consumer Law*, Intersentia, Cambridge, 2014, p. 648.

26 On the issue of constitutionalization and the horizontal application of fundamental rights, *see* A. Hartkamp, *European Law and National Private Law, Effect of EU Law and European Human Rights Law on Legal Relationships between Individuals*, 2nd ed., Intersentia, Cambridge, Antwerp & Portland, 2016; H.-W. Micklitz (Ed.), *Constitutionalisation of European Private Law*, Oxford University Press, Oxford, 2014; U. Bernitz, X. Groussot & F. Schulyok (Eds.), *General Principles of EU law and European Private Law*, Wolters Kluwer, Alphen aan den Rijn, 2013. *See also* AG Opinion of 8 September 2011, *Dominguez*, C-282/10, EU:C:2011:559 and AG Opinion of 18 July 2013, *Association de Médiation Sociale*, C-176/12, EU:C:2013:491.

27 *See* S. Iglesias Sanchez, 'Unfair Terms in Mortgage Loans and Protection of Housing in Times of Economic Crisis: *Aziz* v *Catalunyacaixa*', 51 *Common Mkt L. Rev.* 2014, pp. 955, 970, who rightly observes that this case is "an instance where EU law, in an indirect manner, provides for a higher standard of fundamental rights protection than the national constitutional standard"; D. Blázquez Peinado, 'El procedimiento de ejecución hipotecaria y su adecuación a la normativa europea en materia de protección a los consumidores por cláusulas abusivas. Jurisprudencia reciente del Tribunal de Justicia', 39 *Revista General de Derecho Europeo* 2016, pp. 1-31.

28 Judgment of 17 July 2014, *Sánchez Morcillo and Abril García*, C-169/14, EU:C:2014:2099; Judgment of 29 October 2015, *BBVA*, C-8/14, EU:C:2015:731; Judgment of 26 January 2017, *Banco Primus*, C-421/14, EU:C:2017:60; Order of 11 June 2015, *Banco Bilbao Vizcaya Argentaria*, C-602/13, not published, EU:C:2015:397; Order of 8 July 2015, *Banco Grupo Cajatres*, C-90/14, not published, EU:C:2015:465.

29 As a result of the situation, grassroots movements were born with the objective to prevent evictions ('*anti-desahucios*'), the most active being the *Plataforma de Afectados por la Hipoteca* (PAH).

30 That is to say, before the adoption of Law 1/2013, of 14 May 2013, laying down measures to strengthen the protection of mortgage debtors, debt restructuring and social rents (Ley de medidas para reforzar la protección a los deudores hipotecarios, reestructuración de deuda y alquiler social) (BOE No 116, of 15 May 2013, p. 36373, 'Law 1/2013') amending the Spanish civil procedural law to which reference is made in *Sánchez Morcillo and Abril García*, C-169/14.

undermine the effectiveness of the exercise of rights derived from Union law. By making it impossible for the court from hearing the merits of the objection pertaining to the existence of an unfair term and granting interim relief in order to ensure the full effectiveness of the final decision, the contested Spanish procedural rules undermined the protection sought by the Unfair Terms Directive.[31]

Similarly, in *Banco Popular Español*,[32] the Court found incompatible with the protection afforded by the Unfair Terms Directive, that feature of the Spanish procedural law that precluded the court responsible for the enforcement proceedings from both assessing (of its own motion or at the request of the consumer) the unfairness of a term contained in the contract from which the debt arises and which is the basis for the enforcement order and from granting interim relief guaranteeing the full effectiveness of the final decision of the Court hearing the declaratory proceedings.

To corroborate the strength of the impact of the design of the national mortgage enforcement law upon the effective procedural protection of the consumer-mortgage debtor, the Court in *Aziz* infused its reasoning with considerations relating to the quality of the property as the *family home*.[33] The procedure was fashioned in such a way as to only provide for protection of a merely compensatory nature: according to the then-applicable Spanish legislation, even if Mr. Aziz could eventually win his case regarding the mortgage agreement's unfair terms, that 'win' could only result in the award of damages and interest. Meanwhile, his dwelling would have been lost in a forced sale. The Spanish procedure did not, therefore, make it possible to prevent the "definitive and irreversible loss of that dwelling".[34]

The referring court also sought guidance with regard to the assessment of the terms of the contract. One such term was an 'acceleration' clause, according to which the lender had the right to call in the totality of the loan in case of default in the payment of a single instalment. In order to guide the national court in determining the unfairness of the particular term, the Court explicitly took into account the "*long-term*" nature of the contractual relationship.[35]

In the aftermath of *Aziz*, Spain's procedural law was amended, opening up the scope of grounds on the basis of which enforcement could be challenged.[36] As mentioned

---

31 *Aziz*, C-415/11, para. 58.

32 Order of 14 November 2013, *Banco Popular Español and Banco de Valencia*, C-537/12 and C-116/13, EU:C:2013:759.

33 *Aziz*, C-415/11, para. 61.

34 Id.

35 In that regard, the Court considered that in the assessment of a clause included in such type of a *long-term contract*, concerning the acceleration of repayment on account of events of default occurring within a limited specific period, the courts could take into account whether the non-compliance is sufficiently serious in the light of the term and the amount of the loan, whether the acceleration right derogates from the relevant applicable rules and whether national law provides for adequate and effective means enabling the consumer subject to such a term to remedy the effects of the loan being called in: *Aziz*, C-415/11, para. 73; *see* the analysis of those clauses in Micklitz & Reich, *supra* note 25.

36 For more detail, *see* Fernández Seijo, *supra* note 24.

above, the new provisions governing enforcement became the object of new references for preliminary ruling, including the case in *Sánchez Morcillo and Abril García*.[37] The new Spanish enforcement provisions established a differentiated treatment between the mortgage lender and the mortgage debtor with regard to the right to appeal against a decision on the contract's enforcement. While the mortgage lender was entitled to bring an appeal against a decision upholding the objection raised by the debtor on the ground of the existence of unfair terms in the contract forming the basis of the enforcement order, the mortgage debtor did not have the same right against a judgment dismissing the objection and ordering enforcement. The Court found that such procedural arrangement violated the right to effective judicial protection of the mortgage debtor according to Article 47 of the Charter. The major element that was taken into account was the nature of the asset involved, an asset that meets an "*essential need of the consumer, namely provision of a dwelling*".[38] Although, in principle, there is no right to a second level of review according to said Article 47, this element, along with consideration of the imbalance in procedural rights that accentuated the existing contractual imbalance, led the Court to find a violation of the principle of equality of arms.

The importance of the security subject being the debtor's dwelling is, therefore, a primordial element in testing repossession procedures against the requirements of effective judicial protection and, more broadly, for any contractual relationship where the asset involved is his dwelling. An illustration of that can be found in *Asbeek Brusse*,[39] which involved a residential-tenancy agreement and the question of whether such an agreement concluded between a professional landlord and a tenant acting on nonprofessional basis comes within the scope of the Unfair Terms Directive. To justify its affirmative position, the Court particularly took into account the system of the protection implemented by the said directive. The following passage of the judgment establishes a link between contractual inequality and the need for protection in long-term contractual relationships intended to provide for an *essential need* of the citizen:

> The consequences of the inequality existing between the parties are aggravated by the fact that, from an economic perspective, such a contract relates to an essential need of the consumer, namely to obtain lodging, and involves sums which most frequently, for the tenant, represent one of the most significant items in his budget, while, from a legal perspective, this is a contract which, as a general rule, is covered by complex national rules about which individuals are often poorly informed.[40]

37 *Sánchez Morcillo and Abril García*, C-169/14.
38 Id., para. 38.
39 Judgment of 30 May 2013, *Asbeek Brusse and de Man Garabito*, C-488/11, EU:C:2013:341.
40 Id., para. 32.

It follows from the presented case law that contractual inequality reflects upon procedural inequality and this applies all the more in enforcement proceedings involving the principal residence of the debtor. On account of the importance of his home to the consumer debtor, the national procedural systems must provide a framework under which the debtor may effectively exercise the rights stemming from the Unfair Terms Directive. In view of that, systems that allow for simplified or extrajudicial enforcement proceedings are subject to particular scrutiny as to their ability to meet those requirements. The Court was asked to determine the compatibility with Union law of such an extrajudicial mortgage enforcement scheme in *Kušionová*.[41]

In that case, the Slovak procedural law authorized the voluntary auction of the relevant dwelling, if the parties to the mortgage contract agreed to it, meaning that the creditor had the power to sell the property without a court order. The mortgage debtor had, however, the right to obtain interim relief against unlawful mortgage enforcement proceedings, and to seek a declaration annulling of the sale. This was the decisive element for the Court to reach the finding that Union law did not preclude the particular legislative scheme. The fact that the debtor was required to enter an objection in order to trigger judicial review of the allegedly unfair terms did not, according to the Court, lead to a different conclusion.[42]

The Court further made an important statement on the engagement of fundamental-rights analysis in the interpretation of consumer contract law. When implementing the Unfair Terms Directive, national courts must take into consideration Article 7 of the Charter and the protection of one's *home and family life* enshrined therein.[43] In a sort of direct human rights dialogue with the ECtHR, the Court cited a seminal passage from *McCann v. United Kingdom*:

> The loss of a home is one of the most serious breaches of the right to respect for the home and [...] any person who risks being the victim of such a breach should be able to have the proportionality of such measure reviewed.[44]

A residential immovable property that secures credit is not a mere consumer commodity: it is the family home of the consumer. Satisfying an *essential need* of the citizen, it is, as *Lisa Whitehouse* eloquently puts it, a "precondition of citizenship".[45]

---

41 Judgment of 10 September 2014, *Kušionová*, C-34/13, EU:C:2014:2189.

42 To that effect, the Court recalled previous authorities stating that the principle of effectiveness cannot be stretched so far as to require a compensation for a total passivity on behalf of the consumer: *Kušionová*, C-34/13, para. 56.

43 *See* J. Rutgers, 'The Right to Housing (Article 7 of the Charter) and Unfair Terms in General Conditions', *in* H. Collins (Ed.), *European Contract Law and the Charter of Fundamental Rights*, Intersentia, Cambridge, Antwerp & Portland, 2017, pp. 125-137.

44 ECHR, *McCann v. United Kingdom*, App. No 19009/04, para. 50.

45 Whitehouse 1998, *supra* note 9, p. 200, discussing the rights of the mortgagor from the perspective of the social element of citizenship.

It must be pointed out that, in *Kušionová*, the Court reviewed the standards of effective judicial protection afforded by a specific system of mortgage enforcement, but it did not endorse any particular model of judicial enforcement of contractual obligations coming within the scope of EU law. The judgment seems neutral in that regard. There is nonetheless one unconditional requirement that the debtor must be given an effective remedy when seeking protection from unfair terms. It follows that the requirement to ensure that consumers will not be bound by unfair terms contained in a mortgage credit contract does not preclude the existence of simplified enforcement schemes for as long as they allow for effective judicial protection.

This is confirmed in the judgment of the Court in *Erste Bank Hungary*,[46] which found that Union law does not preclude a system of simplified enforcement, by virtue of which a notary who drew up an authentic instrument concerning a mortgage credit contract, affixes the enforcement clause to that instrument or refuses to cancel it when no review of the unfairness has been performed at any stage. This finding was made, however, subject to the existence, on the one hand, of certain safeguards in relation to the advisory role of the notary and, on the other hand, of provisions enabling consumers to contest the disputed contract including in the enforcement phase.[47]

The approach of the Court attempts to strike a fair balance between, on the one hand, the requirement to ensure effective judicial protection for consumers in proceedings involving contracts that could contain unfair terms and, on the other hand, to leave room for legitimate national procedural preferences in the field of residential repossession, which is not harmonized.[48] While a mandatory court order for repossession would seem to offer higher procedural standards for debtors, Union law, at its current stage of development, does not preclude a procedural scheme by dint of which the consumer debtor is required to make the 'first move'. As the Court holds in *Erste Bank Hungary*:

> [...] the fact that the consumer may rely on the protection of legislative provisions on unfair terms only if he brings court proceedings cannot be regarded in itself [...] as contrary to the principle of effectiveness.[49]

46 Judgment of 1 October 2015, *ERSTE Bank Hungary*, C-32/14, EU:C:2015:637.

47 Id., para. 59, following AG Opinion of 25 June 2015, *ERSTE Bank Hungary*, C-32/14, EU:C:2015:424.

48 One parameter of simplified enforcement schemes is the avoidance of additional costs for the mortgage debtor. *See* AG Opinion of 21 November 2013, *Macinský and Macinská*, C-482/12, EU:C:2013:765, n. 43 (the Court did not proceed with a judgment as the referring court withdrew its question: Order of the President of the Court of 7 February 2014, *Macinský and Macinská*, C-482/12, not published, EU: C:2014:182). It is probable indeed, that the costs of ordinary enforcement proceedings will be shifted, by a standard contractual clause, to the mortgage debtor. Whitehouse 2011, *supra* note 9, p. 151, explains that the practice of English banks in mortgage contracts is to shift the cost of the procedure to the mortgage, thus adding to the financial burden of the borrower.

49 *Erste Bank Hungary*, C-32/14, para. 63.

To give some further illustrations on the matter of *ex ante* judicial review, in Scotland, repossession is possible only with a warrant from the court, save for specified circumstances of voluntary surrender.[50] Such voluntary surrender allows extrajudicial enforcement in circumstances in which the security subject is unoccupied and the debtor consents to the creditor's exercise of his enforcement rights upon the debtor's default. However, the creditor proceeding with a voluntary surrender has to certify that the consent was "given freely and without coercion of any kind".[51] It would, therefore, probably appear that a standard contractual clause in the mortgage contract, according to which the mortgage debtor consents to the extrajudicial enforcement upon default, would not be sufficient alone to prove voluntary surrender. In England and Wales, the ability of the lender to exercise the power to sale without a court order has attracted serious criticism and led the Council of Mortgage Lenders to issue a voluntary statement according to which its members have promised not to seek enforcement without a prior court order for possession.[52, 53]

The cases of the Court that have been discussed up to now allow an assessment of the adequacy of the standards of protection afforded by national mortgage enforcement laws to the extent that they are likely to affect the protection of mortgage debtors from the use of unfair terms. One should not lose sight of the fact that the Union courts do not have jurisdiction to remedy every possible failure of a given national legislative regime governing repossessions and afford adequate protection of mortgage debtors. Judicial review at the European level is limited to the extent to which the respective national legislation interferes with the effective judicial protection of the rights conferred on mortgage debtors by the protective legislation against unfair terms in their capacity as consumers. This means that there are limits to the assessment of national repossession systems against Union law requirements, as exemplified in *Barclays Bank*.[54]

---

50 Home Owner and Debtor Protection (Scotland) Act 2010, Part 1, para. 1, entitled 'Residential Standard Securities: Restriction of Creditor's Remedies'.

51 Id., Sec. 1(3)(1)(b)(iii).

52 The origins of the criticism can be traced to the so-called Horsham Loophole, revealed by *Horsham Properties Limited v. Clark and Beech* [2008] EWHC 2327. In this case, the lender used its power to sell the mortgaged property without a court order and without seeking physical possession, with the borrowers still living in the property. This was a buy-to-let property under the terms of which the borrowers were not entitled to live in the house. Still, the sale of the property exposed concerns arising from the ability to sell without a court order. *See* Note of the House of Commons, *Mortgages Arrears and Repossessions*, SN/SP/4769, 9 January 2014 and L. Whitehouse 2011, *supra* note 9, p. 159.

53 Further, *see* the Polish example, where the simplified system of mortgage enforcement was found unconstitutional by the Polish Constitutional Court, leading to the abolition of the contested legislation. In light of this development, the Court dismissed a case on the compatibility of such law with EU law in its Order of 3 March 2016, *Euro Bank*, C-537/15, not published, EU:C:2016:143. On the earlier judgment of the Polish Constitutional Court regarding banking titles, *see* J. Jemielniak & P. Miklaszewicz, 'Introduction: Capturing the Change: Universalising Tendencies in Legal Interpretation', *in* J. Jemielniak & P. Miklaszewicz (Eds.), *Interpretation of Law in the Global World: From Particularism to a Universal Approach*, Springer, Heidelberg, Dordrecht, London & New York, 2010, pp. 1-27, 6.

54 Judgment of 30 April 2014, *Barclays Bank*, C-280/13, EU:C:2014:279. *See also* order of 5 July 2016, *Banco Popular Español and PL Salvador*, C-7/16, not published, EU:C:2016:523.

In that case, the referring court questioned certain features of the then-applicable Spanish mortgage repossession system. That law entitled the creditor to be awarded the property at 50% of its original value in the absence of a bidder, while leaving the debtor liable for the outstanding amount. The Court found that judicial review of such provision fell outside the jurisdiction of the Union judge. As it is clear from the Unfair Terms Directive, the statutory and regulatory provisions of Member States are excluded from its scope and, in the *Barclays Bank* case, those provisions were applicable "without any modification of the area covered or of the extent of that coverage by means of a contractual term".[55] Unlike the *Aziz* case, the referring court did not question the effect of the national legislation upon the powers of the courts to determine whether a contractual term is unfair or not.

It follows that even if the case-law of the Court made a constructive and purposive interpretation of the Unfair Terms Directive in order to establish the requirements of procedural protection of consumers-mortgage debtors, such interpretation cannot be stretched so far as to challenge national legislative provisions unconnected to the powers of the courts. The limitation of the procedural protection of mortgage debtors within the ambit of the protection provided by the Unfair Terms Directive, takes us to the next issue, namely the added value of the Mortgage Credit Directive in that regard.

12.3 Forbearance and Proportionality in Residential Repossession Proceedings

The Mortgage Credit Directive regulatory reach covers, to a large extent, the precontractual stage of the conclusion of the contract.[56] By means of extended information and transparency requirements, as well as creditworthy assessment controls, this directive aims to prevent the recurrence of irresponsible lending and, thus, to avert future risks associated with such behavior. There are, nevertheless, some provisions that deal with the performance of the mortgage contracts, particularly with the circumstances that can trigger the need for their adaptation.[57] A prominent example is Article 23 of the Mortgage Credit Directive, dealing with the issue of foreign-currency loans and the limitation of the foreign-exchange rate risk inherent in such contracts.[58] The most remarkable provision,

55 *Barclays Bank* (C-280/13), para. 41, referring to judgment of 21 March 2013, *RWE Vertrieb*, C-92/11, EU:C:2013:180.

56 *See* Ferretti, *supra* note 18, p. 849; T. Josipovic, 'Consumer Protection in EU Residential Mortgage Markets: Common EU Rules on Mortgage Credit in the Mortgage Credit Directive', *in* A. Albors-Llorens, K.A. Armstrong & M.W.Gehring (Eds.), *The Cambridge Yearbook of European Legal Studies*, Vol. 16, 2013-2014, pp. 223-253.

57 *Cf.* EuSoCo Principles, Principle 10 on Adaptation.

58 On the unfair terms in the foreign currency contracts *see* Judgment of 20 September 2017, *Andriciuc and others*, C-186/16, EU:C:2017:703 and Judgment of 30 April 2014, *Kásler and Káslerné Rábai*, C-26/13, EU:C:2014:282.

for the purposes of this chapter, however, is Article 28 on arrears and foreclosures. Even though it does not set harmonized rules or mandatory substantive conditions on repossession, it is the first time that a link is established – at the level of European legislation – between credit default, indebtedness, and the family home.

The first paragraph of Article 28 of the Mortgage Credit Directive reads as follows: "Member States shall adopt measures to encourage creditors to exercise reasonable forbearance before foreclosure proceedings are initiated". The requirement of 'reasonable forbearance' (*tolérance raisonnable* in French) is not a new concept. In a broad sense, "forbearance mechanisms"[59] might already exist in the mortgage repossession process, in circumstances where the courts have the powers to suspend possession, particularly when it appears likely that the debtor will be able to clear the arrears within reasonable time. In the Mortgage Credit Directive, forbearance corresponds rather to a 'pre-action' requirement incumbent upon the creditor with the objective to avoid the initiation of repossession proceedings at the first place.[60] In this sense, forbearance may form part of best-practice rules and be set out in credit institutions' codes of conduct. Such rules broadly encourage cooperation between the credit institution and the debtor running arrears, inviting them to engage in discussions at an early stage in the debtor's financial difficulties and reach a solution that would render the mortgage sustainable. This normally involves agreeing to an alternative repayment plan that might include, for instance, capitalization of the arrears, an extension of the term of repayment, and/or interest-only payments for a certain period of time.

The Mortgage Credit Directive leaves, however, up to the Member States to decide on the legal effect of this requirement. Former draft proposals from the European Parliament employed more prescriptive language: "Member States shall *ensure* that creditors exercise reasonable forbearance and make all other reasonable attempts to resolve the position before initiating foreclosure proceedings" (emphasis added).[61] Moreover, in the explanatory statement of a motion for a European Parliament resolution on a new agenda for European Consumer Policy, figured a bold proposal of suspension of evictions or foreclosures arising from defaults in payments in the case of mortgage contracts involving the

59 S. Nield, 'Thumbs Down to the Horizontal Effect of Article 8', *Conv. Prop. Law.* 2015, pp. 77-88, 84, who qualifies s. 36 of the UK Administration of Justice Act 1970 a "usual forbearance mechanism". On this provision and the possibility of its interpretation in light of the right to respect of home, *see* J. Hurford, 'Does Article 8 Broaden the Court's Powers Under Section 36 of the Administration of Justice Act 1970?', 17 (1) *J. Housing Law* 1960, pp. 9-15.

60 Para. 27 of the Preamble to the Mortgage Credit Directive states that "[...] it is appropriate to encourage creditors to deal proactively with emerging credit risk at an early stage and that the necessary measures are in place to ensure that creditors exercise reasonable forbearance and make reasonable attempts to resolve the situation through other means before foreclosure proceedings are initiated".

61 Report of 11 October 2012 on the Proposal for a Directive of the European Parliament and of the Council on Credit Agreements Relating to Residential Property (COM(2011)-C7-0085/2011-2011/0062(COD), Article 18b.

principal home, due to causes not attributable to the consumer, such as unemployment. According to that proposal, the suspension of the foreclosure would have resulted in:

> applying a moratorium on monthly payments until the person concerned finds work, or replacing the mortgage payments with a lease-purchase option on that home, or setting a monthly rent that is less than 20% of that person's income for a period of at least two years.[62]

As Article 28 of the Mortgage Credit Directive now stands, the legal force and the effect of the observance of the requirement of forbearance in enforcement proceedings are a matter for the national legislature. The varying degrees of the prescriptive force of the forbearance requirement can better be understood with reference to three concrete examples (the first two predate the entering into force of said directive).

The first example is the English 'Pre-Action Protocol for Possession Claims based on Mortgage or Home Purchase Plan Arrears in Respect of Residential Property' (the 'Pre-Action Protocol').[63] Although the handling of mortgage arrears was already subject to regulation,[64] the Pre-Action Protocol demonstrates the importance of the role of the courts in "assessing whether the lender is in compliance with the expected regulatory standards at the point where an application for a possession order is made".[65] According to its Preamble, the Pre-Action Protocol describes the behavior that the court will normally expect of the parties prior to the possession claim. The stated objective of the Pre-Action Protocol is to ensure that both the lender and borrower act "fairly and reasonably with each other in resolving any matter concerning mortgage [...] arrears" and that greater "pre-action contact" between the parties is encouraged. Under certain circumstances, the lender "must *consider* not starting a possession claim for mortgage arrears" (emphasis added), such as where the borrower can demonstrate steps taken in view of applying to a government-funded scheme of assistance or where he demonstrates that

62 Report of 17 May 2013 on a New Agenda for European Consumer Policy (2012/2133(INI)), Explanatory Statement, under the heading 'Social and Environmental Responsibility'.

63 The Protocol is available on the UK Judiciary website, retrieved on 3 July 2017 from <www.justice.gov.uk/courts/procedure-rules/civil/protocol/prot_mha>. For more detail, L. Whitehouse, 'The Mortgage Arrears Pre-Action Protocol: An Opportunity Lost', 75 *Modern Law Rev.* 2009, pp. 783-814; and L. Whitehouse, 'Mapping the Boundaries of the Law of Mortgage: The Repossession Process in Practice', *in* C. Twigg-Flesner & G. Villalta-Puig (Eds.), *Boundaries of Commercial and Trade Law*, Sellier European Law Publishers, Munich, 2011, pp. 51-74.

64 *See, in particular*, Section MCOB 13 'Arrears, Payment shortfalls, and repossessions: regulated mortgage contracts and home purchase plans', in Financial Conduct Authority (FCA) *Mortgage and Home Finance: Conduct of Business Sourcebook*, retrieved on 3 July 2017 from <www.handbook.fca.org.uk/handbook/MCOB.pdf>.

65 Civil Justice Council, Consultation Paper, Mortgage Arrears Protocol, 2008, pp. 22-23, retrieved on 3 July 2017 from <www.judiciary.gov.uk/wp-content/uploads/JCO/Documents/CJC/Publications/consultation+papers/CJC+Consultation+paper+mortgage+arrears+pre-action+protocol.pdf>.

reasonable steps are being taken to market the property.[66] The repossession is to be considered "a last resort", which should "not normally be started unless all other reasonable attempts have failed".[67] It is worth noting that the earlier draft of the Pre-Action Protocol employed more prescriptive terms: it provided that "possession proceedings *should not* be started" (emphasis added) under certain conditions.[68]

The second example, one of a more prescriptive approach and more intensive judicial oversight of the forbearance requirement, is Scotland's Home Owner and Debtor Protection Act (Scotland) Act 2010 (hereinafter the 'Home-Owner Protection Act'). The Home-Owner Protection Act restricts creditor remedies in residential securities and qualifies the creditor's right to immediate possession upon default. More particularly, as it has already been hinted to (Section 12.2), the creditor may introduce an action for repossession only with a warrant from the court, save for the case of voluntary surrender. If the debtor does not consent to voluntary surrender, the creditor has to apply to the court in order to exercise the remedies he is entitled to and, before doing so, he *must* comply with the pre-action requirements imposed by the Home-Owner Protection Act.[69] The creditor is obliged to make reasonable efforts to agree with the debtor on a repayment plan. The court may not grant the application for possession unless it is satisfied that the creditor has complied with the pre-action requirements and that it is *reasonable* in the circumstances of the case to do so. The matters that the court needs to consider in that regard are the nature of and reasons for the default, the ability of the debtor to fulfil his obligations within a reasonable time, any action taken by the creditor to assist the debtor to fulfil those obligations, where appropriate, participation by the debtor in a debt payment program approved under the legislation on debt arrangement, and, finally, the ability of the debtor and of any other person residing at the security subjects to secure *reasonable alternative accommodation*.[70]

The third and final example of the level of prescriptive force of the forbearance requirement is taken from Ireland. Under Regulation 29(1) of the European Union (Consumer Mortgage Credit Agreements) Regulations 2016 (the 'Mortgage Regulations'):

> A creditor shall exercise reasonable forbearance before possession proceedings are initiated and shall, at a minimum, comply with the provisions of any code or similar measure put in place by the Central Bank on the handling of arrears.

66 The Pre-Action Protocol, Sec. 6.1.

67 Id., Sec. 7.

68 For a critical view of the Pre-Action Protocol as an "opportunity lost" when compared to the earlier draft of the Pre-Action Protocol, *see* Whitehouse 2009, *supra* note 63.

69 The Home-Owner Protection Act, Sec. 2(2) (1A, 1B & 1 C). The pre-action requirements are set out in Sec. 4 of the Home-Owner Protection Act.

70 The Home-Owner Protection Act, Sec. 2, (5).

For Ireland, such requirements are provided in the Irish Code of Conduct on Mortgage Arrears 2013 (the 'CCMA'). According to the CCMA, a lender may only commence legal proceedings for a borrower's primary residence after (i) it has made every reasonable effort under the CCMA to agree with the borrower on an alternative arrangement and (ii) either (a) the CCMA's specified time delay for the commencement of legal proceedings has expired or (b) the borrower has been classified as not cooperating.[71] Even though legal proceedings have already commenced, a lender must still continue to maintain contact with the borrower to try to come to an alternative repayment arrangement, and if such an agreement is reached, the lender must seek an order from the court putting the legal proceedings on hold.[72]

In a case that predates the Mortgage Regulations, the Irish Supreme Court ruled on the effect of the breach of the codes of conduct upon the lender's right to seek possession,[73] in its judgment of 15 May 2015 in *Irish Life and Permanent Plc v. Gemma Dunne and Kevin Dunne and Irish Life and Permanent Plc v. Dylan Dunphy*.[74] The code of conduct applicable to the case imposed a 12-month moratorium on seeking possession under certain circumstances. The Irish Supreme Court, per Mr. Justice Clarke, held that where the breach of the code of conduct

> involves a failure by the lender to abide by the moratorium referred to in the [c]ode, but in no other case, non-compliance with the [c]ode affects, as a matter of law, a relevant lender's entitlement to obtain an order for possession.[75]

With the exception of the moratorium, the Irish Supreme Court determined that the courts were not, pursuant to the law as it stood at the time,

> given any general jurisdiction to consider whether the actions of a lender might be considered, by reference to whatever criteria one might like to apply, to be reasonable or fair.[76]

The newly adopted Mortgage Regulations, however, makes an explicit reference to the code of conduct as a minimum mandatory standard of compliance with the forbearance requirement. The fact that creditors are required by law to demonstrate their compliance with the reasonable forbearance requirement, in combination with the more detailed

71 CCMA, Provision 56.

72 Id., Provision 59.

73 *See* P. Kenna & K. Lynch-Shally, 'Comparing Mortgage Law in England and Ireland', *Conv.* 2014, pp. 294-316; T. Murphy, 'A Shield or a Sword or Just Soft Law? An Analysis of the Banking Regulatory Codes of Conduct on the Bank/Customer Relationship', 20 *Comm. Law Pract.* 2013, pp. 163-169.

74 [2015] 2 I.L.R.M. 192.

75 Id., para. 5.28.

76 Id., para. 5.22.

provisions of the CCMA, militates in favor of broader jurisdiction for Irish courts in repossession proceedings. On the other hand, Regulation 29(7) only provides a criminal sanction of the breach of the CCMA,[77] and makes no specific reference to the civil consequences of any breach of the reasonable forbearance in the proceedings.[78] Thus, it remains to be seen how this provision will be applied by the Irish courts.

The Irish example demonstrates that even where lender forbearance is elevated to a mandatory pre-action requirement, judicial review of such requirement is not assimilated to a fully fledged *proportionality* check. The latter is indeed the most intensive ground of review in residential repossession proceedings.

Judicial review of the proportionality of an order for eviction has already been elevated, by the ECtHR, to an important factor in the determination of the level of adequate "procedural safeguards" afforded by national legislation to the right to protect one's home under Article 8 ECHR.[79] In the previous section (Section 12.2), reference was made to the ECtHR's landmark case, *McCann v. United Kingdom*, the case that inspired the Court's reasoning in *Kušionová*.[80] However, it has to be stressed out that *McCann v. United Kingdom*, as well as the subsequent Strasbourg cases on eviction, arose in the context of social-housing tenancy law, involving public landlords and tenants.[81] At the time of those judgments, it appeared yet unclear whether the proportionality review would also be applicable in eviction orders initiated by a private party, such as a private landlord or a mortgage creditor. The judgment in *Vrzić v. Croatia*,[82] nuances the approach of the ECtHR in relation to the proportionality test when private interests are at stake in repossession.

Vrzić v Croatia concerned enforcement proceedings between a private creditor and a couple who had used their house as collateral to secure a personal loan and a loan for their company. The couple argued, essentially, that their house should have been ex-

77 Regulation 29 (7) of the Mortgage Regulations: "A creditor who contravenes a provision of this Regulation commits an offence".

78 The proposal of the need for clarification of the impact of the breach of the code in private litigation (and not just administrative or criminal) was made by J. Spooner, in 'Review of the Code of Conduct on Mortgage Arrears: Submission to the Central Bank of Ireland, 10 April 2013, p. 5 (retrieved on 03 July 2017 from <www.centralbank.ie/docs/default-source/publications/CP63/joseph-spooner-submission.pdf?sfvrsn=0)>, who argued that "the auxiliary enforcement of these codes would not only contribute to enhancing compliance levels with the codes, but would also provide redress in individual cases in which a consumer has been harmed by a lender's non-compliance with a code thus providing just outcomes and attributions of responsibility in individual cases in a manner in which the administrative sanctions procedure cannot".

79 *See* the landmark judgments *Connors v. the United Kingdom*, ECHR, App. No. 66746/01, para. 83; *McCann v. United Kingdom*, ECHR, App. No. 19009/04, para. 50, and subsequent cases *Kay v. United Kingdom*, ECHR, App. No. 37341/06, para. 68; *Ivanova and Cherkezov v. Bulgaria*, ECHR, App. No. 46577/15, para. 53; *Sagvolden v. Norway*, ECHR, App. No. 21682/11, para 140.

80 *Kušionová*, C-34/13.

81 For an account of this case law *see* C. Schmid & J. Dinse, 'Towards a Common Core of Residential Tenancy Law in Europe? The Impact of the European Court of Human Rights on Tenancy Law', *in* Nogler & Reifner, *supra* note 8, pp. 627-639; Nield, *supra* note 59.

82 *Vrzić v. Croatia*, ECHR, judgment of 12 July 2016, App. no. 43777/13.

empted from enforcement as it was meeting their basic human needs, relying upon their right to respect for the home and their right to property.

The Strasbourg court recognized that Article 8 ECHR was applicable as long as the debtors were obliged to vacate the house that served as family residence. It then recalled its settled case law on the requirement for the national courts to carry out a proportionality test when adopting an eviction order.[83] In all those cases however, the persons against whom the eviction order was directed "were living in State-owned or socially owned flats and an important aspect of finding a violation was the fact that there was no other private interest at stake".[84] The ECtHR found the *Vrzić v. Croatia* case to be different, as the sale of the house of the debtors "was a consequence of their failure to meet their contractual obligations [...] a consequence to which the applicants had expressly agreed".[85]

However, the absence of proportionality review in private repossession proceedings does not absolve the state, the judgment in *Vrzić v. Croatia* points out, from affording the parties to the dispute "judicial procedures which offer the necessary procedural guarantees".[86] The analysis of the Croatian procedural law on enforcement led to the conclusion that it did offer such guarantees, but that the debtors did not take advantage of them. This was so as the debtors did not participate, for instance, in the assessment of the valuation of the house "even though they had an opportunity to do so".[87] Moreover, they did not challenge the loan agreements, although they could have done so.[88]

The solution given in *Vrzić v. Croatia* can be associated to the approach taken in an earlier decision of the UK Supreme Court in *McDonald*, even if the legal context of the two cases is not the same. The case of the ECtHR concerned mortgage possession proceedings brought by a private lender, while *McDonald*[89] case concerned a possession order brought by a private landlord against a tenant. However, both cases touch upon the difficult question of the possible horizontal effect of the right for respect of one's home in residential repossession involving private parties.

As a preliminary remark, it must be remembered that the English courts have long been wrestling with the question of proportionality in the context of possession claims of

83 Id., para. 65.
84 Id., para. 66.
85 Id., paras. 69-72.
86 Id., para. 101.
87 Id., para. 114.
88 Id., para. 70.
89 *McDonald (by her litigation friend Duncan J McDonald) v. McDonald and others*, [2016] UKSC 28. *See* A. Dymond, 'McDonald – Private Landlords and Article 8', 19 *J. Housing Law* 2016, pp. 93-96; S. Pascoe, 'The end of the road for human rights in private landowners' disputes?', *Conv.* 2017, pp. 269-286; S. Nield, 'Thumbs Down to the Horizontal Effect of Article 8', *Conv.* 2015, pp. 77-88; idem, 'Shutting the Door on Horizontal Effect: Mc Donald v. McDonald', *Conv.* 2017, pp. 60-71.

residential property by local authorities.[90] The judgment in *Pinnock*[91] represented the "resolution of a protracted-judicial dialogue"[92] between the House of Lords and the ECtHR on the issue. In *Pinnock*, it was finally held that the compatibility of UK law with Article 8 [ECHR] would require accepting that:

> where a court is asked to make an order for possession of a person's home at the suit of a local authority, the court must have the power to assess the proportionality of making the order,[93]

even if in "very highly exceptional cases".[94]

The UK Supreme Court had reserved its position with regard to a case where the person seeking an order for possession is a private landlord and not a public authority. *McDonald* provided an opportunity for that Court to address the issue. The property at issue, a flat, served as the home of a woman unable to work due to severe psychiatric problems. Her parents had purchased the flat using a loan secured by a mortgage thereon. The parents granted their daughter an assured tenancy,[95] but they remained liable for the repayment of the loan. Once they started to run behind on their payments owing to financial difficulties, the company appointed a receiver who sought possession of the flat under Section 21(4) of the Housing Act 1988 in the parents' name.[96] The tenant advanced her right to respect of home and argued that even if the mandatory requirements of the law had been met, the court should consider the proportionality of making an order for possession.

The UK Supreme Court did not accept the proportionality defense in repossession proceedings initiated by a private landlord. It held that the legislature had already struck the balance between the rights of residential tenants to respect of home and the property

90 *See* S. Nield, 'Clash of the Titans: Article 8, Occupiers and Their Home', *in* Bright (Ed.), *supra* note 9, pp. 101-129; Lord Walker of Gestingthorpe, 'The Saga of Strasbourg and Social Housing', *in* N. Hopkins (Ed.), *Modern Studies in Property Law*, Vol. 7, Hart Publishing, Oxford and Portland, OR, 2013, pp. 3-14; H.H. Judge N. Madge, 'Small Earthquake in Bulgaria: Not Many Dead', 19 *J. Housing Law* 2016, pp. 61-65; I. Loveland, 'Twenty Years Later – Assessing the Significance of the Human Rights Act 1998 to Residential Possession Proceedings', *Conv.* 2017, pp. 174-194.

91 *Manchester City Council v. Pinnock* [2011] 2 AC 104. See also *Hounslow London Borough Council v. Powell* [2011] 2 AC 186.

92 *McDonald, supra* note 89, para. 34.

93 *Pinnock, supra* note 91, para. 49.

94 Id., para. 51.

95 The definition of an assured tenancy according to Sec. 1(1)(b) of the Housing Act 1988 is a tenancy "under which a dwelling-house is let as a separate dwelling" to one or more individuals, at least one of whom occupies it as her "only or principal home". The provisions on assured tenancies provide for enhanced protection of residential tenants in possession proceedings, described in *McDonald, supra* note 89, paras. 20-28.

96 For this reason, Nield, *supra* note 89, 61 explains that this was not "a straightforward case of a landlord wishing to evict their tenant but a mortgage repossession case which utilised the route of appointing a receiver to initiate repossession as a prelude to sale".

rights of private-sector landlords. The proportionality defense would have added, according to the judgment, an additional layer of requirements to the ones that have already been set by the legislature in a way that would frustrate "consistency of application and certainty of outcome".[97] Echoing older decisions of the European Commission on Human Rights,[98] the judgment held that a court is "merely the forum for the determination of the civil right in dispute between the parties" and, therefore, "once it concludes that the landlord is entitled to an order for possession, there is nothing further to investigate".[99] This would not prejudice, according to the judgment, the right of the tenant to challenge the legality of the statutory regime by virtue of which repossession was ordered, a case which had not yet been advanced.[100]

McDonald illustrates the cautious stance of the judiciary against an approach that could frustrate the balance struck by statute in private relationships or that could be perceived as interfering with fundamental issues of housing policy. The judgment received a critical reception in housing literature.[101] Sarah Nield views its restrictive approach "disappointing to the emergence of human rights protection of the home" and argues that it "takes the human out of home repossession".[102] Another author, Susan Pascoe, argues, in turn, that the approach in *McDonald* does not find support in *Vrzić v. Croatia* because the legislation in question did not offer the necessary procedural guarantees and that the view taken was extremely narrow by not sufficiently considering the implications stemming from the fact that the possession order was due to the mortgage arrears of the parents, who bought the flat for their disabled daughter.[103]

McDonald is definitely not an easy case, raising the problematic of the influence of fundamental rights in private residential repossession cases and the role of the courts. Taking into account the psychiatric problems of the person involved, it is actually a 'hard' case. Such cases urge legislative intervention for the establishment of the grounds and the criteria on the basis of which the courts may consider the proportionality of repossession at least in the presence of exceptional circumstances. However, the legislative intervention might also prove necessary in the exceptional context of deep economic recession. A sharp rise in repossessions' rate within such context is a phenomenon that exceeds the sphere of the specific contractual relationship or the personal situation/hardship of the individual debtor and becomes a matter of public interest.

97 *McDonald, supra* note 89, para. 43.
98 In particular *Wood v. United Kingdom* (1997) 24 EHRR CD 69.
99 *McDonald, supra* note 89, para. 44.
100 Id., para. 45.
101 *See* literature supra note 89.
102 Nield, *supra* note 89, 60.
103 Pascoe, *supra* note 89.

12.4 Urgent Measures of Protection of the Primary Residence against Repossession

The financial crisis revealed the broader economic and societal implications of the repossession of the primary residence. An economy in a recessionary spiral may trigger default factors that affect the personal capacity of the consumer to repay (unemployment or loss-of-earning capacity). The bursting of the housing bubble exacerbated the situation of underwater mortgages. Hans-Wolfgang Micklitz spoke of the collective dimension of household debt that needs to be "reconstructed in its macro-economic context".[104] In the same vein, the risk of mass repossessions exceeds the sphere of the debtor in default. In the absence of State intervention, large-scale repossessions bring along social problems, such as homelessness and blighted communities, as well as widen the gap of an unequal society.[105]

At the height of the economic crisis, governments introduced urgent measures intended to refinance underwater mortgages or restrict the creditor's right to repossess in the event of default. This restriction took, at times, drastic forms in the name of safeguarding the public interest and social peace. Ian Ramsay provides a panorama of the various measures adopted across the Member States, all intended to meet the situation of delinquent residential mortgage credits, ranging from procedural means destined to ensure that repossession would be the last resort and measures governing the circumstances of debt restructuring, to the granting of social benefits in order to support interest payments or, ultimately, to moratoria on repossession.[106] Here, we focus on the moratorium as an illustration of, perhaps, the most drastic measure introduced to protect the debtor's principal residence and, in turn, to restrain the mortgagee right to repossess.

Greece instituted a moratorium on repossessions of the debtor's principal residence amid the unprecedented economic crisis that plunged the country into economic depres-

---

104 H.-W. Micklitz, 'Conclusions: Consumer Over-indebtedness and Consumer Insolvency: From Micro to Macro', *in* Micklitz & Domurath (Eds.), *supra* note 6, p. 233.

105 *See* J. Stiglitz, *The Price of Inequality*, Penguin Books, London/New York, 2013, pp. 212-215; P. Cox, 'Foreclosure Reform Amid Mortgage Lending Turmoil: A Public Purpose Approach', 45 *Hous. L. Rev.* 2008, pp. 683-745. With regard to the impact of the subprime and predatory lending in the United States upon the communities we note the Opinion of the US Supreme Court decided on May 1, 2017 in case *Bank of America Corp. et al. v. City of Miami, Florida* (No. 15-1111), 581 U.S. (2017), consolidated with case *Wells Fargo & Co et al. v. City of Miami, Florida* (No. 15-1115). The City of Miami filed suit alleging it had suffered damages due to the violation by the bank of the Fair Housing Act (FHA). In particular, it alleged that the discriminatory conduct of the banks led to a disproportionate number of foreclosures "which impaired the City's effort to assure racial integration, diminished the City's property-tax revenue, and increased demand for police, fire, and other municipal services". The US Supreme Court accepted the City's standing under the FHA. However it remanded for further proceedings on the issue of causation between the conduct prohibited by the statute and the harm alleged by the City. It found that the lower court erred in concluding that the causation was satisfied solely on the ground that the City's alleged injuries were "foreseeable results" of the Bank's misconduct.

106 I. Ramsay, 'Two Cheers for Europe: Austerity, Mortgage Foreclosures and Personal Insolvency in the EU', *in* Micklitz & Domurath (Eds.), *supra* note 6, pp. 189-227, 207.

sion lasting more than six consecutive years. The extent of the moratorium, in terms of time-length and eligibility conditions, is probably unique in the European Union. In its most absolute form, it lasted from mid-2010 until the end of 2013.[107] Whereas initially eligible for the moratorium were only consumer debtors, the moratorium was then dis-associated from the consumer capacity and became linked to the protected asset, the principal family residence.[108] This can be explained by the impact of the economic depression, which was not restricted to consumer mortgage debtors, but affected a broad base of the Greek population. Moreover, during the same period, the horizontal moratorium was put in place by virtue of which no enforcement proceedings could be initiated by banking institutions for debts below EU 200,000.[109] As from 1 January 2014, the conditions of the moratorium of the principal residence were tightened in order to avert the risk of 'strategic' defaults.[110] A means test was implemented, which considered, in particular, the value of the property (less than EUR 200,000) and the total family revenues and assets in possession, and was further subject to a minimum repayment instalment, except for the unemployed debtors who lacked any source of income. Meanwhile, for consumer debtors in particular, the consumer insolvency law (introduced for the first time in 2010) provided for a more permanent solution in order to shield the principal residence from repossession, as long as the debtor met the debt-restructuring conditions established through that process.[111]

The Greek moratorium was finally replaced, as of 1 January 2016, with a new regime of particular protection of the debtor's primary residence, which will remain applicable until 31 December 2018.[112] By virtue of this regime, protection of the principal residence is now fully embedded within the framework of the law on consumer insolvency,[113] which means that only consumer debtors may qualify. The new regime allows a consu-

107 The moratorium was extended with successive decrees which modified the original moratorium provided for in the transition provisions of the consumer insolvency Law 3869/2010 on debt restructuring of over-indebted natural persons (FEK A 130/03.08.2010) as amended (the 'Law 3869/2010'), so-called Law '*Katseli*' out of the name of the then minister in office that promoted the law. For a commentary of this law, *see*, among others, A. Kritikos, *Debt restructuring of natural persons*, Athens-Thessaloniki, Sakkoulas, 2016 (in Greek, author translation).

108 The extension of the moratorium was brought about by Article 46, para. 2 of Law 3986/2011 (FEK A 152/01.07.2011) which amended Article 19 of Law 3869/2010.

109 The horizontal moratium was instituted by Article 40 of Law 3858/2010 (FEK A 102/01/07/2010) and was extended by successive decrees until the 31st of December 2013.

110 Law 4224/2013 on a Government Council for managing private debt, a Greek Investment Fund managing state property and other urgent provisions (FEK A 288/31.12.2013). For a commentary on this law *see* I.S. Spiridakis, *The Suspension of Auction of the Primary Residence*, Athens-Komotini, Ant. Sakkoulas, 2014 (in Greek, author translation). The moratorium under the conditions instituted by this law was put in place until the 31st of December 2014. During 2015 and the political upheaval in Greece there was a *de facto* moratorium of repossession of the principal residence.

111 Law 3869/2010, Art. 8. *See* G. Mentis & K. Pantazatou, 'Country Report Greece', *in* Micklitz & Domurath (Eds.), *supra* note 6, pp. 29-45.

112 Law 4346/2015 (FEK A 152/20.11.2015) which amended Law 3869/2010.

113 Under Article 9 of Law 3869/2010.

mer debtor to apply to the court to obtain debt restructuring that excludes his principal residence from repossession under very specific circumstances and subject to strict conditions. In sum, the consumer debtor may shield his residence only if the asset serves as his principal residence, his monthly family income does not exceed an amount equal to the statutorily determined "reasonable living expenses"[114] augmented by 70%, the value of the asset does not exceed a certain threshold and in so far as he is classified as "co-operating" in accordance with the Banking Code of Conduct. The debtor is still required to reimburse up to the maximum of his repayment capacity and, in any event, at least the amount that would not be liable to deteriorate the position in which his creditors would have been in the event of repossession.[115] For a restrictively defined category of debtors, who are in a particularly dire economic situation, the law provides the potential of benefitting from a social scheme of debt-repayment support.

Spain offers another example of a legislatively mandated moratorium; unfortunately, it was enacted too late to prevent several instances of suicide by evicted homeowners.[116] The Spanish moratorium had considerably more restrictive eligibility conditions, when compared with its Greek counterpart. The royal decree law 27/2012 (dated as of 15 November 2012)[117] imposed a temporary moratorium on evictions as an urgent measure intended to benefit a very narrowly defined category of "vulnerable debtors" facing a high risk of social exclusion due to specific situations of hardship defined by said law.[118] The moratorium for those persons is in place through 2017.[119]

114 The method of calculation of 'reasonable living expenses' is provided in Art. 5, para. 3 of Law 3869/2010.

115 The concretization of the application of those two criteria is set out in the Decision 54/15-12-2015 of the Bank of Greece. The determination of the "maximum repayment capacity" is based on the actual current and future repayment capacity by the debtor of the entirety of the debt, according to reliable and realistic data which also take into account his own and his family "reasonable living expenses". In order to determine the situation in which the creditors would have been in the event of repossession, it is necessary that the creditors submit an estimation of the commercial value of the pledged asset with reference to the percentage of diminution of such value due to an eventual repossession and the costs related to it.

116 *See* suicide incident reports in the press, retrieved on 03 July 2017 from <www.huffingtonpost.com/2013/02/15/4th-eviction-suicide-spain_n_2697192.html>.

117 Real Decreto-ley 27/2012, de 15 de noviémbre, de medidas urgentes para reforzar la protección a las deudores hipotecarias, BOE 279 of 16 November 2012.

118 *See* P. Gutierrez de Cabiedes & M. Cantero Gamito, 'Country Report Spain', *in* Micklitz & Domurath, *supra* note 6, pp. 67-85.; S. Nasarre-Aznar, 'A Legal Perspective of the Origin and the Globalisation of the Current Financial Crisis and the Resulting Reforms in Spain' and V. Valino, 'Mortgage Foreclosure and Housing Rights in Spain: Crisis or General Deception?' both *in* Kenna (Ed.), *supra* note 10, pp. 37-72 and pp. 101-115.

119 The latest prolongation of the moratorium was brought about by Royal Decree Law 1/2015 of 27 February on a second chance mechanism (Real Decreto-ley 1/2015, de 27 de febrero, de mecanismo de segunda oportunidad, reducción de carga financiera y otras medidas de orden social), BOE 51 of 28 February 2015. This law introduced a limited possibility for mortgage debtors to qualify for the discharge of their mortgage debt in lieu of repossession of the mortgaged property under certain circumstances. This is a more limited form of what has long been vindicated in Spain as the right to '*dación en pago*' or *datio in solutum*, whereby the transfer of the mortgaged property to the bank suffices to repay the outstanding debt. For a detailed account on this mechanism and more broadly on mortgage reform in Spain, *see* Fernández Seijo, *supra* note 24.

A particularly drastic measure restricting the property rights of lenders was adopted by the autonomous government of Andalucía, commonly known as the 'decree to fight evictions'. The measure was intended to reinstate what it called the "social function of the property" by imposing a penalty on institutional lenders holding vacant properties and allowing the state to use such vacant properties to provide housing for evicted families under the condition that they would pay a certain amount of rent.[120] The Andalusian measure was held to be partially unconstitutional by the Spanish Constitutional Court on the grounds that the regional government had over-ridden its competences in the adoption of certain provisions of said legislation, because the issue of the homeowners' protection had already been dealt with at the national level.[121]

In the above illustrations of urgent measures, the national contexts in which the issue of the protection of the primary residence of debtors arose were not identical,[122] just as the causes of the crisis varied between the two countries. However, in both instances, protecting the primary residence was at the heart of the legislative intervention. At the level of Union law, the Mortgage Credit Directive did not go so far as to set specific measures to afford protection of particularly vulnerable debtors of their primary residence, a matter falling – arguably – within the competence of the Member States. However, as has already been stated above, it does make a step toward a more consumer debtor-oriented procedure that takes account of the importance of the security involved.[123] Notably, the Commission Staff Working Paper that accompanied the proposal for that directive concludes[124] that, although foreclosures should constitute a measure of last resort for the lender, when they do take place, "common sense and *humanity* should always prevail at all levels (lender, authorities, courts, etc.) and throughout the whole procedure", taking particularly into account the "intolerable *social and human* implications for both borrowers and their families" (emphasis added).

120 Decreto-ley 6/2013, de 9 de abril, de medidas para asegurar el cumplimiento de la Función Social de la Vivienda (BOE, Num. 69, pag. 67, 11.04.2013), repealed and expanded by the subsequent Law 4/2013 of 1 October on measures to encourage welfare housing schemes (Ley 4/2013, de 1 de octubre, de medidas para asegurar el cumplimiento de la función social de la vivienda, BOE Num. 263, pag. 88451, 02.11.2013).

121 TS Sentencia 93/2015, de 14 de mayo 2015 (BOE 146 of 19 June 2015).

122 For the causes of household debt in Spain, *see*, indicatively, S. Nasarre-Aznar, ?A Legal Perspective of the Origin and the Globalisation of the Current Financial Crisis and the Resulting Reforms in Spain', *in* Kenna (Ed.), *supra* note 10, and in Greece, *see* G. Mentis & K. Pantazatou, 'Country Report Greece', *in* Micklitz & Domurath, *supra* note 6, pp. 29-45.

123 *See* Cherednychenko, *supra* note 17, p. 163, who argues in favor of the further development of what she calls the "positive" side of procedural consumer protection which would complement the "negative" side connected with the setting aside of national procedural legislation incompatible with the effective protection of consumer rights.

124 Commission Staff Working Paper, *National measures and practices to avoid foreclosure procedures for residential mortgage loans*, SEC (2011) 357 final, Brussels, 31.3.2011, page 11.

12.5 Conclusion: A Distinct Framework for Mortgage Repossession Proceedings Involving a Primary Residence

The phenomenon of mortgage repossessions in the aftermath of the 2008 subprime mortgage loan crisis was an occasion to expose gaps in the procedural protection of mortgage debtors and unearth the imbalances in the respective positions of the parties in the contractual and postsigning contractual processes, deeply rooted in the unlimited right of the mortgagee to repossess. It highlighted the need for a specific framework for repossessions for residential mortgage loans, affording enhanced protection. As long as the market assumes the biggest part of giving access to homeownership, the State must ensure a fair process and that proper judicial oversight is in place. That presupposes, in turn, the reconceptualization of that 'asset' as more than a mere commodity and the redesign of procedure accordingly.

This chapter attempted to advance certain core elements of procedural safeguards in proceedings that engage with a citizen's fundamental right to respect of one's home and family life. To that purpose, it examined the Union case law and legislation, as well as national legislative and judicial perspectives, and the Strasbourg Court's case law. Across the different perspectives, the main theme is that national legislation should allow a mortgage debtor to make *effectively* his case to protect his home, to challenge the legality of the (nonjudicial) enforcement title, and, eventually, to challenge the law when it does not afford an appropriate standard of protection.

The legal framework on foreclosures must be designed in a way to ensure adequate protection of the asset involved, which represents a 'basic human need' for lodging. This requirement has been realized, at the EU level of law, through the avenue of the judicial protection of consumers against the use of unfair terms in the mortgage contract and the power of the courts to review such terms. In this way, Union law can operate as one among the levers of inciting legal reform intent on strengthening the protection of the fundamental rights of the mortgage debtors. Union law can also set the tone of a more protective procedural framework with regard to the forbearance constraint on the part of the lender. However, the forbearance requirement loses in effectiveness if it is not rendered a compulsory pre-action requirement in any repossession procedure and if the courts are not vested with the power to refuse to grant a court-ordered repossession when it is sought in violation of such requirement.

Consideration of the 'Basic Needs' principle in repossession proceedings instils a novel procedural ethos, one that takes due account of the constitutional dimensions involved. This may, in turn, herald a new narrative for consumers in the postcrisis era. When viewed against the backdrop of the Court's case law on mortgage repossessions, this narrative reflects an "image"[125] of consumers distinct from the one originally envi-

125 *See* D. Leczykiewicz & S. Weatherill (Eds.), *The Images of the Consumer in EU Law, Legislation, Free Movement and Competition Law*, Hart Publishing, Oxford and Portland, OR, 2016.

saged in connection with the creation of the internal market. It is not the image of a consumer who requires protection so as to gain confidence in the internal market and shop across border. It is, rather, the image of a consumer who has lost confidence in the market and who now requires protection so as to live a decent life. For the time being, the Unfair Terms Directive has taken the lead in protecting the consumer in the framework of 'life time' contracts, as a result of a constitutional reading of the existing secondary legislation in novel societal contexts.

Protecting the essential aspects for the EU citizen-consumer covered by the model of 'life time' contracts, to which this book is devoted, deserves its place among the elements that will shape the discourse of the future shape of a "social Europe", to which EU leaders committed in their Rome Declaration of 25 March 2017.[126] As Hans-Wolfgang Micklitz observed, the "constitutionalized" consumer may enable the EU to turn a new page in the history of private law.[127] His vision can be extrapolated to the history of the Union. In the aftermath of the crisis, the internal market needs to be strongly anchored to the ultimate objective set out in article 3 TEU, from which it is apparent that the EU, as the Court states in Grand Chamber, "has not only an economic, but also a social purpose".[128]

Bibliography

Beka, A., *The Doctrine of the 'Active Consumer Court'*, Cambridge: Intersentia (forthcoming, 2018).

Bernitz, U. *et al.* (Eds.), *General Principles of EU law and European Private Law*, Alphen aan den Rijn: Wolters Kluwer, 2013.

Blázquez Peinado, M. D., 'El procedimiento de ejecución hipotecaria y su adecuación a la normativa europea en materia de protección a los consumidores por cláusulas abusivas. Jurisprudencia reciente del Tribunal de Justicia', 39 *Revista General de Derecho Europeo* 2016, pp. 1-31.

Cherednychenko O., 'The EU Charter of Fundamental Rights and Consumer Credit', *in* H. Collins (Ed.), *European Contract Law and the Charter of Fundamental Rights*, Cambridge/Antwerp/Portland, OR: Intersentia, 2017, pp. 139-166.

126 *See also* the European Commission Reflection Paper on the Social Dimension of Europe (Foreward) acknowledging that while "the economic, social and political case for a social Europe is solid", what will have to be build is "a consensus on its future shape".

127 H.-W. Micklitz, 'The Consumer: Marketised, Fragmentised, Constitutionalised', *in* Leczykiewicz & Weatherill (Eds.), *supra* note 125, pp. 21-42.

128 Judgment of 21 December 2016, *AGET Iraklis*, C-201/15, EU:C:2016:972, para. 77.

Collins, H. (Ed.), *European Contract Law and the Charter of Fundamental Rights*, Cambridge/Antwerp/Portland, OR: Intersentia, 2017.

Countouris, N. & Freedland M. (Eds.), *Resocialising Europe in a Time of Crisis*, Cambridge: Cambridge University Press, 2013.

Cox, P., 'Foreclosure Reform Amid Mortgage Lending Turmoil: A Public Purpose Approach', 45 *Hous. L. Rev.* 2008, pp. 683-745.

Dymond, A., 'McDonald – Private Landlords and Article 8', 19 *J. Housing Law* 2016, pp. 93-96.

Everson, M. & Joerges, C., 'Between Constitutional Command and Technocratic Rule: Post Crisis Governance and the Treaty on Stability, Coordination and Governance ("The Fiscal Compact")', *in* Carol Harlow *et al.* (Eds.), *Research Handbook on EU Administrative Law*, Cheltenham, UK/Northampton, USA: Edward Elgar, 2017.

Fernández Seijo, J.M., *La Tutela de los Consumidores en los Procedimientos Judiciales, Especial Referencia a las Ejecuciones Hipotecarias*, Barcelona: Bosch, 2017.

Ferretti, F., 'The Over-Indebted European Consumers: *Quo Vadis* Personal Insolvency Law?', 41 *E.L. Rev.* 2016, pp. 843-864.

H. H. Judge Madge, N., 'Small Earthquake in Bulgaria: Not Many Dead', 19 *J. Housing Law* 2016, pp. 61-65.

Habermas, J., *The Crisis of the European Union, A Response* (C. Cronin, Trans. From German), Cambridge: Polity Press, 2013.

Hartkamp, A., *European Law and National Private Law, Effect of EU Law and European Human Rights Law on Legal Relationships between Individuals* (2nd ed.), Cambridge/Antwerp/Portland, OR: Intersentia, 2016.

Hartkamp, A. *et al.* (Eds.), *Cases, Materials and Text on European Law and Private Law*, Oxford/Portland, OR: Hart Publishing, 2017.

Hurford, J., 'Does Article 8 Broaden the Court's Powers under Section 36 of the Administration of Justice Act 1970?', 17 (1) *J Housing Law*, pp. 9-15.

Iglesias Sanchez, S., 'Unfair Terms in Mortgage Loans and Protection of Housing in Times of Economic Crisis: *Aziz* v *Catalunyacaixa*', 51 *Common Mkt L. Rev.* 2014, p. 955.

Jemielniak, J. & Miklaszewicz, P., 'Introduction. Capturing the Change: Universalising Tendencies in Legal Interpretation', *in* J. Jemielniak & P. Miklaszewicz (Eds.), *Interpretation of Law in the Global World: From Particularism to a Universal, Approach*, Berlin: Springer, 2010, pp. 1-27.

Josipović, T., 'Consumer Protection in EU Residential Mortgage Markets: Common EU Rules on Mortgage Credit in the Mortgage Credit Directive', *in* A. Albors-Llorens, K.A. Armstrong & M.W.Gehring (Eds.), *The Cambridge Yearbook of European Legal Studies* (Vol. 16), Oxford: Hart Publishing, 2013-2014, pp. 223-253.

Kenna, P. (Ed.), *Contemporary Housing Issues in a Globalised World*, Farnham: Ashgate Publishing, 2014.

Kenna, P. & Lynch-Shally, K., 'Comparing Mortgage Law in England and Ireland', *Conv.* 2014, pp. 294-316.

Kilpatrick, C. & de Witte, B., *Social Rights in Times of Crisis in the Eurozone: The Role of Fundamental Rights' Challenges*, EUI Working Papers, Law 2014/15.

Kritikos, A., *Debt Restructuring of Natural Persons*, Athens-Thessaloniki: Sakkoulas, 2016.

Leczykiewicz, D. & Weatherill, S., *The Images of the Consumer in EU Law, Legislation, Free Movement and Competition Law*, Oxford/Portland, OR: Hart Publishing, 2016, pp. 159-182.

Lord Walker of Gestingthorpe, 'The Saga of Strasbourg and Social Housing', *in* N. Hopkins (Ed.), *Modern Studies in Property Law* (Vol. 7), Oxford/Portland, OR: Hart Publishing, 2013, pp. 3-14.

Loveland, I., 'Twenty Years Later – Assessing the Significance of the Human Rights Act 1998 to Residential Possession Proceedings', *Conv.* 2017, pp. 174-194.

Micklitz, H.-W. (Ed.), *Constitutionalisation of European Private Law*, Oxford: Oxford University Press, 2014.

Micklitz, H.-W. & Domurath, I. (Eds.), *Consumer Debt and Social Exclusion in Europe*, London/New York: Routledge, 2015.

Micklitz, H.-W. & Reich, N., 'The Court and Sleeping Beauty: The Revival of the Unfair Contract Terms Directive', 51 *Common Mkt L. Rev.* 2014, pp. 771-808.

Murphy, T., 'A Shield or a Sword or just Soft Law? An Analysis of the Banking Regulatory Codes of Conduct on the Bank/Customer Relationship', 20 *Comm. Law Pract.* 2013, pp. 163-169.

Nield, S., 'Clash of the Titans: Article 8, Occupiers and Their Home', *in* S. Bright (Ed.), *Modern Studies in Property Law* (Vol. 6), Oxford: Hart Publishing, 2011, pp. 101-129.

Nield, S., 'Thumbs Down to the Horizontal Effect of Article 8', *Conv.* 2015, pp. 77-88.

Nield, S., 'Shutting the Door on Horizontal Effect: Mc Donald v McDonald', *Conv.* 2017, p. 60.

Nogler, L. & Reifner, U. (Eds.), *Life Time Contracts, Social Long Term Contracts in Labour, Tenancy and Consumer Credit Law*, The Hague: Eleven International Publishing, 2014.

Nolan, A. (Ed.), *Economic and Social Rights After the Global Financial Crisis*, Cambridge: Cambridge University Press, 2014.

Pascoe, S., 'The End of the Road for Human Rights in Private Landowners' Disputes?', *Conv.* 2017, pp. 269-286.

Posner, R., *A Failure of Capitalism, The Crisis of '08 and the Descent into Depression*, Cambridge, MA/London: Harvard University Press, 2009.

Ramsay, I., 'Two Cheers for Europe: Austerity, Mortgage Foreclosures and Personal Insolvency Policy in the EU', *in* H.-W. Micklitz & I. Domurath (Eds.), *Consumer Debt and Social Exclusion in Europe*, London/New York: Routledge, 2015, pp. 189-227.

Rolnik, R. & Rabinovich, L., 'Late-Neoliberalism: The Financialisation of Homeownership and the Housing Rights of the Poor', *in* A. Nolan (Ed.), *Economic and Social Rights After the Global Financial Crisis*, Cambridge: Cambridge University Press, 2014, pp. 57-89.

Rutgers, J., 'The Right to Housing (Article 7 of the Charter) and Unfair Terms in General Conditions', *in* H. Collins (Ed.), *European Contract Law and the Charter of Fundamental Rights*, Cambridge/Antwerp/Portland, OR: Intersentia, 2017, pp. 125-137.

Spiridakis, I., *The Suspension of Auction of the Primary Residence*, Athens-Komotini: Ant. Sakkoulas, 2014.

Spooner, J., 'Fresh Start or Stalemate? European Consumer Insolvency Law Reform and the Politics of Household Debt', *ERPL* 2013, pp. 747-794.

Spooner, J., 'Review of the Code of Conduct on Mortgage Arrears: Submission to the Central Bank of Ireland, 10 April 2013.

Stiglitz, J., *The Price of Inequality*, London/New York: Penguin Books, 2013.

Terryn, E. *et al.* (Eds.), *Landmark Cases of EU Consumer Law*, Cambridge: Intersentia, 2014.

Thompson, M., 'Possession Actions and Human Rights', *Conv. Prop. Law.* 2011, pp. 421-440.

Touraine, A., *Après la Crise*, Paris: Éditions du Seuil, 2010.

Trstenjak, V. & Beysen, E., 'European Consumer Protection Law: Curia Semper Dabit Remedium?', 48 *Common Mkt L. Rev.* 2011, pp. 95-124.

Whitehouse, L., 'The Home-Owner: Citizen or Consumer?' *in* S. Bright & J. Dewar (Eds.), *Land Law Themes and Perspectives*, Oxford: Oxford University Press, 1998, pp. 183-205.

Whitehouse, L., 'The Mortgage Arrears Pre-Action Protocol: An Opportunity Lost', 75 *Modern Law Rev.* 2009, pp. 783-814.

Whitehouse, L., 'A Longitudinal Analysis of the Mortgage Repossession Process 1995-2010: Stability, Regulation and Reform', *in* S. Bright (Ed.), *Modern Studies in Property Law* (Vol. 6), Oxford: Hart Publishing, 2011, pp. 151-174.

Whitehouse, L., 'Mapping the Boundaries of the Law of Mortgage: The Repossession Process in Practice', *in* C. Twigg-Flesner & G. Villalta-Puig (Eds.), *Boundaries of Commercial and Trade Law*, Munich: Sellier European Law Publishers, 2011, pp. 51-74.

13 Home Mortgage Loans as Life Time Contracts

Alan M. White[*]

13.1 The Historical Development of the Modern US Home Mortgage Loan Contract Reveals Heavy State Involvement

Today's home mortgage loan in the United States is not a market product. The predominant contract is a fixed interest rate, 30-year amortizing home loan. This contract form was created by federal government agencies in the 1930s, during the New Deal, to reconstruct housing finance after the market collapse of the Great Depression. The Home Owners Loan Corporation purchased defaulted private mortgage loans of the 1920s from failing banks, and then restructured them from the prevailing private market contract, a 5-year, interest-only, balloon payment loan, into loans with monthly payments of principal and interest over a longer term designed to fully amortize the debt over time.[1]

This restructuring of past home loans was followed by state intervention to make these new home mortgage loan structures permanent. Two federal government initiatives that remain essential features of the US home loan market made this possible, one to provide insurance against default for lenders, and one to raise capital for mortgage lending using the borrowing power of the state. The Federal Housing Administration (FHA) and the Veteran's Administration (VA) provided insurance against loan losses to private lenders, to expand the availability of home loans to lower-income borrowers and war veterans.[2] At about the same time, the Federal National Mortgage Association (FNMA or 'Fannie Mae') stimulated a secondary market for home loans, by purchasing the loans from banks and selling bonds backed by the mortgages to raise capital and allow banks to fund more loans. The FNMA was first funded by the federal government in the 1930s, then sold to private investors in the 1960s, and most recently renationalized in 2008.[3] The FHA, VA, and FNMA prescribe the terms of loans, and the qualifications for borrowers, which became the standard form of contract dominating the field. Mortgage loans eligible to be purchased

* Professor of Law, CUNY School of Law.

1 P. Fishback, J. Rose & K. Snowden, *Well Worth Saving: How the New Deal Safeguarded Home Ownership*, University of Chicago Press, Chicago, 2013.

2 R.K. Green & S.M. Wachter, 'The American Mortgage in Historical and International Context', 19 *J. Econ. Persp.* 2005, p. 93.

3 J.R. Hagerty, *The Fateful History of Fannie Mae: New Deal Birth to Mortgage Crisis Fail*, The History Press, Charleston, 2012.

by FNMA came to be known as 'conforming' loans. The standard contract forms approved by FNMA, and its younger sibling, the Federal Home Loan Mortgage Corporation ('Freddie Mac'), are widely used not only for mortgage loans sold to these secondary market agencies, but for many other home loans as well. The FHA and VA mortgage contracts incorporate terms in government-published manuals and regulations, and FNMA mortgages are regulated by manuals and servicer guidelines as well. In 2016, about 60% of outstanding home mortgages were either purchased by FNMA or Freddie Mac, or insured by FHA or VA.[4] The terms of mortgage contracts are highly standardized, and more closely resemble public administrative regulations than privately negotiated contract terms.

The subprime foreclosure crisis of 2007–2008, which led to millions of home foreclosures, was blamed in part on mortgage contract terms that created excessive risk of default, in mortgage contracts that were not conforming (i.e., that were not standardized FNMA or FHA contracts). Indeed, the basic definition of a subprime mortgage was one that was not eligible for FNMA purchase or FHA insurance. The foreclosure crisis resulted, in part, from subprime mortgage contract terms that deviated from the conforming contract norms, including variable-rate loans with artificially low initial rates, loans with balloon payments, interest-only payment loans that did not amortize, prepayment penalties that prevented refinancing, and loans made without documentation or verification of borrower income. Federal legislation passed in response to the crisis has now discouraged or prohibited many of these mortgage loan terms. For example, prepayment penalties are now prohibited or restricted for many categories of home mortgage loans.[5]

Also, as a result of the subprime foreclosure crisis and the widespread problems with how banks and mortgage servicers managed defaulted loans, the new Consumer Financial Protection Bureau issued extensive regulations in 2013 requiring lenders to notify delinquent borrowers of available alternatives to modify their loan terms in order to avoid foreclosure.[6] The new mortgage servicing regulations operate in tandem with various forbearance and workout programs developed by FHA, VA, FNMA, and Freddie Mac, to establish standards for contract modification and forbearance with the aim of preventing unnecessary home losses.

Thus, through direct regulation of mortgage loans, funding of mortgage loans, insuring of mortgage loans, and regulation of mortgage loan enforcement and foreclosure, the government profoundly influences or simply dictates the nature, terms, and enforcement of the American home loan contract. The present home financing system and the contracts that support it are simply inconceivable without this direct and pervasive state involvement. In this context, applying classical doctrines of contracts law to the home loan relationship makes little sense.

4 Urban Institute Housing Finance Policy Center, *Housing Finance at a Glance, a Monthly Chartbook*, 2016, Retrieved on 6 July 2017 from <www.urban.org/sites/default/files/publication/83676/2000909-Housing-Finance-at-a-Glance-A-Monthly-Chartbook-August-2016.pdf>.

5 Dodd-Frank Mortgage Reform and Anti-Predatory Lending Act, Section 1414, 15 U.S.C. §1639c(c).

6 Mortgage Servicing Rules Under the Real Estate Settlement Procedures Act, 12 C.F.R. §1024.41.

13.2 Applying the Life Time Contract Model to the US Home Mortgage Loan

The European Social Contract Group (EuSoCo) has elaborated on a definition and a set of Principles for a distinct category, Life Time Contracts – that is to say, contracts that are essential to human flourishing, and whose human dimension renders the classical liberal framework of contract law inadequate.[7] Life Time Contracts, exemplified by the employment contract, the consumer credit contract, and the residential tenancy contract, have two essential features: their subject and their duration. Life Time Contracts provide access to essential human needs, including housing, employment, and basic consumption, and they are typically long-lived, rather than one-off exchanges. According to this paradigm, these contracts share features that contract law must recognize as imposing special obligations on the parties. Among the Principles proposed for Life Time Contracts[8] are: universal access (Principle 8); a fair or social price (Principle 9); adaptation of contract terms to changes over time (Principle 10), protection from unfair or premature termination (Principle 11), information and communication throughout the life of the contract (Principles 12 and 13), and recognition of collective interests and collective participation in negotiation and administration of Life Time Contracts (Principles 7 and 10).

The Anglo-American law of contracts, premised on the bargained-for exchange, the one-time offer and acceptance, performance or breach and remedy, stands on a libertarian and individualistic foundation, a notion of market activity as the busy interactions of persons and firms, with the aid of the invisible hand, make possible the happy convergence of individual autonomy and collective welfare. In this story of contracts, social intervention and control are limited to clear abuses: fraud, duress, impossibility due to unforeseen events, and so forth. The law cannot and should not, in this classical common law of contracts, view any particular contract outcome, whether performance or breach, success or default, as more or less desirable, so long as the nonbreaching party is made whole for any breach. This classical contract theory has little room for social control over price or terms, protection of the weak from the powerful, or any insistence on adaptation and modification of contracts when parties run into difficulties meeting their obligations.

There is a counter-narrative in the Anglo-American tradition, elaborated by such figures as Ian MacNeil[9] and Stewart Macaulay,[10] called relational contract theory. Contracts, according to relational theorists, exist on a spectrum from discrete, one-off exchanges, viewed as exceptional, to the more typical relational contract, one embedded

7 L. Nogler & U Reifner (Eds.), *Life Time Contracts: Social Long-Term Contracts in Labor, Tenancy and Consumer Credit Law*, The Hague: Eleven Publishing, 2014.

8 *See* 'Principles of Life Time Contracts', *in* Nogler & Reifner (Eds.), *supra* note 7, pp. 5-10.

9 I.R. Macneil, 'Relational Contract Theory, Challenges and Queries', 94 *N.W.U. L. Rev.* 1999, p. 877; I.R. Macneil, 'The Many Futures of Contract', 47 *S. Cal. L. Rev.* 1974, p. 691.

10 S. Macaulay, 'Relational Contracts Floating on a Sea of Custom? Thoughts about the Ideas of Ian Macneil and Lisa Bernstein', 94 *N.W.U. L. Rev.* 1999, p. 775.

in an ongoing relationship between the parties and with other interconnected parties and transactions. Employment contracts are often studied by relational contracts scholars, because they can only be understood in the context of a web of legal relationships, including wage and hour laws, safety, health insurance, pension rights, and union representation. The rules describing and governing contract formation and interpretation must take account of the evolving relationship between the parties, and rules governing breach and remedy in a relational contract must attend to the need of the parties to continue working together and adjust their obligations accordingly. Relational contract theory ascribes much greater importance to solidarity between contracting parties, the need for a robust duty of good faith, and the understanding that contract terms are worked out over time rather than agreed to in a magical contract-formation instant. Its proponents view relational contract as descriptive of a broad range of commercial interactions, including carefully negotiated business-to-business deals as well as the standardized consumer, employment, and housing contracts of mass society. Relational contract theory shares some normative principles with the Life Time Contracts theory. However, relational contract doctrine has remained largely theoretical, and has had little if any impact on the actual development and elaboration of the common law.

It is also worth noting that American law has historically recognized a need for social regulation, including price regulation, of contracts in the public utility sector, meaning contracts for essential infrastructure services, including transportation, energy, and communications services.[11] Public utility law, which concerns millions of contracts for the purchase of these essential services, is founded on principles of universal access at fair and nondiscriminatory prices, social obligations that are completely foreign to contracts law as such. In return for protection from competition, utility companies are subject to extensive social control over price, quality of service, and granting or denial of contracts to customers. Public utility law mediates the relationship between state actors, the regulatory agencies, and the market participants, the utility companies. Although it is viewed as an area of administrative or public law, public utility law necessarily addresses important principles of contract law and structure, not entirely unlike the principles advocated for Life Time Contracts.

The conception of a category of Life Time Contracts governed by a robust set of mutual responsibilities and social principles fits well, both descriptively and as a theoretical model, with the modern United States home mortgage loan contract. Despite the predominant Anglo-American freedom of contract framework, some, although not all, of the Principles of Life Time Contracts can be observed in various forms in the evolution of mortgage loan contracts in the United States, particularly in the periods from the New Deal until the deregulation wave of the 1980s, and again in new legal norms adopted in the wake of the 2008 subprime mortgage crisis.

11 A.M. White, 'Banks as Utilities', 90 *Tulane L. Rev.* 2016, p. 1241.

13.2.1 Universal Access

While in other nations, the security of tenure provided in home and apartment leases serves as the means to pursue the right to shelter for all, the United States has for many decades pursued a policy of homeownership for the broadest possible number of households. The share of households owning a home rose from 40% in the 1930s to nearly 70% in 2005 and around 64% today.[12] More than 70% of White households are homeowners, while the rate is barely above 50% for Black and Hispanic Americans. It is true that several European countries have similar homeownership rates; nevertheless, government housing policy in the United States has strongly favored ownership over rental as the preferred path to decent and affordable housing for everyone. The federal government subsidizes and supports home buyers through the mortgage interest tax deduction, local property tax deduction from federal taxes, very favorable treatment for capital gains from home sales, and federal government aid to mortgage insurance and the secondary mortgage market. On the other hand, government aid for rental housing, either for construction or for direct rental subsidies in public housing, has steadily eroded. Tax subsidies for homeowners are more than quadruple the amount spent by the federal government for low-income rental housing.[13]

Banks and other mortgage lenders are not, of course, required to offer home mortgage loans universally to all applicants. On the other hand, the Fair Housing Act, Equal Credit Opportunity Act, and Community Reinvestment Act establish norms of nondiscrimination and community investment that impel lenders to offer mortgage loans fairly and equally to all qualified borrowers.[14] Federal bank regulators have taken strong enforcement action and imposed fines on banks, who avoided making loans in Black and Hispanic neighborhoods because the banks did not have branches nor did marketing in those neighborhoods.[15] Moreover, the principal obstacle for many low-income applicants, the need for a substantial sum of money as a downpayment on a house, is addressed through the FHA and VA government insurance programs, which permit borrowers to borrow as much as 96% or more of the price of a home.[16]

Any regulated bank making home mortgage loans in the United States, therefore, operates in a context that does not allow the bank to choose arbitrarily with which

12 U.S. Bureau of the Census, *Quarterly Residential Vacancies and Homeownership First Quarter 2017*, Retrieved on 6 July 2017 from <www.census.gov/housing/hvs/files/currenthvspress.pdf>.

13 Center on Budget and Policy Priorities, *Chart Book: Federal Housing Spending is Poorly Matched to Need* 2017, Retrieved on 6 July 2017 from <www.cbpp.org/research/housing/chart-book-federal-housing-spending-is-poorly-matched-to-need>.

14 D. Immergluck, *Credit to the Community, Community Reinvestment Policy and Fair Lending in the United States*, Routledge, Oxon and New York, 2015.

15 R.L. Swarns, 'Biased Lending Evolves, and Blacks Face Trouble Getting Mortgages', *New York Times*, 30 October 2015, Available at: <www.nytimes.com/2015/10/31/nyregion/hudson-city-bank-settlement.html>.

16 The down payment requirement for an FHA-insured mortgage in 2017 is 3.5%, Retrieved on 6 July 2017 from <www.fha.com/fha_article?id=210>.

home buyers it will contract. On the contrary, the social norms reflected in government policies promoting homeownership, and attempting to combat race discrimination and neighborhood exclusion, impose on banks something like a universal access norm.

13.2.2 A Fair or "Social" Price

There are three competing views of how home mortgage loans should be priced. The neoliberal free market view has advocated so-called "risk-based" pricing, according to which borrowers and loans presenting a greater-than-average risk of default must pay higher than average fees and interest rates for their loans. There are two salient critiques of risk-based pricing. First is an efficacy problem, namely that predictions of risk are never precise, and that because of information problems on both the borrower and lender sides, variable loan pricing often results in "opportunity pricing", that is, charging more for loans to borrowers who are less well informed, rather than borrowers who truly present greater risks.[17] The second critique is one of equity: low-income and first-time home buyers are more likely to be, or be perceived to be, at higher risk, so that risk-based pricing means that the poor and new entrants in the housing market will pay more than the wealthy for the home loan contract. This results in slower wealth accumulation for the least wealthy, and aggravation, rather than narrowing, of wealth inequality in society.

The second approach to mortgage pricing is uniform pricing, an approach that predominated in the United States for the FHA and VA mortgage and most of the private mortgage market during the postwar decades, until the deregulation of the 1980s.[18] When mortgage prices for government-insured mortgages were established uniformly, and private market loans were limited by usury caps, applicants were either approved for a very standardized loan contract at a fixed price, or they were denied.

The third approach, the social pricing approach, sets prices according to ability pay, and recognizes that in order to make both secure housing tenure and wealth accumulation possible for families at the bottom of the economic ladder, loan prices should be lower for low-income home buyers and new entrants to home financing. A difference of even 1% in the interest rate for a 30-year mortgage loan can speed or slow debt reduction and wealth accumulation by tens of thousands of dollars. This conception of social pricing finds some expression in certain forms of community development financing in the United States, but these examples are rare and necessarily require government sub-

17 A.M. White, 'Risk-Based Mortgage Pricing, Present and Future Research', 15 *Housing Pol'y Debate* 2004, p. 503.

18 C. Lesser Mansfield, 'The Road to Subprime HEL Was Paved with Good Congressional Intentions: Usury Deregulation and the Subprime Home Equity Market', 51 *S.C. L. Rev.* 1999, p. 473.

sidies.[19] While many terms of the home loan contract are regulated in the United States, the interest rates are not. The financial reforms following the 2008 crisis restored some social controls, but did not undo the deregulation of prices of the 1980s. If mortgage loan interest rates are set by market forces, there is no means without government subsidy to offer lower interest rates to low-income borrowers. Simply put, true social pricing of home loans requires either direct regulation of pricing or state subsidy. Thus, the current context makes it very unlikely that the principle of social pricing will be incorporated into the legal environment for mortgage loans. In this respect, the Life Time Contracts model would require a rethinking of US mortgage contract law.

13.2.3 Adaptation of the Contract Provisions to Changed Circumstances over Time

There are at least two respects in which a typical home mortgage loan, repaid over 30 years, requires adaptation of its terms over time. First, as the homeowner repays the debt and the home value appreciates, the risk of nonpayment to the lender progressively diminishes, as does the cost of administering the loan. Because the predominant mortgage contract bears a fixed rate of interest, and often a fixed mortgage insurance premium, this reduced risk produces something of a windfall for the lender. The homeowner who does not sell the home or refinance the mortgage, but continues paying the initial rate may be overcompensating the lender.

The market solution to this gradual cost reduction is somewhat inefficient. American homeowners can, and frequently do, refinance, that is, enter into a new mortgage loan contract at lower interest rates when the opportunity arises, due to improvements in their credit or changes in market rates. However, refinancing imposes significant transaction costs, as the new lender must appraise the property, examine the property title, evaluate the borrower's credit, and produce extensive documentation. While adjustable-rate mortgage products exist, they are generally indexed to changes in market rates, not to improvements in the borrower's risk profile. A Life Time Contracts view might argue for a need to modify interest rates for the benefit of borrowers whose contract performance warrants a rate reduction.

The second respect in which home loan contracts require adaptation over time is to respond to temporary income loss or other events that prevent the borrower from making the contractual payments. During the 2008 foreclosure crisis, mortgage lenders and investors recognized a need to modify loan terms, when modifications could permit the borrower to continue repaying, albeit at lower interest rates or over longer terms, and prevent a forced home foreclosure sale and the losses to both parties a foreclosure would

19 US Dept. of Housing and Urban Development, 'Increasing Access to Sustainable Mortgages for Low-Income Borrowers, Evidence Matters', 2016, Retrieved on 6 July 2017, from <www.huduser.gov/portal/periodicals/em/spring16/highlight3.html#title>.

yield. Existing mortgage loan contracts made no provision for such modifications, and even when lenders and borrowers agreed to mutually advantageous modifications, some courts struggled with finding those modifications to be valid, enforceable contracts.[20] Moreover, the contracts between mortgage investors and mortgage servicers often made it difficult for the servicers to negotiate home loan modifications, even where loan modifications would reduce the risk of losses and benefit the mortgage investors.[21] The widespread efforts to modify mortgage terms to avoid massive foreclosures have had very mixed results, and the rigidity of contracts, as well as the agency problems created by the separation of lending, investing, and servicing mortgage loans, have been criticized.[22]

It seems self-evident that a fixed repayment schedule that does not and cannot vary over 30 years or more will not be suitable for every home buyer, whose income and life circumstances may vary considerably during that time. When we consider that the family home is at stake, it also seems self-evident that home loan contracts should incorporate the ability, and even the duty, to modify repayment terms, without impairing the primary debt obligation, when the borrower's circumstances warrant. Such a duty could be read into home loan contracts based on an adaptability norm, coupled with a duty of good faith and solidarity for these Life Time Contracts.

13.2.4 Protection from Unfair or Premature Termination

Closely related to a duty to modify repayment terms would be a duty to avoid termination by forced foreclosure sale of the home. Early termination of a home mortgage loan contract obviously will have harsh consequences. Mortgage foreclosures, according to most traditional bankers, are to be avoided at all costs. They are bad for the homeowner, bad for the surrounding community, and generally very bad for the bank, which will typically lose a good deal of money, because foreclosure sales do not usually realize anything like the fair value of the home, and because most borrowers have few, if any other assets from which the lender may collect the deficiency remaining after a foreclosure sale. While existing contract law does not impose any particular obligation to avoid foreclosure, the law establishes the structures for enforcement of the loan contract, and foreclosure law often makes home loan contract enforcement more complex and time-consuming than the legal enforcement of ordinary debts. The bias against foreclosure, which

---

20 *See Wigod v. Wells Fargo Bank, NA* 673 F.3d 547 (7th Cir. 2013) (rejecting bank claims that mortgage modification agreement was not binding); *Gordon v. JP Morgan Chase Bank, NA*, 505 Fed. Appx 361 (5th Cir. 2013) (oral modification agreement was not enforceable).

21 A. Levitin & A. Gelpern, 'Rewriting Frankenstein Contracts: The Workout Prohibition in Residential Mortgage-Backed Securities', 82 *S. Cal. L. Rev.* 2009, p. 1077.

22 D. Peterson & D.C. Harvey, 'Kafkaesque Bureaucracies as Natural Breaching Experiments: Interactional Failures and the Search for Institutional Agency', 38 *Symb. Interact.* 2015, p. 195, Available at: <http://onlinelibrary.wiley.com/doi/10.1002/symb.149/abstract>.

exists in some but not all US states, indirectly protects homeowners from premature and unfair termination of their home loans.

Laws and procedures for enforcing home mortgage loans through foreclosure sales vary to a small extent among the states. Roughly half the states permit nonjudicial foreclosure, that is, a forced sale by the lender after payment default by, and notice to, the borrower, without the need to file a legal action in court. If the borrower objects, the burden is on her to initiate a lawsuit asking a court to prevent the sale. Foreclosure sales in these states can occur in as little as 60 days after a payment default. The remaining states require the filing of a lawsuit, with full due process protections, before a foreclosure sale can take place. In these states, the process typically requires six months or more to be completed. Thus, some states enforce a contractual mechanism that permits the lender to terminate the contract on fairly short notice, while others do not permit contracts to waive judicial intervention.

After the 2008 crisis, many states and localities took additional measures to prevent unfair or wasteful foreclosure sales. Among those measures were many mediation or diversion programs, requiring mortgage servicers and home loan borrowers to meet with a neutral third party to discuss alternatives to a forced sale.[23] There is some evidence that foreclosure mediation programs, in tandem with the incentives offered by the federal Treasury Department to banks to encourage mortgage modifications, were successful in reducing foreclosure sales. On the other hand, the voluntary, incentive-based approach taken by the federal government to address the foreclosure crisis has been roundly criticized as inadequate in preventing the millions of preventable foreclosures that took place in the decade following 2007.[24] In contrast, foreclosure sales in the United Kingdom were kept to a low level due to a combination of lender forbearance, mortgage modification, and government subsidies to homeowners.[25]

Even in states with the most aggressive legislation, no state has mandated that lenders or mortgage servicers offer alternatives to foreclosure sales to defaulting homeowners, even in cases where both lender and homeowner would be better off. The general approach has been to "nudge" mortgage servicers with incentives to negotiation, and with procedural hurdles to foreclosure. This ambivalence about restricting the ability to terminate mortgage loans via foreclosure sales reflects the enduring freedom-of-contract ideology that survives the extensive government involvement in mortgage contracts. Seen through the Life Time Contracts lens, the legal rules for mortgage foreclosures could, and ought to, require rather than nudge lenders and servicers to offer defaulting bor-

23 A.M. White, 'Foreclosure Diversion and Mediation in the States', 33 *Ga. St. L. Rev.* 2017, p. 411.

24 D. Immergluck, 'Too Little, Too Late and Too Timid: The Federal Response to the Foreclosure Crisis at the Five-Year Mark', 23 *Housing Pol'y Debate* 2013, p. 199.

25 K. Blacklock & M. Whittaker, *Hangover Cure, Dealing with the Household Debt Overhand as Interest Rates Rise*, Resolution Foundation Report, 2014, Retrieved on 6 July 2017 from <www.resolutionfoundation.org/publications/hangover-cure-dealing-with-the-household-debt-overhang-as-interest-rates-rise/>.

rowers every possible alternative, including modification of contract terms, to prevent unfair and unnecessary foreclosures.

13.2.5 *Continued Information and Communication through the Contract's Life*

During the 30-year life of a home mortgage loan, the possibility of errors and misinformation is great. This is particularly true with the rise of the mortgage servicing companies, banks, or other entities that are not the lender or investor, but that administer the mortgage loan.[26] The mortgage loan servicer is not only required to account for principle and interest, which may vary annually, but often to collect from the homeowner monthly, and then pay annually, additional amounts for taxes and property insurance.

The frequency of errors by mortgage servicers motivated Congress and the Consumer Financial Protection Bureau to enact detailed rules and regulations requiring mortgage servicers to provide homeowners with monthly loan statements, to respond to borrower information requests promptly, and to correct errors.[27] These statutory obligations, applicable to virtually all home loans administered by banks, are in addition to the basic common law contract, duty of good faith, which requires honesty between contracting partners.[28]

When the homeowner fails to make payments, the availability of payment rescheduling and loan modifications are the subject of complex programs and rules that the servicer must explain and make available. Postcrisis reforms have likewise imposed duties on mortgage servicers to inform home loan borrowers who fail to make payments of the alternatives to foreclosure available to them.[29] The statutory and regulatory context for mortgage lending and servicing in the United States today incorporates extensive duties to inform and communicate over the life of the contract. In this regard, the Life Time Contract Principles 12 (communication) and 13 (continued information and transparency) are already present in US mortgage law.

13.2.6 *Recognition of Collective Interests and Collective Participation in Negotiation and Administration of Life Time Contracts*

The home loan contract has a broad and important impact beyond the parties (i.e., the lender and the borrower). A community where low-cost financing is available, especially with low down payment requirements, will necessarily have a robust and active housing

26 K. Eggert, 'Limiting Abuse and Opportunism by Mortgage Servicers', 15 *Housing Pol'y Debate* 2004, p. 753.

27 Real Estate Settlement Procedures Act, Consumer Financial Protection Bureau, Mortgage Servicing Regulations, 24 CFR Part 1024.

28 *McDonnell Douglas Corp. v. United States*, 323 F.3d 1006, 1020 (Fed. Cir. 2003).

29 Mortgage Servicing Rules Under the Real Estate Settlement Procedures Act, 12 C.F.R. §1024.41.

market. On the positive side, the availability and successful administration of mortgage loans will increase homeownership and investment in housing. On the negative side, perhaps, excessive availability of home loans on unduly lenient terms may simply lead to speculation and housing price bubbles. In any event, there is an obvious and important collective interest in the qualifications established for the creation of home loan contracts, as well as in the terms and conditions of those contracts, because of their secondary effects on communities.

Widespread failure of mortgage loan contracts will also deeply affect the surrounding community. Several US cities have sued mortgage lenders and financers in the wake of the foreclosure crisis, on the grounds that the risky subprime mortgage loans they made led to concentrated foreclosures, housing abandonment, and financial burdens on the city.[30]

Because of these obvious social effects of successful and unsuccessful mortgage loan contracts, the logic of collective negotiation and political control of the home loan contract is apparent. The price and other terms and conditions of mortgage credit, the ability and willingness of parties to renegotiate in the face of repayment problems, and the rules for enforcing contracts and holding foreclosure sales directly affect the accumulation and distribution of wealth and the economic and social health of neighborhoods and communities. The political imperative favoring homeownership by the broadest possible segment of society has motivated the US government's continual involvement in funding, insuring, subsidizing, and regulating the mortgage loan contract. Perpetually seen as exceptional and contrary to market principles, this collective and political negotiation of contract has remained an enduring feature of the US mortgage loan for seven decades or more. A long period of tight social control over mortgage terms followed the foreclosure crisis of the early 1930s and continued until the 1980s, when Reagan–Thatcher deregulation and market liberalism propelled the repeal of interest rate and other controls. The resulting proliferation of mortgage contract terms was widely understood as causing the 2008 crisis, and has led to re-imposition of tight social controls on the home financing contract.

13.3 Conclusion

The home mortgage loan contract has become essential to meeting the vital human need for shelter in the American market-based economy. The sensible norms of the Life Time Contracts paradigm are well adapted to this essential contract. To a certain extent, US residential mortgage law already incorporates principles of universal access, continued information and communication, and adaptation to changed circumstances over the life of the contract. States vary considerably in protecting home loan borrowers from unfair

30 *Bank of America Corp. v. City of Miami*, 137 S.Ct. 1296 (2017).

early termination, although federal regulations require at least some procedural steps to reduce unfair foreclosure sales. On the other hand, the notion of a social price is still alien to US law, with some exceptions. Recognition of a social or collective interest in the negotiation and terms of home loan contracts remains controversial. Although de facto, the US home mortgage contract is largely designed by state and quasi-state bureaucracies (FHA, Fannie Mae), the dominant ideology insists that the private market in mortgages must be restored, that the nationalization of mortgage finance is a temporary aberration that must be reversed at the earliest opportunity,[31] and that economic efficiency via competition among lenders and private contract negotiations should be the norm. The result is a continuing tension between a government role in regulating or limiting mortgage contract terms and the continual pressure to deregulate.[32] An explicit recognition that home mortgage contracts, as a species of Life Time Contracts, are different, and implicate broad societal interests, and adoption of the full set of Principles of Life Time Contracts, would bring coherence to our understanding of the law that structures these contracts. Treating home mortgage loans as Life Time Contracts would permit a clear-headed application of contract law in service of the American dream of affordable and sustainable homeownership for all.

BIBLIOGRAPHY

Blacklock, K. & Whittaker, M., *Hangover Cure, Dealing with the Household Debt Overhand as Interest Rates Rise*, Resolution Foundation Report, 2014, Retrieved on 6 July 2017 from <www.resolutionfoundation.org/publications/hangover-cure-dealing-with-the-household-debt-overhang-as-interest-rates-rise/>.

Center on Budget and Policy Priorities, *Chart Book: Federal Housing Spending is Poorly Matched to Need* 2017, Retrieved on 6 July 2017 from <www.cbpp.org/research/housing/chart-book-federal-housing-spending-is-poorly-matched-to-need>.

Eggert, K., 'Limiting Abuse and Opportunism by Mortgage Servicers', 15 *Housing Pol'y Debate* 2004, p. 753.

Fishback, P., Rose, J. & Snowden, K., *Well Worth Saving: How the New Deal Safeguarded Home Ownership*, Chicago: University of Chicago Press, 2013.

---

31 S. Wachter & P. McCoy, 'A New Coalescence in the Housing Finance Reform Debate', 4 *Penn Wharton Pub. Pol'y Initiative* 2016, p. 1, Retrieved on 6 July 2017 from <http://repository.upenn.edu/pennwhartonppi/3>.

32 B. Protess & J. Hirschfeld Davis, 'Trump Moves to Roll Back Obama-Era Financial Regulations', *New York Times*, 3 February 2017, Available at: <www.nytimes.com/2017/02/03/business/dealbook/trump-congress-financial-regulations.html..>

Green, R.K. & Wachter, S.M., 'The American Mortgage in Historical and International Context', 19 *J. Econ. Persp.* 2005, p. 93.

Hagerty, J.R., *The Fateful History of Fannie Mae: New Deal Birth to Mortgage Crisis Fail*, Charleston: The History Press, 2012.

Immergluck, D., 'Too Little, Too Late and Too Timid: The Federal Response to the Foreclosure Crisis at the Five-Year Mark', 23 *Housing Pol'y Debate* 2013, p 199.

Immergluck, D., *Credit to the Community, Community Reinvestment Policy and Fair Lending in the United States*, Routeledge, Oxon and New York, 2015.

Lesser Mansfield, C., 'The Road to Subprime HEL was Paved with Good Congressional Intentions: Usury Deregulation and the Subprime Home Equity Market', 51 *S.C. L. Rev.* 1999, p. 473.

Levitin, A. & Gelpern, A., 'Rewriting Frankenstein Contracts: The Workout Prohibition in Residential Mortgage-Backed Securities', 82 *S. Cal. L. Rev.* 2009, p. 1077.

Macaulay, S., 'Relational Contracts Floating on a Sea of Custom? Thoughts about the Ideas of Ian Macneil and Lisa Bernstein', 94 *N.W.U. L. Rev.* 1999, p. 775.

Macneil, I.R., 'The Many Futures of Contract', 47 *S. Cal. L. Rev.* 1974, p. 691.

Macneil, I.R., 'Relational Contract Theory, Challenges and Queries', 94 *N.W.U. L. Rev.* 1999, p. 877.

Nogler, L. & Reifner, U. (Eds.), *Life Time Contracts: Social Long-Term Contracts in Labor, Tenancy and Consumer Credit Law*, The Hague: Eleven Publishing, 2014.

Peterson, D. & Harvey, D.C., 'Kafkaesque Bureaucracies as Natural Breaching Experiments: Interactional Failures and the Search for Institutional Agency', 38 *Symb. Interact.* 2015, p. 195, Available at: <http://onlinelibrary.wiley.com/doi/10.1002/symb.149/abstract>.

Protess, B. & Hirschfeld Davis, J. 'Trump Moves to Roll Back Obama-Era Financial Regulations', *New York Times*, 3 February 2017, Available at: <www.nytimes.com/2017/02/03/business/dealbook/trump-congress-financial-regulations.html.>.

Swarns, R.L., 'Biased Lending Evolves, and Blacks Face Trouble Getting Mortgages', *New York Times*, 30 October 2015, Available at: <www.nytimes.com/2015/10/31/nyregion/hudson-city-bank-settlement.html>.

U.S. Bureau of the Census, *Quarterly Residential Vacancies and Homeownership First Quarter 2017*, Retrieved on 6 July 2017 from <www.census.gov/housing/hvs/files/currenthvspress.pdf>.

Urban Institute Housing Finance Policy Center, *Housing Finance at a Glance, a Monthly Chartbook*, 2016, Retrieved on 6 July 2017 from <www.urban.org/sites/default/files/publication/83676/2000909-Housing-Finance-at-a-Glance-A-Monthly-Chartbook-August-2016.pdf>.

US Dept. of Housing and Urban Development, 'Increasing Access to Sustainable Mortgages for Low-Income Borrowers, Evidence Matters', 2016, Retrieved on 6 July 2017, from <www.huduser.gov/portal/periodicals/em/spring16/highlight3.html#title>.

Wachter, S. & McCoy, P., 'A New Coalescence in the Housing Finance Reform Debate', 4 *Penn Wharton Pub. Pol'y Initiative* 2016, p. 1, Retrieved on 6 July 2017 from <http://repository.upenn.edu/pennwhartonppi/3>.

White, A.M., 'Risk-Based Mortgage Pricing, Present and Future Research', 15 *Housing Pol'y Debate* 2004, p. 503.

White, A.M., 'Banks as Utilities', 90 *Tulane L. Rev.* 2016, p. 1241.

White, A.M., 'Foreclosure Diversion and Mediation in the States', 33 *Ga. St. L. Rev.* 2017, p. 411.

14 The Collective Dimension of Life Time Contracts: A Labour Law Perspective

*Orsola Razzolini**

14.1 Meanings and Functions of 'Collective Interest'

In Italy, the concept of 'collective interest' was famously defined by Francesco Santoro Passarelli: "A collective interest is not the sum of individual interests, but their combination".[1] One main feature of the collective interest is its indivisibility; a second is its organization. According to Widar Cesarini Sforza "the collective interest represents and expresses the organizational principle of the group".[2] The collective interest represents the common, indivisible goal whose achievement justifies the group's becoming a 'collectivity', by its setting down rules and creating an organization. The 'indivisibility' of collective interests demands the denial of the individual interests of the group's members, which explains why, in Italian labour law, any discussion about individual, homogeneous interests have been abandoned; an indivisible collective interest cannot coexist with individual, homogeneous interests.[3]

What, then, is the function of a collective interest? In Italy and Germany, the concept of a collective interest, viewed through the lens of private law, is used to justify the priority of collective agreements over individual agreements or their 'inderogability'. According to Mattia Persiani, a private collective organization requires the organization and subordination of the private members' individual interests to the organization's interests.[4]

In Italy and Germany, the concept of collective interest led to the development of 'collective autonomy', which is a tool by which the activity of collective organizations becomes integrated into the formal legal system through the vehicle of contract law.[5] To put it simply, collective autonomy combines a strong requirement for the State's non-interference with the acknowledgement that a certain degree of interference or, perhaps better, of integration, is inevitable for collective bargaining to produce legal effects.

---

* Associate Professor at the University of Genova.

1 F. Santoro Passarelli, *Nozioni di diritto del lavoro*, Jovene, Napoli, 1967, p. 21.

2 W. Cesarini Sforza, *Il diritto dei privati*, Giuffrè, Milano, 1963, p. 108.

3 *See* R. Corrado, *Trattato di diritto del lavoro. Vol. I. Parte generale*, Unione tipografica-editrice torinese, Torino, 1965, p. 236 *et seq.*

4 M. Persiani, *Saggio sull'autonomia privata collettiva*, Cedam, Padova, 1972, p. 141 *et seq.*

5 *See* G. Vardaro, *Contrattazione collettiva e sistema giuridico*, Jovene, Napoli, 1984, p. 12, who speaks of "formal rationalization".

This tension lies beneath the debate about the *erga omnes* effects of collective agreements and the question of their 'inderogability'.[6]

On the contrary, in the legal tradition of the United Kingdom, collective agreements do not normally create binding, legally enforceable contracts and, mostly, they are not understood through private law but, rather, in social terms (the so-called gentleman's agreement).[7] The law might intervene to regulate trade union's abuse or misuse of power against its members[8] or to create the institutional legal framework for collective bargaining to develop and take place,[9] but the doctrine of 'collective laissez-faire' traditionally prevented any form of strong and complete integration of the social parties, their rules, and their agreements (in the social sense) into the legal system.[10] In fact, in the British legal tradition, there is a terminological distinction between 'contract' and (collective) 'agreement', which recalls the French distinction between *contrat* and *convention* (collective); while such distinction does not exist in Italy (*contratto individuale* and *contratto collettivo*) or in Germany (*Arbeitsvertrag* and *Tarifvertrag*).[11]

A unique approach was adopted in France, where the concept of collective autonomy has not been explored or theorized.[12] It is the law (*Code du travail*) that intervenes to assert the binding nature of collective agreements, to measure the trade unions' ability to represent workers (unionized and non-unionized), to include them in the law-making process, and to regulate the relationship between statutes and the different levels of collective bargaining.[13] In the meantime, Article 34 of the French Constitution gives the state exclusive rule-making authority in fixing the fundamental principles (*principes fondamentaux*) of individual and collective labour law and of social security law, while "provisions included in the full set of constitutional regulations do not refer to the collective contract or collective agreement".[14]

---

6 *See* W. Däubler, *Kommentar zum Tarifvertragsgesetz*, Baden-Baden, Nomos, 2003.

7 *See* Lord Wedderburn, 'Inderogability, Collective Agreements and Community Law', 21 *Ind. L.J.*, p. 245.

8 *See* O. Kahn-Freund, 'Trade Unions, the Law and Society', 33 *Mod. L. Rev.* 1970, p. 241 *et seq.*

9 *See* P. Davies & M. Freedland, *Kahn-Freund's Labour and the Law*, 3rd edn, Stevens, London, 1983, p. 88 *et seq.*

10 *See* S. Deakin & F. Wilkinson, *The Law of the Labour Market. Industrialization, Employment, and Legal Evolution*, Oxford University Press, Oxford, 2005, Ch. 4.

11 *See* A. Supiot, 'Un faux dilemme: la loi ou le contrat ?', *Droit Social* 2003, p. 59 *et seq.*

12 *See* M. Le Friant, 'Collective Autonomy: Hope or Danger?', 34 *Comp. Labor L. & Pol'y J.* 2013, p. 627 *et seq.* which provides a comparative overview on the meaning and understanding of collective autonomy in Germany, Italy, Spain, and France.

13 *See* G. Borenfreund & M.A. Souriac, 'Les rapports de la loi et de la convention collective: une mise en perspective', *Droit Social* 2003, p. 72.

14 Le Friant, *supra* note 12, p. 637; I. Odoul-Asorey, 'Négociation collective et droit constitutionnel', *L.G.D.J.* 2013, p. 222 *et seq.*

14.2 Principles 10 and 5 of Life Time Contracts

Principle 10 of Life Time Contracts[15] concerns the 'adaptation' of the content of a Life Time Contract in response to changing circumstances if:

> taking into account all the circumstances of the specific case, and in particular the contractual statutory allocation of risk and fundamental obligation of a human being, one of the parties cannot reasonably be expected to continue to comply with the contract without variation of its terms.

Further, its final sentence provides that "[c]ollective regulation shall take precedence over individual adaptation".[16] The sentence replicates the idea that the 'collective interest' and 'collective autonomy' prevail over individual interests and individual autonomy, but only within certain limits.

This approach is justified by the specific social and human nature of Life Time Contracts – such as labour, consumer, and credit agreements – that involve individuals and their fundamental human and existential needs. Unlike the Italian and German experience, the idea that collective interests prevail over individual interests is provided with a legal foundation, although its application is confined to the very specific case of contract adaptation in response to changing circumstances. One might argue that Principle 10's last sentence provides – contrary to the labour law experience – that the priority of collective agreements over individual agreements is neither a general principle nor an axiom, but rather a principle that applies only to the specific case of a contract's adaptation in light of changing circumstances.

It is not clear what the intention of the Principles' drafters was. A restrictive interpretation of the idea of priority of collective-over-individual interests is not necessarily a paradox (as it might appear at first glance). Suffice it to say that, since the 1990s, Spiros Simitis fathered a new line of thought that underlines the need to 'rediscover the individual'[17] and to protect the individual against 'legal and collective colonialism'.[18] The debate is still present nowadays, in the face of the deep crisis that intermediate groups[19] and trade unions are undergoing.

On the contrary, Principle 5 is much more assertive: it provides that:

15 The English language version of the sixteen 'Principles of Life Time Contracts' can be found in L. Nogler & U Reifner (Eds.), *Life Time Contracts: Social Long-term Contracts in Labor, Tenancy and Consumer Credit Law*, Eleven International Publishing, Oxford, 2014, pp. 5-10.

16 Id., p. 7.

17 S. Simitis, 'Il diritto del lavoro e la riscoperta dell'individuo', *Giornale di diritto del lavoro e delle relazioni industriali* 1990, p. 100.

18 Id.

19 See M.V. De Giorgi, 'Vivere per raccontarla: i gruppi intermedi', *Rivista di diritto civile* 2012, p. 791 *et seq.*

> stringent regulation or other collective rules will secure the degree of social protection needed in line with the subject matter of the contract, its duration, its importance in the life of the individuals concerned.[20]

In the Italian translation of Principle 5,[21] we find the word '*inderogabile*', which word has been directly translated by some as 'inderogability' rather than the more common 'non-derogable', intended to manifest an individual's inability to derogate from the applicable law or collective agreements. Notably, Principle 5 addresses both the state and its social parties, both of whom are called to set forth binding, nonderogable rules intended to protect the weaker or more vulnerable contracting party, according to both the duration and the type of contract.

Neither Principle 10 nor Principle 5 mention the principle of 'favour' that usually governs the hierarchical relationship between collective and individual agreements (namely, that the collective agreement rules prevail unless the individual agreement provides more favourable rules). But, even the omission of the principle of 'favour' could not be regarded as a mere forgetfulness, as the role it plays in the governance of the sources (legal and contractual) of employment rights and duties is almost everywhere under discussion.[22]

14.3 Collective Representation Mechanisms: The Unfair Labour Practice Mechanism and Other Procedural Forms of Collective Action

The theorization of the concepts of collective interest and collective autonomy – the latter being a concept that does not exist in the French legal tradition[23] – leads one to draw a clear line between individual interests and collective interest. Notably, the collective interest has been regarded, more and more, as the interest of the collective organization, namely the trade union, rather than as the synthesis of its members' interests. A number of studies underline the idea that the collective organization is a fiction, as the individual remains the starting point for all dogmatic constructions;[24] nonetheless, collective inter-

20 Principle 5 of Life Time Contracts, *supra* note 15, p. 6.

21 Id., p. 12.

22 For a recent overview of the changing value of this principle in France, *see* A. Jeammaud, 'De l'incidence de l'accord collectif sur le contrat de travail' and P. Ancel, 'L'articulation du contrat du travail et des accords collectifs au regard de la force obligatoire du contrat', *Revue de droit du travail* 2016, p. 228 *et seq.* and p. 240 *et seq.*, respectively; for the Italian debate (although with regard to the relationship between law and collective agreements), *see* G. Centamore, 'Legge e autonomia collettiva: una critica della dottrina dell'inderogabilità bilaterale', *Lavoro e diritto* 2015, p. 491 *et seq.*

23 *See* Le Friant, *supra* note 12, p. 627.

24 *See* R. Flammia, *Contributo all'analisi dei sindacati di fatto. I. Autotutela degli interessi di lavoro*, Giuffrè, Milano, 1963, ch. 1; Persiani, *supra* note 4, p. 109 *et seq.* For a critical view, *see* M.G. Garofalo, *Interessi collettivi e comportamento antisindacale dell'imprenditore*, Jovene, Napoli, 1979, p. 154 *et seq.*

ests have often been conceived as the institutional interests of the organization, regarded as separate from its members' interests.[25]

The ascription of collective interests to trade unions, rather than to their members, also stems from the development of procedural tools by which trade unions are entitled to protect collective interests in the courts.

In Italy, Article 28 of the Italian Statute of Workers, *Statuto dei lavoratori*, (hereinafter, 'Article 28 ISW') provides trade unions with a particular procedural form of collective action: repression of an unfair labour practice (*repression della condotta antisindacale*), which Gino Giugni imported from the American experience with its Wagner Act, also known as the National Labor Relations Act of 1935,[26] Section 8.[27] The unfair-labour-practice mechanism is unique to the Italian and American legal frameworks: trade unions are entitled to bring actions against an employer to obtain an order whose content is defined by the law in general and broad terms. Notably, the judge can order an employer to desist from the unfair conduct and restore the status quo.

Article 28 ISW authorizes trade unions (not individuals) to bring action in court against employer conduct that is capable of infringing the employees' 'freedom of association, the right to carry out collective activity and the right to strike'. In the 1970s, Italian scholars debated the individual versus collective nature of the interests protected by Article 28 ISW. According to one line of thought, it did not protect the institutional interest of trade unions, but rather protected the individual interests of its members, whose protection responded to the interests of all workers as well as of the trade unions.[28] This perspective concluded that the individual and collective interests were strongly interdependent and could not be separated from one another. The second line of thought, on the other hand, concluded that the interest protected by Article 28 ISW was the interest of trade unions themselves, and regarded those interests as separate from their members' individual interests;[29] it was founded, in part, on the general rule of continental European civil procedure *nul ne plaide par procureur*, which is to say that there must be strict coincidence between the holder of the substantial right and the holder of the right of action (i.e., the right to bring a legal action before a court).[30]

Italian case law seems to have embraced the idea of collective interest as the trade union's own interest. More precisely, Italian judges have held that Article 28 ISW is

25 25. In Italy, *see* particularly the theories developed by Garofalo, *supra* note 24; G. Ferraro, *Ordinamento, ruolo del sindacato, dinamica contrattuale di tutela*, Cedam, Padova, 1981, p. 130 *et seq.*

26 The National Labor Relations Act of 1935 (49 Stat. 449), 29 USC §§ 151-169.

27 29 USC § 158.

28 *See* T. Treu, *Condotta antisindacale e atti discriminatori*, Franco Angeli, Milano, 1974, p. 16 *et seq.*; *see also*, L. Lanfranchi, 'Prospettive ricostruttive in tema di art. 28 dello statuto dei lavoratori', *Rivista trimestrale di diritto e procedura civile* 1971, p. 388 *et seq.*, who, from the idea that Article 28 ISW protects individual interests, infers that the legal provision introduces, from a procedural law point of view, a particular case of 'procedural substitution'.

29 *See* Garofalo, *supra* note 24, p. 142 *et seq.*

30 Id.

intended to protect a trade union's collective interest, which is different and autonomous from the interests and rights of workers.[31] Something similar has developed in the German legal system: in a very controversial 1999 decision, the German federal labour court agreed that trade unions were entitled to take legal actions against agreements, determined by work councils, that regulated matters already regulated at the collective bargaining level. Collective freedom of association, regarded as a trade union's prerogative, can be infringed by agreements and measures agreed at the company level that, going beyond the work councils' codetermination prerogatives, aim at frustrating or bypassing collective bargaining.[32]

In France, where the industrial relations system is much more integrated into the legal order, trade unions are granted the capacity to institute legal proceedings to protect their interests and of the 'collective interest of the profession' (*intérêt collectif de la profession*) so as to obtain compensatory damages (Article L. 2132-3 Code du Travail).[33] Broadly speaking, French judges hold that there is a breach of the 'collective interest of the profession' in cases of breach of either normative or obligatory clauses of a collective agreement (e.g., breach of rules regulating days-of-week leaves, and health and safety protection). What matters is that the question must be a general question that can 'interest the members of the profession or of the collectivity as a whole'.[34] The interests of the members of a certain profession are, therefore, different from both the interests of trade unions and the individual interests of the workers.[35]

The difference between the Italian and French approach would likely benefit from an example: the case of an employer's refusal to convert a fixed-term employment contract into an employment contract of permanent duration. According to Italian judges, in case the employer violates legal provisions or normative clauses of collective agreements, his/her conduct can be understood as an unfair labour practice only if it is demonstrated that it was objectively capable to infringe reputation and credibility of the trade union in front of workers; conversely, French judges would not hesitate to recognize that the employer's conduct is in breach of the collective interest of the profession, thereby condemning the employer to pay compensatory damages.[36] In this respect, it is suggested that, in France at least, trade unions play a monitoring role on the employer's conduct, similar to the role played by labour inspection mechanisms.

31 Cass., sez. Un., 27 July 1984, n. 4399; Recently App. Roma, 19 October 2012.

32 *See* M. Weiss & M. Schmidt, *Labour Law and Industrial Relations in Germany*, 4th edn, Wolters Kluwer, Cologne, 2008, p. 242 *et seq.*

33 *See* J. Pélissier, J. Auzero & E. Dockès, *Droit du travail*, 27th edn, Dalloz, Paris, 2013, p. 1039 *et seq.*; M. Henry, 'L'action syndicale en exécution des conventions collectives', *Droit ouvrier* 2007, p. 112 *et seq.*

34 M. Grèvy, 'L'action en justice du syndicat dans l'intérêt collectif de la profession au cœur de la "saga de l'ouverture du dimanche"', *Revue de droit du travail* 2014, p. 486.

35 Id.

36 *See* Cass. soc., 19 February 2016, No. 14-26304.

In all continental European systems, the trade unions' ability to take legal action to protect the individual interests of their members (or even nonmembers) is permitted in only exceptional cases. One such exception is represented by the French *action en substitution* (action in substitution). The Code du Travail provides a number of such cases, for example: moral and sexual harassment,[37] discrimination,[38] agency work,[39] fix-term work,[40] and individual dismissal for economic reasons[41] – in which trade unions can take legal action in the place of an employee, who is given the rights of opposition, intervention, and ending the trade union's proceedings at any time. This type of substitution action represents an exception to the principle of *nul ne plaide par procureur*.

EU Antidiscrimination Law Directives 2000/78/EC of 27 November 2000 and 2000/43/EC of 29 June 2000 also provide a new concept of 'collective discrimination' that, in Italy, has been implemented by Article 5 of Legislative Decrees 215/2003 and 216/2003. Article 5 regulates two different cases: in the first (paragraph 1), the individual worker expressly authorizes the trade union to take legal proceedings on his/her behalf; while paragraph 2, authorizes trade unions to initiate legal proceedings in case of collective discrimination whenever the victims of such discrimination cannot be identified. Such legal actions can be both injunctive and compensatory. Thus, according to paragraph 2, trade union is granted the substitution action in case the victims of discrimination cannot be immediately identified.

In the now-famous *Fiat* case – in which Fiat, the employer, systematically refused to rehire employees who were members of CGIL (the left-wing Italian Union) at its new establishment – the Court of Appeal recognized the legitimate interest of the trade union in bringing a legal action on the behalf of both nominated employees (on the ground of a legal delegation of authority) and other non-identified potential victims of Fiat's discrimination (on the ground of substitution action). Coherently, the Court of Appeal suggested that, in collective discrimination claims, unlike an unfair labour practice claim, the focus is not on trade union's interest and prerogatives, but on the employees' rights and interests.[42]

According to an interesting line of thought, in case of collective discrimination trade union, equality bodies, and other specific organizations against discriminations should be also entitled to bring legal action in order to protect the general/public interest to equality and non-discrimination.[43] The famous EU Court's judgment in *Feryn* seems to conceal

37 Art. L. 1154-2 Cd. Tr.

38 Art. L. 1134-2 Cd. Tr.

39 Art. L. 1251-59 Cd. Tr.

40 Art. L.1247-1 Cd. Tr.

41 Art. L. 1235-8 Cd. Tr.

42 *See* C. App. Roma, 19 October 2012.

43 See C. Rapisarda Sassoon, 'La tutela dei soggetti discriminati. Azione individuale, azione pubblica, tentativo di conciliazione', *Nuove leggi civili e commentate* 1994, p. 73 *et seq.*; F. Borgogelli, 'I consiglieri di parità', *Nuove leggi civili e commentate* 1994, p. 143 *et seq.*

this perspective.[44] Here, the EU Court, by asserting the discriminatory nature of an employer's general public statement that it will not hire any individual of a certain ethnic origin, anticipates the anti-discriminatory protection to the point at which there are no complainants claiming to have been the victim of such discriminatory recruitment policy. The focus here is neither on individual nor on collective interests; the well-functioning of the labour market is rather at stake insofar as discriminatory recruitment policies can hinder the access to the market of certain groups of candidates.

14.4 Class Action and Collective Action in Consumer Law: A Brief Overview

In consumer law, lines have been drawn between diffuse interests, homogeneous individual rights, and collective interests. Diffuse interests cover un- or under-represented interests of groups of people who lack access to justice. Diffuse interests become collective interests once the diffuse-interest holders can be identified in a well-organized group of people that can assume a different legal form. Once again, through an organization, a diffuse interest can turn into a collective interest benefitting from legal protection. It is worth taking note of Directive 2009/22/EC of 23 April 2009 on injunctions for the protection of consumers' interest, according to which actions for an injunction can be brought by a 'qualified entity', meaning:

> any body or organisation which, being properly constituted according to the law of a Member State, has a legitimate interest in ensuring that the provisions referred to in Article 1 are complied with.[45]

According to the new Italian consumer law,[46] consumer associations that (a) are adequately representative at the national level and (b) have been registered on a Ministerial list enjoy the right to bring injunctive collective actions for the protection of the consumers' collective interests. The weight is placed on the *consumers*' interests and not on the *associations'* interests. The wording highlights that the consumers (as individuals), and not the associations of consumers, remain the holders of the collective-interest.[47] This might be an interesting point of comparison between consumer law and labour law: in labour law, trade unions are regarded more as autonomous private entities that have their own institutional rights and interests, while in consumer law, the focus is on consumers' interests rather than on the associations' interests. However, as in labour law, consumer

44 *Feryn*, C-54/07, Judgment, EU:C:2008:397

45 Directive 2009/22/EC of 23 April 2009 on injunctions for the protection of consumers' interest, OJ [2009] L110/30, Art. 3.

46 Italian Consumer Code, Article 139 *et seq.*

47 *See* A. Giussani, 'Voce "Azione collettiva"', *in Enciclopedia del diritto Annali*, 2007, p. 132 *et seq.*

associations cannot bring individual actions; they can only bring collective actions focused on protecting the consumers' indivisible collective interests.

Italian consumer law[48] also outlines the concept of 'homogeneous individual rights' that can be enforced through a class action, which is a compensatory redress mechanism. Such homogeneous individual rights have, apparently, only a collective nature as, in practice, they remain with individuals and they are not indivisibles.[49] Unlike a collective action, a class action is a collective compensatory form of redress that allows each class member to bring an action either (a) individually, (b) through the associations to which he/she grants power, or (c) through committees in which he/she participates, to assess liability and to seek an order of payment of damages. A class member must demonstrate that he/she can adequately represent the interests of the other members that, in any case, must expressly *opt in* (whereas, in the USA, an *opt out* rule applies).[50]

The Italian class action was strongly influenced by the American experience, notably, by Rule 23 of its Federal Rules of Civil Procedure (FRCP), which regulates class actions. Rule 23(a) provides four prerequisites for all class actions: (1) the class must be so numerous that joinder of all members is impracticable ('numerosity'); (2) there must be questions of law or fact common to the class ('commonality'); (3) the claims or defences of the representative parties must be typical of the claims or defences of the class ('typicality'); and (4) the representative parties must fairly and adequately protect the interests of the class ('adequacy of representation'). In labour law cases, an interesting recent example is provided by *In re: National Football League Players' Concussion Injury Litigation*.[51] At this stage in the proceedings, the Third Circuit Court of Appeals was asked to find that the District Court abused its discretion when it certified the class of retired National Football League players (a class of approximately 21,000 members). The Third Circuit affirmed the District Court's class certification, stating that it had ably exercised its discretion when finding that all of FRCP Rule 23(a) prerequisites had been met, and thus rejected claims that it had erred when it certified the class. As to the commonality requirement, the Court of Appeals remarked that:

---

48 Italian Consumer Code, Art. 140*bis*, para. 2 (introduced by Law No. 99/2009).

49 According to Article 140*bis*, homogenous individual rights are (a) contractual rights of a number of consumers and users who find themselves in a homogeneous situation in relation to the same company, including the rights relating to contracts underwritten in accordance with Articles 1341 and 1342 of the Civil Code concerning standard contracts; (b) homogeneous final consumers' rights concerning a given product in relation to its manufacturer, even in the absence of a direct contractual relationship; (c) homogeneous rights to the payment of damages due to these consumers and users and deriving from unfair commercial practices or anti-competitive behaviours.

50 *See*, among others, P. Porreca, 'Ambito soggettivo e oggettivo dell'azione di classe', *Europa e dir. priv.* 2010, p. 541 *et seq.*; C. Belli (Ed.), *Le azioni collettive in Italia. Profili teorici ed aspetti applicativi*, Milano, Giuffrè, 2007; M. Taruffo, 'La tutela collettiva nell'ordinamento italiano: lineamenti generali', *Rivista di diritto processuale civile* 2011, p. 103 *et seq.*; R. Poli, 'Sulla natura e sull'oggetto dell'azione di classe', *Rivista di diritto processuale civile* 2012, p. 38 *et seq.*; A. Giussani, 'L'azione di classe: un primo bilancio', in *Rivista di diritto processuale civile* 2012, p. 1177 *et seq.*

51 *In re National Football League Players Concussion Injury Litigation*, 821 F.3d 410 (2016).

> Even if players particular injuries are unique, their negligence and fraud claims still depend on the same common questions regarding the NFL's conduct. For example, when did the NFL know about the risks of concussion? What did it do to protect players? Did the League conceal the risks of head injuries? These questions are common to the class and capable of class wide resolution.

An FRCP Rule 23 class action differs from a collective action governed by Section 216(b) of the Fair Labor Standards Act (hereinafter FLSA). For such collective actions, the certification process is easier insofar as the certification – or decertification – of the collective action only affects employees who have expressly *opted in* (an 'opt in regime'). The FRCP Rule 23 class certification, on the other hand, is much harder since it affects all individuals belonging to the class who have not *opted out* (an 'opt out regime'). In an FLSA collective action, employees bear the burden of demonstrating that they are 'similarly situated': a requirement treated by courts differently from that of commonality in the light of the very different regime that applies to FLSA collective actions and FRCP Rule 23 class actions.[52]

In the United States, both Rule 23 FRCP class actions and FLSA collective actions demand an individual's initiative to file suit. From a comparative perspective, it has been pointed out that, while the American model works in the United States, it is unlikely to work in the EU, insofar as it implies the existence of a sort of 'altruistic individualism' which appears to be extraneous to the European tradition.[53] Further, so far, the lack of a detailed regulation of contingent attorney's fees makes class actions extremely risky and inconvenient in Europe.[54] Also, in Europe, at least, a collective compensatory form of redress, based on an association's initiative, would seem to be more coherent and effective.

In a mass society, individuals often lack the incentive to access to justice in the face of small economic claims and the high cost of litigation. Furthermore, another aim of collective redress mechanisms is to encourage individuals to aggregate into groups. Of course, collective redress mechanisms may suffer, on their part, of some weaknesses; notably, the possible divergence between the interests of the association and the interests of its members, which might lead to the association's decision not to take any legal action that would bring benefits to its members but not the association itself.[55]

52 *See* W.C. Jhaveri-Weeks & A. Webbert, 'Class Actions under Rule 23 and Collective Actions under the Fair Labor Standard Act: Preventing the Conflation of Two Distinct Tools to Enforce the Wage Laws', 23 *Georgetown J. Poverty L. Pol'y* 2016, p. 233 *et seq.*

53 *See* Taruffo, *supra* note 50, p. 112.

54 In this respect, I the legislative proposal of the Italian 5 Star Movement (Movimento 5 Stelle) in the DDL S. 1950 of 13 September 2016.

55 *See* A. Carratta, 'Effetti Del Giudicato E Tutela Collettiva', *in* Belli (Ed.), *supra* note 50, pp. 109-110.

14.5 Collective Dimension and Collective Representation Mechanisms in Principle of Life Time Contracts

Principle 7 of Life Time Contracts provides:

> Collective and ethical dimensions: Employees and consumers are entitled to expect that the collective aspect of their individual interests is safeguarded by the state through collective representation mechanisms, together with the application of general values of good morals and good faith which influence access, formation, contents, adaptation and dissolution of such relationships.[56]

The 'collective aspect' of workers and consumers' individual interests strongly calls to mind the idea of collective, indivisible interests that can be enforced and protected through collective representation mechanisms established by statute. It can be argued that both homogeneous individual rights and interests and class action mechanisms (based on individual initiative) remain extraneous to the core of Principle 7.

The wording 'collective interest' might turn out to be a little too restrictive when compared with the recent transformations in trade unions' and consumer associations' action. Also, the expression 'collective representation mechanisms' encompasses both representation mechanisms in collective bargaining and judicial collective action. In this respect, two factors should be particularly considered. First, homogeneous individual rights are gaining importance in the trade unions' strategy and action. Second, the trade unions' modern strategy is shifting from representation in collective bargaining to representation in other activities and services, focussed on maximizing the well-being of individuals.[57]

The strong development of so-called 'workplace welfare', mainly intended to increase workers' 'well-being' (a concept that underscores the weight placed on the individual rather than the group) is a forceful example of this trend. Workplace welfare encompasses different solutions provided by the company and negotiated by trade unions in order to meet the employee's personal and familial needs, such as special medical and dental expenses, elder care, children assistance, summer camps, bureaucratic support, and even the provision of a leave period for workers being stalked or who have suffered family violence. A number of agreements also grant special benefits to married or same-sex couples (e.g., holidays, special vacations, or leave). The main idea is that workplace welfare stimulates the worker's productivity, leading to greater convergence of his/her goals with the employer's goals.

---

56 Principle 7 of Life Time Contracts, *supra* note 15, p. 6.

57 See M. Carrieri & P. Feltrin, *Al bivio. Lavoro, sindacato e rappresentanza nell'Italia di oggi*, Donzelli Editore, Rome, 2016, ch. 1.

In the meantime, trade unions have invested in different services – such as accounting, legal counselling, and bureaucratic and administrative support – that can be used to attract new trade union members. Trade unions are becoming a fundamental support for the individual worker and his/her personal and professional choices. For example, at the Italian trade unions' annual conference in 2015, the CISL (the second-largest Italian trade union confederation) highlighted that the trade unions' renewal and survival can be found in their ability to play an important role in 'personal care' services, by developing collective bargaining focussed mainly on maximizing the individual worker's well-being. Even the language used in collective agreements appears to have changed: they now speak of youth, women, and precariousness, rather than of 'workers'. The former productive-economic language has since been replaced with language that is centred more on the individual and his/her personal and existential needs.

These changes can be interestingly explored from a Life Time Contracts perspective. Collective agreements can be regarded, more and more, as long-term contracts that are important for the worker's self-realization and participation at the workplace level. From collective agreements, but also from other services and activities carried out by their representatives, workers receive benefits that are essential to their life and humans needs.

In this evolving scenario, it would be interesting to rediscover and enhance the trade unions' capacity to take judicial collective actions to protect collective, as well as individual homogeneous, interests. On one hand, the changing nature of collective and individual interests should lead to giving trade unions access to compensatory redress mechanisms – not just injunctive redress mechanisms – conceived to protect workers' interests, not just the trade unions' interests. Using the consumer law debate could bring the topic of collective compensatory redress mechanisms into focus. On the other hand, rediscovering judicial collective action might play an important role in counteracting the workers' unequal economic power that, today, is making it more and more difficult for them to access effective protection and remedies.[58] Workers' access to justice and effective protection is threatened nowadays by a number of factors; the decreasing economic value of the single claims (notably, dismissal claims); the increasing costs and risks of the litigation (consider the new Italian procedural rule which increases the economic costs of the adverse outcome). In this framework, Unions' judicial action, turned to protect workers' interests, could fill the gap of (economic) power that negatively affects and conditions workers' access to effective remedy.

BIBLIOGRAPHY

Ancel, P., 'L'articulation du Contrat du Travail et des Accords Collectifs au Regard de la Force Obligatoire du Contrat', *Revue de Droit du Travail* 2016, pp. 240-250.

58 *See, e.g.*, Article 47, Charter of Fundamental Rights of the European Union (CFREU).

Belli, C. (Ed.), *Le Azioni Collettive in Italia. Profili Teorici ed Aspetti Applicativi*, Milano: Giuffrè, 2007.

Borenfreund, G. & Souriac, M.A., 'Les Rapports de la Loi et de la Convention Collective: une Mise en Perspective', *Droit Social* 2003, p. 72.

Borgogelli, F., 'I Consiglieri di Parità', *Nuove Leggi Civili e Commentate* 1994, p. 143 *et seq.*

Carratta, A., 'Effetti Del Giudicato E Tutela Collettiva', *in* C. Belli (Ed.), *Le Azioni Collettive in Italia. Profili Teorici ed Aspetti Applicativi*, Milano: Giuffrè, 2007, pp. 109-110.

Carrieri, M. & Feltrin, P., *Al bivio. Lavoro, Sindacato e Rappresentanza nell'Italia di Oggi*, Rome: Donzelli Editore, 2016.

Centamore, G., 'Legge e Autonomia Collettiva: una Critica della Dottrina dell'Inderogabilità Bilaterale', *Lavoro e Diritto* 2015, p. 491 *et seq.*

Cesarini Sforza, W., *Il Diritto dei Privati*, Milano: Giuffrè, 1963.

Corrado, R., *Trattato di Diritto del Lavoro. Vol. I. Parte Generale*, Torino: Unione Tipografica-Editrice Torinese, 1965, p. 236 *et seq.*

Däubler, W., *Kommentar zum Tarifvertragsgesetz*, Baden-Baden: Nomos, 2003.

Davies, P. & Freedland, M., *Kahn-Freund's Labour and the Law* (3rd ed.), London: Stevens, 1983.

De Giorgi, M.V., 'Vivere per Raccontarla: i Gruppi Intermedi', *Rivista di Diritto Civile* 2012, p. 791 *et seq.*

Deakin, S. & Wilkinson, F., *The Law of the Labour Market. Industrialization, Employment, and Legal Evolution*, Oxford: Oxford University Press, 2005.

Ferraro, G., *Ordinamento, Ruolo del Sindacato, Dinamica Contrattuale di Tutela*, Padova: Cedam, 1981.

Flammia, R., *Contributo all'Analisi dei Sindacati di Fatto. I. Autotutela degli Interessi di Lavoro*, Milano: Giuffrè, 1963.

Garofalo, M.G., *Interessi collettivi e comportamento antisindacale dell'imprenditore*, Napoli: Jovene, 1979.

Giussani, A., 'Voce "Azione collettiva"', *in Enciclopedia del Diritto Annali*, 2007, Milano: Giuffrè, p. 132 *et seq.*

Giussani, A., 'L'azione di Classe: un Primo Bilancio', *Rivista di Diritto Processuale Civile* 2012, p. 1177 *et seq.*

Grèvy, M., 'L'action en Justice du Syndicat dans l'Intérêt Collectif de la Profession au Cœur de la "Saga de l'Ouverture du Dimanche"', *Revue de Droit du Travail* 2014, p. 486.

Henry, M., 'L'action Syndicale en Exécution des Conventions Collectives', *Droit Ouvrier* 2007, p. 112 *et seq.*

Jeammaud, A., 'De l'Incidence de l'Accord Collectif sur le Contrat de Travail', *Revue de Droit du Travail* 2016, pp. 228-239.

Jhaveri-Weeks, W.C. & Webbert, A., 'Class Actions Under Rule 23 and Collective Actions Under the Fair Labor Standard Act: Preventing the Conflation of Two Distinct Tools to Enforce the Wage Laws', 23 *Georgetown J. Poverty L. & Pol'y* 2016, p. 233 *et seq.*

Kahn-Freund, O., 'Trade Unions, the Law and Society', 33 *Mod. L. Rev.* 1970, p. 241 *et seq.*

Lanfranchi, L., 'Prospettive Ricostruttive in Tema di Art. 28 dello Statuto dei Lavoratori', *Rivista Trimestrale di Diritto e Procedura Civile* 1971, p. 388 *et seq.*

Le Friant, M., 'Collective Autonomy: Hope or Danger?', 34 *Comp. Labor L. & Pol'y J.* 2013, p. 627 *et seq.*

Lord Wedderburn, 'Inderogability, Collective Agreements and Community Law', 21 *Ind. L.J.*, p. 245.

Nogler, L. & Reifner, U. (Eds.), *Life Time Contracts: Social Long-term Contracts in Labor, Tenancy and Consumer Credit Law*, The Hague: Eleven International Publishing, 2014.

Odoul-Asorey, I., 'Négociation Collective et Droit Constitutionnel', *L.G.D.J.* 2013, p. 222 *et seq.*

Pélissier, J., Auzero, J. & Dockès, E., *Droit du Travail* (27th ed.), Paris: Dalloz, 2013.

Persiani, M., *Saggio sull'Autonomia Privata Collettiva*, Padova: Cedam, 1972.

Poli, R., 'Sulla Natura e sull'Oggetto dell'Azione di Classe', *Rivista di Diritto Processuale Civile* 2012, p. 38 *et seq.*

Porreca, P.,'Ambito Soggettivo e Oggettivo dell'Azione di Classe', *Europa e Dir. Priv.* 2010, p. 541 *et seq.*

Rapisarda Sassoon, C., 'La Tutela dei Soggetti Discriminati. Azione Individuale, Azione Pubblica, Tentativo di Conciliazione', *Nuove Leggi Civili e Commentate* 1994, p. 73 *et seq.*

Santoro Passarelli, F., *Nozioni di Diritto del Lavoro*, Napoli: Jovene, 1967.

Simitis, S., 'Il Diritto del Lavoro e la Riscoperta dell'Individuo', *Giornale di Diritto del Lavoro e delle Relazioni Industriali* 1990, p. 100.

Supiot, A., 'Un Faux Dilemme: la Loi ou le Contrat ?', *Droit Social* 2003, p. 59 *et seq.*

Taruffo, M., 'La Tutela Collettiva nell'Ordinamento Italiano: Lineamenti Generali', *Rivista di Diritto Processuale Civile* 2011, p. 103 *et seq.*

Treu, T., *Condotta Antisindacale e atti Discriminatori*, Milano: Franco Angeli, 1974.

Vardaro, G., *Contrattazione Collettiva e Sistema Giuridico*, Napoli: Jovene, 1984.

Weiss, M. & Schmidt, M., *Labour Law and Industrial Relations in Germany* (4th ed.), Cologne: Wolters Kluwer, 2008.

15 Postface: Regards d'un Civiliste Français

Pascal Ancel[*]

Lorsque Luca Ratti m'avait demandé, en 2016, de présenter un rapport introductif au séminaire de Luxembourg qui forme la base du présent ouvrage, il m'avait d'abord semblé que je n'étais pas nécessairement le mieux placé pour jouer ce rôle. Civiliste ayant enseigné le droit des contrats français, puis luxembourgeois, pendant plus de trente ans, formaté à une certaine manière, relativement classique, de penser le droit des contrats, je ne me sentais, à première vue, que peu à l'aise avec un concept aussi novateur que celui des Life Time Contracts, et je n'étais pas sûr de pouvoir, ni même de vouloir, comme le titre de ce séminaire semblait y inciter, "repenser le droit des contrats". A la réflexion, cependant, je m'étais dit que, précisément en raison de mon profil "classique", il était peut-être intéressant de porter sur les travaux relatifs aux Life Time Contracts un regard extérieur, à la fois pour mettre en évidence les obstacles à la pénétration de ce nouveau concept au sein de la théorie générale du contrat, et pour contribuer à alimenter la réflexion dans la doctrine traditionnelle. C'est pourquoi, finalement, j'avais accepté de faire cette introduction, et c'est pourquoi j'ai accepté de reprendre mon texte pour, après relecture des différentes contributions de cet ouvrage, en faire une postface.

Jusqu'à présent, la théorie (appelons-là ainsi provisoirement) des Life Time Contracts ne semble pas avoir eu une grande répercussion dans le monde académique français, dont je suis issu. L'ouvrage publié par le groupe sous la direction de Luca Nogler et Udo Reifner[1] ne comptait qu'une seule contribution d'un professeur français – et encore s'agissait-il d'un professeur en poste à l'Université McGill de Montréal, qu'on peut qualifier de marginal dans le milieu universitaire français.[2] Et cet ouvrage n'a, malheureusement, guère trouvé d'écho en France. En cherchant les occurrences de l'expression Life Time Contracts dans les bases de données des différents éditeurs français, on tombe obstinément sur les trois mêmes références: celle du compte-rendu fait de l'ouvrage par David Hiez à la Revue trimestrielle de droit civil,[3] celle d'un article de Muriel Fabre-Magnan (qu'on retrouve sans grande surprise parmi les contributeurs du présent

* Senior Professor at the University of Luxembourg.

1 L. Nogler & U. Reifner (Eds.), *Life Time Contracts: Social Long-Term Contracts in Labour, Tenancy and Consumer Credit Law*, The Hague, Eleven International Publishing, 2014.

2 V. Forray, 'Le "Social" et la Défaisance – Introduction au Problème de la Critique en Droit Européen des Contrats', *in* L. Nogler & U. Reifner (Eds.), *Life Time Contracts: Social Long-Term Contracts in Labour, Tenancy and Consumer Credit Law*, The Hague, Eleven International Publishing, 2014, p. 221 *et seq.*

3 D. Hiez, "À Propos des Life Time Contracts", 2014 *RTD Civ.*, p. 817.

ouvrage), qui l'évoque à l'occasion de sa critique de la notion de contenu du contrat,[4] et celle d'une contribution de colloque dont je suis l'auteur, où j'en parle très brièvement pour inciter les travaillistes à penser autrement la force obligatoire du contrat.[5] De manière significative, un article récemment paru en France, et portant le même intitulé que le présent ouvrage, ne fait aucune allusion aux travaux du groupe EuSoCo.[6]

Cette indifférence de la doctrine française à l'égard de la catégorie des Life Time contracts est d'autant plus remarquable que, à la suite de l'entrée en vigueur de la récente réforme du droit des obligations, nous pouvons avoir l'impression que nous venons, en France, de "repenser le droit des contrats". Cela aurait pu en être l'occasion: un auteur français prônait ainsi que le législateur profite de la réforme pour "se saisir d'un programme idéologique audacieux susceptible de provoquer un changement de paradigme: une notion de contrat plus réaliste, dans laquelle le contractant ne serait plus une abstraction mais une personne appréhendée dans son contexte, et plus sociale, dans laquelle la loi des parties ne serait plus la seule mesure de la justice contractuelle pour laisser une place à l'intérêt général".[7] On n'était pas si loin de l'esprit du groupe porteur de la notion des Life Time Contracts, qui – comme en témoignent pratiquement toutes les contributions de cet ouvrage – visent principalement à remettre l'humain et le social au cœur de la théorie du contrat. Cependant, l'étude de la réforme française révèle assez vite que celle-ci n'a guère permis d'inscrire dans le droit civil une nouvelle conception du contrat, en tout cas pas dans le sens prôné par ce groupe. Pour l'essentiel, la réforme française est une codification des solutions jurisprudentielles existantes, revues à la marge pour intégrer quelques solutions tirées des textes internationaux (notamment les Principes Unidroit) et des projets européens, dans le but (assez illusoire sans doute) de rendre le droit français des contrats plus attractif sur le plan international. Aussi bien, comme ces textes et ces projets, le texte français (par ailleurs techniquement plutôt bien fait) continue-t-il de penser le contrat de droit commun sur le modèle traditionnel d'un contrat ayant pour objet un échange économique de biens ou de services contre de l'argent. Il serait sans doute excessif d'écrire que ce modèle se ramène, comme dans le Code civil, à celui de la vente, contrat instantané, qui se dénoue aussitôt qu'il est formé ou du moins en un seul moment par l'exécution des obligations qu'il fait naître. Le droit positif et la dogmatique juridique française ont depuis longtemps intégré, dans le droit commun des contrats, les contrats de durée, notamment à travers la distinction des contrats à exécution instantanée et des contrats à exécution successive. Et l'un des apports de la réforme est d'insérer dans le Code civil plusieurs articles relatifs à la durée des contrats. Mais cette intégration s'est réalisée d'un point de vue strictement tech-

4 M. Fabre-Magnan, "Critique de la Notion d'Objet du Contrat", *RDC* 2015/3, p. 639 *et seq.*, spec. p. 644.

5 P. Ancel, "L'articulation du Contrat de Travail et des Accords Collectifs au Regard de la Force Obligatoire du Contrat", 2016 *Revue de Droit du Travail*, p. 240 *et seq.*, spec. p. 249 n. 58.

6 F. Chénédé, "Repenser le Droit des Contrats. Le Titre III du Livre III du Code Civil à l'Epreuve des Ordres Juridiques Européens", *in* B. Bonnet (Ed.), *Traité des Rapports entre Ordres Juridiques*, Issy-les-Moulineaux, LGDJ, 2016.

7 J.P. Chazal, "Quel programme idéologique pour la réforme du droit des contrats?", 12 *Recueil Dalloz* 2015, p. 673.

nique, sans aucune considération de l'utilité concrète que ces contrats présentent pour ceux qui les passent. Les articles relatifs à la durée du contrat sont même, de ce point de vue, parmi les moins audacieux de la réforme: contrairement au projet initial, le texte ne prévoit plus expressément la responsabilité du contractant qui rompt de manière abusive un contrat à durée indéterminée, et il n'introduit aucune obligation de motivation en cas de non-renouvellement des contrats à durée déterminée, alors même que certains de ces contrats présentent un intérêt vital pour un contractant (une telle obligation n'apparaissant, que dans le cadre limité de la résolution pour inexécution par déclaration unilatérale, et non dans celui de la résiliation des contrats à durée indéterminée). Par ailleurs, même si le nouveau texte marque un souci accru, et très louable, de veiller à l'équilibre des relations contractuelles en protégeant les contractants faibles, il reste très loin, dans son esprit, de l'idée centrale des concepteurs de la théorie des Life Time Contracts. Les règles posées à cet égard, dont le domaine d'application dépasse très largement celui des Life Time Contracts (en ce qu'elles visent tout aussi bien les contrats passés par les personnes morales et les contrats instantanés), ne connaissent pas de modulation particulière en fonction de la durée des contrats concernés et de leur importance pour la vie d'un des contractants.

Cette indifférence du nouveau texte français aux situations concrètes, cet attachement au modèle conceptuel traditionnel, ne frappent guère, d'une manière générale, ses multiples commentateurs, parce qu'ils sont eux-mêmes, pour la plupart, formatés par ce modèle, qui leur semble naturel, comme il l'est pour les rédacteurs des principes européens et internationaux, et parce que le texte contient par ailleurs suffisamment de nouveautés techniques pour donner l'illusion d'un certain renouvellement.[8] A cet égard, la confrontation du nouveau texte français avec les principes dégagés par le groupe Life Time Contracts joue comme un révélateur de la faible originalité du texte, elle amène à réfléchir sur ce qu'il aurait pu être, en même temps que – de manière plus positive – elle permet d'ouvrir de nouvelles perspectives d'interprétation de certaines de ces dispositions.

C'est de ce point de vue que la lecture du présent ouvrage s'avère particulièrement stimulante pour un civiliste traditionnel . C'est sans doute avec un regard extérieur qu'on mesure le mieux l'originalité de cette nouvelle approche, son caractère détonant, perturbant par rapport à la vision classique du droit des contrats, qu'on mesure le mieux aussi les obstacles auxquels elle peut se heurter si ses tenants souhaitent traduire en règles de droit positif les principes qu'ils mettent en avant.

Il me semble que cette originalité, cette perturbation de l'approche classique, et les obstacles que cela induit, se situent à deux niveaux, celui de la dogmatique juridique, et celui de la science du droit. Au premier niveau le concept de Life Time Contracts amène un **dépassement des catégories contractuelles techniques** (15.1). Au second, elle suppose **un décloisonnement entre les disciplines** (15.2).

8 Pour un petit catalogue des nouveautés introduites par la réforme V. par exemple: O. Deshayes, T. Génicon & Y.M. Laithier, *Réforme du Droit des Contrats, du Régime Général et de la Preuve des Obligations. Commentaire Article par Article*, Lexis Nexis, Paris, 2016, pp. 4-5.

15.1 Un Dépassement des Catégories Contractuelles

L'originalité fondamentale du concept de Life Time Contracts est de mettre sur le même plan, au sein de la théorie générale des contrats, des types de contrats qu'on ne met généralement pas ensemble, qui relèvent de catégories techniques différentes. Dans sa version première, le concept recouvrait trois types de contrats: le contrat de travail, le contrat de bail d'habitation, et les contrats de crédit aux consommateurs. Ce que ces contrats ont en commun, d'un point de vue concret, humain, c'est, d'une part qu'ils s'exécutent nécessairement dans une durée plus ou moins longue (ce sont des "Time contracts"), d'autre part qu'ils sont nécessaires à la satisfaction de besoins élémentaires de l'un des contractants (se loger, se nourrir, se déplacer, avoir accès à la santé, à la culture, aux loisirs…) – ce sont des "Life contracts". C'est la combinaison de ces deux aspects, la durée et la satisfaction des besoins (Time et Life) qui permet de cerner le concept, intraduisible en beaucoup de langues comme cela a été souvent relevé. A cet égard la proposition faite dans le présent ouvrage par Muriel Fabre-Magnan de traduire en français par "contrats cruciaux" mérite d'être saluée, même s'il me semble que cette traduction intègre plus clairement l'élément "Life" que l'élément "Time" de la dénomination anglaise.

A partir de ces deux éléments, on peut se demander si la catégorie ne devrait pas être élargie, et c'est du reste ce que proposent plusieurs contributeurs du présent ouvrage, comme l'avait déjà fait David Hiez dans son article précité: Andrea Nicolussi suggère d'y intégrer les dons d'organes ou de produits du corps humain, Alexander Flos traite sous cet angle du contrat de mariage, qu'il rapproche du contrat de bail, et Antonio Albanese s'interroge sur l'extension de la catégorie aux contrats d'affaires qui instaurent une relation de dépendance entre entreprises. Luca Nogler et Udo Reifner eux-mêmes, dans leur texte introductif, s'interrogent sur une extension possible aux contrats de service visant à satisfaire des besoins élémentaires (l'eau, l'électricité, les moyens de communication…), mais ils se montrent réticents à admettre une telle extension. C'est, je crois, faire preuve de sagesse: il est sans doute prudent de vérifier d'abord la viabilité du concept à travers les trois types initiaux, avant de l'élargir, éventuellement, à d'autres contrats. Une telle extension paraît en tout cas problématique si on souhaite que la notion de Life Time Contracts ne soit pas seulement une construction intellectuelle, mais, comme le propose notamment Muriel Fabre-Magnan, et comme l'envisagent, à terme du moins, Luca Nogler et Udo Reifner, une véritable catégorie technique entraînant l'application d'un régime juridique spécifique (au même titre que les contrats-cadres ou les contrats d'adhésion par exemple). Il est clair que toute extension risque de rendre plus difficile l'utilisation technique d'un concept, qui, même limité à son champ d'application initial, est déjà suffisamment perturbant au regard des catégories techniques traditionnelles.

Il l'est déjà si on considère chacun des trois types de contrats qui y sont inclus, dans la mesure où le concept de Life Time Contracts amène à traiter ensemble des formes de travail, de bail, ou de crédit, qui relèvent traditionnellement de catégories techniques différentes, et qui relèvent donc de régimes juridiques différents. Elisabeth Brameshuber et Julien-Alexis Defromont traitent ainsi de la manière dont le concept de Life Time Contracts permettrait de dépasser la distinction entre le travail subordonné, qui relève directement du droit du travail, et le travail indépendant dès lors que le contexte concret révèle une dépendance de fait à l'égard du cocontractant. Le contexte de la "nouvelle économie" étudié ici par Charles F. Szymanski dans le contexte américain donne à ce dépassement une grande actualité. De même, les contrats de crédit qui entreront dans la catégorie peuvent prendre la forme d'un prêt d'argent classique, mais aussi d'un leasing – c'est à dire, techniquement, d'un contrat de location de bien. Ces rapprochements, cependant, ne sont pas trop dérangeants, et ils sont déjà largement faits dans les droits nationaux, soit par le biais de requalifications, soit par l'édiction de règles communes destinées à protéger la partie faible quelle que soit la forme juridique adoptée.

Beaucoup plus perturbante, pour un juriste classique, est la volonté d'inclure les trois types de contrats considérés (travail, bail, crédit) au sein d'une catégorie nouvelle de la théorie générale du contrat, qui transcenderait les distinctions habituellement faites, d'un point de vue technique, entre les différents contrats de durée. Ce rapprochement ne suscite pas de difficultés particulières lorsqu'il fonde une protection particulière du contractant au stade de la conclusion du contrat (obligation d'information, absence de discrimination, équilibre des obligations réciproques, condamnation des clauses abusives) parce que ces règles peuvent s'appliquer de la même manière quelle que soit la structure du contrat. Beaucoup de ces règles, du reste, existent déjà, dans les droits nationaux et en droit européen, dans l'optique de la protection des contractants en situation de faiblesse (qui n'est pas l'aspect le plus spécifique de la catégorie des Life Time Contracts), mais la catégorie permettrait sans doute de les dépasser, notamment en posant des règles relatives à l'accès à de tels contrats (Muriel Fabre-Magnan) ou en intégrant une exigence de formation (au sens d'éducation) des contractants protégés qui pourrait se prolonger tout au long de la vie du contrat (Giulia Merlo). De même, l'intégration d'une dimension collective dans les Life Time Contracts, sur le modèle de ce qui existe déjà en droit du travail, dont l'importance est notamment soulignée par Charles F. Szymanski et Orsola Razzolini, ne devrait pas susciter de difficultés techniques particulières, même si elle devrait sans doute prendre des formes différenciées selon le type de contrat.

L'élaboration d'un régime spécifique d'ensemble applicable aux Life Time Contracts semble en revanche plus problématique pour les règles applicables aux effets de ces contrats, parce que ces règles ne peuvent difficilement être pensées en faisant abstraction de la structure technique de la relation contractuelle. Je voudrais prendre ici deux exemples, qui sont au cœur des Principes élaborés par le groupe, et qui reviennent à plusieurs reprises dans les contributions de cet ouvrage, celui des règles relatives à la rupture du contrat et celui de son adaptation au changement de circonstances.

S'agissant de la rupture, l'article 11 des principes pose que "la résiliation des contrats d'existence doit être transparente, responsable et socialement acceptable. La rupture anticipée contre la volonté du consommateur, du locataire ou du salarié doit avoir lieu en dernière extrémité". Le texte exige en conséquence de justes motifs de résiliation ainsi qu'un délai raisonnable de préavis. L'article 3 pose par ailleurs que la rupture anticipée ne peut avoir d'effet que pour l'avenir. Un juriste français ne verra aucune difficulté à appliquer ces règles au contrat de bail et au contrat de travail, qu'il a déjà l'habitude de rapprocher au sein de la même catégorie technique des contrats à exécution successive. Et beaucoup de droits nationaux (notamment le droit français) connaissent déjà des règles destinées à protéger le salarié et le locataire contre une rupture brutale et non motivée du contrat, qu'on peut facilement mettre en parallèle même si elles prennent des formes techniques différentes. On est *a priori* beaucoup plus embarrassé avec le cas du contrat de crédit, parce que ce contrat, bien que son exécution soit étalée dans la durée, a de prime abord une structure complètement différente des deux autres: les remboursements périodiques que fait l'emprunteur ne sont pas la traduction d'obligations qui se renouvellent continuellement dans le temps, elles représentent des fractions d'une obligation globale de remboursement de la somme prêtée. Aussi bien, la rupture anticipée du contrat par le prêteur, en cas de défaillance de l'emprunteur, est-elle techniquement très différente de la résiliation d'un contrat de bail ou d'un contrat de travail. Elle prend la forme d'une déchéance du terme qui aboutit normalement à obliger l'emprunteur à rembourser immédiatement l'intégralité des sommes dues, pour le passé et pour l'avenir ce qui peut conduire à la saisie du bien acquis grâce au crédit non remboursé – sauf le jeu des règles relatives au surendettement. De même, si on regarde la situation inverse, où c'est le contractant dont le contrat assure la subsistance qui désire mettre fin à la relation, le remboursement anticipé du crédit paraît techniquement très différent de la démission du salarié ou de la résiliation du bail par le locataire. On peut bien, on doit même, comme nous y incitent Anthi Beka (dans le cadre du droit européen) et Alan M. White (dans le contexte des Etats-Unis), renforcer les mesures de protection du preneur de crédit contre la saisie de son immeuble lorsque celui-ci lui sert de résidence principale. De même, la liberté du remboursement anticipé du crédit pourrait être assurée de la même manière qu'on assure celle de la démission du salarié ou du départ du locataire avant la fin de son bail. Et c'est tout le mérite du concept de Time Life contracts de nous amener à dépasser les différences techniques entre ces contrats, et, parce qu'elles ont des incidences concrètes du même type, à penser l'encadrement de la fin du contrat de crédit de la même manière que celui de la fin du contrat de travail ou de bail. Il faut néanmoins avoir conscience que ce rapprochement (particulièrement stimulant) ne pourra guère se faire qu'au niveau de principes généraux servant d'inspiration pour les règles techniques, dont on a du mal à penser qu'elles pourraient être les mêmes pour les trois contrats.

Il en va sans doute de même, quoique de manière moins évidente, lorsqu'on envisage l'autre question cruciale relative aux Life Time Contracts, celle de l'adaptation de ces contrats aux changements de circonstances qui affectent le contractant, et notamment aux changements qui affectent sa vie personnelle. Les rédacteurs des principes ont conçu sur cette question un texte visiblement inspiré du § 313 du BGB et de l'idée de disparition du fondement contractuel (Wegfall der Geschäftsgrundlage). Cependant, comme le montrent des contributions de Alvise Schiavon et Nuno Manuel Pinto Oliveira, un tel texte semble assez éloigné de la vision dominante de l'imprévision (hardship), telle qu'elle s'exprime dans les Principes Unidroit ou dans les projets européens (PECL, DCFR), dont s'inspire clairement le nouvel article 1195 du Code civil français. Les rédacteurs du texte français, notamment, n'ont sans doute pas imaginé que la possibilité de révision judiciaire qu'ouvre ce texte pourrait s'appliquer aux contrats entrant dans la catégorie des Life Time Contracts, pour lesquels existent déjà, de manière plus ou moins développée, des mécanismes spécifiques d'adaptation au changement de circonstances. Par ailleurs, dans l'opinion commune, le "changement de circonstances" visé par ces différents textes ne recouvre que les changements de circonstances extérieures, d'ordre économique et social. On n'a semble-t-il jamais pensé que cela pourrait également concerner "l'augmentation des contraintes matérielles", également prise en compte par les auteurs des Principes of Life Time Contracts, et qui pourrait tenir aussi bien à la survenance de problèmes personnels au contractant (chômage, maladie, perte du logement etc.) – la "force majeure sociale" pour reprendre l'expression de Wilhelmson relayée ici par Nuno Manuel Pinto Oliveira. Là encore, le concept de Life Time Contracts agit comme un révélateur, comme un stimulant permettant de penser autrement, de rapprocher des situations qu'on ne traite habituellement que de manière cloisonnée. Il permet par exemple de regarder avec des yeux neufs le nouvel article 1195 du Code civil, en observant que rien dans la rédaction du texte ne limite son champ d'application (et ne l'exclut donc pas pour les contrats ici considérés) et que la notion de "changement de circonstances" qu'il vise, même si elle a été pensée par ses rédacteurs dans l'optique habituelle des débats sur l'imprévision, pourrait tout aussi bien s'appliquer aux changements de circonstances personnelles. Cela ne signifie pas, cependant, qu'on doive aller dans ce sens, et, même s'il n'y a pas ici de véritable impossibilité technique à introduire un mécanisme de révision pour imprévision commun aux différents Life Time Contracts, on peut se demander si la mise en place de mécanismes d'adaptation spécifiques à chacun des contrats considérés n'est pas une meilleure solution: il n'est tout de même pas évident que les conséquences du surendettement pour un preneur de crédit immobilier doivent être, techniquement, les mêmes que ceux du chômage pour un locataire ou de la longue maladie pour un salarié.[9] Mais au moins, en bousculant les catégories habituelles, le concept de Life Time Contracts ouvre sur ce point comme sur bien d'autres de nouvelles perspectives d'interprétation des dispositifs existants ainsi que de création de nouveaux dispositifs.

9 Je rejoins complètement ici la position de G. Howells, 'Change of Circumstances in Consumer Credit Contracts – The United Kingdom Experience and a Call for the Maintenance of Sector Specific Rules', *in* Nogler & Reifner, *supra* note 1, p. 451 *et seq.*, spec p. 463.

Ces nouvelles perspectives, cependant, ne peuvent être envisagées qu'au prix d'un décloisonnement des disciplines juridiques dont le présent ouvrage offre un remarquable exemple.

15.2 Un Décloisonnement des Disciplines Juridiques

Chacun sait que la construction des catégories juridiques n'est pas seulement fonction du contenu des règles, elle relève de choix opérés par les juristes, en tout premier lieu par les membres de la doctrine et ces choix peuvent eux-mêmes être largement influencés par l'appartenance de ceux-ci à telle ou telle discipline de la science juridique. On sait aussi que la complexification croissante des différentes branches du droit, la multiplication des sources des règles, leur obsolescence de plus en plus rapide, ont entraîné, au sein du monde académique, une spécialisation disciplinaire de plus en plus poussée.

Une telle spécialisation est de nature à faire obstacle à l'implantation, au sein de la théorie générale du contrat, d'un concept transversal qui englobe à la fois des opérations relevant du droit du travail, du droit des baux, du droit de la consommation, et du droit commercial, et qui ne sont, habituellement, jamais étudiées par les mêmes personnes. L'approfondissement du concept de Life Time Contracts suppose un dialogue interdisciplinaire dont on connaît la difficulté, même lorsqu'on veut se limiter à une interdisciplinarité interne au droit.

Il faut d'abord un dialogue entre les spécialistes des différentes disciplines juridiques qui s'intéressent aux trois types de contrats regroupés (en attendant une éventuelle extension) sous l'étiquette des Life Time Contracts. Le présent ouvrage, coordonné par un travailliste italien en poste à Luxembourg, qui prolonge des travaux initiés par un autre travailliste italien et par un spécialiste allemand du droit de la consommation, et qui ont rassemblé des auteurs venus d'horizons divers, est un exemple magnifique d'un tel dialogue interdisciplinaire. La diversité des origines géographiques des contributeurs est tout aussi remarquable, tant il est vrai que, dans le monde actuel, une telle réflexion ne peut plus se concevoir dans un cadre exclusivement national – même si un des buts est que cette réflexion trouve ensuite des traductions concrètes dans le cadre des différents droits nationaux.

Mais il faut aussi – et c'est une question à laquelle je suis, en tant que civiliste, particulièrement sensible – un dialogue entre, d'un côté les spécialistes de ces différentes disciplines, et d'un autre côté les auteurs qui travaillent principalement sur la théorie générale du contrat. C'est peut-être sur ce terrain qu'on risque de rencontrer les plus grandes difficultés, du moins si j'en juge par ce que j'ai pu observer au sein du monde académique français.

En France, où le droit civil continue d'occuper une place prépondérante dans la formation des juristes, et dans le recrutement des professeurs, le droit des contrats (entendez la théorie générale du contrat comme construction intellectuelle traitant des règles du droit commun des contrats) est souvent considéré comme la "discipline-reine", celle qui permet de s'assurer le premier rang dans le monde académique. Il en résulte la constitution d'une sorte de "caste" de professeurs spécialistes du droit commun des contrats, "spécialistes du général" en quelque sorte, qui ne sont pas toujours assez ouverts aux réglementations spéciales. Par ailleurs, beaucoup de ces civilistes ont tendance, surtout dans la période récente, à raisonner sur le modèle des contrats d'affaires, ce qui ne facilite guère l'intégration d'un concept comme celui des Life Time Contracts, sans doute plus facile à admettre par les auteurs orientés du côté du droit de la consommation. Au-delà même de leur orientation, il faut noter que les porteurs de la théorie générale du contrat restent souvent très enclins à mettre au premier plan de leur réflexion les catégories techniques abstraites, derrière lesquelles le contenu social, humain, tend à s'effacer. L'entreprise poursuivie par les concepteurs des Life Time Contracts, qui tend au contraire à valoriser ce contenu social et humain concret, ne peut réussir que si les tenants de la théorie générale cessent de considérer les catégories comme des sortes de vérités, comme des dogmes, alors qu'elles ne sont que le produit d'une évolution historique souvent assez récente – comme l'avait montré de manière remarquable, dans le premier ouvrage consacré aux Life Time Contracts, l'étude conduite par Udo Reifner sur la *locatio conductio*.[10] Ces catégories civilistes – et en tout premier la catégorie du contrat – nous devons constamment accepter de les repenser en les nourrissant des évolutions, des déformations, des distorsions, qu'elles connaissent dans le droit des contrats spéciaux, et dans les autres branches, en droit du travail, en droit de la consommation, en droit bancaire etc.

Cette interdisciplinarité, cependant, ne doit pas fonctionner à sens unique. Il ne suffit pas que les "spécialistes de théorie générale" s'ouvrent davantage au social et aux autres disciplines qui travaillent sur les différents contrats dont il est ici question. Il faut aussi qu'à l'inverse les spécialistes de ces disciplines acceptent davantage d'entrer dans la logique de la théorie générale, d'en approfondir les concepts pour pouvoir les repenser. Beaucoup de contributions publiées dans cet ouvrage reposent sur cette réappropriation des concepts civilistes. On notera tout particulièrement celle d'Elisabeth Brameshuber qui cherche à montrer comment la réinscription du droit du travail au sein du droit civil pourrait être de nature à empêcher l'éviction du droit du travail par le recours de plus en plus fréquent aux contrats de prestation de services. Mais en même temps, comme le montre précisément cette contribution, les concepts du droit civil doivent être repensés, retravaillés, pour tenir compte des besoins spécifiques que les contrats concernés doivent satisfaire: même si on admet, avec l'auteur, que l'employeur puisse se servir du concept civiliste d'imprévision pour baisser le salaire des employés , ce ne peut être que dans des circonstances très exceptionnelles, que l'article 10 des Principes relatifs aux Life Time Contracts devraient permettre de circonscrire. Comme l'écrit l'auteure "As LTC Principle

10 U. Reifner, 'Darlehensvertrag als Kapitalmiete (Locatio Conductio Specialis)', *in* Nogler & Reifner, *supra* note 1, p. 419 *et seq.*

No. 10 (Adaptation) shows, the specificities of the labour relationship prevent the employer from recourse to that adjustment option in the majority of cases. It limits that possibility by simultaneously recognising the employee's need for protection".[11]

Quelque temps avant le séminaire dont le présent ouvrage est l'aboutissement, j'avais été chargé de réfléchir dans le cadre d'un colloque de droit du travail sur le problème très actuel de l'articulation des accords collectifs et des contrats de travail individuels au regard du concept civiliste de la force obligatoire du contrat.[12] Beaucoup de travaillistes, en France, ont du mal à admettre qu'un accord collectif (et notamment un accord d'entreprise) puisse modifier un contrat de travail antérieurement passé même dans un sens défavorable au salarié. Pour s'opposer à une telle solution (que les récentes ordonnances modifiant le Code du travail français ont en partie consacrée), ils invoquent volontiers la force obligatoire du contrat, qui interdirait qu'un contrat de travail puisse être modifié contre le gré du salarié. Le problème, que j'avais essayé de mettre à jour, est que la force obligatoire du Code civil, brandie comme un talisman, est en réalité un principe bien fragile lorsqu'on l'applique aux contrats à exécution successive et à durée indéterminée, puisque (en raison de la prohibition des contrats perpétuels), ces contrats sont normalement résiliables à tout moment par une partie, et que celle-ci a donc, en fait, le pouvoir d'imposer à l'autre une modification des termes du contrat. Si on veut qu'il n'en aille pas ainsi en matière de contrat de travail, on peut précisément mettre en avant l'idée que celui-ci est un "contrat crucial" pour la vie du salarié, ce qui justifie une force obligatoire renforcée limitant considérablement le droit de mettre fin au contrat contre le gré du salarié. Le dialogue avec les civilistes permet ici d'approfondir la théorie générale, de montrer ses insuffisances, au lieu de s'en servir comme d'un rempart illusoire contre certaines évolutions législatives. Et ce n'est que par ce dialogue qu'on peut, faire évoluer les concepts de la théorie générale – comme celui de la force obligatoire-, les nourrir des exigences du droit spécial, qu'on peut repenser le droit des contrats, pour y intégrer du concret, du social, de l'humain. La théorie des Life Time Contracts, au cœur du présent ouvrage, est un puissant outil pour ce renouvellement.

BIBLIOGRAPHY

Ancel, P., "L'articulation du Contrat de Travail et des Accords Collectifs au Regard de la Force Obligatoire du Contrat", 2016 *Revue de Droit du Travail*, p. 240 *et seq*.

11 E. Brameshuber, *supra* Ch. 10.

12 Cette contribution a été publiée à la *Revue de Droit du Travail* 2016, p. 240 *et seq*. avec le titre *L'articulation du contrat de travail et des accords collectifs au regard de la force obligatoire du contrat.*

Chénédé, F., "Repenser le Droit des Contrats. Le Titre III du Livre III du Code Civil à l'Epreuve des Ordres Juridiques Européens", *in* B. Bonnet (Ed.), *Traité des Rapports entre Ordres Juridiques*, Issy-les-Moulineaux> LGDJ, 2016.

Chazal, J.P., "Quel Programme Idéologique pour la Réforme du Droit des Contrats?", 12 *Recueil Dalloz* 2015, p. 673.

Deshayes, O., Génicon, T., & Laithier, Y.M., *Réforme du Droit des Contrats, du Régime Général et de la Preuve des Obligations. Commentaire Article par Article*, Paris: Lexis Nexis, 2016.

Fabre-Magnan, M., "Critique de la Notion d'Objet du Contrat", RDC 2015/3, p. 639 et seq.

Forray, V., 'Le "Social" et la Défaisance – Introduction au Problème de la Critique en Droit Européen des Contrats', in L. Nogler & U. Reifner (Eds.), Life Time Contracts: Social Long-Term Contracts in Labour, Tenancy and Consumer Credit Law, The Hague: Eleven International Publishing, 2014, p. 221 et seq.

Hiez, D., "À Propos des Life Time Contracts", 2014 RTD Civ., p. 817.

Howells, G., 'Change of Circumstances in Consumer Credit Contracts – The United Kingdom Experience and a Call for the Maintenance of Sector Specific Rules', *in* L. Nogler & U. Reifner (Eds.), *Life Time Contracts: Social Long-Term Contracts in Labour, Tenancy and Consumer Credit Law*, The Hague: Eleven International Publishing, 2014, p. 451 *et seq.*

Nogler, L., & Reifner, U. (Eds.), Life Time Contracts: Social Long-Term Contracts in Labour, Tenancy and Consumer Credit Law, The Hague: Eleven International Publishing, 2014.

Reifner, U., 'Darlehensvertrag als Kapitalmiete (Locatio Conductio Specialis)', *in* L. Nogler & U. Reifner (Eds.), *Life Time Contracts: Social Long-Term Contracts in Labour, Tenancy and Consumer Credit Law*, The Hague: Eleven International Publishing, 2014, p. 419 *et seq.*

Principles of Life Time Contracts (de/en/fr/it/es)

Prinzipien sozialer Dauerschuldverhältnisse

1. *Lebenszeitverträge:* Lebenszeitverträge sind soziale Dauerschuldverhältnisse, die mit Bezug zu einem Teil der Lebenszeit natürlicher Personen lebenswichtige Güter, Dienstleistungen, Arbeit und Einkommensmöglichkeiten zur Selbstverwirklichung und sozialen Teilhabe bereitstellen.

2. *Humanität:* Lebenszeitverträge stellen den Menschen in seiner Wirklichkeit und humanen Ausbildung in den Mittelpunkt. Es ist daher nicht nur der Vertragsabschluss, sondern vor allem die dauerhafte Kooperation unter Berücksichtigung der Machtverhältnisse, die es im Recht zu steuern gilt. Persönliche Verhältnisse zu Dritten (insbesondere in der Familie) müssen Berücksichtigung finden.

3. *Langfristigkeit:* Das Vertrauen beider Vertragspartner in den Bestand des langfristigen Lebenszeitvertrages wird geschützt (z.B. Kündigungsschutz), so dass Vertragsauflösungen nur mit der Wirkung „ex nunc" erfolgen. Eine Eingrenzung erfährt dieser Vertrauensschutz durch die Privatautonomie insoweit, als ein Mindestmaß an Entscheidungs- und Handlungsfreiheit eine vorzeitige Aufkündigung erforderlich machen.

4. *Verbundene Verträge*: Die Einbettung der jeweiligen Vertragsverhältnisse in ein Netzwerk von Verträgen erfordert deren

Principles of Social Long-Term Contracts

1. *Life time contracts:* Life time contracts are long-term social relationships providing goods, services and opportunities for work and income creation. They are essential for the self-realisation of individuals and their participation in society at various stages in their life.

2. *Human Dimension:* The subject matter of life time contracts is real-life circumstances. The role of the law governing them is to frame the power relationships of those contracts in terms of human development, so that on-going co-operation rather than the formation of the contract lies at the heart of the contractual relationship. Personal relations (such as the family) have to be taken into account.

3. *Long-term relationship:* Mutual trust between the parties as to the durability of the long-term relationship must be protected, and early termination must have only future effect, having no bearing on the contract prior to that point. Early termination must be restricted to circumstances in which the freedom and the autonomy of the individual is at issue and makes early termination necessary.

4. *Linked contracts:* Life time contracts are embedded in a network of linked contracts to which the law must have regard when legal questions fall to be decided.

Einbeziehung und Beachtung bei der Lösung rechtlicher Fragen.

5. *Rücksichtnahme:* Die Bereitstellung von Nutzungsmöglichkeiten für Verbraucher und Arbeitnehmer erfordert soziale Rücksichtnahme auf die konkreten körperlichen und seelischen Belange zum Schutz des Schwächeren. Das Gesetz oder andere kollektive Regeln sehen nach Art, Dauer und dem Grad der Bedeutung dieser Verträge für die Lebensverhältnisse der Betroffenen in zwingender Form verschiedene Stufen der Rücksichtnahme vor.

6. *Produktive Nutzung:* Wer im Rahmen von Lebenszeitverträgen Nutzungen und Einkommensmöglichkeiten bereitstellt, hat alles zu unterlassen, was deren sozialen Zweck gefährdet.

7. *Kollektivität und Ethik*: Arbeitnehmer und Verbraucher können vom Staat verlangen, dass kollektive Systeme zu ihrer Interessenwahrung ebenso wie kollektive Wertsysteme von Treu und Glauben sowie den guten Sitten in den Prozessen von Abschluss, Gestaltung und Auflösung sozialer Dauerschuldverhältnisse Eingang und Berücksichtigung finden.

8. *Zugang*: Wer Lebenszeitverträge anbietet, muss in Ankündigung, Vorbereitung und Abschluss sowohl bei der Definition der Gruppe, für die diese Nutzung bereitgestellt wird, als auch innerhalb der Gruppe jede Diskriminierung nach persönlichen wie sozialen Merkmalen unterlassen. Die Bedeutung der Lebenszeitverträge für die Befriedigung menschlicher Grundbedürfnisse wie Wohnen, Arbeit, Teilhabe an der Wirtschaft erfordert ein Menschenrecht

5. *Basic needs:* The provision of essential goods and services for basic needs related to consumption and employment requires that physical, social and psychological considerations be taken into account in order to ensure the protection of the weaker party to the contract. Stringent regulation or other collective rules will secure the degree of social protection needed in line with the subject matter of the contract, its duration and its importance in the life of the individuals concerned.

6. *Productive use:* The provider of essential goods and services or income-generating opportunities under a life time contract must avoid taking any action that will jeopardise the social purpose of the contract and the productive use of the rendered services.

7. *Collective and ethical dimensions:* Employees and consumers are entitled to expect that the collective aspect of their individual interests is safeguarded by the state through collective representation mechanisms, together with the application of general values of good morals and good faith that influence access, formation, contents, adaptation and dissolution of such relationships.

8. *Access:* Providers of life time contracts must refrain from discrimination in terms of the personal and social characteristics at all stages of the contract, from access to termination, including discrimination in terms of the group of intended users of the contract, or individual members of that group. The importance of life time contracts in meeting the basic human needs

auf Zugang zu diesen Gütern und Dienstleistungen.

9. *Entgelt:* Leistung und Gegenleistung der Lebenszeitverträge dürfen nicht in einem auffälligen Missverhältnis stehen. Der Preis muss nach transparenten und diskriminierungsfreien Gesichtspunkten bemessen sein.

10. *Anpassung:* Haben sich die sozialen und wirtschaftlichen Umstände, die die Grundlage des Lebenszeitvertrags bilden, nach Vertragsschluss schwerwiegend verändert oder stellen sich wesentliche Umstände, die zur Grundlage des Vertrags geworden sind, als falsch heraus und hätten die Parteien den Vertrag nicht oder mit anderem Inhalt schließen müssen, wenn sie diese Veränderung vorausgesehen hätten, so kann Anpassung des Vertrags verlangt werden, soweit einem Teil unter Berücksichtigung aller Umstände des Einzelfalls, insbesondere der vertraglichen oder gesetzlichen Risikoverteilung und seines sozialen Zwecks sowie der grundlegenden Pflichten der Person, das Festhalten am unveränderten Vertrag nicht zugemutet werden kann. Kollektive Regelungen haben den Vorrang.

11. *Kündigung*: Die Kündigung von Lebenszeitverträgen muss transparent, nachvollziehbar und sozial verträglich gestaltet sein. Sie ist ultima ratio. Sie muss die wahren und angemessenen Gründe nennen und diskriminierungsfrei erfolgen. Sie soll sich nur an Gründen in der Person oder im Verhalten des Nutzenden sowie der Wirtschaftlichkeit der Bereitstellung für den Anbieter orientieren. Bei

of subsistence, employment and participation in economic life gives access to these goods, services and income opportunities the status of fundamental human right (distributive justice).

9. *Remuneration:* The mutual obligations of life time contracts shall not be grossly disproportionate. Prices must be transparent and non-discriminatory.

10. *Adaptation:* If the social and economic circumstances upon which a life time contract is based have changed significantly since the contract was entered into, or if material circumstances from which the parties derived have arisen that are found to be at variance with its original situation to such an extent that the social nature of the contract is jeopardised, and if the parties would not have entered into the contract or would have entered into it on different terms had they foreseen this change, adaptation of the contract may be required if, taking into account all the circumstances of the specific case, and in particular the contractual or statutory allocation of risk and the fundamental obligation of a human being, one of the parties cannot reasonably be expected to continue to comply with the contract without variation of its terms. Collective regulation shall take precedence over individual adaptation.

11 *Termination:* Termination of life time contracts must be transparent, accountable and socially responsible. Early termination against the will of the consumer, tenant or worker must be a measure of last resort. Disclosure of true and fair grounds for termination must be non-discriminatory and be

wirtschaftlichen Gründen sind kollektive Mechanismen des Interessenausgleichs zu suchen. Der einzelne und seine Interessenvertretung sind zu hören. Es ist Gelegenheit und Zeit für Vorschläge zur Vermeidung von Kündigung und/oder Kündigungsfolgen zu schaffen. Soweit die Kündigung im Interesse der Partei liegt, die den Vertrag erstellt und die Dienstleistung organisiert hat, muss sie die Interessen der anderen Partei gebührend berücksichtigen.

12. *Kommunikation*: Vom Beginn der Vertragsverhandlungen, während der Geschäftsbeziehungund bis hin zur Abwicklung des Lebenszeitvertrages soll der Dialog zwischen den Vertragspartnern auf einer gleichrangig, kooperativ an der Erfüllung des Vertragszwecks sachorientiert sowie einer direkt persönlich geführten Kommunikation beruhen. Vor jeder Vertragsgestaltung (Abschluss, Anpassung, Kündigung etc.) hat eine diesen Maßstäben entsprechende Anhörung zu erfolgen, die dem Grundsatz vertrauensgetragener Kommunikation Rechnung trägt.

13. *Information und Transparenz*: Während der Vertragsverhandlungen, der Vertragslaufzeit sowie nachvertraglich soll eine an den Bedürfnissen des Vertragspartners orientierte hinreichende, wahrheitsgemäße, vollständige, rechtzeitige und verständliche Information erfolgen, die bestehende Informationsasymmetrien überwindet.

14. *Existenzsicherung*: Soweit Lebenszeitverträge regelmäßige Einkommen verschaffen, diese zeitlich und örtlich verfügbar machen oder sich auf Zahlungen

provided a reasonable period before termination comes into effect. The only grounds for termination are personal behaviour of such significance as to merit termination, or financial circumstances or interests on the part of the provider that materially affect the viability of the subject matter of the contract. Where the reasons for termination are financial in nature, users are entitled to have recourse to mechanisms of collective redress, including the right of the individual to be heard or represented. This procedure must allow sufficient time for users to put forward measures preventing termination and/or its consequences. As far as the termination is in the interest of that party which has developed the contract and organised the service, it has to consider the interest of the other party with due diligence.

12. *Communication:* Throughout the contractual relationship, from the beginning of the process of negotiation of the contract to its termination, a continuing and co-operative dialogue must be established on an equal basis and at a personal level between the parties with regard to fulfilling the purpose of the contract. Such a discussion must take place before each stage in the contract (formation, adaptation, termination), and communications must at all times be based on the principle of trust and confidence.

13. *Information and Transparency:* During the negotiation of the contract and for the life time of the contract, accurate, complete, timely and understandable information must be provided that is adequate to overcome any information asymmetry that arises.

aus solchem Einkommen beziehen, ist zu gewährleisten, dass das für die Sicherung des Existenzminimums notwendige Einkommen durch fortdauernde Zahlungen bzw. Schutz vor Pfändungen, Verjährungsregeln und Ausgleich nicht geschmälert wird.

15. *Soziale Not*: Die sozialen Risiken der Arbeitslosigkeit, Obdachlosigkeit und überschuldung müssen in der individuellen wie kollektiven Gestaltung der Nutzungsverträge entsprechend ihrer gesellschaftlichen Verursachung angemessen berücksichtigt und durch das öffentliche Recht ergänzt werden

16. *Vertraulichkeit*: Die während der Geschäftsbeziehung eines Lebenszeitvertrages erlangten persönlichen Daten und darauf beruhende Bewertungen sind vertraulich zu behandeln und dürfen nur zur Erfüllung des Vertragszwecks benutzt werden.

14. *Securing livelihood:* Where life time contracts provide for regular income, making it available according to time and place, or for payments to be drawn from that income, a minimum level of income must be guaranteed in the form of continuing payments sufficient to meet the consumer's subsistence needs and, if applicable, protection must be provided from attachment of income, seizure and individual voluntary arrangements with creditors.

15. *Exclusion:* The social risks of unemployment, homelessness and over-indebtedness must be taken into account in both the individual and the collective forms of the contract with due regard to its social origin and in line with public law.

16. *Confidentiality:* Personal data obtained during a life time contractual relationship and assessments based on such data must be treated confidentially and only be used for the purpose of the contract.

Principes des contrats à temps essentiels à l'existence de la personne

1. *Contrats d'existence*: Les contrats d'existence sont des relations sociales à long terme par lesquelles les individus se fournissent des biens ou des services, accèdent à un travail ou à une source de revenus. Ces contrats sont essentiels à la réalisation et l'insertion de l'individu dans la vie sociale, à différents stades de celle-ci.

2. *Dimension humaine*: ce sont les conditions concrètes de vie qui constituent la matière des contrats d'existence. Le droit qui les régit a pour fonction de contrôler le pouvoir qui s'exerce lors de la relation contractuelle afin de permettre le développement personnel des individus qui y participent. C'est donc la coopération continue des parties au cœur de la relation qu'il s'agit de régler, plutôt que le processus de formation du contrat. Les relations intimes (telles que les relations familiales) doivent être prises en compte.

3. *Relation à long terme*: la confiance mutuelle doit être protégée pendant toute la durée de la relation. Toute rupture anticipée ne doit produire d'effet que pour l'avenir et n'avoir aucune incidence sur la relation contractuelle antérieure à la rupture. La rupture anticipée doit être réservée aux circonstances dans lesquelles la liberté et l'autonomie de la personne sont en cause et rendent ainsi nécessaire une telle rupture.

4. *Contrats connexes*: les contrats d'existence sont insérés dans un réseau de contrats

Principi sui contratti "di durata" per l'esistenza della persona

1. *Contratti "di durata" per l'esistenza della persona:* i contratti di durata per l'esistenza della persona sono contratti socialmente rilevanti i quali hanno per oggetto la soddisfazione di esigenze delle persone relative a beni e servizi primari, al lavoro ed alla capacità economica necessaria allo sviluppo della persona come individuo e nella sua vita di relazione.

2. *Dimensione umana:* punto di riferimento centrale dei contratti per l'esistenza della persona è la persona umana colta nella sua concreta realtà materiale e culturale. Il diritto non deve, quindi, preoccuparsi di regolare soltanto la conclusione del contratto, ma soprattutto la cooperazione duratura tra le parti facendo sì che essa non sia compromessa o distorta dalla eventuale differenza di potere (contrattuale) indotta dai rapporti di forza che sussistono tra le parti stesse. Si deve tener conto anche dei rapporti personali altamente significativi per la vita delle persone (come ad esempio, le relazioni familiari).

3. *Durata:* deve essere tutelato l'affidamento reciproco tra le parti circa il permanere nel tempo del contratto per l'esistenza della persona (prevedendo, ad esempio, una tutela in caso di recesso), in modo tale che il recesso o la risoluzione del contratto abbiano effetto solo "ex nunc". Tale regola può essere derogata dall'autonomia privata solo per i casi in cui lo scioglimento

connexes qui doivent être pris en considération lorsque qu'un problème juridique doit être réglé.

5. *Besoins essentiels*: la fourniture de biens et services visant à la satisfaction des besoins essentiels de l'individu, dans le contexte d'une opération de consommation ou d'une relation de travail, suppose que soient pris en compte des considérations d'ordre physique, social et psychologique afin d'assurer la protection de la partie la plus faible au contrat.

6. *Clause d'utilité*: le fournisseur de biens ou de services essentiels à l'existence, ou bien celui qui offre l'accès à une source de revenus doit s'abstenir de toute action qui pourrait compromettre la dimension sociale du contrat ou l'utilité des prestations contractuelles.

7. *Aspects collectifs et éthiques*: les salariés et les consommateurs sont fondés à attendre de l'Etat que la dimension collective de leurs intérêts individuels soit sauvegardée au moyen de mécanismes de représentation collective, ainsi que par l'application des valeurs générales d'une bonne morale et de la bonne foi, qu'il s'agisse de l'accès, la formation, du contenu, de l'adaptation et de la dissolution des relations contractuelles.

8. *Accès*: ceux qui offrent des contrats d'existence doivent s'abstenir de toute discrimination quant aux caractéristiques personnelles ou sociales des consommateurs à quelque étape du contrat que ce soit, depuis l'accès à celui-ci jusqu'à son terme. Ceci concerne tant la discrimination à l'égard du groupe auquel appartient la partie visée que la discrimination à

anticipato del rapporto risulta necessario per non mortificare la libertà di decisione e di azione delle persone.

4. *Collegamento contrattuale:* il fatto che i contratti per l'esistenza della persona si inseriscano in una rete di contratti impone di affrontare le questioni giuridiche che li riguardano considerando sistematicamente anche il collegamento negoziale.

5. *Farsi carico della situazione della controparte:* la messa a disposizione di beni e di possibilità di godimento a favore di consumatori e lavoratori presuppone la disponibilità a farsi carico in modo solidale della tutela della parte più debole, con riguardo alla sua integrità fisica e morale. Tenendo conto del tipo, della durata e dell'importanza di tali contratti per le condizioni di vita degli interessati, la legge e le discipline collettive devono prevedere in modo inderogabile, vari gradi di rispetto e protezione della controparte.

6. *Uso produttivo:* chi nell'ambito di contratti per l'esistenza della persona concede l'utilizzazione di beni o la disponibilità di denaro deve astenersi dal fare tutto ciò che possa compromettere gli scopi cooperativi degli stessi.

7. *Dimensione collettiva e clausole etiche:* i lavoratori dipendenti ed i consumatori possono pretendere che lo Stato predisponga e prenda in considerazione nelle fasi della conclusione, dello svolgimento e della cessazione dei contratti per l'esistenza della persona meccanismi collettivi di tutela dei loro interessi e che sia sempre dato rilievo ai valori richiamati dalla buona fede e dal buon costume.

l'égard du membre d'un groupe. Du fait de l'importance des contrats d'existence pour la satisfaction des besoins humains en termes de subsistance, de travail et de participation à la vie économique, il convient de donner à l'accès à ces biens et services ainsi qu'à ces sources de revenus le statut d'un droit de la personne humaine.

9. *Prix*: les obligations réciproques dans un contrat d'existence ne doivent pas être grossièrement disproportionnées. Les frais doivent demeurer abordables et alignés sur les coûts.

10. *Adaptation*: en cas de changement significatif des conditions sociales ou économiques qui constituent le fondement du contrat d'existence, ou en cas d'augmentation des contraintes matérielles envisagées par les parties, de telle sorte que la nature sociale du contrat serait remise en cause, et de telle sorte que les parties ne se seraient pas engagées si elles avaient su que des modifications de cette ampleur pouvaient survenir, l'adaptation du contrat peut être requise à condition que, tenant compte de toutes les spécificités du contrat en cause, en particulier de la manière dont le contrat ou les lois répartissent la charge des risques contractuels, et en tenant compte des obligations fondamentales qui pèsent sur les personnes, on ne saurait raisonnablement attendre d'une partie qu'elle se conforme au contrat sans que son contenu ait été modifié. Les règles collectives d'adaptation doivent primer sur les adaptations individuelles.

11. *Résiliation*: la résiliation des contrats d'existence doit être transparente,

8. *Accesso:* chi offre contratti per l'esistenza delle persone non deve compiere nessuna discriminazione personale o sociale. Ciò vale sia nel momento della predisposizione, sia in quello della pubblicità, sia nella conclusione, inclusa la eventuale definizione della categoria di destinatari. La rilevanza che hanno i contratti per l'esistenza della persona, avendo essi ad oggetto il soddisfacimento di bisogni primari della persona quali l'abitazione, il lavoro e la partecipazione alla vita economica, esige il riconoscimento di un diritto umano all'accesso mediante il contratto a tali beni e servizi.

9. *Corrispettivo:* la prestazione e la controprestazione relative al contratto di durata per l'esistenza della persona non possono risultare manifestamente sproporzionate tra loro. Il corrispettivo deve essere determinato secondo criteri trasparenti.

10. *Adeguamento e inesigibilità:* può essere chiesto l'adeguamento del contratto se le circostanze sociali ed economiche che oggettivamente rappresentano il sostrato del contratto per l'esistenza della persona si sono notevolmente modificate dopo la conclusione del contratto stesso oppure se le circostanze che hanno costituito i presupposti fondamentali del contratto si rivelano diverse da quelle considerate dalle parti tanto da far ritenere ragionevolmente che le parti o non avrebbero concluso il contratto o l'avrebbero concluso a condizioni significativamente diverse. La richiesta può aver luogo se, tenendo conto di tutte le circostanze del caso concreto ed in particolare della distribuzione contrattuale

responsable et socialement acceptable. La rupture anticipée contre la volonté du consommateur, du locataire ou du salarié doit avoir lieu en dernière extrémité. La déclaration des motifs sincères et équitables de rupture du contrat doit être non-discriminatoire et prévoir un délai de préavis raisonnable avant que celle-ci ne prenne effet. Seuls le comportement d'une partie justifiant une rupture de contrat, les conditions économiques ou l'atteinte aux intérêts du cocontractant de telle sorte que la continuité de l'objet du contrat se trouve compromise constituent des motifs de résiliation. Lorsque la résiliation a lieu pour des raisons économiques, l'autre partie a un droit de recours dans le cadre des procédures collectives de règlement, y compris le droit d'être entendue ou représentée. Le processus doit laisser un temps suffisant à l'autre partie afin de prendre les mesures propres à préparer la résiliation et / ou ses conséquences. Dans la mesure où la résiliation a lieu dans l'intérêt de la partie qui a élaboré le contrat et organisé la fourniture des prestations, les intérêts de l'autre partie doivent être pris en considération, avec toute la diligence attendue lors de la résiliation.

12. *Communication*: tout au long de la relation contractuelle, depuis le début des négociations jusqu'au terme du contrat, le dialogue et la coopération des parties doivent être établis sur des bases égalitaires, et individuelles, en ce qui concerne l'accomplissement des objectifs

e legale del rischio, nonché dello scopo cooperativo del contratto e di eventuali obblighi fondamentali della persona, non si può esigere che una delle parti rimanga vincolata al contratto col contenuto immutato. Devono essere prioritariamente applicate eventuali regolamentazioni collettive.

11. *Recesso:* il recesso da un contratto per l'esistenza della persona deve essere trasparente, controllabile e socialmente accettabile. Esso deve rappresentare l'extrema ratio. Il recesso deve, inoltre, indicare i motivi reali ed adeguati, nonché evitare sempre discriminazioni. L'atto di recesso deve essere giustificato solo da ragioni attinenti, rispettivamente, alle condizioni fisiche del debitore, al suo comportamento oppure ad un eccesso di costo economico della cooperazione creditoria. Se il recesso dipende da motivi economici devono essere privilegiati meccanismi collettivi di conciliazione. Il debitore ed i suoi rappresentanti devono essere previamente sentiti. Deve essere prevista la facoltà, ed il tempo necessario per esercitarla, di avanzare proposte per evitare il recesso o mitigarne le conseguenze. Quando il recesso è nell'interesse della parte che ha predisposto il contratto e ha organizzato il servizio il suo esercizio fa sempre sorgere obblighi di protezione della controparte.

12. *Comunicazione:* il dialogo e il confronto tra le parti contrattuali deve essere improntato, già a partire dall'inizio delle trattative precontrattuali, nel corso del rapporto contrattuale e fino alla cessazione degli effetti del contratto per l'esistenza della

contractuels. La discussion doit être mise en place à chaque étape du contrat (formation, adaptation, résiliation) et la communication doit être basée sur la confiance.

13. *Information et transparence*: afin de remédier aux asymétries de l'information qui pourraient survenir entre les parties, une information adéquate, complète, opportune et compréhensible doit être fournie, au cours de la négociation et pour toute la durée du contrat.

14. *Garantie des moyens de subsistance*: lorsque le contrat d'existence prévoit le versement de revenus réguliers, les mettant à disposition à un temps et en un lieu déterminés, ou prévoit le prélèvement des paiements sur les revenus d'une partie, il doit être garanti que la partie concernée conserve un montant minimum de ressources afin d'assurer sa subsistance. Le cas échéant, une telle protection doit s'étendre aux voies d'exécution, aux mesures de saisie et aux accords passés avec les créanciers pour l'apurement des dettes.

15. *Exclusion*: les risques sociaux du chômage, du surendettement et de la perte de logement doivent être pris en compte dans toutes les formes individuelles ou collectives de contrat, en considérant les origines sociales de la personne, et conformément aux dispositions du droit public.

16. *Confidentialité*: les données communiquées dans le cadre d'un contrat d'existence et les estimations faites à

persona, al modello di una comunicazione paritaria, orientata in modo cooperativo alla realizzazione degli scopi contrattuali. Tale comunicazione dev'essere condotta in modo personale e diretto tra le parti. Prima del compimento di qualsiasi atto unilaterale attinente al contratto (adeguamento, recesso etc.) deve essere sentita la controparte con modalità che rispettino i canoni enunciati, e in ogni caso il principio di tutela dell'affidamento reciproco.

13. *Informazione e trasparenza:* durante le trattative precontrattuali, lo svolgimento del contratto, così come nel periodo successivo alla cessazione, la parte che predispone e organizza il contratto deve prestare costantemente informazione in modo veritiero, esauriente, puntuale, comprensibile e attento ai bisogni della controparte.

14. *Garanzia del minimo vitale:* se il contratto per l'esistenza della persona procura con regolarità delle somme di danaro (che ad esempio possono formare un reddito o una rendita), o le rende disponibili in un determinato tempo e luogo, oppure fa riferimento a prelievi da tali somme per effettuare dei pagamenti, deve essere preservato il reddito minimo vitale escludendo obblighi di pagamento periodico, pignoramenti, forme di prescrizione e compensazione che intacchino tale minimo vitale.

15. *Esclusione sociale:* nella strutturazione individuale e collettiva dei contratti per l'esistenza della persona devono trovare adeguata considerazione, in rapporto alle loro cause socio-economiche, i rischi di

partir de ces données doivent faire l'objet d'un traitement confidentiel et ne doivent être utilisés que dans le cadre de l'objectif contractuel.

disoccupazione, di mancanza di alloggio e di sovra-indebitamento. La relativa disciplina deve essere integrata da quella di diritto pubblico.

16. *Trattamento confidenziale dei dati:* i dati personali acquisiti in occasione del contratto per l'esistenza della persona, così come le valutazioni inerenti a tali dati devono essere trattati in modo riservato e possono essere utilizzati solo per l'esecuzione del contratto.

Principios de los contratos sociales a largo plazo

1. *Los "contratos para la existencia"* se definen como relaciones jurídicas contractuales de larga duración cuyo objeto es satisfacer necesidades humanas esenciales a través de bienes y servicios. Facilitan la integración y participación de las personas en la sociedad, a lo largo de su vida.

2. *Dimensión humana.* Las circunstancias de la vida real de las personas contribuyen a configurar el contenido de los "contratos para la existencia". Corresponde al derecho establecer el marco para que las relaciones de poder subyacentes en tales contratos se orienten al desarrollo humano, para que la cooperación entre las partes contractuales ocupe un lugar central en la relación (más allá de las reglas jurídicas sobre conclusión del contrato); y para que se tenga en cuenta el contexto personal en el que estos "contratos para la existencia" se desarrollan (incluidas las relaciones familiares)

3. *Relaciones duraderas.* Debe protegerse la confianza recíproca entre las partes en cuanto a la duración de los "contratos para la existencia". La rescisión, revocación o cancelación contractual !únicamente pueden desplegar efectos de cara al futuro, pero nunca retroactivos. La cancelación sólo puede admitirse en circunstancias en las que, de no permitirse, se afectaría negativamente a la libertad y la autonomía de los individuos estén en juego.

4. *Contratos vinculados.* Los "contratos para la existencia" se desarrollan en el contexto de redes de relaciones contractuales vinculadas, que son relevantes para interpretar la problemática jurídica derivada de tales "contratos para la existencia".

5. *Necesidades básicas.* En los "contratos para la existencia" relativos a bienes y servicios para satisfacer las necesidades esenciales de las personas (consumo, relaciones laborales, vivienda) deben tomarse en consideración las circunstancias materiales, sociales y psicológicas para proteger a la parte contractual más débil. Corresponde al derecho garantizar un nivel de protección adecuada al objeto del contrato, a su duración y a su importancia para la vida de los individuos afectados.

6. *Cláusula de utilidad.* Los proveedores de bienes o de servicios, o de rentas para satisfacer necesidades esenciales de las personas, deben evitar cualquier actuación que comprometa la dimensión social de los "contratos para la existencia" y/o para favorecer el uso productivo de las prestaciones.

7. *Aspectos colectivos y éticos.* Los asalariados y los consumidores tienen derecho a la protección del Estado y a que se salvaguarden sus intereses por medio de mecanismos de representación colectiva, así como de la aplicación de los principios generales de ética y buena fe a los "contratos para la existencia" en todas sus fases (acceso , formación, contenido, adaptación, y resolución).

8. *Acceso.* Los proveedores que ofrecen "contratos para la existencia" deben abstenerse, en cualquiera de las fases del contrato (desde el acceso a la relación contractual hasta su término) de toda discriminación basada en

las características personales o sociales de los consumidores, es decir, discriminaciones por motivo del grupo al que pertenezca el individuo afectado, o por causa de su posición dentro del mismo. El acceso a los bienes, servicios y rentas mediante "contratos para la existencia" debe gozar del estatuto de los derechos humanos y de la justicia distributiva, por su importancia para la satisfacción de las necesidades humanas, subsistencia, empleo y participación en la vida económica de las personas.

9. *Precio.* Las obligaciones recíprocas que tienen su fuente en los "contratos para la existencia" deben ser equilibradas y proporcionadas. Los precios han de ser transparentes y no discriminatorios.

10. *Adaptación.* Puede exigirse la adaptación de los "contratos para la existencia" en caso de cambio significativo de las condiciones sociales o económicas que concurren en su desarrollo, cuando tales modificaciones afecten a la propia naturaleza de "contratos para la existencia" y cuando, de haberse conocido tales modificaciones las partes no se habrían comprometido. Será una condición para la adaptación el que tenidas en cuenta las especificidades del contrato y en particular el reparto legal o contractual de los riesgos contractuales, así como las obligaciones contractuales derivadas para las personas, pueda deducirse razonablemente que el individuo no se hubiera comprometido, sin mediar una modificación del contrato. Las reglas colectivas de adaptación prevalecerán sobre las adaptaciones individuales.

11. *Resoluciòn.* La resoluciòn de los "contratos para la existencia" debe ser transparente, responsable y socialmente aceptable. La rescisión anticipada contra la voluntad del consumidor, del inquilino o del asalariado sólo será posible en situaciones extraordinarias y excepcionales, y mediando motivos explícitos y equitativos. Nunca será discriminatoria, su efectividad irá precedida de un plazo de preaviso razonable. Sólo es posible cuando el comportamiento de una de las partes sea tan grave que lo justifique, o cuando las circunstancias financieras que afecten al proveedor hagan materialmente inviable el desarrollo del contrato. Cuando la resoluciòn se base en motivos financieros, el consumidor contará con procedimientos colectivos de defensa en lo que ser escuchado y representado. El proceso debe garantizar que las partes dispongan de tiempo suficiente para adoptar medidas de preparación frente a la resoluciòn y / o sus consecuencias. En tanto que la resoluciòn se efectúa en interés de la parte que redactó el contrato y organizó el abastecimiento de las prestaciones, ésta debe respetar los intereses de la otra parte.

12. *Comunicación.* A lo largo de la relación contractual en los "contratos para la existencia", desde el comienzo de las negociaciones hasta su terminación, el diálogo y la cooperación entre las partes se basarán en la igualdad en el cumplimiento de los objetivos contractuales, la comunicación y la confianza.

13. *Información y transparencia.* Para solventar posibles asimetrías de información entre las partes, en las negociaciones

precontractuales y en cada fase de los "contratos para la existencia" se facilitará información adecuada, completa, oportuna y comprensible.

14. *Garantía de los medios de subsistencia.* Cuando los "contratos para la existencia" den lugar al abono de rentas regulares, en tiempo y lugar determinados; o prevén deducciones sobre las rentas disponibles por las personas; la parte afectada conservará siempre un mínimo de recursos con el fin de asegurar su subsistencia. Esta protección se mantendrá en vía de ejecución, en los embargos, y en los acuerdos con acreedores.

15. En la interpretación de *"contratos para la existencia"* se tendrán en cuenta los riesgos sociales derivados del desempleo, del sobreendeudamiento y de la pérdida de vivienda, a la luz de la perspectiva social de la persona, y de las disposiciones del derecho.

16. *Confidencialidad.* Los datos comunicados en el marco de los "contratos para la existencia" así como las estimaciones realizadas por el proveedor, deben ser objeto de un tratamiento confidencial. Sólo pueden utilizarse en el desarrollo contractual.